Rebels in Arms

EARLY
AMERICAN
PLACES

ADVISORY BOARD

Vincent Brown, *Harvard University*

Cornelia Hughes Dayton, *University of Connecticut*

Nicole Eustace, *New York University*

Amy S. Greenberg, *Pennsylvania State University*

Ramón A. Gutiérrez, *University of Chicago*

Peter Charles Hoffer, *University of Georgia*

Karen Ordahl Kupperman, *New York University*

Mark M. Smith, *University of South Carolina*

Rosemarie Zagarri, *George Mason University*

Rebels in Arms

*Black Resistance and the Fight for
Freedom in the Anglo-Atlantic*

JUSTIN IVERSON

The University of Georgia Press
ATHENS

Chapter 1 originally appeared, in a different form, as "Enslaved Rebels Fight for Freedom: Nathaniel Bacon's 1676 Slave Rebellion" in *Atlantic Studies* 18, no. 2 (2020): 271–288, and is reprinted here by permission of Informa UK Limited, trading as Taylor & Francis Group, www.tandfonline.com.

© 2022 by the University of Georgia Press
Athens, Georgia 30602
www.ugapress.org
All rights reserved

Designed by Kaelin Chappell Broaddus
Set in 10.5/13.5 Adobe Caslon Pro Regular
by Kaelin Chappell Broaddus

Most University of Georgia Press titles are
available from popular e-book vendors.

Printed digitally

Library of Congress Cataloging-in-Publication Data

Names: Iverson, Justin, 1987– author.
Title: Rebels in arms : Black resistance and the fight for freedom in the Anglo-Atlantic / Justin Iverson.
Description: Athens, Georgia : The University of Georgia Press, [2022] | Series: Early American places | Includes bibliographical references and index.
Identifiers: LCCN 2022013679 | ISBN 9780820362793 (hardback) | ISBN 9780820362809 (paperback) | ISBN 9780820362786 (ebook)
Subjects: LCSH: Slavery—America—History. | Slavery—Atlantic Ocean Region—History. | Slave soldiers—America—Case studies. | Slave soldiers—Atlantic Ocean Region—Case studies. | Slave insurrections—America—Case studies. | Slave insurrections—Atlantic Ocean Region—Case studies.
Classification: LCC HT1048 .I94 2022 | DDC 306.3/62097—dc23/eng/20220610
LC record available at https://lccn.loc.gov/2022013679

CONTENTS

LIST OF ILLUSTRATIONS ix

ACKNOWLEDGMENTS xi

NOTE ON TERMINOLOGY xiii

INTRODUCTION 1

CHAPTER 1
Enslaved Rebels Fight for Freedom
Nathaniel Bacon's Slave Rebellion
15

CHAPTER 2
"Negroes Plundered by the Indians from Carolina"
*Slave Soldiers in the South Carolina
Yamasee War, 1715–1717*
29

CHAPTER 3
Liberty to Slaves
Lord Dunmore's Ethiopian Regiment, 1775–1776
64

CHAPTER 4
Mutiny in the Caribbean
*Saltwater Slave Soldiers in the
Eighth West India Regiment, Dominica, 1802*
91

CHAPTER 5
Fugitives on the Front
Maroons in the Gulf Coast Borderlands War, 1812–1823
122

CHAPTER 6
Resistance Militarized
*Slaves Soldiers in the First
South Carolina Volunteers, 1862–1865*
166

EPILOGUE   207

NOTES   213

BIBLIOGRAPHY   243

INDEX   291

ILLUSTRATIONS

Figures

1. Portrait of Great Bridge, 1775 — 69
2. Sergeant William Bronson of Company A — 173
3. Company A at Beaufort, South Carolina — 174
4. Engagement at the Doboy River, Georgia — 177
5. Emancipation Day with the First South Carolina Volunteers — 178

Maps

1. Cases of Armed Resistance in the Anglo-Atlantic, 1676–1865 — 12
2. Map of Virginia during Bacon's Rebellion, 1676 — 21
3. Map of Revolutionary Virginia, 1775–1776 — 67
4. Sketch Map of Gwynn's Island by Thomas Jefferson — 74
5. Gwynn's Island in the Chesapeake Bay — 76
6. Plan of the Island of Dominica — 103
7. Fort Shirley at Prince Rupert's Head — 104
8. Prince Rupert's Head — 104
9. Cabrits at Prince Rupert's Head — 105
10. Sketch of Maroon Towns along the Suwannee River in North-Central Florida, 1818 — 129
11. Gulf Coast Maroon Settlements, Movements, and Battles, 1812–1823 — 141

12. St. Mary's River Area of Operations — 182
13. Jacksonville and St. Johns River Area of Operations — 184
14. Palatka and St. Johns River Area of Operations — 186
15. Map of Charleston Area Sea Islands — 189

Tables

1. Members of the Ethiopian Regiment on Gwynn's Island by Sex — 81
2. Estimated Members of the Ethiopian Regiment Who Survived the War, by Age and Sex — 81
3. Slaves Imported from Africa to Virginia, 1750–1776 — 83
4. Slaves Imported from Africa to Virginia, 1701–1776 — 83

ACKNOWLEDGMENTS

This book is the culmination of hard work and great assistance from so many people over several years that I am extremely grateful to have received. First and foremost, I am thankful to my doctoral advisor, Aaron Fogleman, who was amazing to study with in graduate school, where this project first developed. He has provided keen vision and plentiful feedback and has always been available for support. His guidance is a model to follow. I am also deeply appreciative to members on my dissertation committee who supported my ideas from the very beginning. Jim Schmidt's unique talent to reframe thoughts and ask difficult questions has sparked even more curiosity. Ismael Montana has also always been available to help, and his great insight has consistently pushed me to dig deeper. I have enjoyed Doug Egerton's intellectual enthusiasm from the moment I met him, and his vision and passion for my thoughts and for the field has been incredibly helpful and infectious. I have also benefited from the support of other scholars during this process who have provided critical feedback in early iterations of chapters and who have so generously given me their time and expertise to strengthen my research, my teaching, and my writing, as well as to prepare me for life as a historian. I am thankful to John Shy, Andrea Smalley, Brian Sandberg, Sean Farrell, Beatrix Hoffman, Andy Bruno, Emma Kuby, Nancy Wingfield, Eric Jones, Taylor Atkins, Valerie Garver, Kristin Huffine, Stan Arnold, Eric Hall, and Ann Hanley. Nathaniel Holly at the University of Georgia Press has also been extremely helpful and supportive since the moment I met him. Meanwhile, my frequent conversations with friends B. J. Marach and Nicole

Dressler have also spurred more meaning, and I am grateful to have learned so much with them over the years.

I have also benefited from financial support for this project and the expertise of library and archive personnel throughout the world. I am deeply thankful to the Northern Illinois University History Department and Graduate School, as well as the Newberry Library Center for Renaissance Studies, for this support. I am indebted to Lia Markey and Christopher Fletcher at the Newberry Library, as well as Michele Willbanks and James Cusick at the P. K. Yonge Library of Florida History and David Grabarek at the Library of Virginia, for all their help navigating the extensive collections that each library holds.

Finally, I am also extremely thankful to my wonderful family for their love and support along the way. My mother, Lisa Nelson, has especially fostered my interest in history since as long as I could read, and her continued support for these interests has been unwavering. For that I am forever grateful.

NOTE ON TERMINOLOGY

I have taken care to use the adjectival phrase "enslaved" instead of "slave" to refer to the unfree people of the African diaspora featured in this work. Conversely, I have tried to refer to people who owned enslaved people as "slave owners" or "slaveholders" instead of the term "master." I believe it is important to highlight this power dynamic and restore agency and humanity to people kept in bondage in the Atlantic world. However, out of sheer preference for greater lexical diversity and style, I do use the terms "slave" and occasionally "master" throughout this work. Additionally, while the term "rebel" typically refers to enslaved people who were resisting their own enslavement featured in this work, in chapter 1 I occasionally use this term to refer to Nathaniel Bacon's forces more broadly, which contemporaries and historians since have often employed. Likewise, I sometimes refer to Confederate forces in chapter 6 as "rebels." Finally, the soldiers and slave rebels in this work were both African- and American-born. Some were also biracial (see especially this discussion of the Gulf Coast borderlands Maroons in chapter 5). In cases where it is probable that some slave soldiers were born in Africa, the Caribbean, or mainland North America, I therefore use "African" and "African American" to denote their origin. I do not, however, use these terms to signify acculturation or creolization among these people. More broadly, I also use the terms "Blacks" or "Black people" interchangeably with "African" and "African American." The term "Whites" is also used generally to refer to European colonists and American-born people of European descent. For consistency, I also capitalize all racial and ethnic groups as proper nouns. Finally, I use the terms "uprising," "rebellion," "revolt," and "insurrection" interchangeably.

Rebels in Arms

INTRODUCTION

In 1863 Sergeant Prince Rivers, a soldier in the Union army's all-Black First South Carolina Volunteer Infantry Regiment, spoke about why he decided to run away from his owner and fight in the Union army. As a soldier, Rivers told his comrades at St. Helena Island, "Now we can look our old masters in de face. They used to sell and whip us, and we did not dare say one word. Now we an't afraid, if they meet us, to run the bayonet through them." Rivers also said that he would not stop fighting until all enslaved people in the South were free. Another soldier in the regiment echoed the sentiment later in the war. Corporal Thomas Long delivered a sermon to his companions in 1864 in which he explained that fighting for the Union army when it promoted Black freedom was essential to achieving emancipation. He said that "if we hadn't become sojers, all might have gone back as it was before; our freedom might have slipped through de two houses of Congress & President Linkum's four years might have passed by & notin been done for we. But now tings can never go back, because we have showed our energy & our courage." Fighting for the First South became a way for enslaved people to attack the chattel slave system and free millions of enslaved Black people.[1]

While enslaved people like Rivers, Long, and others in the First South finally broke the chattel slave system in the United States, they actually followed in the footsteps of thousands of other enslaved people who took up arms and became soldiers to fight for Black freedom for nearly two hundred years in the Anglo-Atlantic world. They followed the paths of people like Billy and Lally and their children Cressy, Flora, Beck, Cynthia, and Nero.

The family had run away from their owner, John Forbes, in northern Florida to fight with the British army and Seminole Maroons at the fort at Prospect Bluff, which had become a stronghold for Maroons to defend the Gulf Coast borderlands from American enslavers between 1812 and 1816. Veterans of the First South were also following in the footsteps of people like Private Hypolite, an enslaved soldier of the Eighth West India Regiment (WIR) who participated in a massive mutiny in the British colony of Dominica in April 1802 and later joined the island's Maroons.[2]

Soldiers of the First South carried the torch of still others before them who used military service to fight for Black freedom. They trailed people like slave soldiers in Lord Dunmore's Ethiopian Regiment, who engaged their former owner, Colonel Joseph Hutchings, at the battle of Kemp's Landing near Norfolk on November 15, 1775, or like seventy-year-old Jane Thompson, who fled from owner Robert Tucker in Norfolk in 1776 to join Dunmore's lines during the American Revolutionary War. Soldiers in the First South succeeded people like Francisco Menéndez, an enslaved man who took up arms for the Yamasees and Spanish against English enslavers in Carolina during the Yamasee War in 1715–1717. Finally, they shadowed hundreds of enslaved people who took up arms for Nathaniel Bacon in exchange for freedom during his rebellion in Virginia in 1676–1677.[3]

Enslaved Black people took up arms and fought in nearly every colonial conflict in early British North America. They fought in Nathaniel Bacon's Rebellion in Virginia in 1676, in the Tuscarora and Yamasee Wars in the Carolinas and Georgia in the second decade of the eighteenth century, in Florida during the War of Jenkins' Ear in 1740, in Virginia and Pennsylvania in the French and Indian War from 1754 to 1763, and throughout North America and the Caribbean during the American Revolutionary War, among many other conflicts. They participated in several other armed engagements elsewhere in the British Atlantic in the seventeenth, eighteenth, and early nineteenth centuries as well. They attacked enemy positions in the sixteenth century, and they defended Caribbean colonies from French, Spanish, and Dutch assaults as early as 1640. They helped colonial militias fight Maroons by the early eighteenth century in Jamaica, and they routinely assisted slaveholders in stopping slave insurrection. By the early nineteenth century, thousands of enslaved soldiers served in the British army in North and South America, in the Caribbean, and in Africa for various interests of the British Empire. They often fought for their owners as ordered or in hopes of being manumitted for faithful and good service. Others were sometimes forced to arm and participate in armed conflict, and some used the opportunity that violent conflict produced to run away from slavery. Still others turned coat and served for their masters' enemies.[4]

Slave soldiers fought for every other European colonial empire in the Atlantic as well, and they took part in some of the first conquests in the Caribbean and the Americas. During the rise of Atlantic slave trading, they also guarded European slave forts along the Atlantic coast in Africa, and they served to protect the developing slave trade. Yet they also fought against the slave trade in Africa, and many were enslaved due to war and armed conflict in the continent. Their role with respect to White empires built on Black slavery in the Atlantic has perplexed historians for decades, who have studied how and why enslaved soldiers participated in conflicts that seemingly reinforced White colonization and Black slavery throughout the littoral.[5]

Historians have long been familiar with some of these soldiers' exploits since as early as the mid-nineteenth century, when abolitionists like William Cooper Nell wrote some of the first histories of enslaved people's contributions to early American war efforts. Since the modern civil rights movement, there has been a steady surge in research on free Black and enslaved soldiers in early America, and scholars have further sought to demonstrate how Black soldiers contributed to American military history.[6]

Conversely, throughout the history of slavery in North America, enslaved people took up arms to rebel against Atlantic chattel slavery and attack their owners. While successful rebellion was a rare exception, during insurrection some rebels successfully ran away and formed Maroon communities in outlying swamps, mountains, and forests, where they could evade their former owners and escape the horrors of chattel slavery. Scholars have studied slave rebellions and Maroons in the Atlantic world for more than a century to better understand the nature of Atlantic slavery and to assess its impact on the people who endured it.[7]

A new wave of scholarship has emerged in the last twenty-five years that reconceptualizes the frequency and scope of slave rebellions and Maroon societies and has tied resistance in both to warfare. While some have found slave revolts in conventional warfare, others have asked what slave rebellions meant for enslaved Africans and have tied rebellion to war by highlighting how enslaved rebels fought like soldiers. These episodes thus revealed that slave resistance could be acts of war against slavery and that enslaved Africans repeatedly made war against the Atlantic slave system.[8]

In short, military histories of early America and the British Atlantic, histories of slave rebellions and Maroons, and interpretations of warfare in the African diaspora and transatlantic slave trade remain disconnected, but scholars have begun to flesh out warfare in enslaved resistance movements, while also finding resistance in times of war and armed conflict. Thus, an emerging swell of scholars seeks to further our understanding of the relationship between resistance and war and how slaves interpreted and acted on these opportunities.

This work contributes to this new surge of scholarship to show how slave soldiers interpreted these violent upheavals in ways that challenge us to reconsider how we think about large-scale armed conflict and Black resistance. It brings military histories of early America, histories of slave rebellions and *marronnage*, and histories of warfare in the African Diaspora together to show that slave soldiers and plantation slave and Maroon rebels were sometimes one and the same. How did some slave and Maroon soldiers in early America and the British Atlantic turn colonial and imperial warfare and rebellion into opportunities to achieve and preserve their own freedom? How did these goals or methods of slave soldiers involved in armed resistance change over time from the early period of establishing the Atlantic slave system to the age of emancipation? Did armed resistance differ in the British Atlantic based on geography or in conflicts involving Native Americans? Did armed resistance differ when other European imperial powers were involved?

This book examines approximately two hundred years of enslaved people taking up arms in times of war and rebellion to resist the Atlantic chattel slave system. It investigates six cases in early America and the British Atlantic in which slaves took up arms and participated as soldiers in conflicts traditionally thought to have been fought over colonial or imperial policy or as "Indian wars." In each conflict, slave soldiers and Maroons took up arms for Anglo-Americans and served as soldiers to fight for them to serve various interests in the British Empire and the United States. But in each conflict, some soldiers also fought against their owners. To be sure, still others fought for other interests, and perspectives were diverse. We know a lot about these conflicts from White and Native American perspectives, but we know much less about how all enslaved Black soldiers and Maroons interpreted them. Yet each case captures a moment of armed resistance in the Anglo-American Atlantic and shows how many enslaved people and Maroons viewed soldiering or the process of becoming a soldier or armed military combatant. In each case, some slave and Maroon soldiers used military conflict as an avenue to challenge the slave system and turned war and rebellion into battles about Black liberation. In each case they used armed conflict to further slave insurrection or Maroon war.

At times Black soldiers took up arms in exchange for freedom, often running away to their owner's imperial and Native American enemies to further challenge the slave system. At other times they created conflict or allied themselves with forces willing to promote Black freedom, albeit often on a limited basis. The cases thereby give us a better sense of the relationship between war and slavery and how people living in difficult or desperate circumstances mobilize for conflicts seemingly unrelated to them. They give us a better sense of how slavery influenced war and how war can transform slavery, because in the Anglo-Atlantic world, armed conflict often raised the specter of the future of chattel slavery and freedom from it. The cases give us a better sense of soldiering as a form of resistance to slavery, while examining enslaved soldiers also gives us a deeper understanding of the meaning and experience of slavery and war altogether. These many thousands of people who risked everything to acquire and protect their individual freedom and end slavery laid the groundwork for the freedom of many others. It also meant that military service developed a special meaning for African Americans in their struggles for freedom, equality, and opportunity, especially in the United States.

This work uses case studies to examine how slave soldiers fought in early America and in the British Atlantic. Each case represents a different type of armed conflict that slave soldiers used to fight for freedom in various places in the Atlantic world. These conflicts include internal imperial rebellions, wars with Native American allies and enemies, conflicts with other European allies and enemies, and civil war. Each case also represents a different type of military service that slave soldiers used in various places in the Atlantic world. They fought in colonial militias, in professional armies in times of crisis, and in professional armies during times of relative peace. The cases provide comparative analytical value in and of themselves, and part of the contribution this work makes is with its comparative Atlantic analysis. I compare and contrast each case to other incidents of slave insurrection and Maroon warfare throughout the Atlantic littoral and over time. Although there are some general patterns across time and space, I try to compare each case to incidents of rebellion and *marronnage* that were closely related in terms of both geography and time. Each case represents a collective act of slave resistance to Atlantic chattel slavery, similar in form to slave rebellion or Maroon war. While each case in this work represents collective resistance, each case does not represent an entire history of the many slaves, Maroons, and free soldiers who participated in each conflict. Indeed, Black perspectives were diverse, and even when some enslaved soldiers turned warfare into opportunities to resist chattel slavery, others chose not to do so or fought for other reasons and interests. Additionally, the cases do not represent a comprehensive history of the Black military experience in the Anglo-Atlantic. Nonetheless, these cases are a significant part of that story as well as the long road to abolition.

The comparative framework is also grounded in a basic anatomization of Atlantic slave revolts that gives more meaning to some general patterns of militarized slave insurrection against which each case study can be measured. While Atlantic slave revolts changed over time and were affected by the creolization of enslaved rebels and their appropriation of revolutionary ideology, among other things, there were at least four static features of slave insurrection that help make sense of the Atlantic chattel slave system and how slave soldiers responded to similar conditions. These features include collective participation, material deprivation, goals and objectives, and tactics and methods.[9]

The first feature that characterized Atlantic slave revolts was the collective participation of enslaved rebels. Slave revolts were collective endeavors and they occurred on a less frequent basis than other individual and collective acts of resistance. Exactly how many rebels constituted an uprising or what their proportion of the larger enslaved population actually meant has been the subject of debate among slaveholders and modern historians alike. What is at least clear is that slave rebellion required more than just one or two conspirators to form, and when they erupted generally only a small proportion of the total enslaved population decided to participate. Rarely did rebels represent a majority of the total enslaved population, and in many cases, the participation rate hovered around 10 to 20 percent of the total local, state, or colonial slave population. For example, during the massive uprising in St. John in 1733, approximately 10 percent of the island's slave population participated in the rebellion. Likewise, census data show approximately 8 percent of slaves in the German Coast area participated in the large revolt outside New Orleans in 1811, and roughly 10 percent of slaves in Southampton County participated in Nat Turner's 1831 Virginia rebellion. Rebels' decisions to take part were based on a multitude of factors, not least being their desire to use violence and risk their lives since almost all rebellions ultimately failed and rebels died. Slave soldiers, like plantation rebels, mobilized collectively and only significantly challenged the slave system when they fought collectively.[10]

Most historians of slavery in the Atlantic, Ottoman, and Indian Ocean worlds now agree that material deprivation also often influenced precisely where, when, and why slaves revolted. When owners shifted the economic burden to their slaves or increased their work requirements, slaves were more likely to rebel. If war or natural disasters destroyed homes and crops, or if enslaved people were starving, they were more likely to rebel. If they endured more physical abuse or maltreatment from their owners, they were more likely to rebel. The absence of some of these conditions in the Ottoman and Indian Ocean worlds helps explain the absence of major slave insurrections in those regions, unlike what happened in the Atlantic littoral. Thus material deprivation was often present before militarized slave revolts occurred. For example, in 1639 in St. Kitts, slaves conspired to rise up because of their "brutal treatment." In Barbados in 1675 a violent storm destroyed hundreds of homes and killed several people in the summer before a rebel conspiracy there. Similarly, in 1691 and 1692 a disease "swept away" sailors, planters, and slaves on the island and created high mortality rates and "truly deplorable" conditions before the 1692 conspiracy there. Before the 1733 St. John uprising, a drought ravaged the island and a hurricane destroyed food and crops. In Berbice in 1763 dysentery wreaked havoc on the enslaved population before the enormous rebellion there. To be sure, material suffering was relative, and there were numerous cases in which the conditions for enslaved people had not bottomed out before insurrections erupted. For example, several uprisings broke out during holidays when enslaved people were often on reduced work schedules or enjoyed larger food rations. Deprivation could also be a personal motivator in ways that differed from general economic conditions. Sometimes enslaved people formed insurrection because of their own personal sufferings that did not affect the larger enslaved population in the same ways.[11]

These cases also represent just a drop in the bucket of the thousands of Atlantic slave insurrections, but they comport with a general feature of Atlantic slave revolts also shown below in each chapter. Conditions were harsher for enslaved people in the Atlantic world than in other systems of slavery around the globe, which encouraged insurrections that were unique to the Atlantic littoral. When these conditions worsened even further, either generally or personally, rebellions were often more likely to occur. This was true too for enslaved people who took up arms and became soldiers to resist the chattel system.[12]

Another feature that typified Atlantic slave revolts was the goals and objectives that slave rebels shared when they mobilized. Rebels generally desired to achieve freedom or some form of relief from the chattel system, either for themselves or to larger ends. Rebels in the Stono Rebellion were "calling out liberty" as they marched from plantation to plantation in Carolina in 1739. Likewise, Gabriel and his followers planned on carrying a flag with the words "death or liberty" inscribed on it in Virginia in 1800. Slave rebels who created Maroon communities in Jamaica, Saint-Domingue, or Brazil removed themselves from planter control altogether even though chattel slavery survived nearby. Slave soldiers, like slave rebels, fought to achieve freedom for themselves, and in some cases freedom for everyone in the immediate area.[13]

While not every Atlantic slave rebellion was necessarily violent, militarized rebellions generally followed a basic pattern that relied on military violence to achieve rebel goals. Enslaved rebels usually met in advance to rise up. Even spontaneous rebellions required some degree of coordination. Once rebels banded together, they usually killed a planter and White overseers on one plantation and ransacked the house to gather weapons. In most cases, acquiring firearms or even cannons at these early stages of insurrection was vital. When the rebels were fully armed, either with firearms or other weapons such as farm implements, knives, and lances, they moved to nearby plantations to recruit more slaves and kill more enemies. They often moved in military formations and used military tactics and procedures to further their goals. Military violence became central to accomplishing their objectives. In most cases, they forced other enslaved people to join them by threatening to kill them or destroy their homes if they did not participate. In many militarized revolts, rebels also relied on military oathing ceremonies that also solidified allegiance and commitment to combat. Such oaths were often rooted in African military traditions. Once mobilized, if the rebels were lucky, they could fight their way to mountains, forests, or swamps to escape White retribution. If they were unfortunate, they often faced White militias in pitched battles that resulted in the utter destruction of the rebel forces. In many ways militarized rebellions demonstrated some of the same tactics and violence that slave soldiers chose to resist the chattel system.[14]

While the comparative framework in this book uses revolts and Maroon wars throughout the Atlantic for analysis, it examines cases of slave soldiers only in the United States and British realm of the Atlantic world because military slavery and the manner in which Whites were willing to arm free and enslaved Black people differed in the Anglo-Atlantic than elsewhere in the littoral, or in the rest of the British global empire. Indeed, historians have shown that, unlike the Spanish, Portuguese, French, and others, British colonists and imperial authorities were reluctant to permit free Black and enslaved people to take up arms and serve in military units in the Atlantic world. While every European empire employed enslaved soldiers on the coast of Africa to protect slave forts and defend their slave-trading operations, British colonists became reluctant to employ slave soldiers on the other side of the Atlantic and to develop independent free Black and slave military units like their European counterparts. Enslaved soldiers participated in Spanish conquests in the Americas in the sixteenth century, and formal all-Black militias were formed in almost every Spanish colony by the seventeenth century. Aside from protecting Spanish colonists from Native American, British, French, and Dutch attacks, they also fought Maroons and tracked runaway slaves. Similarly, enslaved soldiers fought for Portuguese interests in all-Black units like the *Terço de Gente Preta* in northeastern Brazil in the mid-seventeenth century. Enslaved soldiers were also used to fight the Palmares Maroons as early as the 1640s. The Dutch too employed slave soldiers in the mid-seventeenth century in Brazil, and they even considered conscripting African veterans to serve in the militia in Curaçao near the end of the seventeenth century. Slaves were definitely serving in the island's militia by the first decade of the eighteenth century, while they also served in militias in Suriname in the early eighteenth century. Slaves and free Blacks served in their own militias in the French Atlantic by the early eighteenth century as well, such as in the Maréchausée in Saint-Domingue in 1721. A permanent free Black militia existed in French Louisiana by 1739. The Danish also established an all-Black "corps" on St. John as early as 1721.[15]

But in the British Atlantic, colonial authorities more often prohibited free Black and enslaved people from arming or serving in colonial militias. To be sure, English privateers like Sir Francis Drake relied on Maroon soldiers for help fighting against the Spanish in Panama as early as the late sixteenth century, and in times of crisis English colonists did enlist the help of enslaved soldiers by the mid-seventeenth century. By 1640 slaves helped the English defend Providence Island near present-day Colombia from a Spanish attack, and some slaves helped the English fight in Santo Domingo in 1654. In the 1660s slaves were first incorporated into the Barbados militia in what may be the earliest case of slave soldiers in the British Atlantic. The 1681 Militia Act in Jamaica also required Black people to help defend the colony, while Deputy Governor Charles Lyllton proclaimed Maroon leader Juan de Bolas to be the leader of some sort of Maroon "militia" in the 1660s and 1670s. But all too often enslaved people did not serve as soldiers but as military laborers, and they were often prohibited from carrying firearms. All too often they returned to their previous status once peace returned, and permanent free Black and slave militias did not develop as early or as widely as they did in French, Spanish, Portuguese, or Dutch colonies. "Black Shot" slave soldiers who fought against Maroons in Jamaica did not muster until the 1720s during the First Maroon War, but Jamaican colonists still recruited Indians to fight the rebels throughout the conflict. Once peace was reached with the Maroons, the Maroons essentially made Black units obsolete as the Maroons promised to provide military assistance in case of foreign invasion and slave insurrection. While Maria Bollettino has recently demonstrated that English colonists were willing to use slave soldiers earlier than previously thought, the general pattern persists that British colonists only used slave soldiers in times of crisis and conflict throughout the seventeenth and eighteenth centuries. This contrasted significantly with other European imperial forces in the Americas, who had been using large numbers of enslaved Black people for military purposes since the late seventeenth century and seemed to have fewer reservations about it. Indeed, it was not until the end of the American Revolutionary War that the first permanent peacetime enslaved army developed in the Anglo-Atlantic with the establishment of the West India Regiments, which also became the largest professional slave army in the Atlantic world. Consequently, the ways in which slave soldiers served and took up arms in the Anglo-Atlantic were unique in the larger Atlantic world. In addition, while Black slaves served in British military units around the world, the nature of chattel slavery and slave resistance was unique in the Atlantic world, where conditions for enslaved Black people were worse and where slave insurrection was not uncommon.[16]

Finally, while this is a story about enslaved people who used military service and took up arms, it excludes Black sailors, including pirates, those who served for merchants, on slave ships, and those who eventually served in the Royal Navy, all of whom were ultimately part of a different narrative. Indeed, Europeans of all sorts relied on Black sailors since the beginning of Atlantic history to support trade, colonization, and slavery, and there did not appear to be the same reservations about their military use as there were about employing slave soldiers on land.[17]

I argue that slave resistance in the British Atlantic and United States was increasingly militarized, by which I mean that over the course of nearly two centuries, enslaved soldiers, Maroons, and plantation rebels together relied increasingly on military institutions and operations to achieve their goals. Enslaved soldiers relied on military service to attack the slave system, and Maroons and plantation rebels used martial tactics, techniques, and procedures to do the same. Organized and militarized violence increasingly became their modus operandi. The militarization of slave resistance increased significantly in the mid- to late seventeenth century and continued to rise throughout the eighteenth century and well into the age of revolution. It surged with the rise of the Atlantic chattel slave system, and it survived the first assaults on slavery that revolutionary ideology wrought. It swelled in conjunction with other resistance efforts like running away, work slowdowns, and other day-to-day acts of insubordination that were also parts of the much larger story of resistance to slavery. It increased even after the abolition movement, along with others who relied on nonviolence and the rhetoric of revolution to promote Black freedom. The militarization of resistance reached its peak in the Anglo-Atlantic during the American Civil War, when nearly two hundred thousand enslaved people joined the Union army and navy to fight for freedom. Enslaved people took up arms and became soldiers in various conflicts in the British Atlantic, and they turned them into conflicts about Black liberation. The long history of abolition and Black emancipation was thus deeply connected to slave soldiers and the militarization of resistance.

This story of armed resistance begins with Nathaniel Bacon's rebellion in Virginia in 1676, what most historians describe as a revolt by lower-class White settlers against their superiors and against Native Americans. Bacon's Rebellion marked the first major conflict in British North American history in which enslaved Africans and African Americans took up arms as a group and participated in a major, lengthy, violent conflagration. It may have also been the first time in British Atlantic history in which Black slaves revolted in the midst of a White rebellion. As a case study, the conflict also shows how enslaved people began using military service and military methods to resist the chattel system, and how they began turning armed conflict into struggles about slavery. For slave soldiers in Bacon's army, this conflict in Virginia was a *slave rebellion*.[18]

The story moves farther south in chapter 2 to South Carolina in 1715, where armed conflict erupted between colonists and the Yamasee. The Yamasee War from 1715 to 1717 shows how "Indian war" affected Black armed resistance and how it operated differently in the Lowcountry than in the Chesapeake in the early eighteenth century. Here too, slave soldiers served in colonial militias and used war as an opportunity to fight for Black freedom, and dozens if not hundreds ran away and fought with Yamasee and Spanish soldiers in the conflict. But a more developed and liberal militia system in South Carolina, as well as the presence of Spanish and Indian rivals in South Carolina, Georgia, and Florida, presented slave soldiers with more options than forty years earlier in Virginia. In this case, they could run to Indian communities, seek refuge with Spanish allies at Saint Augustine, or

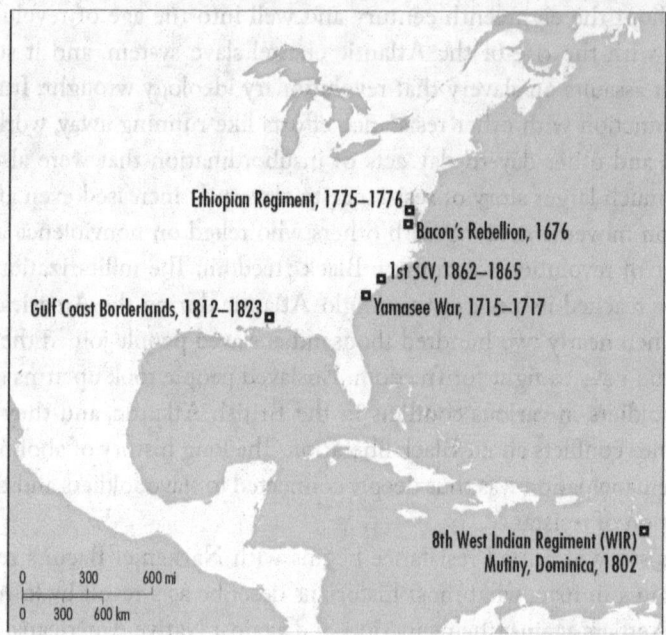

MAP 1. Cases of Armed Resistance in the Anglo-Atlantic, 1676–1865. Map created by the author.

protect their masters and earn their freedom via loyal military service. These influences enabled more enslaved people without previous military experiences to learn martial tactics, techniques, and procedures.

Chapter 3 returns to Virginia in 1775 and 1776 to examine Lord Dunmore's Ethiopian Regiment and how revolution affected armed resistance and slave soldiering. Whereas slave soldiers in 1676 Virginia and 1715 South Carolina served in colonial militias, soldiers in the Ethiopian Regiment became official members of the British army in North America. Revolution further militarized slave rebels, as fighting for the British army during the Revolutionary War became the most viable option for enslaved rebels in early America to attack slavery. Moreover, the Revolutionary War transformed soldiering and led to the professionalization of slave soldiers who served in the British army, instead of in colonial militias. The success of Black Loyalist soldiers during the war, like soldiers in the Ethiopian Regiment, led to the creation of the first permanent peacetime professional slave soldiers in the British Atlantic with the Carolina Black Corps and then later the West India Regiments. Slave soldiers were learning how to use professional military service to advance their own agendas, and revolutionary conflict opened more opportunities for enslaved people to fight for freedom.[19]

The British professionalization of slave soldiers that developed in the American Revolution leads to chapter 4, which addresses slave soldiers in the Eighth West India Regiment who mutinied in Dominica in 1802. The West India Regiments became the largest peacetime slave army in the Atlantic world, and they primarily saw military action in the Caribbean, where White colonists were more open to arming enslaved people than on the mainland due to manpower shortages, demographic imbalances, and the near-constant threat of imperial attack.[20] In Dominica slave soldiers learned how to use permanent military service to advance their own agendas as opposed to taking up arms in times of crisis. The 1802 mutiny was one of only three mutinies in the West India Regiments before emancipation in the British Atlantic, and it was the only mutiny before the 1807 Mutiny Act that made all slave soldiers in the British army free for all intents and purposes. Slave soldiers in the Eighth WIR, most of whom were African-born, mutinied in April 1802 because they feared they were about to be disbanded and transformed into plantation slaves. They did not view military service itself as a safety valve from chattel slavery, which was often the case for enslaved soldiers in professional armies elsewhere in the Atlantic during the period.

This story returns to the mainland in chapter 5, which traces the development of Maroons in the Gulf Coast borderlands of northern Florida, southern Georgia, Alabama, and Mississippi Territory in the second decade of the nineteenth century, thereby showing how some runaway slaves turned imperial warfare among competing imperial powers and Native Americans into opportunities to fight against slavery. Like the parallels in Virginia from 1676 to 1776 in chapters 1 and 3, chapter 5 examines developments in slave soldiering in some of the same areas as soldiers involved in the Yamasee war a hundred years earlier seen in chapter 2. In the borderlands, enslaved people caught up in armed conflict fled to allies who promoted their freedom, including the Spanish at Saint Augustine and the British at Pensacola. Some runaway slaves also joined Seminole and Creek Indian allies to form the largest Maroon society in United States history. These Maroons participated in continuous warfare from 1812 to 1823 to prevent U.S. Americans from invading their territory and forcing their re-enslavement. As the fighting unfolded, the Seminole Maroons also allied with the Creek, Seminole, British, and Spanish armies and took up arms with them to resist American imperial ambitions in the area.

The next large-scale opportunity in the Anglo-American Atlantic to use military service to resist chattel slavery also became the scene for the largest efforts that enslaved soldiers led to achieve their goals. The militarization of resistance in the Anglo-Atlantic world reached its apex during the American Civil War. The final chapter focuses on slave soldiers who served in the First South Carolina Volunteer Infantry Regiment, which began organizing on the Sea Islands of South Carolina, Georgia, and Florida in the spring and summer of 1862. Importantly, soldiers in the First South Carolina Volunteers were also the first slave soldiers to organize en masse and begin fighting their former owners and slaveholders during the Civil War. They began fighting months before the Emancipation Proclamation, and they helped persuade many Northerners that slave soldiers would be vital to winning the Civil War. Slave soldiers helped make the Civil War a conflict about the future of chattel slavery, and they nearly exclusively tied resistance to slavery to military service. They advanced the important goal of Black emancipation, and they finally achieved their centuries-long goal of abolition in 1865.[21]

The age of revolution created more war and conflict, which also provided more opportunities for slave soldiers to serve and to turn more conflicts into events that supported their own agendas. Militarization of resistance increased due in part to these developments. As slave soldiers relied on military service to challenge the slave system, Maroons and plantation slave rebels concomitantly attacked the system with some of the same methods. In many cases the two types of rebel soldiers were one and the same. Armed resistance became one of the most significant approaches to achieve emancipation. In 1866 one anonymous veteran of the First South wrote to Union general Daniel Sickles expressing how important soldiering was to ending chattel slavery. The man wrote that he and other enslaved people fled from slavery "under the Bondage of Soldiers life" and that they had "run right out of Slavery in to Soldiery." Armed resistance had become one of the most significant approaches to achieve emancipation.[22]

From Black perspectives, the world changed dramatically during the ages of revolution and emancipation, when slavery expanded in some areas and contracted in others. As war and revolution advanced, opportunities to take up arms and to attack chattel slavery advanced as well, and slave soldiers seized those opportunities time after time. By doing so, they became a part of the larger abolition movement in the British Atlantic that finally culminated in emancipation in the Caribbean by 1838 and in the United States by 1865.

CHAPTER 1

Enslaved Rebels Fight for Freedom
Nathaniel Bacon's Slave Rebellion

Early in September 1676, Virginia planter Nathaniel Bacon led 136 armed followers toward the colonial capital at Jamestown, Virginia, where Governor William Berkeley and his army of loyal supporters anxiously awaited the rebels. To deter desertion among his ranks and to possibly recruit more soldiers while marching, Bacon "proclam'd liberty" to all Black slaves and White indentured servants who already served in his army or who would join him in his fight against Berkeley. As the rebels continued to advance toward the city, they recruited hundreds of followers who responded to the proclamation. According to one account, enslaved people and White servants "chiefly formed his army," and when they arrived outside the city's wooden palisades, Bacon ordered all of his men to build trenches and prepare cannons to bombard Berkeley's Loyalist supporters. His soldiers worked under cover of darkness on the night of September 17 to build the bulwarks, while others also helped Bacon sneak into the city. In fear of the upcoming attack, all but twenty of Berkeley's followers deserted and slipped through the siege lines on the evening of September 18 to watch how the town might react as it faced imminent destruction. The following morning, Bacon and his soldiers entered Jamestown unopposed and burned it to the ground, including the church, the statehouse, twelve new brick houses, and several wooden framed homes. From sloops on the James River, Loyalists watched the flames light up the evening sky.[1]

The fall of Jamestown in September 1676 represented the height of Bacon's power in his eighteen-month rebellion against Governor Berkeley from 1675 to 1677. The assault also represented how much Bacon's Rebellion had changed since its beginnings in July 1675, when colonist Thomas Mathew killed several Doeg Indians in retaliation for the theft of his hogs. Tensions between White planters and Native Americans escalated, which led to murder and retaliatory raids between the colonists and Indians in late 1675. By March 1676 Governor Berkeley declared war on the Natives. But the governor also refused to grant Bacon a military commission to attack Indians since Berkeley thought that Bacon's unrestrained strategy would cause a massive conflict similar to what New England colonists endured in King Philip's War. As a consequence, the governor's refusal to support Bacon's aggressive strategy enticed a new wave of dissent from planters who supported Bacon's cause and who bore the brunt of Indian attacks in Virginia. By the end of June 1676 many Virginia colonists had mobilized with Bacon to continue to fight Native Americans and to attack Berkeley's Loyalists. In just a year a White-Indian frontier conflict morphed into a colonial rebellion fought over issues of class and colonial administration, among other things. The fighting did not end even after Bacon's death from dysentery in October 1676. Only after more troops from London arrived in November did peace appear near, and by January 1677 British captain Thomas Grantham secured the surrender of the last of the rebels, which included eighty Black slaves and twenty White indentured servants who were heavily armed with muskets, gunpowder, and cannons.[2]

Despite the presence of enslaved people taking up arms against their owners, they have often not been the main subject of historical inquiry for scholars studying Bacon's Rebellion. Scores of studies have argued that Bacon's Rebellion was a civil war among English colonists, an Indian war, a sectarian conflict, or some sort of revolt that challenged imperial rule. To be sure, most who have examined the events of 1675–1677 have noted that Black slaves and White servants fought in Bacon's army, including most notably Edmund Morgan, who long ago argued that the rebellion transformed Virginia and facilitated the rise of Black chattel slavery in the colony. Although a number of historians have acknowledged the presence of enslaved people in the ranks of Bacon's army and noted their potential importance, no one has fully investigated the meaning of their presence from Black perspectives, or how their activities compared to those of other enslaved people in the Atlantic world to gain insight into their activities and motives.[3]

This chapter explores the Black rebel experience in Bacon's army and asks what Bacon's Rebellion meant for the enslaved soldiers who participated in it. Were they loyal soldiers concerned about Indians and British imperial strategy, or were they trying to accomplish something else? Bacon's Rebellion was the first major conflict in British North America in which enslaved Black people took up arms as a large group and participated in the fighting. This early conflict also shows how slave soldiers at the beginning of the rise of the Atlantic chattel slave system took up arms during internal imperial conflict. It offers a glimpse into how slave soldiers perceived military status in the seventeenth century, and into the beginnings of the militarization of slavery and slave resistance in the Anglo-Atlantic. While Bacon and many of his White allies fought in an imperial rebellion, enslaved Africans and African Americans marching in Bacon's army were also engaged in a slave insurrection to secure their own freedom.

Rebellion within a Rebellion

The Black slaves who joined Bacon's army were a diverse set of African- and American-born people. Privateers brought the first recorded shipment of African slaves to Virginia—some "20. and odd Negroes"—in 1619. These first Africans in Virginia were probably enslaved and taken across the Atlantic by the Portuguese, who traded for slaves in Angola. Slave names in Virginia in the 1630s and 1640s also reflected Iberian designators, which suggest that English traders transshipped them from colonies that relied on Portuguese and Spanish slave traders who brought enslaved people from West-Central Africa. Given that direct slave imports from Africa to Virginia were rare in the seventeenth century, the first generation of Africans was probably a somewhat coherent ethnic group from West-Central Africa but also a group of Atlantic Creoles. However, the supply of African slaves in the English Atlantic shifted in the 1640s, as British colonists began to import more Africans using Dutch traders working on the Gold Coast at Elmina. They also transshipped several thousand African- and American-born people from the British Caribbean via the intercolonial slave trade. In addition, they imported a substantial number of people taken from European coastal forts in the Bight of Biafra, the Gulf of Guinea, and Senegambia during the period. All told, in 1670 Berkeley estimated that there were two thousand enslaved Black people in the colony.[4]

Precisely when African and African American slaves became involved in Bacon's Rebellion is not clear in the historical record. Extant records are limited and even somewhat contradictory as to when, where, and how many Black slaves fought in the rebellion. There is no direct evidence that shows enslaved people joined Governor Berkeley's army, though some were taken by Berkeley's supporters during attacks on Baconite plantations. According to John Harold Sprinkle Jr., White servants were probably ordered to fight in Berkeley's army too. Notwithstanding these orders, reports appear to confirm the fact that most servants joined Bacon's army during the rebellion and took advantage of the "loosness and liberty of the tymes." In the spring of 1676 Bacon had mobilized several hundred followers, most of whom were male landowners who lived on the frontier. Though treated as the "scum of the country" and "rabble of the basest sort" by Loyalists who overwhelmingly came from the Virginia elite, several Baconites did own slaves and a few were fairly wealthy, including Nathaniel Bacon himself. Together they marched against the Occaneechee and then the Susquehanna, before they petitioned Berkeley to give Bacon a military commission, which Berkeley denied him. By June 5 Bacon went to Jamestown again with about forty followers, and after the unit's small altercation with the town's militia, Berkeley declared Bacon a rebel. Captain Thomas Gardner captured him just days later, but Berkeley pardoned Bacon and released him on parole. Weeks later, he returned to Jamestown again with nearly five hundred supporters to again demand a commission, but by June 25 both Bacon and Berkeley left Jamestown after news that Indians had killed eight White colonists in the area. Campaigns in July and August were also directed at Indians and at Berkeley's supporters as Bacon's soldiers chased Berkeley to Gloucester and Accomack Counties. By then Loyalists took up arms, attacked the Baconites, and destroyed their homes. It had become clear that the fighting was no longer just about an "Indian War." It is unclear if enslaved people had taken up arms yet in the rebellion, although they were clearly caught up in the plantation raids and attacks.[5]

By September 7 Berkeley returned to Jamestown and reclaimed it from rebel control. On his return, the governor offered to pardon the rebels and set servants and slaves free if they deserted Bacon, and if others not involved "would (in Arms) owne the Governours cause." Berkeley also promised to give Baconites' land to and exempt taxes for anyone who would fight for the governor. This was the first time during the rebellion in which either side called on servants and enslaved people to fight for either cause. But fearing mass desertion and potential defeat, Bacon responded with his own emancipation proclamation, the exact provisions or details of which are unknown except that he promised "liberty to all Servants and Negro's" and that many servants "and other persons of desperate fortunes" ran away from their owners to join the rebellion "upon the invitation and encouragement of libertie." According to Berkeley, Bacon bound his followers with "a most horrid oath" in which he declared that he would not give quarter to the enemy. Bacon also administered loyalty oaths near present-day Williamsburg, in which he demanded that Virginians join him or return to their homes on the arrival of reinforcements from London. They were also prohibited from assisting Berkeley. He also demanded they swear that the governor had been acting illegally. By the time Bacon reached Jamestown to lay siege on it, his forces had nearly doubled, indicating that servants and slaves likely joined his ranks. According to one account, enslaved people and servants "chiefly formed his army" by the time Bacon's forces burned Jamestown. The proclamation was the beginning of a turn from a White rebellion to a Black slave rebellion. It is possible that slaves were not with Bacon for the sacking of Jamestown given the limited details of when they joined Bacon's army, but it is reasonable to believe that they would have joined by then given Bacon's emancipation offer. Indeed, enslaved rebels responded similarly to rumors of emancipation throughout the Atlantic for nearly two centuries starting as early as 1669. According to Steven Saunders Webb, servants and slaves made up two-thirds of Bacon's forces after the burning of Jamestown, and according to one contemporary account, they were part of Bacon's army since at least when Berkeley left Jamestown shortly before Bacon's assault. Before Bacon ordered the siege on the settlement on September 15, 1676, Bacon's rebels kidnapped Loyalist women to use as human shields as they prepared fortifications and fixed guns on the city. The origins of such a tactic remain unknown, but accounts of the rebellion made it clear that Loyalists were "not well acquainted" with that "method in war." The tactic, which also humiliated Loyalist women and their husbands, was subject to intense scrutiny in petitions and grievances after the rebellion. Four days later, Bacon and his soldiers razed Jamestown, and homes inside the city were destroyed or burned to the ground. Though many residents suffered from the destruction of the city, among the more eminent victims were Colonel Thomas Swann, Major Theop. Hone, and Mr. William Sherwood, all of whose homes and provisions were burned. With the Loyalists on the run, Bacon moved on to Gloucester and Charles City Counties and continued to plunder Loyalist plantations.[6]

As the rebels burned houses and barns, they stole as many provisions as they could carry. Among the important supplies that the rebels took were weapons and ammunition as they armed themselves and prepared for more attacks against Berkeley and his supporters. The rebels destroyed much of what they could not take with them. The plunder was also a method to recruit more slave rebels to join the movement, and Bacon and his men "carryed away" at least a handful of slaves as they plundered. The rebel approach to individual plantations was both a terrorizing and liberating experience for enslaved Virginians. On the one hand, enslaved people confronted a violent, angry, and well-armed mob whose members wanted to destroy plantations in their path. On the other hand, the rebels were offering a pathway out of bondage, and at the very least slaves could use the chaos as an opportunity to flee from their owners. Faced with these options, many enslaved people chose to join.[7]

After Bacon's proclamation, slaves were also probably involved in the fighting on the Elizabeth, York, and James Rivers, and on the Chesapeake shore where sailors in the Royal Navy arrived in September 1676 to help suppress the rebellion. They were possibly among Bacon's forces that fired at Captain Robert Morris near Newport News at the end of the month in an attempt to entice the enemy to land and fight. They were also possibly among those who engaged Captain Thomas Larrimore's sloop on September 29. A handful of them may have even been the "runaways" captured in the fighting on the Elizabeth River just days later in early October. The rebels continued to battle Berkeley and the Royal Navy near Newport News, Elizabeth City, and up the Hampton River in southeastern Virginia for the rest of the month. Enslaved people even continued to join the rebel forces after Bacon's untimely death on October 26. Just a day later, Captain Morris moved to Nansemond to cut off the remaining rebels, and by November 4 he arrived at Craney Island to prepare for peace. More rebels were captured later in November, though the fighting still continued. By December 28 rebel garrisons were on the run and the end appeared near.[8]

Further inland, enslaved soldiers were definitively among Bacon's last rebels. After Captain Grantham secured the surrender of a large rebel faction at West Point on January 2, he marched three miles to Colonel John West's house, where he found four hundred Black and White rebels who were upset about the previous capitulation. Grantham noted that some of the enslaved soldiers "were for shooting me, and others for cutting me in pieces," and he surrendered himself to them to calm them down. He later recalled that he had to reassure the enslaved rebels that they would be pardoned and freed from slavery to keep them calm. Indeed, the Royal Commissioners investigating the rebellion believed that Grantham was "in jeopardy of beinge killed by the Negroe slaves who were dissatisfied with the said Treaty beinge in distrest of their hoped for liberty." Presumably out of fear of either being returned to bondage to vindictive owners or executed for participating in the rebellion, the enslaved soldiers knew that surrender without the prom-

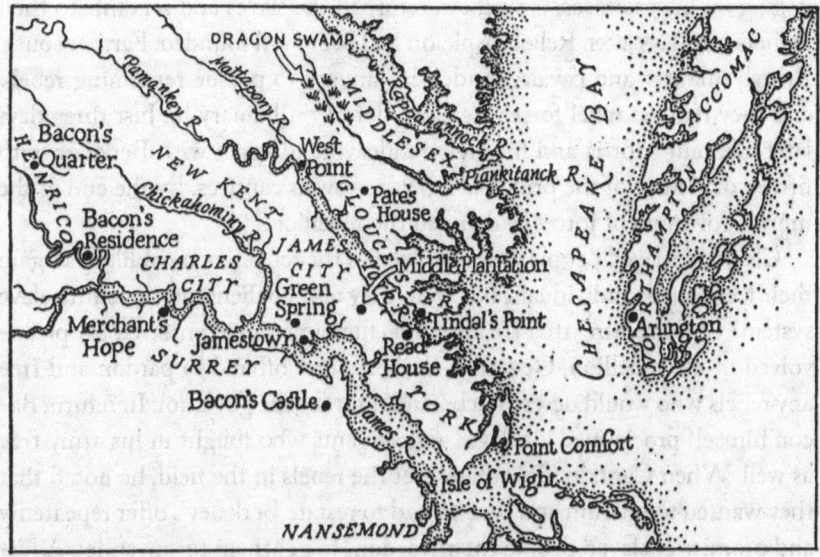

MAP 2. Map of Virginia during Bacon's Rebellion, 1676. From Wertenbaker, *Torchbearer of the Revolution*, 224. Courtesy of Princeton University Press.

ise of freedom was not an option, and they threatened to kill if their demands were not met. In order to further assuage them, Grantham promised the remaining White rebels that they could return home with their arms if they wished to keep fighting enemy Indians. He also promised that masters would be compensated for every servant and slave who was discharged from their bondage. For most of the rebels these assurances were enough, and they marched back toward their homes.⁹

Grantham successfully took control of the garrison, capturing approximately five hundred muskets, powder and shot, and three large cannons. But eighty remaining Black slaves and twenty English servants refused to surrender. Grantham cajoled them into boarding his sloop and promised that he would deliver them to the Brick House Garrison downriver from Colonel West's house. Probably betting that this might be the best chance to preserve their own goals, the slaves and servants finally agreed to board and Grantham ordered his men to treat the rebels "civilly." But it soon became apparent that Grantham did not intend to keep his promise once he refused to land them on shore. Instead, he kept them on board while he left for another ship, and once he was safe from rebel retaliation Grantham aimed four pieces of cannon on the remaining rebels, telling them he would fire if they did not submit. Facing surrender or death, the rebels chose the former. Reneging on his promises, Grantham returned the slaves and servants to their owners just days later. Rebel suspicion had been well founded. Farther south, British infantry and cavalry landed in January to pursue remaining rebels, and they handed rebel forces a sizable defeat on January 16. Just three days later Captain Morris and his crew rendezvoused again with Berkeley with fifteen or sixteen of the principal rebels in tow as captives. By the end of the month government forces had ended the rebellion.[10]

Clearly enslaved people were involved in the rebellion, most likely to gain their freedom as individuals, but were they also challenging the entire slave system? Underscoring that freedom was fundamental to enslaved people involved in the rebellion, Governor Berkeley first offered to pardon and free any rebels who would desert Bacon and fight for the governor. In return, Bacon himself proclaimed all slaves and servants who fought in his army free as well. When Captain Grantham met the rebels in the field, he noted that they wanted to kill him and that he had to restate Berkeley's offer repeatedly and promise enslaved people their freedom to get them to surrender. Additionally, Berkeley's officers seized slaves and servants from other rebels, ostensibly to prevent them from revolting with the rest. In fact, freedom was so important for this rebellion that even King Charles II issued an emancipation proclamation to enslaved rebels in October 1676, in hopes that it would end the insurrection. Only slow communication and Berkeley's reluctance rendered the king's proclamation irrelevant by the time it reached Virginia shores. So many slaves fought in this rebellion that they threatened to destroy planter authority and wealth, and they nearly did destroy Virginia's largest settlements. Although they may not have initially intended to overthrow the slave system, eventually so many enslaved people joined the revolt that they did, indeed, threaten it.[11]

Like Other Slave Rebellions in the Atlantic

Enslaved people fought in Bacon's Rebellion much like other enslaved people involved in militarized revolts during the period. Colonial accounts detail Bacon's army marching toward Jamestown and then dividing itself into multiple wings in the frontier. If slaves were present for the attack on Jamestown, they were perhaps among the six soldiers who probed the town's sentinels and fired at them before retreating back to safety, which paralleled how rebels employed fire-and-withdraw tactics against Europeans in revolts in Jamaica and in St. John in the late seventeenth and early eighteenth centuries. Furthermore, the rebels used firearms, cannons, and other weapons effectively in battle. They also dug trenches and built siege lines when they surrounded the settlement in September. The military character and utility of firearms in Bacon's Rebellion bear a resemblance to the 1675 and 1692 plots in Barbados, the 1673, 1685, and 1690 revolts in Jamaica, the 1733 St. John revolt, and the Stono Rebellion in South Carolina in 1739.[12]

Enslaved soldiers in the Virginia rebellion fought much like the "Amina" slaves during the 1733 St. John rebellion and the Akan rebels in Barbados and in Jamaica at the end of the seventeenth century. Rebels in Barbados in 1675 plotted to fight for their freedom in a militarized manner. They reportedly planned their militarized uprising for three years. According to English accounts, enslaved Black people planned to kill their owners and set sugarcane fields on fire before they would take military control of the island. Once they conquered colonial authorities, they would appoint a man named Cuffee as their own ruler. Similarly, both Africans and Creoles again led a revolt in Barbados in 1692 and hoped to elect a king. The rebels, who primary lived in St. Michael, Christ Church, and St. George Parishes, planned to infiltrate Bridgetown's magazine, where a Black armorer inside would provide them with 400 barrels of gunpowder, 300 muskets, and 160 swords. From there they would move to Needham's Fort, where Irish servants would open the doors for them and help them gain military control of the island. They would also seize control of British ships and communication lines. The rebels had reportedly organized themselves into four infantry regiments and two cavalry regiments in an English fashion. They had also timed their rebellion with the departure of British soldiers from the island, which would ensure military success.[13]

In Jamaica in 1673, two hundred Akan rebels rose up on Major Lobby's plantation (St. Ann's), killing him and twelve White men before they seized arms and ammunition and fled to the mountains for safety, where they remained hidden from colonial militias. Similarly in Jamaica in 1685, approximately 150 Akan slaves rose up at Widow Grey's plantation at Guanaboa (present-day St. Catherine). The rebels immediately seized at least twenty-five firearms from Grey's house, and they killed two White men nearby. From there the rebels moved to the neighboring Price plantation, where they again engaged two colonists. The rebels at first evaded a White counterattack, and they retreated into thick forest where they knew mounted soldiers could not reach them. They broke into two or three groups, and at least one faction fought off the first counterattack launched by the White militia. They continued to raid plantations before they disappeared into the mountains for safety. By the end of the revolt, several hundred laid down their arms and surrendered. Those who did not were captured and executed. Likewise, in 1690, nearly five hundred Coromantee rebelled on Thomas Sutton's plantation (Clarendon) and killed their owner and all the White servants at the plantation. They seized nearly fifty muskets and even four pieces of field artillery before moving to the next plantation to kill more. A colonial militia soon defeated them at Sutton's house, and thirty or forty who did not surrender fled into the surrounding mountains where they lived as Maroons. In St. John in 1733, Akwamu rebels also used cannons to ambush planters, and they successfully engaged French and Danish forces for months. They too elected a king and planned on establishing their own government had the rebellion succeeded. Like these other rebellions, enslaved soldiers in Bacon's army colluded with White servants to accomplish their goals. In military fashion, they also attacked major settlements in the colony, seized arms and ammunition, and attempted to install a new leader. They also used military violence to achieve their goals.[14]

A general pattern thus emerged in the seventeenth and early eighteenth centuries in mostly African-led and militarized slave revolts in the Atlantic, and the behavior of enslaved soldiers in Bacon's army conforms to that pattern. On multiple occasions in Barbados, Jamaica, and St. John, rebels organized in military fashion and used firearms and even cannons to attack the fortifications in the area. After seizing control of the primary military threat, rebels planned to kill White authorities and then appoint their own rulers to create their own political state. Recruits were enlisted with coercive practices as the rebellions developed, and those who refused to join faced violence from the rebels. Rebels also attacked the main population centers and burned and ransacked their masters' homes. Bacon's rebels also marched into battle with him at Jamestown and Williamsburg, and then in the frontier. They too used firearms and cannons to fight Governor Berkeley and their former masters. They also drove Berkeley out of the capital, and the rebellion as a whole was a clear attempt to unseat authorities in the colony. We know that Europeans behaved in similar ways in colonial rebellions during the period, and that Europeans and Africans revolted together in Virginia. But should we not pay more attention to African perspectives, not just the European?

The development of law in Virginia after the rebellion also indicates how enslaved rebels had threatened the slave system, which was the case after militarized slave rebellions elsewhere in the Atlantic world, like in colonial South Carolina and Barbados. As with other revolts and conspiracies, authorities often passed new legislation to restrict slaves in hopes that they could prevent future insurrections. These laws were often immediately implemented after insurrections, such as the Act for the Better Ordering and Governing of Negroes that planters in South Carolina passed in May 1740, just months after the Stono Rebellion. But sometimes enslaved rebels influenced legislation several years after they revolted, as was the case in Barbados in 1676 and 1677, when planters continued to pass new restrictions on slaves following the 1675 conspiracy on the island. In 1676 Barbadian authorities passed "An Act to prevent the people called Quakers, from bringing Negroes to their Meeting" after the 1675 conspiracy on the island. They also passed an "Act for the better ordering and governing of Negroes" to further regulate enslaved people. In Virginia the Royal Commissioners recommended new laws that would address runaway "servants" in the colony and suggested that they should "serve as a public Servant and Slave of the Colony." The House of Burgesses therefore passed "An Act Concerning Servants who were out in rebellion" in 1677 that added time to servants' contracts for their desertion during the rebellion. In addition, servants who were "assisters in the said rebellion" were to restitute owners for the damages they caused during the uprising, and "horses, sloopes, boates, armes, servants, slaves or other goods" taken during the rebellion were to be posted at each county courthouse "in faire writeing" so that owners could claim them. Native Americans captured during the rebellion could also be kept enslaved. In 1680 the House passed "An Act for Preventing Negroes Insurrections" in June. The new law prohibited enslaved people from carrying weapons of any kind and restricted their unsupervised congregations. The law came four years after Bacon's Rebellion, but the timing of its adoption suggested that lawmakers were still concerned about Bacon's enslaved rebels. Authorities in Virginia did not detect another plot to rebel among servants and slaves in the colony until 1687 in the Northern Neck, and records do not otherwise indicate that planters were concerned that enslaved people were becoming increasingly rebellious or agitated in 1680.[15]

Material deprivation of enslaved people often preceded militarized slave revolts during the period, and material deprivation also affected enslaved soldiers in Bacon's army. Rebels in Bacon's army in 1676 faced economic loss and deprivation. Tobacco prices in Virginia had fallen, and Governor Berkeley increased taxes to help pay for colonial expenditures. Furthermore, tobacco overproduction and navigation acts further decreased tobacco prices, while war with the Dutch in the 1660s and 1670s increased colonial debt. Underscoring how financially strained the colony was, Berkeley stated to the king that because the previous year's crops were so bad and because tobacco prices had fallen, he and his advisors did not think they had enough money to adequately fund an army against Bacon or hostile Natives. At the very least, it is clear that economic decay was present in the colony in 1675. Warren Billings has described it as having probably affected all segments of Virginia society and made living at even subsistence levels difficult. More importantly, Virginia colonists and their slaves suffered substantial threats to food security leading up to Bacon's Rebellion. In October 1675 Barbados governor Atkins described his frustration in a letter to Sir Joseph Williamson about the lack of provisions on the island, as English ships sent supplies to Virginia that had "been in a starving condition." In two other letters to Williamson that same month, R. I. Watts and Nathaniel Osborne observed that ships returning from Virginia reported that the colony had lost a great amount of its Indian corn and tobacco crops, and that the majority of pigs and other livestock were dead. Furthermore, New Englanders enforced high prices on foods that they exported to Virginia, which further strained Virginia's fiscal stability. Osborne reported to Williamson in April 1676 that sailors returning from Jamestown described an illness wreaking havoc in Virginia. The outbreak, which some sailors believed was similar to the plague, caused fever, head and stomachaches, and colds before killing many Virginia men, women, and children. To make matters worse, colonial reports indicated an abnormally hot summer and autumn, and a colder than average winter during the rebellion. Indeed, conditions in the colony were very poor, as both planters and enslaved people suffered more from pestilence, crop failures, and mortality rates in 1675 and 1676 than they ever had in the colony since the Starving Time in 1609. Aside from disease and a threatened food supply, it is also likely that the Virginia planters who endured substantial economic stress passed more of the burdens down to their slaves just as planters did elsewhere in the Atlantic, including in the many cases in which enslaved people responded by rebelling.[16]

Aside from economic loss, starvation, and disease, planters passed a series of acts in the House of Burgesses in the early 1660s that worsened living conditions for slaves. New legislation in March 1661 required that White servants who ran away with enslaved Africans and African Americans would serve additional time of service in their contracts, and that they would be fined if any enslaved person was lost or died in flight. The intent of the law was to deter collusion between servants and slaves and make it more difficult for enslaved people to resist. Planters passed another law that same month that prohibited colonists from trading with servants and slaves without their owner's consent, which limited potential transactions among servants and slaves. Given that an enslaved person's ability to trade food and goods often increased bondpeople's standard of living and that surpluses could help them purchase their freedom, the new restriction undermined their material comfort. It also limited their ability to escape bondage. Perhaps more importantly, another 1661 act proscribed colonists from keeping Native Americans as slaves and ordered Indians to serve sentences no longer than English servants of the same age. White Virginians continued to hold Indians as slaves despite the law, but the legislation itself suggests the beginning of a labor transition, as planters shifted toward Black slaves instead of Natives as a labor source. Additionally, an act passed in December 1662 declared that the status of Black children would be inherited according to the condition of the mother. Establishing a lifelong condition of bondage, the act made enslaved children bondspeople for life and contributed to the worsening conditions for enslaved people in Virginia leading up to Bacon's Rebellion. Furthermore, another act in 1667 ensured that baptisms among slaves would not change their condition in bondage. Christian slaves would remain slaves. The Black chattel system was already in ascendance in the colony before enslaved rebels mobilized in Bacon's army.[17]

Conclusion

Bacon's Rebellion was something different for Black slaves involved in the fighting. While Whites continued to fight each other and local Indians, dozens if not hundreds of Black slaves revolted for their liberty in one of the largest slave insurrections in British North American history. Consistent with other militarized slave insurrections in the Atlantic, slaves endured material deprivation connected to the rise of the Black chattel system at the onset of Bacon's Rebellion, and they were more likely to rise up against those at the top of the system. The rebellion was not a cause of the rise of Black chattel slavery in Virginia but rather a symptom of its already having developed, and many White and Black people were prepared to resist it violently. In addition, Bacon's enslaved rebels fought collectively and proportionately as other slaves did in revolts throughout the Atlantic world. The rebels, both Black and White, threatened to destroy the planter regime in colonial Virginia. They fought alongside servants as they had done earlier in Barbados, and they razed, plundered, and fought like rebels in many other revolts in the littoral.[18]

Finally, like other enslaved rebels across the Atlantic, the rebels in Virginia fought in order to escape bondage. Notably, enslaved people were among the last holdouts who kept fighting Captain Grantham well after Bacon had died. In distress that Berkeley and Grantham might renege on their pardons, the enslaved rebels refused to give up and forced Grantham to promise them their freedom. By doing so, servants and slaves also made Bacon's Rebellion a conflict about slavery itself. Slavery in Virginia continued for almost two hundred more years, but revolting slaves in Bacon's army demonstrated that they could confront their masters with the issue of emancipation. In fear that the insurrection would intensify, Berkeley's men seized servants and slaves before they could join in the fight, while servants and slaves also forced Bacon, Berkeley, and King Charles II to consider their freedom in order to end the fighting. The rebellion was the first major conflict in British North America in which slave soldiers fought in large numbers and were able to push the issue of emancipation. It was also one of the first major conflicts in which enslaved people used military service to challenge the chattel system.

In Bacon's case, a slave revolt was part of another war, and while enslaved people fought in the conflict, the cause and character of their fighting was distinct from that of other belligerents involved. Although affected by White-Indian frontier warfare, Virginia slaves had a more important goal: they wanted their own emancipation. Their ability to raise the specter of emancipation among Virginia planters demonstrates the power and negotiating space that enslaved rebels held, but it also attests to how much influence slave revolts had on promoting Black emancipation in the Atlantic. The wedge that Bacon's enslaved soldiers created for themselves would also be one of the first of many attempts in which enslaved people used warfare in slave societies and the practice of arming slaves to challenge their bondage and promote their freedom. From Black perspectives, Bacon's Rebellion was much more than an Indian conflict or resistance to government policy. It was the beginning of a series of armed slave revolts that were part of the history of slavery and the militarization of slave resistance in the Anglo-Atlantic.

CHAPTER 2

"Negroes Plundered by the Indians from Carolina"

Slave Soldiers in the South Carolina Yamasee War, 1715–1717

Approximately forty years after enslaved soldiers rose up in Virginia as part of Nathanial Bacon's army, enslaved people farther south also seized the opportunity that violent conflict offered to achieve emancipation. Whereas rebels in Bacon's army joined the fray in an Indian-imperial conflict in Virginia, in South Carolina violence flared up when the Yamasee Indians rebelled against English colonists in the spring of 1715. The ensuing Yamasee War, which lasted until 1717, was one of the largest and most violent Indian wars in early American history.[1]

The war, which historians have noted had significant consequences on European-Native imperial relations in the Southeast and on the Indian slave trade, also had substantial implications for Black slaves in the region as loyal slave soldiers helped defend the British territory from Native and Spanish attacks. Their success in defense of the colony seemingly helped solidify Black chattel slavery in Carolina, while those who chose to run away and fight for the Spanish in nearby Florida were increasingly called on to defend Spanish interests in the area. For their assistance to the Spanish Empire, they could live free in Florida.[2]

The Yamasee War offered enslaved Black people in Carolina an opportunity to defend plantations and earn their owners' good favor, and we are beginning to understand that the conflict additionally offered enslaved people an opportunity to run from or even fight against their owners as they allied with warring Yamasee who also sided with the Spanish in Florida. But we still do not fully know what this conflict meant to the enslaved Black people who chose from these options, and especially not how the activities of enslaved people compared to those of other enslaved people in the Atlantic world in times of war and rebellion. How did slave soldiers use military service in the Carolina Lowcountry to challenge the slave system?

This story of slave soldiers moves from Virginia to South Carolina where slave soldiers in the Lowcountry experienced war and armed conflict in different ways than in the Chesapeake decades earlier. While Jane Landers has shown that some slaves in Carolina were willing to join the Yamasee against British colonists, this chapter goes deeper to compare and examine the range of options slave soldiers had in Carolina in 1715–1717. The Yamasee War was also a conflict in which several Native American groups fought each other as well as British colonists, and in which Spanish imperial rivals were heavily involved. Thus, it also offers insight into how slave soldiering worked in the British Atlantic with so many competing interests and actors at play, especially the presence of imperial rivals, who were absent in Virginia in 1676. How could and did enslaved people exploit such circumstances, which recurred frequently in the Atlantic world, to further their own goals? What did the Yamasee War mean for the enslaved soldiers who participated in it, and what were slave soldiers trying to accomplish by participating in this conflict? How did they compare to the enslaved soldiers who participated in other incidents of armed conflict in the Atlantic? How did slave soldiers interpret military service when Native Americans and European rivals offered other alternatives?

While British colonists and Yamasee Indians were engaged in a frontier war in South Carolina, significant numbers of enslaved Africans and African Americans took to soldiering to achieve something else. For those who took up arms with the Yamasee and Spaniards in Florida, the conflict morphed into something similar to what happened forty years earlier in Virginia, despite some important differences between the Lowcountry and the Chesapeake. Instead of an internal imperial rebellion like Bacon's Rebellion in Virginia, in Carolina enslaved soldiers exploited an Indian war and took advantage of a White imperial rival in Florida to fight for something else. For them, taking up arms was about challenging their owners and fighting for freedom, and the manner in which they did so bore striking resemblance to how militarized slave rebels created insurrections in the Lowcountry and elsewhere in the Atlantic in the early eighteenth century. Thus, in Carolina in 1715–1717, warfare and soldiering became another opportunity to strike at chattel slavery and demonstrated a rise in the militarization of slave rebels.

South Carolina at the Outbreak of War

On the eve of the Yamasee War, South Carolina's White and Black populations were growing rapidly. By the end of the first decade of the eighteenth century, there were almost 10,000 Black and White people living in the colony, including more than 3,900 free White men, women, and children, more than 100 White servants, 4,100 enslaved Black people, and 1,400 Indian slaves. By 1715 there were roughly six thousand White people and eight thousand Black slaves living near the Yamasee, Creek, Cherokee, and Yuchi. From 1700 to the end of the war, a little more than fourteen hundred enslaved Africans arrived via the transatlantic slave trade, of which a little more than 56 percent and 43 percent were imported from the Gold Coast and Senegambia, respectively. However, many of the enslaved people living in South Carolina had been imported via the intercolonial slave trade from Barbados, Jamaica, and Antigua. In the first twenty years of the eighteenth century, Carolina planters imported a little fewer than nine hundred enslaved people this way, of which more than five hundred were transshipped from Jamaica and Barbados. Ninety-nine more came from Antigua. During the same period, enslaved people embarking from the Gold Coast constituted almost 45 percent of the people brought to Jamaica, Barbados, and Antigua via the transatlantic slave trade, while people from the Bight of Benin represented the next largest group at almost 29 percent. Taken together during this early period of Carolina history, a large faction of the enslaved people in South Carolina who were not American-born were probably Akan, Twi, or Gā speakers from the Gold Coast, who were likely taken as prisoners during the many wars that erupted in the region during the period.[3]

By English estimates there were 1,215 Yamasee, including 413 men, 345 women, 234 boys, and 233 girls living in the region. There were also 214 Apalachicola, 638 Apalatchee, 233 Savana, 400 Yuchi, 2,406 Ochesee or Creek, 1,773 Abikaw, 2,313 Talliboose, 770 Alabama, and 9,992 Cherokee, among many others, totaling 28,041 Natives within seven hundred miles of Charleston, many of whom could fight against White planters if they wanted to. The Cherokee alone had about four thousand warriors in more than thirty separate towns in the Carolinas, Georgia, and present-day southeastern Tennessee, while the Catawba northwest of Charleston could mobilize more than five hundred soldiers spread out in seven towns. The Apalachee near Augusta, Georgia, had almost three hundred soldiers, and the Yamasee themselves had more than four hundred men who could fight.[4]

Tensions between the British colonists and Yamasee and Timucua Indians had been simmering for decades before the war erupted. Long before the Yamasee challenged British expansion in Carolina, the Timucua also fought back English encroachment in northern Florida and southern Georgia. Like the Yamasee, the Timucua had faced English aggression in the late seventeenth and early eighteenth centuries, forcing them to flee to Saint Augustine and the Spanish, who relied on them as allies against other Indian nations. English expansion in Carolina also encouraged a rise in Indian slave trading in the region. English slave traders targeted Natives who were not British allies, and they worked with Native American allies to secure more people to keep as slaves. For a brief period the Yamasee themselves served English traders in this way and worked against the Spanish in Florida. However, shortly before the Yamasee War, Westo Indian slave raiders who were allied with the English led a series of raids and attacks in Carolina that drove many Indian groups farther south to avoid enslavement. It was these refugees that joined the nascent Yamasee confederacy in the last decades of the seventeenth century. By the 1680s there were over three hundred Yamasee living in the mission towns along the St. Johns River watershed and near Saint Augustine. By 1711 a census showed that there were more than four hundred Native Americans living south of Saint Augustine with the Spanish, a significant reduction from previous decades. By the time the rebellion actually started, the Yamasee confederation consisted of five different groups, including the Lower Creek, Apalachicola, Apalachee, Savannah, and Yuchi. It was these people who fought against the British colonists in 1715.[5]

Most English accounts of the Yamasee War periodize the conflict as starting on Good Friday, April 15, 1715, when Yamasee warriors ambushed English commissioners and traders William Bray, Samuel Warner, Thomas Nairne, and John Wright at the Yamasee village Pocotaligo near Port Royal in South Carolina. The White men had visited the town four days earlier after colonists became alarmed that the Natives were upset and were plotting an uprising against them. When the Yamasee told them they were upset about English traders threatening to enslave Yamasee women and children and that they wanted to meet Governor Charles Craven, Bray and Warner returned to Craven, who sent the men back to Pocotaligo to set up a more formal meeting. The traders had arrived there on a Thursday to assure the Yamasee that their concerns and demands would be satisfied, but the next morning the Natives ambushed them. While the commissioners and traders slept, Yamasee warriors attacked with hatchets and muskets and captured nearly all of those they did not kill. Seymour Burrows was able to escape despite being wounded, and he fled to John Barnwell's plantation on Port Royal Island to alert everyone else. Thereafter, planters prepared for war as the Good Friday Massacre morphed into a much larger conflict between the Natives and English colonists.[6]

According to at least one English account, some colonists even told the Natives before the massacre that the colonists would make war on them, which inculcated the idea among the Yamasee that they had to preemptively strike the English to survive. These rumors were part of a longer history of Yamasee grievances against the traders and Whites in South Carolina decades before. In 1711 and 1712 the Yamasee repeatedly complained about White encroachment, settling debts, and Indians taken as slaves. The Natives also resented English traders who tracked runaway slaves all the way to Saint Augustine in 1714 where people were supposed to be safe from re-enslavement.[7]

According to four Yamasee Caciques who petitioned Spanish governor Francisco de Córcoles y Martínez for help at Saint Augustine later in 1715, they believed the conflict erupted in part due to the Indian slave trade. The four men, Ysiopole, Yfallaquisca or Perro Bravo, Alonso, and Gabriel, informed the governor that they understood Carolina traders were increasingly upset over the Indian slave trade. Yamasee raiders were apparently not providing enough slaves to feed the English plantation system, and when the Yamasee could not satisfy the planters with other goods, the traders threatened to make the Natives slaves themselves, including women and children. Thus they had prepared to make war against the English, and they thought a preemptive strike at Pocotaligo was the best course of action. The chiefs also complained about the destruction of their towns from English attacks, and that they and a confederation of 161 Indian towns had given their name to Spain and would execute the orders of the governor.[8]

Immediately after the Good Friday Massacre, the Yamasee moved on to Port Royal Island and plundered its plantations on Saturday and Sunday. There they killed about sixty White colonists before the rest escaped on canoes. The Yamasee and fleeing White survivors exchanged a round of gunfire, resulting in three Natives being killed. Approximately two hundred White settlers escaped. After the attack on Port Royal, Governor Craven ordered troops to counterattack the Yamasee at Pocotaligo. In about a week a force of around two hundred men marched to the Indian town, but they were spotted by Yamasee warriors near Captain Woodward's plantation and a small skirmish ensued. On April 21 or 22 a major battle occurred at a Sadkeche town during which the Yamasee fled despite nearly trapping Craven's detachment. According to Craven, approximately eleven militiamen were killed and twenty-one were wounded in the early engagement. Several Yamasee warriors were also killed and wounded in the fight. After this small defeat, the Yamasee retreated into the woods and swamps where White soldiers struggled to pursue them. The rest of the colonists then spent their time fortifying several positions along the frontier. In the process they armed several Black slaves in the colony to assist in its defense. By this point, Black slaves were probably both eager and reluctant to join the fray. They were undoubtedly affected by Yamasee raids near Port Royal that also threatened their safety and security, which probably motivated them to take up arms to defend themselves and even seek revenge. On the other hand, others probably disdained having to serve for their White owners, and still others viewed the Yamasee as a potential ally against White colonists in Carolina. Given these options, enslaved Black people began taking up arms in the conflict.[9]

A few weeks later, on May 15, 1715, militia captain Thomas Barker moved with ninety White and twelve Black militiamen toward Hearn's plantation along the Santee River north of Charleston. Just a day earlier Indians had attacked and killed Hearn, unbeknownst to Barker. On May 16 his Black and White battalion arrived near the Santee River under the guidance of an Indian scout named Wateree Jack. Wateree Jack then betrayed the battalion and fled. Barker and his men subsequently moved along the river through a beaten path devastated by a recent hurricane. As they marched, Indian warriors hidden behind the felled trees and bushes ambushed them. Despite the advantage of complete surprise, the Natives possibly attacked too soon, which enabled the Black and White militiamen to return fire. After a short exchange of gunfire, the Black and White soldiers forced the Yamasee warriors to flee, although more than two dozen militiamen were dead, including Barker. Ten were also taken prisoner.[10]

Just days after Barker's defeat, Natives continued their march south toward Thomas Broughton's plantation, where one of his slaves named Jemmy served in the militia to defend it. By June 5, 1715, northern Indians approached Schenkingh's Fort under pretense of peace. Inside the fort, Commander Redwood entertained ideas of a peaceful meeting and allowed the warriors to approach. When the Natives suddenly attacked, at least one enslaved soldier named Wallace who belonged to Benjamin Godin helped fight back before he escaped. Wallace was probably aware of potential rewards for good service, and sure enough Wallace later earned an award for his role. Slave soldiers also helped repel an Indian attack near Charleston that same summer.[11]

Enslaved soldiers also marched with Colonel John Barnwell and Colonel Alexander Mackay, and they helped ambush the Yamasee to retaliate for the Good Friday Massacre. This Black, Indian, and White force attacked several Yamasee towns and helped take at least one prisoner. Later that summer, several enslaved soldiers marched with Colonel John Fenwick against hostile Indians along the Combahee River, and they marched with him to Pond Bridge and to Jackson's plantation, where one enslaved soldier was wounded. About a hundred enslaved soldiers marched with Governor Craven during an expedition across the Santee River in 1715. They had decided to march with him to counterattack their common Indian enemies, while later that same year a company of Black soldiers under the command of Captain John Pight marched with Maurice Moore against the Cherokee.[12]

That same month, Captain George Chicken and his men marched to the Ponds, a plantation also known as Weston Hall, northwest of Charleston, where the Black and White and enslaved and free militia force would guard against further Indian attacks on the northern frontier. At this point, enslaved soldiers saw multiple military options in the conflict. Some continued to serve White commanders, but at least two enslaved soldiers, Pope and Pompey, had joined the northern Indians against the English. By June 12 Chicken led his 120-man battalion to the Ashley River, where he divided his men in a pincer movement to surround the enemy. Among the men serving in Chicken's battalion were forty Black and seventy White soldiers. On the next day, Chicken had hoped to ambush the Natives but they discovered him early, and he was forced to attack too soon. After several hours of close fighting that afternoon, Chicken's men killed several dozen warriors and took two prisoners. As the Indians fled into the swamps, Chicken's men gave chase, but the warriors were able to evade them under cover of darkness. Nevertheless, they had left their weapons and plunder behind them. Chicken's men were also able to rescue several captives from Schenkingh's Fort. Enslaved soldiers were fighting with alacrity and were willing to sacrifice for the colonial cause. Chicken lost two men, including Thomas Broughton's enslaved soldier named Jemmy. He apparently died loyal to his owner despite opportunities to run away and turn coat as others like Pope and Pompey had done.[13]

Despite Chicken's success in June, the fighting caused great consternation among Carolina planters in late spring and early summer. In May the General Assembly of South Carolina supplicated to King George I that they wanted to declare war against the Indians and that he should issue a royal edict to the other British colonies in North America to come to the aid of the South Carolinians, especially rich Virginia. That same month Governor Charles Eden of North Carolina called on volunteers to rise and help their neighbors to the south. But their help was not enough, and by July Governor Craven sent emissaries to Virginia and New England for more assistance. By then the HMS *Valour* had arrived in Charleston with 160 small arms, ten barrels of gunpowder, and twenty-five casks of shot. That same month Virginians finally agreed to send Captain Arthur Middleton and 120 men to South Carolina, while New Yorkers pledged one hundred muskets. The violence that the summer of 1715 brought also encouraged leaders in South Carolina to raise more troops, including enslaved soldiers, who could help defend the colony from hostile Indians. By August 1715 the commissioners of the Commons House Assembly advocated raising twelve hundred White and Black soldiers for the task.[14]

Enslaved soldiers continued to serve as the fighting raged on. Colonel Maurice Moore marched with sixty White soldiers and sixty Native soldiers against the northern Indians, where he was joined in late July by Governor Craven and Thomas Broughton and their accompanying hundred White soldiers and hundred enslaved Black and Indian soldiers. Once Governor Craven marched to the Santee, he forced the Indians to flee over the Ponpon Bridge, though they killed four or five White colonists and burned the crossing. To the south, the Yamasee continued their attacks on plantations near Port Royal and New London, destroying most near the latter. In St. Paul's Parish they destroyed at least twenty plantations and turned the parish into a deserted frontier. Later that summer, Captain William Stone sent one hundred militiamen to Port Royal to cut off Indian canoes and chase the enemy into the woods. On at least two separate engagements in August and September, the English defeated the Yamasee in the area. In late summer or early fall 1715, Colonel John Fenwick marched up to the Pond Bridge and met the enemy Indians at Jackson's house near a ferry. On attacking them at dawn, the English killed nine Natives and took two prisoners, while one White militiamen and one Black soldier were wounded.[15]

The summer of 1715 was disastrous for English colonists in South Carolina. Six to seven hundred Yamasee laid waste to English plantations in the colony. They attacked and destroyed all the settlements near Port Royal, and along the Combahee River, the plantations south of the Edisto River, and all those on the Santee River felt the blow of the Yamasee. They had burned plantations on their way to New London, where they burned even more on arrival. Almost all the plantations in St. Bartholomew's and St. Helen's Parishes were destroyed during the war. Port Royal Island was also abandoned. Approximately a hundred colonists were killed in St. Bartholomew's Parish in the first southern attack alone. As the Yamasee moved through the southern parishes, some colonists and their slaves were barely able to escape. In St. Helen's Parish, English ships had to carry the colonists up to Charleston as they narrowly escaped the attacks.[16]

However, in New London a garrison of fifty to sixty militiamen stopped the Indian advance and forced them to spread out along the Stono River, where they resumed more plunder elsewhere. The Yamasee were so easily able to plunder the southern plantations because Whites had not detected them, so Governor Craven raised seven hundred men to march to the Wincaw River and meet Colonel Moore in the north. By then the *Success* had arrived from Virginia with thirty more Virginian soldiers and eighty White and sixty Indian fighters from North Carolina. The South Carolina Assembly also passed an act to pay for the forces and to raise several White officers, six hundred rank-and-file White soldiers, and four hundred enslaved Black soldiers that were divided into sixty-man companies to go after the Indian threat. By November colonists reported that the enemy Indians had resorted to bush fighting and that they had not been seen in full force for quite some time.[17]

Late 1715 and early 1716 marked a change in the conflict. The Cherokee turned on the Yamasee and agreed to fight with the English against them. The Cherokee's superior numbers in the region marked doom for the smaller Yamasee confederacy, and the English-Cherokee alliance pushed the Yamasee south and out of Carolina. The Yamasee stayed near the Spanish in Florida as refugees. In the meantime, English planters rebuilt several plantations and constructed new forts to protect the shattered frontier. Enslaved soldiers probably helped staff the garrisons along the new line of defense. With the expulsion of the Yamasee and the turn of the Cherokee in 1716, the war was all but over, although official peace treaties were not formalized until 1717. By March 1716 the war had already cost the colony £140,000.[18]

Although there were still skirmishes in 1716 and 1717, including some that resulted in the deaths of Major Henry Quintyne and several of his men at the Port Royal Fort in July 1716, as well as the deaths of planters near the Edisto River in 1717, much of the fighting had dissipated. By April 1717 Secretary of State Joseph Addison informed the Council of Trade and Plantations that the enemy Indians had killed about two hundred people in South Carolina in 1715 and that the colony was paid or owed more than £200,000 in the war. More than four hundred White South Carolinians had died by war's end, or about one in forty living in the colony. Many enslaved people had died or were captured, and several others had fled to Saint Augustine as well.[19]

The Cherokee intervention also changed the tide of Indian diplomacy in the region. The Creek, who had associated themselves with the Yamasee during the war, had gained a new enemy in the Cherokee and were forced to cool relations with the English as a result. Subsequently, they signed for peace in 1717. Meanwhile, the Cherokee were reduced to ten thousand people, while the northern nations were left with 2,500 people. Smaller tribes like the Congeree, Santee, Seawee, Pedee, Waxaw, and Corsaboy were wiped out entirely. In the South the Alabama, Apalatchee, Yamasee, and Creek seemingly solidified their alliances with the French and Spanish against the English despite their losses and displacement in the war. Many of them actually emerged from the war in better diplomatic and strategic positions. They had received gifts without developing new and strict alliances with the English, and they could continue to pit European imperial rivalries against themselves for Indian interests. The Yamasee were significantly dispersed after the conflict, and more than five hundred survivors had to flee farther south to the Spanish at Saint Augustine. Their numbers continued to decline in the ensuing decades, which left a void in the area that the Creek would fill.[20]

The war also changed the military posture of the colony for enslaved soldiers and fugitive slaves in its aftermath. Planters established garrisons at the Congaree River north of Charleston, another barracks forty miles from there, one at Savannah, and another at Port Royal to prevent enslaved people from deserting and reaching Saint Augustine via inland water passages. Planters also put two scout boats and twenty men on patrol to prevent these desertions, and they also built garrisons at Johnson's Fort on James Island for the same reason. The new garrison system, especially the patrols at Port Royal, clearly demonstrated that some enslaved Black people in the colony had turned against their masters during the war, and that they might continue to rebel in the future and flee to Saint Augustine to meet their Indian and Spanish allies. Some enslaved soldiers remained loyal to the colonists during the war, but some took up arms against English interests in the colony.[21]

Carolina planters also resented the Spanish who had built a fort at Apalatchee, where they could support their Apalatchee and Creek allies. English colonists were angered that three to four hundred Indian soldiers whom the Spanish armed and who fought in the Yamasee War resided in four or five villages near Saint Augustine. Black slaves had also apparently joined them. The warriors' main task was to help defend Spanish Florida from English counterattacks. Indeed, from English perspectives, the Spanish appeared well positioned after the war. They continued to produce pitch and tar with the "help of the Negroes plundered by the Indians from Carolina." Although enslaved soldiers had defended plantations and fought in the British militias, it was also clear that some enslaved Black and Indian people and free Natives had used the conflict to support the Spanish, and in its aftermath they helped produce for them in ways that hurt Carolina trading interests. Spanish encouragements for the Yamasee to "murder" and "plunder" South Carolina planters, and their "harbouring rebells, fellons, debtors, servants, and Negro slaves," forced Carolina planters to keep large garrisons on guard at a great cost to the treasury. It seemed that the only solution would be to drive the Spanish and their Black rebel allies out of the continent if the Carolina plantation system were to survive.[22]

Steadfast Slave Soldiers

Some enslaved soldiers were loyal during the Yamasee War, and their service in the defense of the colony was significant. They served in some of the first engagements of the war in 1715, and some earned rewards for their valiant efforts. They also demonstrated to British slave owners that they were crucial for the defense of the colony by 1716. In 1717 there were other indications that enslaved soldiers served with distinction for their English owners. Farther south and west in Florida in September, Spanish lieutenant Diego Peña met several Indians who informed him that twelve Englishmen and one enslaved Black man had arrived in the area as a consequence of the Yamasee War. The Indians reported to Peña that they wanted to take these people to the Spanish governor at Saint Augustine for good favor. The Black prisoner also confessed that he had left Charleston in June 1717 on a boat and two canoes with English militiamen in pursuit of Yamasee fighters. He was apparently willing to chase Indians far from English territory and into a region in which he might have found refuge with English enemies. The enslaved man's account demonstrated that even on forays into Florida to track enemy Indians, enslaved people in the Yamasee War proved themselves loyal soldiers to their English owners.[23]

After the fighting had died down and Governor Robert Johnson reported that peace had "concluded" by July 1716, he also recognized that the colony's Black and Indian allies were absolutely critical for the Yamasee defeat. Not only had the Cherokee and other Indian allies provided provisions that helped defeat the Yamasee and Creek, but Black slave soldiers were reliable, and Johnson noted that to "be able to upon any great emergency to arm their negroes," planters in South Carolina would be "impowered to resist a greater force than the Indian enemy will in all humane probability be able at any time to bring against them." Slave soldiers who remained loyal in South Carolina would have a strengthened role in defending the colony from future Native and Spanish aggression. Notwithstanding their valorous efforts in the war, most of the enslaved Black people who did serve in the militia during the war returned to plantation work after it ended. However, a handful did receive some benefits for their fealty. As noted above, Wallace of Benjamin Godin received a shirt and a hat for his service defending Schenkingh's Fort. Meanwhile, at least three other Black slaves who were captured and taken to Saint Augustine during the war or shortly thereafter were rewarded for their return to Carolina. Buff Moore, who belonged to Captain John Woodward, escaped from Saint Augustine in 1716, and the Commons House approved his freedom on his return to Carolina. Similarly, a man named Harry who belonged to Widow Perry escaped from Saint Augustine in 1721 and was given at least £5 for his return. An enslaved man named Coffee received £10 for his return in 1728 as well. At least two Indian slaves were freed for their service in the war as well.[24]

The Yamasee War was not the first time in which enslaved soldiers fought for their owners in Carolina. It was also not the first time that the English decided to raise more slaves to serve as soldiers for the colony's defense. As early as 1704, South Carolina legislators passed an act to muster "trusty" slaves who could be used as soldiers to defend the colony. The act also required freeholders to make a list of Black, biracial, and Indian slaves who could serve for this purpose and allowed officers to summon slave owners to show why certain enslaved people were chosen for service. Additionally, owners would arm enslaved soldiers with a lance, hatchet, or firearm, and with sufficient ammunition for them to report to their units ready to fight. If slaveholders refused the summons, they were required to appear before commissioners themselves to explain why, and if they refused to send their enslaved people or give them arms during times of alarm, they would forfeit £5 to the militia captain or a different value appraised by nearby freeholders. The act also stipulated that if enslaved soldiers were killed or maimed in service, the public would pay their owners, but not a soldier's family, a fair value for the loss. A similar act in 1708 renewed the earlier law with much of the same mechanisms, except that militia officers were required to arm enslaved soldiers themselves. More importantly, the new act allowed for rewards for valiant service of enslaved soldiers, and if any enslaved soldier killed or took an enemy soldier prisoner, verified by a White comrade, they could earn their freedom. Their owner would be compensated for their manumission. In addition, if an enslaved soldier was wounded or disabled due to military service, they would also be set free at the public's expense.[25]

These provisions encouraged enslaved loyalty, and assuredly enslaved people in Carolina understood military service as a potential avenue to escape chattel slavery in the colony. The act also prohibited freeholders of military age from traveling outside the colony or risk a £50 fine. Owners were also paid £2 per month for each month of service that their enslaved people provided in the militia. Despite these articles that rewarded loyal military service and renewed older legislation to raise enslaved Black soldiers in the colony, the 1708 act also considered what to do if enslaved soldiers were disloyal or chose to resist their enslaved status. If any slave soldier deserted or would "run over to the enemy," their owner would be compensated. These acts, passed during Queen Anne's War, reiterated the dire need to raise enough soldiers in defense of the colony and the practice of using Black slaves against Spanish, French, and Indian enemies nearby. While they incentivized loyal Black military service, they also put safeguards against Black rebellion in place, which demonstrated that enslaved soldiers were willing to betray their owners, or at least that White planters suspected that they would. By 1708 the colony had a militia force consisting of approximately 950 White men spread out through sixteen companies and two regiments. There were also two companies of enslaved Black soldiers who could carry firearms and lances into battle.[26]

The decision to use Black slaves as soldiers in the Yamasee War also reflected insufficient White military manpower. Governor Craven had informed Lord Townshend that he simply did not have enough White men in the country to match the numerically superior Yamasee, so he ordered about two hundred "stout negro men" to muster and march with White soldiers and Indian allies against the hostile Indians. The lords proprietors agreed and petitioned King George I in 1715, reiterating that they did not have enough White men or enough arms and ammunition "for their negroes" to defend the province, which would result in the loss of the colony if the Crown did not react swiftly. Needless to say, all these issues point to the fact that enslaved soldiers served admirably during the Yamasee War for their owners and for various incentives. It was also clear that Carolina planters understood how valuable and reliable enslaved soldiers were, and in February 1719–1720 the South Carolina Assembly passed an "act for the enlisting [of] such trusty slaves," who could be mustered for the colony in "time of alarms" not unlike what they endured during the Yamasee War. The more developed militia system in Carolina compared to what existed in Virginia forty years earlier gave more options for enslaved soldiers and mitigated Black armed resistance.[27]

Ultimately, it was not peculiar why enslaved people willingly fought for their owners when they shared potential Spanish and Indian allies. It is reasonable to believe that some enslaved people preferred to serve as loyal soldiers and that they resented Indian attacks. Indeed, several slaves in Port Royal and St. Bartholomew's Parishes suffered from Indian attacks, while Catawba and Cherokee raids in the Santee region also resulted in enslaved casualties. After the battle of Schenkingh's Fort, Huguenot reverend Mr. Richebourg wrote that the trusted Indians betrayed colonists "by burning a plantation and killing negroes in our settlement" in St. James Parish.[28] Undoubtedly some enslaved people were shaken by the violence that this conflict produced, and many were probably hurt during plantation raids or were even separated from friends and family members. The unknown of what life would be like in Florida, or what punishment their British masters might mete out to them should the Spanish and Yamasee collapse, probably also factored into how enslaved people made decisions in 1715–1717. Some may have liked the prestige of military service, or understood the laws in place, which they knew they could earn recognition and maybe even manumission for their good service. Perhaps some even hoped they would be disabled in war, thus rendering them free from bondage. We cannot know all the motives behind why slave soldiers chose to fight for their English owners, but it is also clear that many enslaved people in South Carolina saw the large-scale conflict as an opportunity to escape from their owners and to join their owners' Indian and European imperial rivals to undermine slaveholding power in South Carolina.

Insurgent Soldiers

Despite loyal military service that enslaved soldiers rendered to the English during the Yamasee War, we know from English, Indian, and Spanish accounts that enslaved people in Carolina also fled from their masters to fight with the Yamasee and Spanish and to fight their former owners. Curiously, during the Yamasee War English authorities declared the Native Americans engaged in a "revolt" or an "insurrection of many nations of Indians," but they did not do the same for the Black slaves who fought in the war with the Yamasee. Planters and authorities did acknowledge that Black slaves were also actively running away during the war and were siding with the Yamasee and Spanish enemies at Saint Augustine. Hugh Bryan was captured during the conflict and reported to authorities in Charleston once his Yamasee captor returned him as part of a peace negotiation. After he had been captured and taken to Saint Augustine and a nearby Creek village, Bryan relayed that he heard the Spaniards in Florida tell the Yamasee to kill the English colonists, and that they would furnish the Indians with "whatever they wanted to carry on the war" against the Carolinians. According to members of the Assembly of Carolina, the Spanish at Saint Augustine were therefore violating the recent Treaty of Utrecht in which Great Britain and Spain agreed not to arm or encourage hostile Natives to attack each other. According to the Assembly members, Spanish behavior at Saint Augustine also directly encouraged the Yamasee to take enslaved people from English plantations. Authorities reiterated Bryan's report that there was an "abundance of slaves taken from us by the Yamasees and carried to Augustine." But they also acknowledged that this was not just a case of enemy Indians stealing passive plantation slaves to take to the Spanish. Indeed, they acknowledged that "many more run away to that place," which demonstrates that many had *chosen* to run away with the Indians and to join the Spanish.[29]

Since most plantations in South Carolina were adjacent to waterways that Carolina Indians used for travel, their location ensured that enslaved people in Carolina, both African and Indian, had close contact with free Indians on frequent occasions. Their work tracking cattle and pathfinding also gave them more mobility, which encouraged interaction with free Natives in Carolina. Such a set-up ensured that enslaved people frequently saw and understood who their potential allies and enemies were, and what paths they might take if they chose to desert or rise up in rebellion. For many this meant running away of their own accord.[30]

English accounts of enslaved interactions with the Yamasee demonstrated both a belief that Black slaves were captives of Indian and Spanish raiders and that they willingly took up arms with the Indians against Carolina planters. In one incident English authorities reported that some plantation slaves "taken" to Saint Augustine flocked to diplomatic agent Major James Cochran when he visited the Spanish fort to "have liberty to go home with their master." Yet they also reported that the Spanish authorities in Saint Augustine refused to deliver any enslaved person who had made it to the fort, which also encouraged "a great many more lately to run away to that place." While we cannot discount the possibility that some enslaved Black people were taken to Florida against their will, we should also be suspicious of White accounts that expected enslaved fealty at all times. To many enslaved people the Spanish fort had become a place where they could escape the evils of the British plantation system in South Carolina. English planters also noted that the "negroes plundered by the Indians from Carolina" during the Yamasee War helped bolster the Spanish garrison at Saint Augustine. The fact that Carolina slaves stayed with the Spanish in Florida and strengthened the Spanish fort there must have also angered Carolina planters, especially since the Yamasee had just as recently as 1712 agreed to "restrain all slaves belonging to any White men from going to warr." Their reneging on the agreement and alliance with enslaved people and the Spanish both undermined English power in the Southeast and strengthened Spanish power in Florida.[31]

Some Carolina slaves fought vigorously with the Yamasee and against the English during the war, as was the case for Francisco Menéndez. Menéndez had potentially served as an enslaved soldier in the Carolina militia a decade before the Yamasee conflict broke out during Queen Anne's War, but he decided that his best chance for freedom was to side with the rebel Indians later on in life. For three years Menéndez willingly fought with Yamasee chief Jospo, though another Yamasee leader named Perro Bravo claimed ownership over him when they visited Saint Augustine. Years later Jospo claimed that the Yamasee allied with enslaved Black people and that the Black slaves helped the Yamasee fight the English in Carolina. The Spanish at Saint Augustine eventually sold Menéndez to Don Francisco Menéndez Marquez due to a fear of English reprisals against Florida for taking Carolina slaves. Though Spanish officials had denied Menéndez his hard-fought freedom after the Yamasee War, he did not give up on these dreams and successfully petitioned for his manumission decades later. Notwithstanding his new Spanish owners, Menéndez understood he lived under better circumstances with the Spanish in Florida, which seemingly transformed this enslaved rebel soldier into a loyal one. Menéndez later served as the leader of the Black militia at the Spanish fort.[32] Although he still petitioned for his freedom, something he did not achieve until 1738, he does not appear to have ever revolted against his Spanish owners as an enslaved soldier, like he did against the English during the Yamasee War. In his case the Yamasee War was a conflict that could turn the loyalties of enslaved soldiers. He had revolted against the English in 1715 but stayed loyal to the Spanish thereafter.

Indeed, Carolina colonists understood the potential for enslaved loyalties to change during the Yamasee War, and they used great caution when they decided to let enslaved soldiers fight. When Carolinians reached out to Virginians for reinforcements during the war, Virginians refused outright to send soldiers and bartered for their service. They first demanded that the Carolinians send them one Black woman for each White Virginia soldier sent to Carolina. At first delegates in the Carolina Assembly found such a measure impracticable as breaking up enslaved families might anger the Black husbands who remained in South Carolina, "wch. might have occasioned a revolt also of the slaves." William Pulteney reported in July 1715 that the French and Spanish were both assisting the Yamasee, who were already too numerous for the South Carolina planters and Black slaves to withstand. Pulteney pondered if enslaved Blacks could be armed for the colony's defense but could also use arms to "become our masters."[33] Pulteney's comments encapsulated the nature of enslaved soldiers in the conflict. They could be both loyal and rebellious.

When the conflict affected Virginia to the north, trader Henry Atherton deposed that he had met with a former slave of Carolina traders who had joined the Yamasee. The Black rebel had also informed Atherton that unscrupulous traders in Virginia had stirred up the Catawba to wage war against Virginians during the conflict. The Council of Colonial Virginia dismissed any evidence that Virginia traders were provoking Indians to war against the colony because the only evidence that was presented came from a "renegado negro who is now actually engaged with the Indians against his Majesties Subjects." Virginia lieutenant governor Alexander Spotswood also informed the Virginia Council that the Catawba and Cheraw Indians were willing to side with the English because of Yamasee aggression and that they were in the process of delivering the two Black "rogues" Pope and Pompey, who, along with a White indentured servant in South Carolina, "had taken arms with the Indians agt the People of that Province." Runaway slaves also fled west with the Yamasee during the war and its aftermath, including to Pallachocola Town near present-day Columbus, Georgia. An English traveler spotted at least one Black fugitive accompanied by a Spaniard there. The area would later develop as a safe haven for Maroons.[34]

Similarly, there were other reports of Black and enslaved soldier rebelliousness during the war. George Duckett, a shipwright from Port Royal, deposed that he saw several of his neighbors' slaves at Saint Augustine, where he had voyaged several times during the war. More specifically, he reported that the slaves of Major James Cochran, James Patterson, Colonel Barnwell, Mrs. Ford, Mr. Dicks, Mr. Graham, Mr. Adams, and one of his own bondmen were all present at Saint Augustine and under Spanish possession. Moreover, the Yamasee had assured him that the Spaniards supplied them with gunpowder and musket balls when they asked for them in exchange for the plunder they brought back to Saint Augustine. There were also indications that Black and Indian slaves attempted to seize the Charleston magazine after the first Yamasee attack. In 1723 South Carolinian authorities listed how many Black and Indian slaves were "taken" and "carryed" to Saint Augustine during the Yamasee War and then again in 1720–1721. During the war at least ninety-eight enslaved people moved from South Carolina to Florida, though it is unclear how many were Black or Indian. Most of them came from plantations owned by John Barnwell, John Cochran, Robert Graham, William Bray, and others from Port Royal. The Yamasee also captured Mrs. Borrows and took her to Saint Augustine. Her husband later traveled there to ensure her return and reported back to Governor Johnson that the Spanish had ordered the Yamasee to "spare no white man, but to bring every negroe alive to Augustine." The Spanish bounties encouraged the Yamasee to continue plantation raids and attacks and bring back enslaved Black people as captives or those who willingly left their owners in Carolina.[35]

Other reports indicated that quite a few enslaved people willingly chose to run with the Indians and join the Spanish instead of being "taken." By 1718 the lieutenant governor of Bermuda, Benjamin Bennett, informed Mr. Popple that the *Trial* had arrived in South Carolina, but its commander, Captain Willington, had relayed that South Carolinians were "very apprehensive that the Cherikees Indians in conjunction with the negros (many haveing already run away from their masters into the woods) would invade them." Captain Willington's information clearly demonstrated that enslaved people on South Carolina plantations had already fled en masse by the end of the Yamasee War, and in collusion with local Native Americans. Perhaps underscoring how important Black rebels involved in the war were, planters in South Carolina struck peace with the Creek in 1717. With the new peace treaty, the Creek agreed to return "all the Negroes and horses they have taken during the War" and all the Black slaves who were "in possession" of the Chickasaw and "Western Indians" as well. English authorities believed they had fewer than forty enslaved Black people with them, but the treaty made clear that the enslaved people had not just run to the Yamasee and to Saint Augustine during the war. They were also living in rebellion among other nations on the frontier.[36]

If there were any doubts about the role of Black rebels involved in the Yamasee War, British planters in South Carolina passed a series of new laws to crack down on the enslaved population. New laws in 1717 targeted White servants who ran away with Black slaves, prohibited interracial marriages, and codified the blackness of biracial Indian-Black children. These measures certainly suggested that repressing rebellious slaves, and their potential Indian and White allies, was very important in the aftermath of the Yamasee War. These measures were also similar to laws that planters used to regulate enslaved people in the aftermath of conventional rebellions and Maroon wars.[37]

Much like some slaves who stayed loyal, others chose to fight against the English. As the Yamasee approached plantations and raids and plunder ensued, while some enslaved people found the experience terrorizing or antagonistic, others must have thought of it as liberating. Natives offered a way out of bondage to Carolina planters, while the chaos that the conflict and plantation plunder produced at least offered an opportunity for enslaved people to flee from their owners. They potentially thought the Yamasee warriors were stronger than the Carolina militia, while they also probably heard about the Spanish decree that gave safe haven to Carolina slaves in Florida. As the warriors moved from plantation to plantation, killing White colonists and taking livestock, enslaved Black people perhaps thought they might be killed too if they did not join the Indians. Since crops and livestock were taken or destroyed, perhaps they chose to run away with the Natives to secure their own food source. It may have been their best chance for survival. Even if the Natives did not give them an option, they were perhaps willing to exchange one owner for another, and they hoped that their new Indian or Spanish masters would treat them better than their English owners had. In any case, they were willing to take the risks associated with leaving their plantations and fighting with allies to undermine English planter power in Carolina.[38]

While English colonists armed "trusty" enslaved people as a defense mechanism against European imperial rivals and hostile Native Americans, the Spanish decision to arm the Yamasee and any fugitive Black slaves who fought with them or who ran to Saint Augustine followed decades of precedent as well. The precedent also helped militarize slave resistance in Carolina by encouraging so many Black slaves to take up arms for the Spanish. Spanish authorities hoped that their allies would defend Florida but also undermine British settlement in the Southeast. By 1683 Black militiamen served at the fort and also joined in attacks against South Carolina in 1686. They also took in runaways from South Carolina to reduce British influence on the mainland. The first recorded runaway slaves from the colony arrived at Saint Augustine in 1687. Just six years later, Spanish king Charles II decreed Florida a religious sanctuary for British slaves from the Carolinas. They could be free if they arrived at the doors at the Spanish fort. Some would later serve in the Black militia, and some of these Black militiamen fought against English planters during Queen Anne's War from 1702 to 1704.[39]

Even after the Yamasee War came to an end, enslaved rebels refused to return to their owners or leave their Indian and Spanish allies in Florida. British colonists in South Carolina still complained about the Spanish arming and supplying the enemy Yamasee Indians, who in turn plundered plantations for enslaved people. Governor Johnson complained in late June 1718 that despite peace with the Creek, they had still moved further south toward Saint Augustine, and the Spanish had still encouraged the Yamasee already there to plunder plantations and bring Black slaves to the fortress in Florida. Even worse, Johnson complained that "servants, slaves, robbers, and debtors frequently escape from hence there," and the Spanish authorities at Saint Augustine refused to return enslaved people who ran to them or those who had potentially served as soldiers with the Yamasee in the recent conflict. The fact that there was only one dubious English account of collective attempts for enslaved people to return to their English owners further suggests that most were willing to stay with the Spanish in Florida. More than six months later Johnson still complained that the Spanish were encouraging the Yamasee to "murder and plunder" Carolinians, and that they were harboring "rebells, fellons, debters, servants and negro slaves," which forced colonists in Carolina to maintain an armed force to defend the frontier—a costly venture. These problems persisted well into the 1720s. Others like George Rodd, Governor Craven, and Captain Chicken also suspected the Spanish and even the French at Mobile were more involved in instigating the Black-Indian rebellion in order to "knock" the English on their heads. South Carolina trading agents Joseph Boone and Richard Beresford reiterated these concerns that the Spanish were arming the Yamasee, which enabled the Natives to plunder English plantations and "rob" them of their slaves and livestock, which "they carry to St. Augustine and are there openly bought by the Spaniards."[40]

These accusations came on the heels of a long history of imperial rivalries, which included French fears at Mobile that the English in South Carolina were instigating enemy Indians to attack them in the decade leading up to the Yamasee War. The fear, real or imagined, encouraged the French in Louisiana to order their Choctaw allies to "plunder" all the English traders living nearby. By September 1715 Governor Jean-Baptiste Le Moyne de Bienville further ordered his Indian allies to kill more English traders and bring in more captives. It is not clear if the French were encouraging plantation slaves to rebel or if Carolina slaves sought refuge or assistance from French officials, but the French were in effect actively supporting British enemies in South Carolina, much like the Spanish in Florida were doing, and it is possible some enslaved people were "taken" or joined forces with Indians also allied with the French during the Yamasee War. By encouraging Native allies to attack British colonists in Carolina, it is possible that the French in the Lower South may have also contributed to further militarized slave resistance in Carolina during the Yamasee War.[41]

For their part, the Spanish at Saint Augustine denied that they were arming any rebellious Indians involved in the Yamasee War and any Black slaves caught up in the fighting. Governor Córcoles y Martínez informed Lieutenant Governor Spotswood in 1716 that he was abiding by the Treaty of Utrecht and that he was not permitted to give arms or ammunition to the rebellious Natives or Black slaves. Yet he also warned Spotswood not to punish any who came to Florida, and he threatened Spotswood that if Carolina planters kept attacking Yamasee who approached Saint Augustine, perhaps including those who brought enslaved rebels with them, he would "punish" the White "aggressors" in the future. In August 1717 the new governor of Florida, Antonio Benavides Bazán y Molina, continued to supply Indian war parties with firearms and ammunition and other supplies, including one party that attacked Henry Mushoe's plantation in Colleton County and took back ten enslaved people. According to Governor Benavides, the end of the Yamasee War was only a culmination of European imperial rivalry in the Southeast in which the English and Spanish were constantly fighting each other and encouraging Native Americans to attack the other.[42] Any enslaved person who wanted to join their war effort was openly accepted. If they did not want to, then they might be conscripted.

Despite Spanish acceptance of rebel slaves in Florida, it was clear there were also differing visions of Black freedom near Saint Augustine and of how the fugitive slaves would be treated. Chief Perro Bravo brought several Black slaves with him to Florida during the war, and together they stayed in Sergeant Major Juan de Ayala y Escobar's home near the fort. Perro Bravo later complained to Governor Benavides that the sergeant major refused to pay him for some of the plantation fugitives he brought back from Carolina. Because he stayed at Ayala's house, he gave an enslaved Black woman to him for his gratitude, but he expected to be paid for the three other enslaved Black people whom be brought. Perro Bravo even threatened to kill them if the sergeant did not pay his debt, which Governor Benavides later ordered to be paid. The incident underscored the corruption of Ayala, whom Benavides also ordered incarcerated on other charges. It also illustrated the competing visions or ideas of enslaved Black participation in the Yamasee War and against English colonists. While the Spanish had promised safe haven for runaway slaves from Carolina since 1693, some Spaniards contravened the royal decree and "purchased" fugitives whom the Yamasee brought. In addition, it was clear that not all Yamasee necessarily viewed enslaved Black people as equal allies or peers in their rebellion against the English. Leaders like Perro Bravo tried to sell them at Saint Augustine and even threatened to kill them if he did not get paid. Whether or not enslaved Black people were aware of these differing visions on their arrival at Saint Augustine is not clear, even though many chose to run to the Spanish during the war anyway. Many took the initiative themselves and fled in hopes of freedom despite this risk. They were only betrayed once they reached Saint Augustine by unscrupulous Spaniards and Indians. Those who were betrayed could still petition for their freedom later on, like Francisco Menéndez did years later.[43]

Black slaves were also not the only enslaved people working on Carolina plantations, nor were they only ones who decided to rebel against White planter power during the Yamasee War. In 1713 St. Thomas Parish had an enslaved population of little more than a thousand people, of which at least sixty were Indians, and according to one estimate, as much as 25 percent of the enslaved population in the entire colony was Indian. It is not clear how many ran away during the fighting, but the Journal of the Commissioners of the Indian Trade noted that Catawba slaves were escaping from Carolina plantations during the war in 1717. Many of these enslaved people were probably better off than their Black counterparts. If they successfully escaped, they could more easily reintroduce themselves back into their nearby communities and reconstitute their ties to friends, family members, and kinship networks.[44]

No matter the reasons why enslaved people chose to rebel, their decision to do so perhaps informed a second wave of rebels that chose a similar path in the 1720s. In 1720 White planters detected a conspiracy among slaves who aimed to reach Saint Augustine just like those who ran away during the Yamasee War. Planters believed the principal conspirators were Mr. Persevall's slaves, who hoped to kill all the White planters and then use a Creek

Indian as a pilot and sail down to Saint Augustine for refuge. The episode was thwarted only when the garrison at Savannah Town stopped the slaves, and when the starving Creek nearby refused to be pilots. However, White South Carolinians acknowledged that the Yamasee were still sending pirogues to Saint Augustine, which encouraged enslaved Black people to go to the Spanish fortress. Planters also believed that it encouraged them to engage in more plunder and be "rogue[s]."[45]

There can be no doubt that enslaved Black people in South Carolina increasingly viewed Saint Augustine as a refuge from British planters shortly after the Yamasee War. In the 1720s several reports indicated that Black slaves continued to collude with Native Americans and flee to the Spanish in northern Florida. By 1727 there were several Black slaves living at the fort who had deserted from South Carolina, including at least ten who had joined a Black-Indian force with Black and Indian commanders.[46] The fact that plantation rebels increasingly fled to Florida in the aftermath of the Yamasee War underscores how parallel their motives, objectives, and methods were to the slave soldiers who did the same during the Yamasee conflict. It also demonstrated a rise in the militarization of resistance in early America since Bacon's Rebellion decades earlier, as more and more rebels took to military service or formed militarized slave insurrections to resist the chattel system.

Yamasee Rebels Like Other Atlantic Slave Rebels

In some ways, the Black experiences in the Yamasee War and the ways that slave soldiers fought in Carolina were similar to how enslaved rebels rose up against their owners in several other militarized slave insurrections in the Atlantic during the period. Coromantee rebels in New York in 1712 led a violent insurrection. On March 25 several dozen enslaved people conspired to kill their White owners and participated in an Akan oathing ceremony to solidify their commitment to the plan. Less than two weeks later the rebels met again at John Crooke's orchard, where they gathered guns, knives, and tools they could use for their assault. Then Cuffee and a Creole slave named John who belonged to Peter Vantilborough set Vantilborough's house in East Ward on fire while the rest of the rebels lay in wait. When several White men arrived to put it out, the armed rebels ambushed them. Augustus Grasset, Adrian Beckmen, Joris Marschalck, William Asht, Henry Brasier Jr., John Corbett, Johannes Low, and John Cure were all shot, stabbed, or bludgeoned to death. The rebels wounded several others. After a few men of the fire team were able to escape to warn the others, Governor Robert Hunter mustered the militia and chased after the rebels, who retreated into the woods. Some committed suicide instead of surrendering. In the end, more than forty enslaved people were tried for their participation in the revolt, and eighteen were executed. Like the rebels in South Carolina, the rebels in New York used military violence, firearms, and military tactics to attack White owners.[47]

The size and scale of the 1712 revolt was much smaller than what rebels in Carolina were conducting, but in both cases enslaved people participated in coordinated and militarized attacks against their owners. As had been the case in South Carolina three years later, the enslaved rebels in New York used weapons, including firearms, to fight their owners. While predominantly led by enslaved Africans, at least two Indian slaves were also involved, much like the Black-Indian cooperation in Carolina in 1715. Both cases were also militarized in character.[48]

The actions of enslaved people in the Yamasee War probably most paralleled the actions of enslaved people during the Natchez revolt in Louisiana in 1729–1730. Much like the Yamasee War, the Natchez revolt demonstrated two types of enslaved soldiers: loyal and rebel. The beginning of the Natchez revolt was also similar to how the Yamasee conflict erupted. French colonists suspected an uprising among the Natives, and Monsieurs Bailly, Ricard, Bourbeaux, and Ducoder all traveled to the Natchez to confirm the rumor, which the Natchez at first denied, much like the Yamasee did before the Good Friday Massacre. As was the case with the Yamasee, tensions between the French and the Natchez escalated in November 1729 when White colonists demanded more from the Natives. Situated on the Lower Mississippi River at Fort Rosalie, Commandant Sr. Étienne de Chépart demanded land from the Indians to build his own estate. The French also gave the Natives an ultimatum to deliver up the lands, and by the end of the month Monsieur Jean-Daniel Kolly and his son met with the Natives to trade. That same day, Commandant Chépart traveled with Sr. Bailly and warehouse keeper Ricard to the Grand Village of the Natchez to trade. The men enjoyed a fun night of eating and drinking with the Natives, although they were tipped off about an upcoming attack. Chépart refused to believe it, and on his return to Fort Rosalie the next night he went to sleep without sounding any alarms.[49]

Inside Fort Rosalie, there were twenty-five White soldiers and 280 Black slaves charged with defending the post, much like enslaved soldiers charged with defending garrisons along the South Carolina frontier during the Yamasee War. On the morning of November 29, the Natchez left their villages and arrived at the French post at nine o'clock in the morning, ostensibly to trade before a hunting trip. The Natchez chief came into Fort Rosalie with thirty men who brought poultry, deerskins, and corn with them, along with a calumet to symbolize their peaceful intentions. They also asked to borrow firearms from the French colonists and promised to give them back when they returned. They walked into Chépart's residence by 9:30, where he greeted them. Suddenly violence erupted. Warriors on the river's shore attacked a trading boat, which signaled to the Natchez inside Rosalie to attack the others. Bailly was killed in his sleep, and even as the fighting died down quickly, the Natchez executed Chépart. Most of the French men were killed, while the Natchez left alive women, children, and Black slaves. Instead the Natchez "made certain of several negroes" and assured them that "they would be free with the Indians," to encourage their participation and cooperation. In all, only twelve Natchez fighters died during the ambush, while almost 250 French colonists were killed.[50]

The initial attack was over by four o'clock in the afternoon. Thereafter, only twenty White men and five or six Black slaves escaped to New Orleans to warn other settlers. Some of the enslaved people caught up in the Indian attack chose not to flee with their owners and stayed inside the French houses. By the end of January they were still living with the Indians at Rosalie. They were similar to the Black slaves still living with the various Indian groups in Carolina and Florida during the Yamasee War. It is intriguing to wonder if these enslaved people were actually captives of the Natchez or if their decision to stay behind and not follow their French owners who fled from the Natives was an act of rebellion in and of itself. By January 1730 the Natchez continued to attack French colonists, while they also demanded ransom for the Black slaves, women, and children whom they had captured. Like the Black slaves that the Yamasee brought to the Spanish at Saint Augustine, it is reasonable to believe that some of these enslaved people were not just passive captives to Indian warriors but instead chose to stay with the Indians against the interests of their former White owners. Like Perro Bravo in Saint Augustine who tried to sell Black slaves who accompanied him, the Natchez were also willing to deliver Black slaves back to White owners for the right price, and it is unclear in both cases if Black rebels were aware of these designs. In any case, the French were more successful than the English in recouping enslaved people, and at the end of January 1730 a French-Chaquetas Indian force successfully attacked the Natchez by surprise and retrieved the women and children and more than one hundred enslaved people.⁵¹

While these slaves may have been Indian captives, it is clearer later on in the rebellion that French colonists understood their Black slaves to be cooperating with the Natchez much like the English did with their slaves cooperating with the Spanish during the Yamasee War. Some accounts pointed to enslaved Black people carrying merchandise from White homes that the Natchez plundered during the rebellion. Nearly three hundred Black slaves were taken or fled to the Natchez, and they helped the Indians escape French counterattacks in January 1730 as well. By June 25, 1730, Natchez defector Taotal visited Monsieur Henri de Louboëy who was leading a French counterattack. Taotal came with several of the French women and Black slaves "captured" in the fighting. French officers noted that it was especially difficult for the Native man to deliver the Black slaves, who were "very much attached to his people, and who had fired at us." They had also been cannoneers and were more "stalwart" than the Natchez themselves. Without a doubt these Black slave rebels used the Indian revolt as an opportunity to flee and to join with the Indians to attack their White owners. When they faced being returned to their masters, they tried to resist again, though unsuccessfully. Others even committed suicide before their White owners could recapture them.⁵²

At the end of the rebellion and after the Natchez defeat in 1731, the French were able to recover the enslaved Black rebels still with the Natchez, including "those who had taken part against us." French colonists punished "the most mutinous negroes those who had been most outspokenly for the Natchez," and they gave three of them to the Choctaw to burn alive. This punishment inflicted "such a horror of the Indians" that the French believed it made enslaved people docile and loyal.⁵³ Aside from the gruesomeness of the punishment, the penalty also demonstrated that like the Yamasee further east, enslaved Black people in the Lower South readily took up arms during Indian wars or rebellions and used the conflicts as opportunities to fight for freedom for themselves. In Louisiana, to do so meant soldiering with Native Americans against their White owners.

But some enslaved people stayed loyal and served as soldiers for their French owners like Carolina slaves did during the Yamasee War. At Tunica near New Orleans, Lieutenant Jean-François-Benjamin Dumont de Montigny later wrote that the Natchez had "found a way to win over our negro slaves and convince them to murder us and make themselves masters of all." A "plot" was uncovered when dozens of Natchez Indians offered peace to Commandant General Étienne Périer. Périer feared the Indians would be able to recruit Black slaves to further fight against White planters, so he had the Black ringleaders, two men and one woman, burned at the stake to make an example of them to other slaves. Périer also discovered that the plot was more widespread than just at Tunica, and slaves as far as the Chaouacha Concession were implicated. To ensure enslaved loyalty, Périer ordered his own enslaved soldiers there to attack a small group of about thirty Indian men, which they did, killing eight or nine men and several women. Périer's intent was to sow division among Black slaves and potential Indian allies. Périer was also pleased with his enslaved soldiers, who executed the task with "a respectable attitude." Slave soldiers probably feared facing brutal treatment like the rebels who were burned at the stake, so they fought with alacrity to appease Périer. He believed he could use them again to destroy all the smaller nations along the Mississippi River in case they too might "cause our negroes to revolt as we see by the example of the Natchez."[54] Périer's comments underscored how in the Southeast, enslaved soldiers were a double-edged sword. With the right circumstances and forceful White orders, they could be successful combatants who could discourage other enemies, namely Native Americans, from resisting White power. With the wrong encouragement, namely from rebellious Natives, enslaved people could turn on their White owners just as easily and cause utter destruction.

There were other reports of loyal enslaved soldiers during the revolt, just like the Yamasee War too. During a French counterattack Commandant Sieur Baron de Cresnay led three battalions of marines, militia, and engineers. Black slaves served some auxiliary function on board the force's boats on the Mississippi River. In July 1730 approximately a hundred Natchez fighters attacked about twenty Black slaves and eleven White guards working nearby Fort Rosalie, killing all but two guardsmen and five enslaved people who escaped. There was also one spectacular report of enslaved loyalty in which an enslaved man escaped the Natchez attack with his Canadian owner. Together they fled from the Natives and even ambushed a party chasing them. The full account of this, which also described the men killing at least ten Indians and the enslaved man killing a bear, is specious, but it is probable that in the heat of the Indian attack, enslaved people did side with their owners or chose to flee instead of face an unknown Indian adversary, much like what some plantation slaves did during the Yamasee War. Enslaved soldiers could prove their loyalty and earn the good graces of their owners by fighting the enemy Indians. Or they could resist in another way and join Indians against White power. For those who chose to do so, the Natchez revolt was an opportunity to fight for freedom in Louisiana.[55]

Aside from the cases in New York and Louisiana, how enslaved rebels participated in the Yamasee War was of course remarkably parallel to other rebellions in South Carolina in the early eighteenth century. Enslaved people in the colony were without doubt agitated, and on many occasions around the time of the Yamasee War they attempted to earn their freedom by attacking White planters. In 1713 planters in Goose Creek detected a plot among the enslaved people. Twelve to fifteen enslaved Black people living along the Cooper River were arrested for conspiring to get "liberty by force." The ringleader was executed, while two others were punished. Similarly, several years after the Yamasee War ended, Black rebels in Charleston conspired in 1722 to kill their masters and take control of the country. In both these conspiracies, Black slaves desired to obtain liberty and even take control of the colony before and after the Yamasee War.[56]

Decades after the Yamasee War, enslaved rebels in Carolina were still trying to reach the Spanish in Saint Augustine like the rebel slave soldiers in 1715–1717. There were several group attempts in Carolina to flee and reach the Spanish in the 1720s as well. At least four enslaved people did this in 1726 and ten more in 1727. In 1739 four or five slaves belonging to Captain Macpherson took several horses and ran away to the woods, wounding Macpherson's son and killing another man in the process. Like the Black rebels who joined the Yamasee before them, they desired to reach the Spanish at Saint Augustine, where they knew they would find refuge.[57]

The most notable incident among these attempts was the Stono Rebellion in 1739, which was also militarized and involved slave rebels who fought like slave soldiers in the Yamasee War. On September 9, 1739, roughly twenty rebels assembled under the leadership of a man named Jemy. They then attacked Mr. Hutchenson's warehouse and killed Mr. Robert Bathurst and Mr. Gibbs, taking guns and gunpowder stored there. Afterward they marched south to reach Saint Augustine and attacked planters on their way, except for Mr. Wallace, who was "a good man." But they also attacked Mr. Lemy's plantation, killing Lemy and his wife and child. At Mr. Rose's house they were joined by several more enslaved people, and together they marched with military colors, beat drums, and "called out" for liberty. They attacked several more plantations along the Pons Road on their way to Saint Augustine, growing in strength from sixty to one hundred in number. After continuing the rebellion for ten miles, a White militia mustered and attacked them, killing several and causing many rebels to disperse. At least thirty escaped and one detachment continued south another thirty miles before planters were able to attack them again and finally defeat them. The Stono Rebellion was one of the largest slave rebellions in early American history, but the actions and goals of the enslaved rebels were not new. They were following decades of precedent in which enslaved people in South Carolina understood they could use military violence and martial tactics, techniques, and procedures to fight for liberty and achieve it if they could only reach the Spanish at Saint Augustine.[58]

Not only were the methods, tactics, and objectives of rebel slave soldiers in the Yamasee War similar to those of other militarized Atlantic rebels, but the conditions they responded to were also similar to conditions confronted by rebels before other militarized slave revolts. Material conditions deteriorated just before enslaved people revolted in Barbados in 1675, in Virginia in 1676, and in St. John in 1733, among many others. These conditions were present for rebellions similar to the Yamasee War as well. Queen Anne's War from 1702 to 1713 produced some economic hardships in New York by 1712, particularly heavy debts, a trade deficit, and a maritime labor shortage that affected the Black slaves there. Further "hard usage" of enslaved people in the city preceded the rebellion there that year. The city also had one of the largest slave populations in the Northeast, which encouraged Black and Indian slaves to rebel against White owners.[59]

In Louisiana before Black slaves revolted with the Natchez Indians in 1729 and 1730, the colony underwent a surge in slaveholding. Throughout the 1720s there was a significant rise in African slave imports into the colony, and as Gwendolyn Midlo Hall has noted, enslaved people suffered from sickness and disease on their arrival in Louisiana. The rise of African imports also helped create a Black majority conducive to slave rebellion. In Natchez specifically, the African slave population increased to 280 people from 1726 to 1729, which was a little more than one hundred fewer people than the number of French colonists who lived there. The population boom in the 1720s also strained the food supply, and although there is no indication of a food shortage in 1729 immediately before the Natchez revolt, there were shortages in the few years preceding it. Meanwhile, exports in slave-produced crops in the colony also surged, which indicated how hard planters pushed their slaves to produce for their own profits. Indeed, planters felt pressured to produce as much tobacco as Virginia to feed the demand in France. All these signs indicate that the Black chattel system was surging on the eve of the Natchez rebellion, which favored conditions for revolt like it did elsewhere in the Atlantic.[60]

Similar conditions were extant in South Carolina shortly before the Stono Rebellion erupted in 1739. Demand for indigo and rice intensified slave labor in the colony, which made life harder for enslaved people. Moreover, the colony experienced two waves of smallpox and yellow fever in the summer of 1739. The epidemics probably hit White planters harder than Black slaves, but the diseases indicated that all people in the colony were suffering. Enslaved people's material conditions were deteriorating. Perhaps most importantly, the timing of the Stono Rebellion was probably tied to the upcoming implementation of a new security act in which White people were required to carry firearms to church on Sundays. The act was a step toward further cracking down on the Black population, and enslaved rebels probably understood that their conditions would worsen after the act took effect. Their best chances for success were probably before the act could be implemented.[61]

The Black chattel system was worsening in South Carolina in the years before the Yamasee War, which demonstrated deteriorating material conditions for enslaved people, as was the case in other rebellions. Like Louisiana before the Natchez revolt, South Carolina's exports to Great Britain surged in the 1710s, leading to significant trade surpluses for the colony, which suggested that the plantation system was working, and that meant enslaved people likely faced more strenuous labor conditions. Moreover, in 1712 the colony's General Assembly passed a new act that missionary Francis Le Jau called "very severe." The 1712 Act for the Better Ordering and Governing of Negroes and Slaves was the fifth iteration of similar laws that were in place as early as 1690 to regulate and monitor enslaved people in Carolina. It reiterated that all "negroes, mulatoes, mustizoes, or Indians" who had been sold or bought as slaves were to be kept as slaves for life. The 1712 version also ensured that enslaved children inherited the condition of their mother. Enslaved people who traveled without a pass could be whipped, and if they resisted arrest they could be killed. Another article required slave owners to search slave quarters for Maroons and weapons every fourteen days. People who stole goods and contraband with slaves would be punished, and enslaved people were not allowed to carry firearms outside plantation limits unless ordered by their owner and in possession of a certificate. Planters who did not punish their slaves enough would also face fines.[62]

Furthermore, the act required planters to hide firearms or restrict access to them, and constables in Charleston were permitted to deputize men to patrol the city on Sundays and on holidays when enslaved people traveled to markets there. Those who refused a constable's summons would be fined twenty shillings. Enslaved people were also required to carry a ticket to travel to the city, and if they were convicted of murder, burglary, robbery, arson, or lesser crimes such as stealing livestock or trespassing, they could face the death penalty. They could even be mutilated for petty larceny. Any enslaved person who participated in mutiny or insurrection would be put to death unless they confessed or gave good testimony. The act also demonstrated planters' fear of imperial rivals influencing enslaved people, and Article 14 of the act enforced a fine for any person convicted of taking enslaved people out of the colony. Another article mandated the death penalty for runaway slaves who attempted to reach rivals such as the Spanish in Florida. If a slave hit a White person they could be whipped, and if they did it more than twice they could be put to death. Any enslaved person over the age of sixteen who ran away for more than twenty days would be whipped. Upon a second offense, they would be branded with the letter R on their right cheek and could have their heels cut for further offenses.[63]

The act also significantly cracked down on enslaved resistance. Militia captains were permitted to raise patrols to track runaways and to take them dead or alive. White patrolmen could even receive disability pay if injured while tracking and apprehending runaways and Maroons. Any plantation slave that harbored a runaway could be whipped, but if they delivered them to their owners they could receive twenty shillings. Enslaved people could also face punishment for working together in a "disorderly way," while plantation managers were required to live within six miles of their plantation. Unlike the act planters enforced in 1701, in which at least one White person was required to live on a plantation, pen, or stock house, the 1712 act tightened White control and required at least one White person to oversee six plantation slaves. The 1712 act further strengthened the legal separation of White and Black people, and much of the draconian punishments were harsher than earlier iterations of the legislation, such as in 1690 and 1701.[64]

The act also created a public welfare fund to care for the poor. Half of the monies paid from violations of the act were to go to the church wardens or overseers of the poor in the parish where the perpetrator lived. This was a change from the 1701 legislation, in which fines were to support a public account to purchase gunpowder and ammunition to be used in defense of the colony. Strikingly, planters in Carolina created an early welfare system in which poor White people could be taken care of at the expense of violence directed at enslaved Black people. Welfare and disability funds were also raised at the expense of even killing Black people who resisted the system.[65]

Just two years after the act was passed, Carolina legislators added additional legislation to further monitor and regulate the liberties of enslaved Black people in the colony. Article 9 imposed a tariff for every enslaved person over twelve years old imported into the colony, and Article 11 prohibited masters from allowing their enslaved people to plant provision grounds of corn, peas, or rice or to keep livestock at a £20 penalty.[66] These provisions demonstrated that conditions for enslaved people in South Carolina were worsening on the eve of the Yamasee War, while planters were also increasingly concerned about the rapidly increasing enslaved population. In both cases, these stipulations reiterated that material deprivation and a higher Black-to-White population ratio that often precipitated revolts elsewhere in the Atlantic were in place just before enslaved people in Carolina joined the Yamasee and revolted against White planters.

A few years after the war ended, legislators seemingly acknowledged that the draconian parts of the 1712 act had encouraged slave rebelliousness. Legislators thus passed a more balanced slave code by 1722, although they still prohibited enslaved people from certain activities, particularly from keeping or selling horses because of their perceived ability to use them to carry intelligence, engage in insurrection, and reach the Spanish in Florida, as had happened during the war.[67]

A hurricane hit the colony in the autumn of 1715 and laid waste to the landscape, similar to how a hurricane made conditions worse for enslaved people on St. John before the rebellion there in 1733. In Carolina the hurricane felled trees and destroyed several structures. Preacher Gideon Johnston wrote to the secretary of the Society of the Propagation of the Gospel in December 1715 that the hurricane destroyed a local church. The church was already in debt, and parishioners could not rebuild it because of the great costs the war had produced. The fact that planters could not rebuild also demonstrated that they were strapped for cash and probably passed down their economic hardships to enslaved people as they had done elsewhere in the Atlantic. Certainly enslaved people bore the brunt of losses from plantation raids and attacks during the war, and those who did not immediately leave plantations with Indian warriors would have faced the arduous tasks of rebuilding and repairing the plantations where they lived. Moreover, these losses scared investors, and in Charleston prices rose and merchants declined to lend credit. As was frequently the case elsewhere in the Atlantic, Carolina planters probably passed these worsening economic conditions down to their slaves, as they would have less money to spend on food, health care, and shelter for enslaved people.[68]

In Carolina in 1715 White power was clearly under threat during Indian attacks, and colonists faced both Spanish and French imperial threats from Florida and Alabama. Even early on during the war, some authorities in South Carolina showed little confidence in Governor Charles Craven's ability to govern, and they were divided on how to handle the conflict. Lieutenant James Fellow complained in August 1716 that Craven seemed "to take very little notice" of the Indian movements in both the northern and southern parts of the colony and that the prosperous colony would be lost unless King George I would take control of it and send a "prudent Governor, a man of resolution," with soldiers to save it. Other colonists also thought the Carolina proprietors acted too slowly against the Yamasee, while some even called for the king to take control to save Carolina from Indian destruction. These conflicts showed division among Whites in the colony at the onset of the Yamasee War, which paralleled the division that was present in Virginia years earlier. Such division was common in many Atlantic slave revolts as well, militarized or not.[69]

Conclusion

For enslaved soldiers involved, the Yamasee War was more than just a White-Indian frontier conflict that typified early American society. While they experienced the violence in many of the same ways as Native Americans and European colonists, the conflict also presented unique opportunities for enslaved soldiers in the emergent Carolina slave society. Slave soldiers were presented with two options: serve as loyal soldiers for their owners and protect themselves and the chattel system in Carolina, or betray their owners and flee and fight for the Yamasee and Spanish in Florida to undermine slaveholding power in the English colony. While this was not the first time they were presented with these choices in the Lowcountry, the Yamasee War was so large a conflict that it presented even greater opportunities to fight or flee for slave soldiers. Fighting their owners threatened to undermine the slave system in Carolina, as did running away to the Spanish in Florida. For slave soldiers who chose to fight and run, the Yamasee War became a militarized slave revolt not unlike others in the Atlantic during the period.

Enslaved rebels joined collectively in groups to run from and fight their owners, and at least one hundred enslaved rebels left Carolina for Spanish Florida. Like the 1712 New York revolt, the Natchez revolt in 1729, and the 1739 Stono Rebellion, enslaved rebels in Carolina endured conditions that made them more likely to rise up against the planter class. A Black plantation slave majority was developing at the start of the war, and Black slaves in Carolina suffered material deprivation associated with the rise of the Black chattel system in the colony before the war began. As the war raged on, they suffered worsening conditions that encouraged them to confront their owners.

Importantly, slave soldiers in Carolina were establishing a method to use warfare, flee, and connect with the Spanish in Florida that would last for another hundred years. Their case in Carolina was not unlike that of the slave soldiers in Bacon's army in Virginia just forty years earlier. They had been able to morph a White-Indian frontier conflict into one about Black emancipation. They had done so in the Lowcountry much as other rebels did in the Chesapeake. Slave soldier rebels in the Yamasee War show that armed resistance could operate in the same ways in the Lowcountry as it did in the Chesapeake, despite a different kind of "Indian War" and the influence of European imperial rivals. Enslaved soldiers were willing to join Native and European allies against English slave owners, despite the option to fight for their owner and potentially earn manumission. As the Atlantic chattel slave system was tightening, slave soldiers increasingly used militarized methods to challenge it.

But there were also important differences between the Carolina slave soldiers and rebels in Bacon's army years earlier. The conflict they joined was primarily an "Indian war" heavily influenced by European imperial rivalries instead of a Native American–White conflict turned into an internal-British imperial rebellion. They could fight for freedom, but they would have to leave Carolina and live with the Natives or the French or Spanish to achieve it together. In Bacon's Rebellion, they could have stayed in Virginia had they defeated Berkeley's Loyalist forces. The presence of strong imperial rivals in the Lower South also encouraged more armed resistance than what was possible in the Chesapeake decades earlier. The Spanish in Florida and to a lesser extent the French near Mobile could promote slave soldiers to turn coat, fight with Natives, and flee from the English. Once in Florida, slave soldiers were provided with even more support to include arms and ammunition and the opportunity to serve as soldiers for the Spanish garrison at Saint Augustine. Slave soldiers' loyalties could be flipped in Carolina.

The conditions in Carolina also affected slave soldier loyalties in a different way. Whereas rebels in Virginia fled predominantly wealthy Loyalists in Berkeley's army, a substantial number of enslaved people soldiered for their owners in Carolina during the Yamasee War. Temporary yet structured military policies in the colony permitted slave soldiers to fight for their owners and earn their own individual freedom. For those who were conscripted into militia service for British colonists, their desire to turn coat for Natives or Spanish rivals and fight against their owners diminished. Thus, armed resistance could be diluted. Nevertheless, the militarization of slave rebels surged in the early eighteenth century as enslaved people increasingly used the military and militarized tactics against their owners to challenge the slave system. In the end, the Yamasee War was another episode of Black armed resistance that followed several incidents before it in Carolina and Virginia, and it was an episode that set the stage for even greater moments of militarized Black resistance that would spike again in Virginia in 1775, Dominica in 1802, the Gulf Coast borderlands in 1812, and the Sea Islands in 1862.

CHAPTER 3

Liberty to Slaves
Lord Dunmore's Ethiopian Regiment, 1775–1776

Preparing to depart from New York City for Nova Scotia in August 1783, British inspectors identified Jane Thompson aboard the ship *L'Abondance*. Cataloged in the *Book of Negroes*, the massive ledger that the British army used to record Black Loyalists being evacuated at the end of the American Revolutionary War, Jane was listed as seventy years old and described as "worn out." She was traveling with her five-year-old grandson Peter to Nova Scotia, where the British army was sending thousands of runaway American slaves who were attached to the army. Jane had fled from her owner, Robert Tucker of Norfolk, Virginia, in 1776 after Virginia governor John Murray, the fourth Earl of Dunmore, promised to free slaves from Patriot owners if they joined his "Ethiopian Regiment" to fight American rebels. She was certainly anxious to leave New York given rumors that Patriot masters were coming to recoup their fugitive slaves.[1]

Jane was one of almost eight hundred enslaved people who fled from their owners in 1775 and 1776 to join Lord Dunmore and become part of his newly formed Ethiopian Regiment. The regiment was made up entirely of slaves and free Blacks under the command of White officers, and Dunmore formally mustered the regiment in late 1775 after months of dozens of runaway slaves had already served as ship pilots and helped raid and pilfer Patriot plantations along the Virginia coast. Although Dunmore aimed his emancipation offer only at slaves, servants, and convicts who could bear arms, many elderly people, women, and children ran to him to escape bondage too. As they reached British lines, those who were not combatants served as washerwomen or in other various auxiliary roles in support of the regiment and Dunmore's Loyalist followers. In almost a year of fighting along Virginia's shore, these runaway slaves razed Patriot settlements, recruited more enslaved people to flee, and fought against and even captured their former owners in combat. The few like Jane and her family who were not captured or who did not die during the war embarked for Nova Scotia in 1783 to take their hard-fought freedom.

Historians have long noted the exploits of soldiers in the Ethiopian Regiment and other Black Loyalists and how fighting for the British army during the Revolutionary War brought concrete opportunities for Black freedom. While thousands of enslaved people ran away to the British army, military service otherwise seemingly mitigated conventional acts of slave rebelliousness during the period. But what exactly did soldiering in the Ethiopian Regiment really mean for enslaved people in the Chesapeake, and how did they view the increasing militarization of resistance near the end of the eighteenth century and during the age of revolution? How did the increasing militarization affect men, women, and children who ran to Dunmore?[2]

Black experiences during the American Revolutionary War were diverse, but the Ethiopian Regiment was one of the earliest moments of slave soldiering and armed resistance during the war. Soldiers in the regiment were not hermetically sealed from enslaved people elsewhere on the continent, nor was their case the only act of armed resistance during the war. But their case was mostly localized to the Chesapeake and one of the first incidents during the war in which professional slave soldiering became an option. It was also one of the clearest cases in which professional military service was tied to slave rebelliousness during the war. Finally, the Ethiopian Regiment offers a glimpse into how slave soldiering in Virginia had changed from the end of the seventeenth century to the end of the colonial era.

Unfortunately, there are no known narratives or memoirs written by members of the Ethiopian Regiment that show how they left slavery and eventually made it to New York or Nova Scotia, like those written by other Black Loyalists such as Boston King or David George. Nevertheless, extrapolating the accounts of Black Loyalists from other units in the British army, including successor units to the Ethiopian Regiment, can help show how enslaved people ran away and joined the regiment, their overall military experiences, and their motivations to fight.[3]

Runaway slaves who joined the Ethiopian Regiment used military service to challenge slavery in Virginia. For perhaps the first time in the Anglo-Atlantic, slave resistance became professionally militarized as revolution expanded the pathways for slave soldiers to test the system as they joined the British army. The militarization of resistance reached its peak in the eighteenth century during the American Revolutionary War. The new and peculiar conditions in Virginia early in the war gave enslaved people the first chance to attack slavery in large numbers while in uniform, as part of a professional army.

Slave Soldiering in the Ethiopian Regiment

As early as September 1775 Captain Mathew Squire skirmished with Patriot forces on the Virginia shore. On board the *Otter*, Squire patrolled the Virginia coast and runaway slaves served as pilots to help him navigate. After another ship under his command, the *Liberty*, ran aground on the Back River in Elizabeth County due to a hurricane, Patriots from the nearby town of Hampton seized many of the supplies on the ship, including several firearms, cutlasses, powder, and ammunition. Patriots accused Squire of leading runaway slaves and British sailors on plunder and pillaging operations in the area. They told Squire that they would not provide restitution for lost supplies unless Squire met a series of conditions, the first of which included returning slave Joseph Harris and other Black fugitives who had worked for Squire to pillage plantations of livestock under the cover of darkness. Harris had reportedly "applied [to the British] for protection" after Patriot slave owners discovered that he was slipping intelligence to the British and helping them navigate the small rivers that fed into the Chesapeake.[4] Harris and the other fugitive soldiers were probably terrified that they would be returned to Patriot owners for their role in the fighting.

But Squire refused to return the fugitives, and with the issue unresolved Squire continued raiding plantations in the area with enslaved soldiers serving with him. On October 26 slave soldiers with Squire attacked Hampton with a small force of six vessels. Despite their efforts, enslaved rebels with Squire lost the battle against the Patriots. During the small engagement, slave soldiers were forced to retreat after intense volleys of Patriot fire for more than an hour and after the capture of the *Hawke*, which had also run aground. On board the ship were at least two Black rebels, while Patriots also found two more with Lieutenant Wright, who had jumped overboard and went on shore. As the men fled for their lives, at least one was shot from a distance by a Patriot marksman. In the end, nine slave rebels were killed in the fighting, along with several British Regulars, and several others were captured. Although the battle of Hampton was a military engagement, Patriot planters in

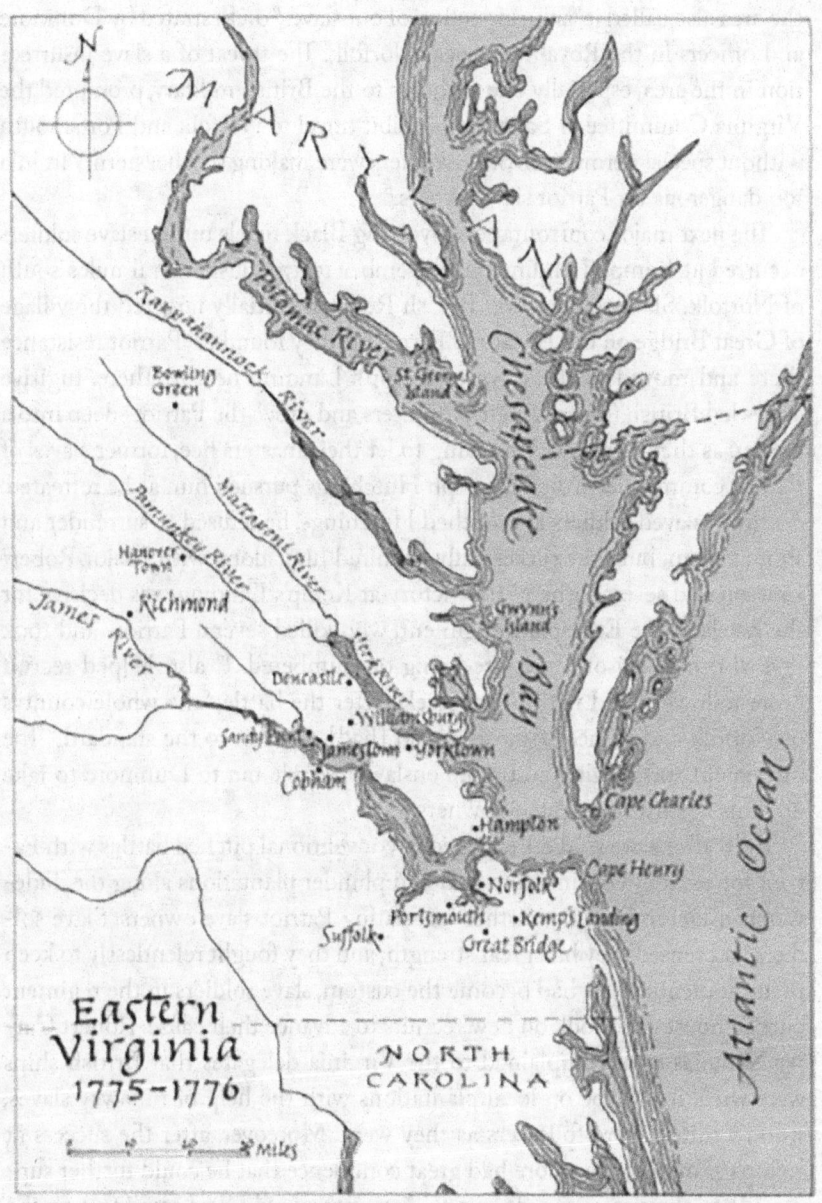

MAP 3. Map of Revolutionary Virginia, 1775–1776. "Eastern Virginia, 1775–1776," designed by Richard J. Stinely, 1988 (originally published in Selby, *Revolution in Virginia*). Reproduced courtesy of the Colonial Williamsburg Foundation.

the area also called it "an insurrection of our slaves" orchestrated by Dunmore and officers in the Royal Navy near Norfolk. The threat of a slave insurrection in the area, especially one with ties to the British military, prompted the Virginia Committee of Safety to prohibit travel to Norfolk and Portsmouth without special permission. Slave soldiers were making southeastern Virginia too dangerous for Patriot slave owners.[5]

The next major confrontation involving Black rebels turned slave soldiers occurred at Kemp's Landing on November 15, 1775, just several miles south of Norfolk. Slave soldiers and British Regulars initially targeted the village of Great Bridge on the Elizabeth River, but they found no Patriot resistance there and moved to the town of Kemp's Landing nearby. There, fugitive slaves led British forces to Patriot fighters and drove the Patriots deep into a swamp as they retreated. Unwilling to let their masters flee, former slaves of Patriot commander Colonel Joseph Hutchings pursued him as he retreated. As the enslaved soldiers approached Hutchings, he refused to surrender and shot at them, but they successfully captured him, along with Major Robert Lawson and several others. The victory at Kemp's Landing was decisive for the rebels in the Ethiopian Regiment, who killed several Patriots and took several others prisoner despite being outnumbered. It also helped recruit more followers, and within just weeks after the battle, "the whole countys of Norfolk and Princes Ann to a man [had] come in to the standard." The movement was surging and more enslaved people ran to Dunmore to take up arms against their Patriot owners.[6]

Even after slave soldiers engaged in conventional pitched battles with Patriot forces, they continued to raid and plunder plantations along the Tidewater in December 1775, further infuriating Patriot slave owners. Slave soldiers had sensed they had great strength, and they fought relentlessly to keep their momentum. As had become the custom, slave soldiers in the regiment burned houses and took on new recruits to advance their cause. Robert Carter Nicholas even complained to the Virginia delegates that British ships were wreaking havoc on local plantations with the help of runaway slaves, who recruited more followers as they went. Moreover, after the success at Kemp's Landing, Dunmore had great confidence that he could further suppress Patriot resistance, and slave soldiers moved to build a small fort on the northern end of Great Bridge, near the southern branch of the Elizabeth River, twelve miles from Norfolk. Dunmore's soldiers, Black and White, had also burned several homes near the river before the Patriots could mobilize. From there they confronted more than two hundred Patriot soldiers under Lieutenant Colonel Charles Scott by November 28, 1775. Within a

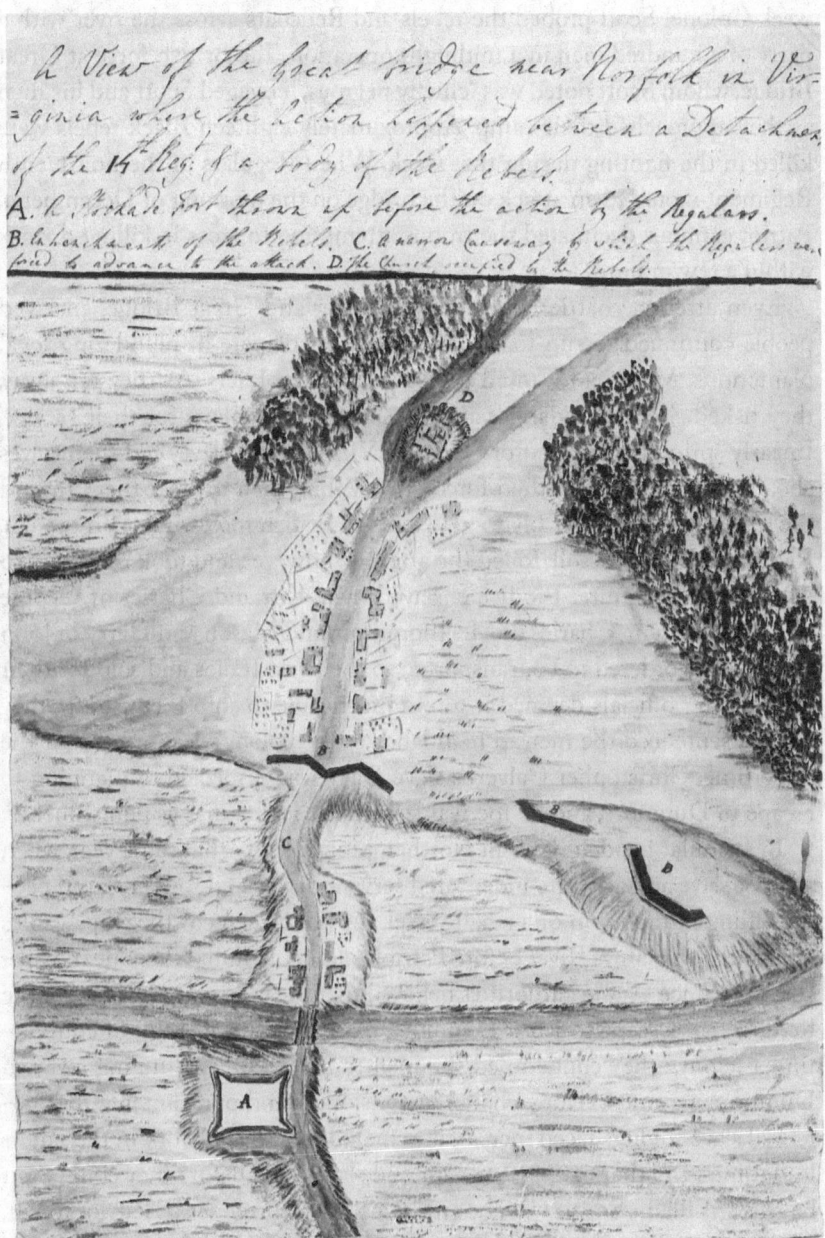

FIGURE 1. Portrait of Great Bridge, 1775. From Rawdon-Hastings, "A View of the Great Bridge." William L. Clements Library, University of Michigan.

week Colonel Scott probed the rebels and Redcoats across the river with a party of a hundred men in a midnight operation. The British force at Great Bridge, whom Scott noted was "chiefly negroes," engaged Scott and his men as they approached their camp. Approximately eighteen Black rebels were killed in the fighting during that week. When Regulars in the Fourteenth Regiment mounted an attack on the bridge on the morning of December 9, Patriot cannons decimated the troops attempting to cross it, killing dozens within a few minutes.[7]

Even after the battles at Kemp's Landing and Great Bridge, enslaved people continued to run to Dunmore and participate in plundering local plantations. More had wanted to become slave soldiers. As they ran away, they risked significant danger and potential punishments for their service. In early spring 1776 in Stafford County, Virginia, five slaves hid themselves aboard a small ship and then forced two White men to steer them toward the Coon River, presumably to get closer to British forces. The White men, Ralph and John Grissoll, foiled the attempt, however, and took the slaves to Maryland for capture. The five enslaved men, Kitt and Charles of George and Robert Brent, Charles of Mr. Thompson, and Mason and Harry of John Ratliff, were ordered to be transported to the West Indies and sold for their crime. After officials deemed it too impracticable to ship them south, they instead sentenced the men to hard labor in the colony's lead mines. At the same time, Christopher Calvert's slave Davy was suspected of planning to escape to Dunmore, and he too was sent to the lead mines as punishment.[8]

In a similar incident later in Northampton County that same year, when a Black slave and a White indentured servant discovered four enslaved people hiding in the cabin of a small vessel, the bondsmen cut the ships' cables and fled to the James River before Patriot soldiers captured them near Mobjack Bay. Since White authorities believed that the men took the vessel more to "effect an Escape to Lord Dunmore, than any other Design of committing a felony," they condemned the men to be executed. Running away to Dunmore became a felony charge of conspiracy, and punishments that potential slave soldiers faced increased to include death and work in the salt or lead mines. In other cases, some captured slaves died before they could even be tried. William Smith was shot for refusing to surrender to Patriot forces, while Arthur Boush's slave Harry was captured but died from wounds before his trial. By December 15, 1775, the Virginia General Assembly declared that "all negro or other slaves, conspiring to rebel or make insurrection, shall suffer death" and that "all slaves who have been, or shall be seduced, by his lordship's proclamation . . . shall be liable to such punishments."[9] If enslaved people wanted to become soldiers for Dunmore, they would be treated as slave rebels. Slave soldiers probably expected this response, and they ran away to join Dunmore regardless of the risks.

In Elizabeth City County in 1775, runaways who had made it to Dunmore's lines and were recaptured at Hampton were deemed too dangerous to keep in the colony, and they were transported to Antigua to be sold. Several days before the battle of Great Bridge, Colonel William Woodford wrote to Edmund Pendleton concerning the treatment of slave soldiers already captured. While he ordered his men to accord them the treatment laid out by the rules of war, he noted that his officers unanimously wanted to "make an immediate example of them." Presumably, they wanted to execute them. Woodford was able to calm his officers down, and slave soldiers captured during the battle of Great Bridge were sentenced to transportation and resale in Honduras for their "crime," even though several of them had been exonerated from having ever borne arms in the Ethiopian Regiment. According to Frey, only after compensation claims to owners whose slaves were executed became too costly for the colonial government did Virginians shift punishments to transportation and hard labor in the mines. The shift reduced costs and still kept slaves, whom Whites considered rebellious, under strict and constant supervision and sequestered from others in a way that inhibited the organizing of insurrection. After a declaration published in mid-December 1775, only slaves who returned to their owners without appearing armed would be pardoned and saved from brutal punishment. Punishments that slave soldiers in the regiment faced were seemingly harsher than what Patriots meted out to other Loyalists and Tories in the area.[10]

The intensification of punishments for potential slave soldiers was also seemingly tied to talk of slave insurrection among planters and soldiers in Virginia in these early moments in 1775 and 1776. There was talk that slaves who ran to the British and who took up arms with the British army were engaged in slave insurrection. William Bradford warned James Madison in January 1775 that Madison's "fear" of an "insurrection being excited among the slaves seems too well founded," because of word that "gentlemen" in England might declare slaves free if they took up arms against the Patriots. Madison concurred that the Patriots would "fall with Achilles" if enslaved people were willing to take up arms with the British. Some Virginia Tories too were worried about Dunmore's Proclamation and that it would become a slave insurrection. John Johnson thought that Dunmore's offer would probably mobilize planters for the Patriot cause in order to "suppress any Insurrection amongst the slaves," which delegates mentioned to the Virginia Convention in Richmond in August 1775. Even before rebel slaves participated in these major battles in the Chesapeake, Virginia planters pondered if runaway slaves joining British officers in the area and pillaging Patriot plantations were involved in "actual rebellion." Curiously this question even begged the same planters to wonder if it were time to arm their own slaves in their defense.[11]

Many planters and slaveholders in the area resented that so many enslaved people had fled to Dunmore and were attacking Patriot soldiers. On Wednesday, June 26, 1776, Landon Carter detailed in his diary at Sabine Hall how eleven of his nearly five hundred slaves ran away the night before. The eleven slaves, all men, snuck into their master's quarters and stole his son's gun, a bag of bullets, gunpowder, and a stack of clothes before absconding on a petty auger. Presumably they joined enslaved people from the neighboring Robinson plantation in the night and were on their way "to be sure, to Ld. Dunmore." They stayed on the run for several days until they were detected by Patriot militia aboard a small ship. They took heavy fire from the White soldiers and were forced to land and flee by foot. As they ran they were fired at again, resulting in the death of three and the surrender of five more. The rest remained at large, and the putative leader of the escape, Moses, never returned to Carter's plantation despite Carter's efforts to recapture Moses for several months. The group was remarkable on Carter's plantation for their attempt to reach Dunmore and to fight, which apparently did not happen again throughout 1776 and 1777. Other people on his plantation did run away, but they did not join British military units. They ostensibly took advantage of the chaos and confusion that war wrought and escaped to somewhere else. In many ways, Moses and his followers were treated more seriously than others on his plantation, suggesting that both Black and White people understood the Ethiopian Regiment to be a grave threat to slavery in the colony. The Virginia Committee of Safety even reported that Dunmore was "exciting an insurrection of our slaves," while one planter opined in John Pinkney's *Virginia Gazette*, "Are not the negro slaves, now on board the *Fowey*, which are under the g——'s protection, in actual rebellion, and punishable as such?" Indeed, slaveholders throughout the Chesapeake believed that the Ethiopian Regiment was engaged in insurrection, and they punished runaways trying to join it as such.[12]

To be sure, British strategists never wanted to incite an actual slave insurrection, but even talk of Dunmore and slaves taking up arms for the British army in spring 1775 alarmed colonial planters who feared that it would lead to slave insurrection. To add to this fear, when Dunmore moved to seize the gunpowder at the Williamsburg magazine in late April 1775, Patriots worried that it was an attempt to undermine their ability to thwart slave insurrections in the colony, which had seemingly intensified that year. Fear of slave insurrection may have even been a grievance in the Declaration of Independence in the next year. Enslaved people also seemingly understood the opportunity in similar ways, and attempts to fight for freedom and rebel increased with the rhetoric of potential slave armies forming. At least two slave conspiracies were detected in Norfolk and Prince Edward Counties in early 1775 before Dunmore's Proclamation, and a couple more were discovered in the James River watershed at the same time.[13]

Enslaved people continued to run away and serve as soldiers for Dunmore in the Chesapeake. Though they were defeated at Great Bridge, one of the more destructive phases of the fighting began at the start of 1776 as slave soldiers and plantation slaves took part in the burning of Norfolk on New Year's Day 1776. As one of Virginia's major cities, it was of great strategic value for both the British and the Patriots, and Dunmore's forces initiated an artillery barrage from the sea between three and four o'clock that afternoon. After more than twelve hours of firing, Dunmore landed a small amphibious assault force to set fire to houses and destroy the city's wharves the next day. In an attempt to deny the enemy the important city and harbor, Patriots inside the city also set wooden structures ablaze. To be sure, the Patriots were responsible for most of the damage, as only a few dozen homes were destroyed by slave soldiers, even though more than thirteen hundred structures were ruined in the city. Nevertheless, enslaved people, both those who had already joined the Ethiopian Regiment and those who had remained with their owners, were caught up in the destruction.[14]

Although Dunmore and his Loyalist supporters razed Norfolk to start the New Year in 1776, the defeat at Great Bridge had essentially made anything more than plantation raids and coastal harassment untenable for British soldiers in the Chesapeake and in southern Virginia. Moreover, Dunmore's hundred-ship flotilla, which included civilian Loyalists, needed substantial military assistance to protect it from Patriot attacks and to supply the noncombatants with food and water. By late May 1776 Dunmore and his soldiers dropped anchor off the coast of Gwynn's Island, a small four-square-mile island south of the mouth of the Rappahannock River. As part of the invading force, enslaved soldiers in the Ethiopian Regiment took the island with very little opposition. They began to build earthworks to protect Dunmore's newly established headquarters on the island from Patriot artillery that was only a few hundred yards away. Along with Royal Marines, sol-

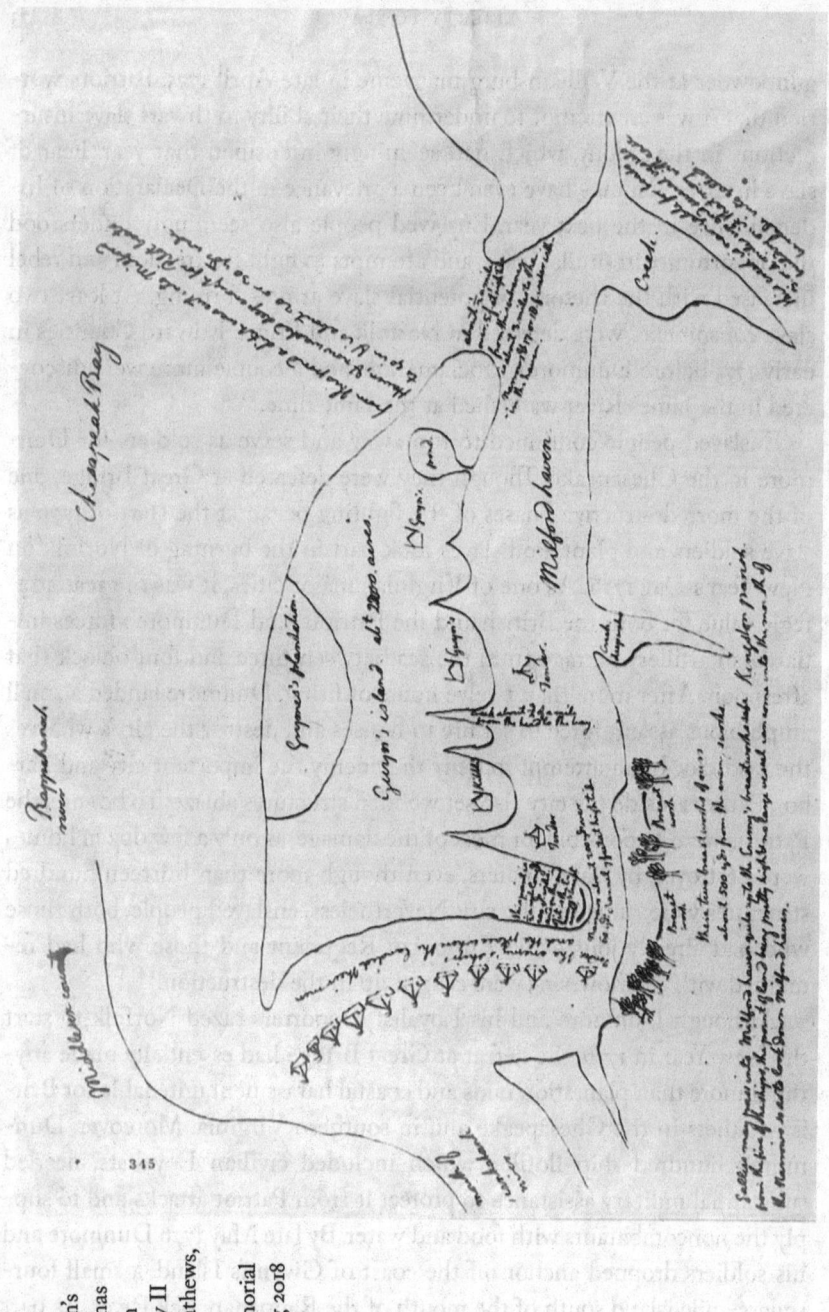

MAP 4. Sketch Map of Gwynn's Island by Thomas Jefferson. From Milton Murray II Collection, Mathews, VA Archives, Mathews Memorial Library, Spring 2018 Newsletter.

diers in the Ethiopian Regiment worked every day to fortify the island under constant harassing fire by Patriot fighters on the mainland just across the Millford Haven channel.[15]

By then slave soldiers in the regiment were already suffering from smallpox and a fever that made its way through the ranks. Just a week earlier in Norfolk, British surgeons had suggested that it was time to inoculate the soldiers in case the illnesses should spread. Despite their caution, illnesses spread and began to wreak havoc on both Black and White soldiers occupying the city. Nearly two hundred slave soldiers died just on the voyage from Norfolk to Gwynn's Island alone. Though the regiment continued to recruit more runaway slaves, approximately six to eight each day, mortality rates from the fever were so high that there were hardly any "effective men" who could actually fight. Slave soldiers were suffering and dying. Within a week British officers noted how dire the situation was becoming, as provisions like food and fresh water were also scarce. By early July conditions did not improve, and Dunmore employed his Loyalist forces, both Black and White, to make inroads onto the mainland to forage for food and fresh water. Some Patriots even suspected Dunmore sent sickened Black rebels onshore to infect the enemy in an early attempt at biological warfare.[16]

Patriots had also made note of fugitive slaves joining the Ethiopian Regiment and Dunmore's presence on Gwynn's Island, and they planned to attack the enslaved rebels as soon as reinforcements arrived. In the meantime they fired harassing shots at the Loyalists on a daily basis for nearly six weeks. At approximately ten o'clock in the morning on July 9, slave soldiers in the regiment felt the first shells from Patriot artillery. They took cover as two eighteen-pound cannons and four nine-pounders began hammering their positions. The barrage lasted for nearly two hours and did substantial damage to British ships patrolling the island nearby, including Dunmore's flagship *The Dunmore*, which had to be towed away. But a shortage of gunpowder and landing craft prevented a Patriot amphibious assault until the next morning. Slave soldiers likely knew the battle would be a defeat, but they returned fire nevertheless with muskets and a six-pound piece of cannon. Unfortunately for them, their fire had little effect, and Dunmore noted how useless it would be to stay on the island while taking on such heavy casualties. He therefore ordered his followers to evacuate. The Patriot delay enabled Dunmore and his soldiers, free and enslaved, to flee later that night under cover of darkness. Likely anticipating the Patriot attack, the Black soldiers were probably anxious and eager to leave the island. At the very least, they knew it was better to leave the disease-ridden place than to stay there.[17]

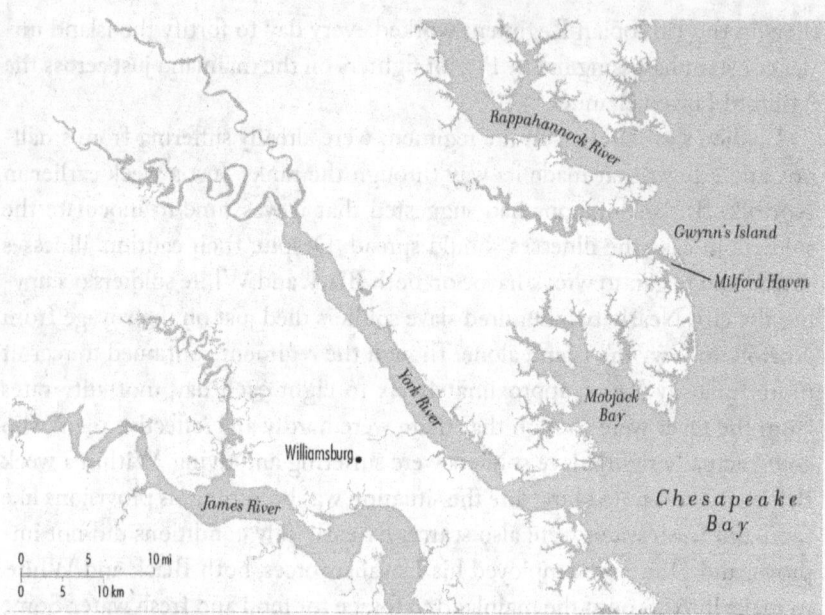

MAP 5. Gwynn's Island in the Chesapeake Bay. Map created by the author.

The next morning roughly 250 Patriots onboard thirty canoes crossed the channel and made landfall on Gwynn's Island. They faced little opposition as everyone who could fight had left, and those who were left behind were mostly noncombatants or were too sick to resist. Patriot captain Thomas Posey took part in the assault and would later describe how tattered much of the Ethiopian Regiment was on Gwynn's Island. He wrote that he "never saw more distress in my life, than what I found among some of the poor deluded Negroes which they could not take time, or did not chuse to cary off with them, they being sick. Those that I saw, some were dying, and many calling out for help; and throughout the whole Island we found them strew'd about, many of them torn to pieces by wild beasts—great numbers of the bodies having never been buried."[18]

Other slave soldiers were buried on the island, totally devastated by illness. At least 150 were buried, while twelve more were dead, "lying in the open air," from a "dreadful fever amongst them." Perhaps as many as four to five hundred slave soldiers died on the island, along with 150 Whites. One Patriot officer who was also part of the attacking force recorded in his journal how "deplorable" the situation was for Black rebels who were sick and were left on the island. He found many of them on the island "dying of the putrid fever; others dead in the open fields; a child was found sucking at the breast of its dead mother. In one place you might see a poor wretch half dead making signs for water, in another, others endeavauring to crawl away from the intolerable stench of dead bodies lying by their sides; in short it was a shocking scene." Yet another officer noted that he found 130 shallow graves on the island and that even the commander, Major Thomas Byrd, fled from the island sick. "In short, such a scene of misery, distress, and cruelty, my eyes never beheld." Like other Black Loyalists who contracted smallpox during the conflict, they had perhaps spent entire days lying on the ground "without any thing to eat or drink." In their desperate state, slave soldiers were unable to kill a single Patriot soldier during the invasion. They were too sick to care, and those who could fight had left them behind, along with the six-pound piece of cannon, baggage, cables, anchors, iron, and fifty head of cattle.[19]

Although many enslaved soldiers in the Ethiopian Regiment had died on Gwynn's Island or were left behind, those who escaped with British forces carried on their fight farther north in the Chesapeake. The rebels sailed to St. George's Island at the mouth of the Potomac River to find fresh food and water again. Even more plantation slaves fled to their standard and joined their ranks. Once again, Black rebels on the island received harassing fire from Patriot fighters nearby on a daily basis. They also did not find an adequate supply of water on the Island, and Dunmore ordered Captain Andrew Hamond to go farther up the Potomac in search of more and to harass Patriot planters. Once again, members of the Ethiopian Regiment took part in the fighting and joined Hamond's 108-man expedition. On board the HMS *Roebuck*, Hamond led the excursion nearly a hundred miles before reaching William Brent's plantation. Aside from an opportunity to plunder the Patriot's property for supplies, nearly three hundred Patriot soldiers had assembled at the plantation and a successful Loyalist attack could boost morale after the disgraceful defeat at Gwynn's Island.[20]

Soldiers with Hamond first cannonaded Brent's house by sea before making landfall, driving away the Patriots harbored inside. Once on land, the Black rebels and British Regulars burned the house and slave quarters on the plantation. Approximately four or five men were wounded, while they also found three dead Patriots on site. The skirmish amounted to little more, and the rebels returned to St. George's Island to reorganize and continue plantation raids elsewhere, which Hamond complained decided "nothing" for the broader British military strategy.[21]

In the end, the fighting near St. George's Island also proved largely unsuccessful for the Ethiopian Regiment and the British military. Provisions were still hard to come by, while fever and illnesses continued to wreak havoc among the ranks. Dunmore's fleet departed St. George's by August 2 and sailed south to evacuate the Chesapeake entirely. When the last of his forces sailed past the Virginia Capes on August 6, only one-third of his soldiers were actually healthy enough to fight. The British had lost twenty vessels in the fighting of the summer of 1776, while Dunmore reported that he had taken or destroyed at least thirty Patriot ships. But close to half of the men and women who joined the Ethiopian Regiment and Dunmore's fleet had perished. Those who were still alive would continue to suffer as they reached New York, and there was not a ship in Dunmore's fleet "that did not throw one two three or more dead overboard every night." They had left Virginia free, but many did not live long enough to enjoy their hard-earned liberty.[22]

Some survivors of 1775 and 1776 continued the fight later in the war. One member of the regiment, Titus or Colonel Tye, led bloody raids and retaliatory strikes against Patriot masters in New Jersey in 1779, with several attacks directly targeting the slaves' former owners. Tye and his followers even killed Patriots as retribution for the death of Black Loyalists in battle. Relentless in fighting as state-sponsored rebels, Tye and the surviving regiment's soldiers avenged their bondage and punished their former owners for their maltreatment. Underscoring the intense personal and vindictive nature of the fighting in which slave soldiers in the regiment participated, they wore "liberty to slaves" inscribed on their uniforms as they fought their former owners.[23]

Running Away to Become a Soldier: Regiment Composition

Issued on November 7, 1775, Dunmore's Proclamation caused widespread and spontaneous slave flight in the Chesapeake. Enslaved people who ran to Dunmore and joined the Ethiopian Regiment thereafter created their own community. Whether or not they fled as individuals or in groups, they came together for a united cause as the regiment formed. Additionally, whether they left alone or in groups, by the time they reached Dunmore's lines, many had formed collective bands. One man named George claimed to have escaped from Norfolk with fifty-five other Black men and two White men after he was captured and interrogated by Patriot forces in late 1775. His comrade, a man named Ted from Kemp's Landing, told Patriot officers that he had fled Norfolk with twenty other Black men and a few White men as well. Indeed, Dunmore's call to arms was causing rampant flight throughout the colony. Within a week, the Virginia Committee of Safety estimated that almost a hundred enslaved people had already joined Dunmore, while by mid-February 1776 Dunmore estimated that he could have as many as three thousand slaves within his ranks. Those who could not reach the British by land stole canoes and small boats and approached by water. Many fled in family groups, like Jane Thompson and her grandson Peter, although there is evidence that family flight to Dunmore was sometimes incremental. Fathers and husbands generally fled first when their families were unsure about joining the rebellion, and after British officers reassured them, the men offered intelligence about Patriot masters and returned to their plantations to bring back their partners and children. Some also returned with food and new recruits to join the regiment. Nearly half of the estimated runaways who fought in the regiment and who survived the war were from Norfolk County, and the vast majority of the regiment came from Norfolk and Princess Ann Counties. Considering the slave population in the two counties, approximately 25 percent of enslaved people closest to Dunmore actually fled to Dunmore's lines.[24]

Despite Dunmore's Proclamation that assured enslaved people their liberty if they reached his forces, running away was still a dangerous and frightening endeavor for many slaves in the Chesapeake in 1775 and 1776. While members of the Ethiopian Regiment left no account describing their fear or obstacles in reaching Dunmore, Boston King recounted his path to freedom in South Carolina in 1780, which was probably similar in many ways to how members of the Ethiopian Regiment reached Dunmore and British forces. King had at first run away to escape the harsh treatment of his owner, and when he escaped to Charlestown he "began to feel the happiness of liberty." As liberating as it must have felt, King was still "much grieved at first," having left his friends behind and being forced to live among "strangers." Escaping from slavery could result in the temporary and even permanent loss of friends and family members. Moreover, what life would be like with the British army during a violent war was unknown. Notwithstanding these uncertainties and the potential loss of kith and kin, enslaved people in the Chesapeake fled to join the Ethiopian Regiment to earn their freedom.[25]

Returns of the Ethiopian Regiment on Gwynn's Island, which the regiment occupied for the better part of six weeks in the summer of 1776, indicate that at least a few enslaved families were part of or followed the regiment. Phillis Thorowgood was at the Mill Point camp on the island with her daughter, also named Phillis, as was Patience Butt, who was listed with a child. Meanwhile, Sergeant Curry served in Dunmore's own company with his unnamed son. The enslaved soldiers and camp followers were otherwise listed by their owners' surnames, but it is reasonable to speculate that several other enslaved family groups were on the island given the simple fact that enslaved people formed their own families on Virginia plantations, and that several enslaved men and women from the same owners were listed as present on the island. It is possible that many ran away to British lines much like David George and his wife Phyllis did in Georgia years later. When George's master left the plantation to escape British advances, George, Phyllis, their two children, and more than fifty other enslaved people left to reach British soldiers near Savannah. While they were in British lines, Phyllis served as a washerwoman for General Henry Clinton before they eventually evacuated Charleston for Nova Scotia at war's end. Women who ran away to the Ethiopian Regiment served in similar roles, as did Phyllis farther south.[26]

To be sure, only Robert Tucker and Bristoll Mitchell are listed on both the returns at Gwynn's Island and in the *Book of Negroes* as having fought in the Ethiopian Regiment. But it is also clear that other people not listed at Gwynn's Island joined Dunmore in family units. Others like Jane Thompson ran away to Dunmore with young children by their side. In a few cases, grandparents also joined the movement. The *Book of Negroes* lists 128 people who probably served with the Ethiopian Regiment at some point. Eighteen are listed as having served with or come to New York with Dunmore, while the others fled from parts of the Chesapeake where the Ethiopian Regiment served and took action in 1775 and 1776. While this method has its limits, it offers a glimpse into who made up the regiment at the start of the Revolutionary War. Of those who probably served, 60 percent were male and 40 percent were female. The ratio may have even been closer to one-half female by other estimates. Most male members were in their twenties when they joined, but sizable numbers were teenagers or in their thirties and forties. Meanwhile, almost half of the women were teenagers, and almost a quarter were older and in their twenties. At least fourteen enslaved people listed in 1783 were under the age of ten when they escaped with their relatives in Virginia, and survivors took little time to build and expand their families living within British lines for the rest of the war. Now that they had earned their freedom and had the opportunity to rekindle relationships with partners or start new relationships altogether, these likely survivors of the regiment had another thirty-one children by the time they evacuated New York for Nova Scotia in 1783. Their numbers also paint a different picture than what was reported after Dunmore's forces evacuated Gwynn's Island, in which close to two-thirds of the enslaved people on the island were men.[27]

TABLE 1. Members of the Ethiopian Regiment on
Gwynn's Island by Sex

	N	% of Known
Male	130	72
Female	51	28
Unknown	64	—
TOTAL	245	—

Source: *Virginia Gazette* (Dixon and Hunter), Williamsburg, August 31, 1776.
Note: Adjustments were made for rounding errors.

TABLE 2. Estimated Members of the Ethiopian Regiment Who Survived the War, by Age and Sex

Men			Women		
Age	N	%	Age	N	%
0–9	10	13	0–9	4	8
10–19	10	13	10–19	24	46
20–29	22	29	20–29	12	23
30–39	14	18	30–39	5	10
40–49	7	9	40–49	3	6
50–59	5	6	50–59	2	4
60–69	2	3	60–69	0	0
Unknown	6	8	Unknown	2	4
TOTAL	76	100		52	100

Source: *Book of Negroes* [1783], Sir Guy Carleton Papers, Nova Scotia Archives Microfilm no. 10149. http://novascotia.ca/archives/africans/archives.
Note: Adjustments were made for rounding errors.

The somewhat balanced sex ratio in the regiment is striking, considering that over the broader history of runaway slaves in the United States, nearly 80 percent were male. The ratio also attests to how important it was for mothers, daughters, sisters, and wives to participate in the regiment, even though they were excluded from carrying firearms in the British army. That so many of them joined also shows how militarized resistance was increasing during the American Revolutionary War. Whereas before slave soldiers in Virginia in 1676 and in South Carolina in 1715 were exclusively men, in the Ethiopian Regiment women and children could participate in more roles than ever before. In the case of the Ethiopian Regiment, women and children could use military service to attack the chattel system, which was an option they did not have access to in earlier cases (see tables 1 and 2).[28]

Despite these hundreds who responded to Dunmore's immediate call, others were already fighting with him or were contemplating joining him before he made his intentions public. Notably, slaves Aaron, Johnny, and Joe Harris were already aboard the British tender *Otter* with Captain Mathew Squire by the summer of 1775, with Harris earning a reputation as a skilled pilot during the fighting at Hampton Roads. Judith Jackson had already been on the run for two years before she decided to join the regiment as a washerwoman. Similarly, Robert Brent's slave Charles fled just after Dunmore issued his proclamation, but Brent assumed that his flight was premeditated. Nor was Dunmore's reach limited to Virginia. Titus or Tye, the slave of John Corlis in Monmouth County, New Jersey, ran away only a day after Dunmore issued his proclamation, and it was impossible for him to have heard the news so rapidly. Furthermore, while Dunmore's Proclamation caused mass flight, not all slaves in Virginia fled to Dunmore to fight their former owners. Of John Willoughby Jr.'s eighty-seven slaves who ran away during the war, only fourteen actually joined the Ethiopian Regiment. The others simply took advantage of the chaos of war and fled.[29]

Most enslaved people who joined the Ethiopian Regiment were probably American-born. People listed on military returns, the *Book of Negroes*, and land applications for Sierra Leone in 1791 have Anglicized names, while approximately 6 percent of Virginia's black population in 1775 was African-born. Virginia planters imported nearly a thousand African slaves per year in the twenty-five years before Dunmore's Proclamation, but there was no African ethnic majority in Virginia by the time the regiment mustered. Africans embarking from the Bight of Biafra, the Gulf of Guinea Islands, and the Windward Coast accounted for the largest groups sent to the colony via the transatlantic slave trade, while Virginians also imported thousands of Gold Coast peoples from Barbados and Jamaica via the intercolonial slave trade (see tables 3 and 4). It would seem that those who did reach the regiment also did not have prior military experience as Dunmore complained that only one-tenth of the rebel slaves who reached his lines were actually capable of bearing arms and that they "hardly ever made use of the gun."[30]

Though Dunmore inspired many of the Ethiopian rebels to join him, and while they were technically under the command of white Loyalist Major Thomas Byrd, Black leaders did emerge during the fighting. Returns of the regiment on Gwynn's Island show that there were at least four Black noncommissioned officers, including Corporals Crouch and Curry, and Sergeants Britain and John Royal. But little more is known of them, and there

TABLE 3. Slaves Imported from Africa to Virginia, 1750–1776

Region of Departure in Africa	N	%
Sierra Leone	1,479	7
Windward Coast	5,038	22
Gold Coast	1,755	8
Bight of Benin	608	2
Bight of Biafra and Gulf of Guinea Islands	5,418	24
West Central Africa and St. Helena	3,999	18
Other Africa	4,160	19
TOTAL	22,457	100

Source: Estimates Database, 2016, Slave Voyages, https://www.slavevoyages.org/assessment/estimates.
Note: Adjustments were made for rounding errors.

TABLE 4. Slaves Imported from Africa to Virginia, 1701–1776

Region of Departure in Africa	N	%
Senegambia	10,500	11
Sierra Leone	1,852	2
Windward Coast	2,591	3
Gold Coast	5,237	5
Bight of Benin	1,745	2
Bight of Biafra and Gulf of Guinea Islands	28,494	30
West Central Africa and St. Helena	10,600	11
Southeast Africa and Indian Ocean Islands	1,767	2
Other Africa	32,088	34
TOTAL	94,874	100

Source: Estimates Database, 2016, Slave Voyages, https://www.slavevoyages.org/assessment/estimates.
Note: Adjustments were made for rounding errors.

do not appear to be any runaway slave advertisements published for their return from potential owners. They may have even been free.[31]

Moses "Daddy" Wilkinson of Miles Wilkinson in Nansemond County also became a leader. He attracted dozens of followers in 1776, and he survived the war to eventually embark from Nova Scotia to Sierra Leone in 1792. At the time of his flight, he was twenty-nine years old and described as blind and lame in the *Book of Negroes*. Not a fighter, Moses was a Methodist preacher and a skilled orator who could communicate and appeal to religious beliefs. Moses remained a leader in Nova Scotia with other Black Loyalists, and in Sierra Leone when the last slave rebels attempted to start a new life in Africa.[32]

The Regiment in Greater Atlantic Perspective

The plundering of plantations and razing of crops in Virginia by soldiers in the Ethiopian Regiment was at least in part the product of a violent and intense war. But their actions also resembled militarized slave rebels elsewhere in the Atlantic world pursuing similar objectives. The hundreds of slaves who joined Dunmore matched the nearly one thousand who fought for Tacky in his massive Jamaican rebellion in 1760, and they exceeded the dozen or so slaves tried for conspiracy with Thomas Jeremiah in Charleston in 1775. They were larger than the group of more than a hundred slaves implicated in the Hanover Parish conspiracy in Jamaica in 1776. They were at least as large as the hundreds of Coromantin rebels who rose up in Jamaica in several insurrections in the late seventeenth century as well.

Aside from their numbers, soldiers in the Ethiopian Regiment followed similar methods, tactics, techniques, and procedures to achieve their goals like militarized slave rebels. At the onset of Tacky's Revolt in St. Mary's Parish, Jamaica, slaves captured muskets and gunpowder and then set fire to the sugar works and cane fields on the Heywood-Hall plantation. As they progressed through Jamaican parishes, they circled individual plantations and recruited more slaves step by step. They planned to live on plantation provisions they plundered to sustain their movement and recruit more rebels. More than a hundred rebels joined in the first phase of insurrection and killed at least a dozen Whites. In most attacks, plantation houses, estate buildings, and sugarcane fields were all destroyed and burned, just like what occurred in several of the Ethiopian Regiment's attacks on Patriot plantations. Rebels also fought White soldiers in several large engagements on the island. When a new faction of rebels rose up in Westmoreland Parish in late May 1760, they routed White militias dispatched after them and successfully defended fortified positions. Their successes on the battlefields also enabled them to capture more firearms and ammunition to sustain their cause. Like the soldiers in the Ethiopian Regiment who recruited more slaves as they moved through the Chesapeake and as word spread of Dunmore's Proclamation, more enslaved people in Elizabeth, St. James, St. Johns, St. Dorothy's, St. Thomas, Clarendon, and Hanover Parishes attempted to join the fighting during Tacky's Revolt.[33]

The soldiers in the regiment were probably most similar to rebels who conspired in Thomas Jeremiah's plot in South Carolina in 1775 and those who conspired in Jamaica in 1776. Jeremiah's conspiracy, either real or imagined, was uncovered in mid-August when some enslaved people betrayed the plot and informed their owners. Though Jeremiah was a wealthy free Black in Charleston, he reportedly solicited an enslaved man named Jemmy at Prioleau's Wharf to steal gunpowder and give it to a fugitive slave in town to help the incoming British. Jemmy's testimony was corroborated by another man named Sambo who stated that two to three months earlier Jeremiah had approached him at Simmons Wharf and asked him about the upcoming war with the British. He told Sambo that such a conflict would benefit Blacks and that Sambo should escape to a schooner and set it on fire, after which he could swim to the British and join the army. The plot was remarkably similar to how some slaves managed to join Dunmore's forces early on, although nothing materialized and Jeremiah was executed. Similarly, the rebels who conspired in Hanover Parish, Jamaica, in 1776 were also armed with cutlasses and were timing their rebellion based on British military movements. They wanted to start the rebellion with the departure of the Fiftieth Regiment for mainland North America. Once British soldiers were to leave the island, the rebels planned on running to the woods to rendezvous with the Leeward Maroons who would assist them in gathering arms and ammunition for continued engagements against White soldiers. They understood, like the Ethiopian Regiment soldiers, that they could turn a war of empire into something else for themselves.[34]

Though the combatants in the Ethiopian Regiment were all men, the roles of women and children attached to the regiment were also consistent with other militarized resistance movements occurring at the time as well. Black women throughout the Revolutionary War served as cooks and washerwomen for male fighters, while children were employed to smother fuses and carry shells to soldiers on the front lines. Though the British military sponsored their activities in these roles, they were not significantly different from what slave rebels did elsewhere on their own, as Marjoleine Kars and Vanessa Holden have recently shown for rebels in Berbice in 1763 and in Virginia in 1831. In addition, enslaved women helped carry provisions and baggage in Jamaica in 1760 during Tacky's Revolt. They also helped prepare food and dressed victuals for rebel fighters, and even after Tacky's death fighters allegedly appointed a queen named Cubah to replace him. Women performed the same auxiliary and logistical positions in rebel forces in Haiti and Guadelupe at the end of the eighteenth century as well, and they carried ammunition and food, and nursed the injured too. Notably, female Haitian rebels even prostituted themselves to French soldiers to steal ammunition and gather intelligence for Black fighters. Undoubtedly and despite their young age or position as auxiliaries in the British army, enslaved women and children actively joined and supported the Ethiopian Regiment in Virginia and contributed to Black Loyalist success by the end of the war just like rebel women and children did all around the Atlantic.[35]

Soldiers in the Ethiopian Regiment shared other experiences with slave soldiers in the Haitian Revolution. In Haiti insurgents first took up arms in late August 1791 with Dutty Bookman near Cap-Français. After a voodoo ceremony at Bois Caïman, the rebels attacked the manager of La Gossette plantation. As the rebellion gained momentum, insurgents marched from plantation to plantation in the Plaine du Nord Parish. They attacked every White person they encountered and any Black slave who stood against them. In just days, thousands of rebels joined and the parish was in flames. As the fighting unfolded, insurgent forces were filled with African veterans who utilized their military experience to sustain the movement. Later on, and much like the soldiers in the Ethiopian Regiment who attacked and plundered Patriot plantations, insurgent soldiers in Haiti attacked plantations and towns controlled by slave owners and enemy forces. By the end of the conflict, thousands of slave soldiers had mobilized to fight for Haitian independence and for freedom from slavery.[36]

Conditions for enslaved people to take up arms and rise up with the British army in Virginia in 1775 and 1776 were also consistent with other militarized resistance movements in the Atlantic during the period. Undoubtedly the planter class was divided in Virginia by the time the Ethiopian Regiment mustered. Whites in Virginia had already been weakened by war with the Shawnee Indians in 1774, and tensions were rising between colonists on proper British imperial policy in the colony. Loyalist and Patriot factions were already in place by 1775, and it was clear that enslaved people were well aware of the political tensions and the start of the Revolutionary War. By the time Lord Dunmore removed the gunpowder from the Williamsburg magazine in April 1775, Patriot and Loyalist camps were entrenching and political cohesion in Virginia had eroded.[37]

In addition to the deteriorating situation that divided White Virginians, a powerful hurricane in August 1775 hit the Chesapeake and caused substantial damage to the region. Itinerant preacher Francis Asbury noted late that month that several ships had been washed up on shore, and houses, docks, and bridges had all been destroyed. Trees and crops had also been lifted from the ground. While planters suffered the inclement weather too, they probably passed the burden on to their slaves, who were left with repairing the damage and who suffered the most from the deterioration of shelter and the poor food and water supply. These conditions were similar to conditions present for other militarized slave rebels who challenged the master regime elsewhere in the Atlantic. Just as had been the case in Virginia for the Ethiopian rebels, slaves who followed Thomas Jeremiah in Charleston exploited the disruptions of war and political division in 1775 too. So too did the slaves in Hanover Parish, Jamaica, in summer 1776. They also suffered from a food shortage after provision lines were cut off from mainland North America, and they waited to rebel until British soldiers and ships left the island and made planters vulnerable. The trade embargo during the Revolutionary War also severely limited provision supplies to Jamaica and prices skyrocketed. Enslaved people on the island were nearly starving. Enslaved Creoles who conspired with African-born slaves in August 1776 also waited for British military forces to leave the island for North America. They reportedly believed "that the mother country was too much employed in America to be able to assist Jamaica" and that "the English were engaged in a desperate war, which would require all their force elsewhere." White planters were vulnerable with the empire at war on the mainland. Similarly, sixteen years earlier on the island, Tacky's followers took advantage of the Seven Years' War to challenge their masters. Slaves in Virginia in 1775 endured unusually difficult material conditions as the Ethiopian Regiment mustered, similar to the conditions that preceded several militarized slave rebellions during the period. White authorities were also divided and vulnerable, much like the conditions present for other rebels during the period.[38]

Conclusion

Though members served as soldiers in the British military during the Revolutionary War, they fought for freedom in a way that resembled militarized slave rebellions throughout the Atlantic world. Common preconditions for militarized rebellions were also present in Virginia in 1775 and 1776, as soldiers in the Ethiopian Regiment endured harsher conditions and witnessed the master class divide at the onset of Dunmore's Proclamation. As was the case elsewhere in the Atlantic, slave soldiers also fought collectively and proportionately along Virginia's shore, and planters, officials, and militiamen thought they were committing rebellion and treated them accordingly. Unlike their Patriot masters who would remember the fighting as a revolution for independence, slaves remembered the Ethiopian Regiment as part of a longer movement to attack the chattel system. In Nova Scotia and in Sierra Leone, veterans of the Ethiopian Regiment and other Black Loyalists refused to be treated like slaves and feared they were being turned into slaves again in Freetown. David George recounted that White authorities in Freetown had treated the Black veterans "as bad as though we had been slaves" and that they would "be made slaves again" if they ran away from the fledgling settlement. Similarly, others petitioned the Sierra Leone Company in London that their freedom seemed fragile at best. They wrote that they wanted to make their "children free and happy after us," but if the directors of the company continued to deny Black leadership of the settlement, their "children may be in bondage after us." The veterans also petitioned against Governor William Dawes, whom they claimed "seems to wish to rule us just as bad as if we were all Slaves which we cannot bear." By 1794 and 1795, survivors of the Ethiopian Regiment like Moses Wilkinson appealed further that Freetown had become "A Town of Slavery" and that they were tired of being "empressed upon with Tyranny and Emprision." They were determined to "Enjoy the privileges of Freedom," which they had fought for so vigorously in North America years earlier.[39]

At the same time in Virginia, Gabriel had planned on waving a larger banner in Richmond with the words "Death or Liberty" inscribed on it, just as the Ethiopian rebels had fought with "liberty to slaves" emblazoned on their uniforms. Their experiences also point to how differences between war and rebellion were sometimes blurred for slaves in the Atlantic World. Slave soldiers in the Ethiopian Regiment used military service to attack the chattel system during the Revolutionary War, but they also fought like militarized slave rebels elsewhere in the Atlantic during the period. Plantation rebels who succeeded them linked their own rebellions to the cause of the slave soldiers in the regiment.[40]

The regiment also demonstrated a surge in militarized slave resistance during the age of revolution. The Revolutionary War brought new ideologies and strategies to early America, and slave soldiers became an increasingly better military option for both the rank and file and for commanders at the top. But the expansion of options for enslaved people during the Revolutionary War also increasingly militarized enslaved families as more roles became open to women and children serving in slave units, and as more enslaved women and children took these opportunities to challenge their status. A professional army gave more enslaved people an opportunity to use military service to challenge the chattel system. In many cases, if they did not choose militarization, families could be separated and divided. In other cases, slave soldiers, be they men, women, or children, formed new ties and strengthened existing ones based on their military service during the war. In mainland British North America, the militarization of slave resistance in the eighteenth century had reached its peak. In the broader British Atlantic, revolution bolstered it and led to a surge in the nineteenth century with the development of permanent, peacetime, and professional slave soldiers and the West India Regiments.

What is further remarkable about the Ethiopian rebels was their success. Though hundreds died from a smallpox epidemic, approximately 250 enslaved people still evacuated with Dunmore in the summer of 1776 and were free from their owners and the abuses of White planters in Virginia. The 128 slaves who appear in the *Book of Negroes* likely served in the regiment and were evacuated to Nova Scotia in 1783. Many of them had married runaways from other parts of the country and started new families since they left Virginia. As many found life in Nova Scotia unappealing, at least nineteen of these likely Ethiopian rebels applied for land in Freetown, Sierra Leone, where the British prepared a settlement in 1792. Among those who made it were Moses Wilkinson, Chloe and Henry Walker, Captain Nathaniel Snowball, Violet Snowball, Bettsey, Henry, Abigail and Lydia Newton, Robert, Jane, and Hannah Jackson, Jenny Bush, Hannah Blair, and Judith Evans. Patrick Henry's slave Ralph and George Washington's bondsman Harry were also among those who reached Sierra Leone more than a decade after leaving their masters in Virginia. In a revolution in which Patrick Henry proclaimed "Give me liberty or give me death," and in a war in which General Washington fought to secure American liberty from British "tyranny," their slaves had fought for their own liberty from the tyranny of their owners, and they were prepared to die if they did not obtain it.[41]

Soldiers in the Ethiopian Regiment had successfully challenged the slave system in Virginia. Their success on the battlefield and utility in the Revolutionary War led to the creation of more slave soldier units in the British army during the war, with which slaves could further challenge slavery in early America. While they did not succeed in ending slavery on the mainland, many had at least escaped from it and found new lives elsewhere. With the help of an uneasy ally in the British army, many were also able to successfully evacuate at war's end and move to safe havens in London and Nova Scotia before eventually reaching Sierra Leone. They were able to integrate themselves into the broader Atlantic world no longer as slaves but as free former soldiers who had earned their liberty by taking up arms. Their ability to do this was matched only by rebels involved in the Haitian Revolution just years later.

Their success also altered slave soldiering in the Anglo-Atlantic. It eventually led to the development of the West India Regiments, which became the first permanent peacetime slave army in the Anglo-Atlantic a decade after the Revolutionary War finally ended. But freedom did not come with service in the regiments and during times of crisis. Enslaved people could no longer just take advantage of exigent circumstances and take up arms with Native or European enemies to fight for freedom. After the American Revolution slave soldiers in the West India Regiments were still shackled to the chattel system. They were therefore forced to take other options to keep attacking slavery.

CHAPTER 4

Mutiny in the Caribbean
*Saltwater Slave Soldiers in the Eighth
West India Regiment, Dominica, 1802*

Travelers who visit Cabrits National Park in Dominica can also visit the restored remains of the famous garrison and ramparts of Fort Shirley, which was the center of European defenses on the island in the eighteenth and nineteenth centuries. The fort is a UNESCO world heritage site, and both UNESCO and tourism partners with Dominica's Ministry of Tourism advertise the fort as a site of both scenic and historic significance. Importantly, it is a place where a "revolt by African slave soldiers in 1802" led to the "freeing of all British slave soldiers in 1807." Since restoration efforts in 2007 visitors to the fort can also read a commemorative plaque dedicated to this revolt, or mutiny, in which soldiers of the Eighth West India Regiment "were killed or executed in their fight for freedom." Slave soldiers in the West India Regiments became part of the largest professional slave army in the Atlantic world, which the British built in the wake of the American Revolution. The plaque in part further reads, "As a result of their action here some 10,000 slave soldiers in the British Army were freed in 1807. It was the first act of mass emancipation in the British empire."[1]

It is surprising, given the mutiny's significance to the history of Dominica and to slavery in the British Empire, as well as its UNESCO recognition, that the mutiny of the Eighth West India Regiment in April 1802 has received scant attention from historians studying slavery and resistance in the Atlantic world. This is not to say that historians studying Dominica or those examining the history of enslaved soldiers in the West Indies are unfamiliar with the mutiny; however, the episode has generally not been characterized as collective slave resistance.[2]

But what exactly did the mutiny mean to the slave soldiers who participated in it? Moreover, how did it compare to other incidents in which enslaved people rose up and challenged the Atlantic chattel system, and how did it compare to other cases of armed resistance in mainland British North America?

By focusing on the Eighth WIR mutiny, this story of armed resistance also moves from mainland British North America to the Caribbean to better evaluate how armed resistance operated elsewhere in the Anglo-Atlantic. While slave soldiers took up arms in British armies and militias throughout the Anglo-Atlantic, the practice operated differently in the Caribbean than in mainland North America. Because of White manpower shortages, large enslaved Black populations, or the constant threat of imperial enemies, British colonists more readily armed slave soldiers in the Caribbean compared to mainland North America. As early as 1640 enslaved soldiers helped British colonists defend colonial possessions in the Caribbean, while by the 1660s enslaved soldiers were incorporated into the Barbados militia. Some mainland colonial authorities such as in Massachusetts considered requiring free Black people and slaves to serve in militias as early as 1652, but generally these ideas were short lived. In other colonies like Virginia, enslaved people were prohibited from serving in the militia as early as 1639. As the seventeenth century progressed, several colonial legislatures barred Black people from military service, which became a trend well into the eighteenth century. Although in a few places enslaved people were permitted to take up arms in times of crisis, as noted above in Virginia and South Carolina, they were still excluded from serving during the French and Indian War in many places, and the specter of permanent and independent Black units did not rise until the American Revolutionary War. Indeed, colonists in the Caribbean were seemingly less restrictive when it came to enslaved people serving in colonial militias while permanent, independent all-Black units also developed.[3]

The West India Regiments became the largest professional slave army that Europeans wielded in the Atlantic world in the early nineteenth century, and this chapter examines professional slave soldiers in the Eighth WIR instead of those who took up arms in militias or in times of emergency such as in chapters 1, 2, and 3, thus offering greater insight into how the professional militarization of slaves affected armed resistance. It also examines the Eighth WIR mutiny because it was one of only three mutinies in the West India Regiments before total emancipation, and it was the only mutiny in the West India Regiments before the 1807 Mutiny Act, which declared all enslaved soldiers who served in the British army free for all intents and purposes. The mutiny thus captures a unique moment in British Atlantic history in which professional armed slaves challenged their owners. In addition, the 1802 mutiny helps better explain armed resistance that occurred after the American Revolution. Thus it helps us understand how the age of revolution influenced how slave soldiers took up arms to fight for freedom and emancipation and the impact of the professional militarization of slaves at that time. The Eighth WIR mutiny was yet another militarized slave revolt in the Anglo-Atlantic, one not unlike others in which enslaved soldiers took up arms to fight for Black liberation. African soldiers involved in the mutiny did not seemingly appropriate revolutionary ideology to further their own cause, while the mutiny also shows that professional slave soldiers in the Eighth WIR did not interpret military service itself as a vehicle for freedom and emancipation.

Saltwater Slave Soldiers: Recruiting Strategies and the Beginnings of the Eighth West India Regiment

How the West India Regiments developed, how slave soldiers were recruited, and how they lived, trained, and fought in the regiments helps explain why soldiers in the Eighth WIR mutinied in Dominica in 1802. As demonstrated in chapters 1, 2, and 3, British authorities had long understood the utility of loyal enslaved soldiers, and throughout the seventeenth and eighteenth centuries, colonists and colonial officials frequently employed slaves in military functions. Yet the success of Black Loyalists during the American Revolutionary War, and subsequent units like the Black Rangers and Carolina Black Corps who helped the British defend Saint Vincent, Tobago, and Grenada from French attacks at the end of the eighteenth century, reinforced the notion that a larger and permanent free Black and enslaved fighting force could be used to great effect in the Caribbean. By the 1790s the British Empire in the Caribbean was also under crisis. The French had made great military strides against the British in the region, and they had successfully employed a large enslaved military force to achieve their imperial goals. By 1794 and 1795, War Secretary Sir Henry Dundas and Commander of the West Indies Sir John Vaughan agreed that the security situation in the West Indies was "critical" and that they needed more troops or else they risked losing British possessions in the Caribbean to the French.[4]

Officials initially wanted to recruit nine thousand slaves from British colonies in the Caribbean to serve as soldiers, which could be achieved by enforcing recruitment quotas on each island. Vaughan also had the authority to take more recruits if a governor refused or did not reach his quota. But mustering several thousand enslaved people to be soldiers in the plantation colonies raised fears among planters that they could agitate the larger plantation slave population. Planters were also concerned about how loyal some slave soldiers would be, while if Black slaves were treated as equals to White soldiers in a permanent military unit, they could undermine ideas of White supremacy.[5]

British military leaders also decided to raise Black troops based on their ideas of science, race, and the Caribbean environment. More than half of the British troops sent to the West Indies from 1793 to 1801 died from tropical diseases in the area, and it was a long-held assumption among White authorities, planters, and travelers alike that Africans and Black Creoles seemed better at tolerating hot temperatures and tropical maladies than Whites. Conscripting enslaved Black people to serve in the military would thus cut down on White casualties and promote stability and security for British colonists in the Caribbean. Officers also thought the move would be more politically popular than sending more White soldiers from Great Britain, and it would alleviate what would be a "vast drain" on Great Britain's White population if Black people were not used. In Dominica especially, Governor Andrew James Cochrane Johnstone claimed that he would save many White lives by raising units of Black soldiers to serve on the island. Initial returns of saltwater slave soldiers in the regiments demonstrated that these ideas were not accurate and that African soldiers were actually more susceptible to illness than White soldiers. But over time and after proper inoculations and seasoning, enslaved Africans in the West India Regiments did become a relatively healthy body of combatants who supported British military ambitions in the region.[6]

Even before the West India Regiments could be raised, Governor Johnstone employed mostly Creole and some African slaves in another military unit known as the Loyal Dominican Rangers. Some of the men were later absorbed into the West India Regiments when they first mustered in April and May 1795. The Eighth WIR rose to full strength by September 15, 1795, under the command of Lieutenant Colonel John Skerrett in Dominica. Soldiers in the Eighth occupied Fort Shirley at Prince Rupert's Bay in Dominica, which was the strongest military position on the island. The Bay was on the northern end of the island and adjacent to the Cabrits, an extinct volcanic rock formation that jutted out of the sea (see maps 6–9).[7]

Each West India Regiment consisted of approximately ten companies with ninety-five privates, along with officers, staff, a quartermaster, an adjutant, a surgeon, and a chaplain. Even though some of the Loyal Dominican Rangers were absorbed into WIR service, taking enslaved recruits from the islands and from oppositional planters presented an obstacle to raising the intended recruitment goals of the West India Regiments altogether. Manumitted soldiers could not be used since they would raise the specter of emancipation. British military authorities also thought that Africans were better for the job. They were cheaper to purchase than Creoles, and they had not yet endured the harsh conditions of plantation slavery, which made them better suited to military discipline. As "New Negroes" they were also "unacquainted with and uncontaminated" by Creoles. Despite their reputation for tenacity and militarization in previous Caribbean slave revolts, officers also believed that Africans in general, and specifically Coromantee, Fante, and Angolans, would be the best soldiers to serve in the regiments.[8]

The British army thus resorted to purchasing African-born slaves directly via the transatlantic slave trade to fill the ranks of the West India Regiments. Though these African soldiers were not skilled or seasoned like Creoles, they could be cheaper and would allow army officials to avoid confrontation with obstinate planters. Enslaved Africans had to be purchased in secrecy, however, because men like Secretary Dundas did not want the public to know that the British government was directly involved in procuring enslaved people from Africa as the abolition movement was gaining momentum. By 1798 Governor Johnstone reported that the army purchased 340 enslaved people to serve on the island at a cost of £22,465. The 295 Africans purchased for £66 each had been inspected and were deemed worthy of their cost, while ninety-one more Creole slaves were also purchased for £73 each. African slaves were predominant in the regiments during these early years, and in some regiments they outnumbered Creole slaves by more than ten to one. It is probable that more than half of all the soldiers in the West India Regiments were African-born, although the precise locations are unknown. The Eighth WIR was particularly known for how many enslaved Africans were purchased for service in the unit.[9]

Acquiring enslaved people solely for military service on a scale as large as what British officers were thinking was not an easy task. Government regulations limited officers from spending more than £75 per person, and they could not compete with planters who were willing to spend much more for bulk purchases. Brigadier General Thomas Hislop also thought that purchasing enslaved women was a good idea so as to encourage marriage as a benefit for enslaved soldiers. Women would also help run garrisons smoothly, while more importantly, the children they had with enslaved soldiers would become property of the British government. Hislop imagined a breeding operation in which young enslaved boys could be "trained to arms" as "excellent soldiers" who could replenish British forces when their fathers died or grew too old to fight. Enslaved girls could also be trained to undertake the same duties as their mothers and help the West India Regiments operate efficiently.[10]

The recruitment project also envisioned keeping enslaved soldiers busy so that they would not "cause trouble" in towns, as well as a support system for elderly soldiers to ensure their cooperation in supporting the chattel system. Finally, Hislop and others believed that enslaved soldiers would have to be subjected to a different set of rules than their plantation slave counterparts. If they were treated the same as plantation slaves the great experiment would never work and soldiers would be disobedient. Accordingly, officers wanted their soldiers to be subject to the Mutiny Acts like White soldiers and not to the Caribbean slave codes. Doing so would help reinforce their elevated prestige and status over plantation slaves, which would earn their loyalty while also protecting them from Caribbean planters who did not like the idea of thousands of enslaved Black soldiers living among them.[11]

The army developed a bureaucratic apparatus for purchasing, examining, and then training the enslaved recruits. Once they were purchased, enslaved people marched in front of officials who examined their bodies to make sure they were healthy and capable of bearing arms. They had just survived the Middle Passage and were now put through a gauntlet of tests and examinations to determine their fate. Recruits had to be at least sixteen years old and five feet three inches tall. They were not supposed to have family members. One can only imagine the fear and chaos that potential recruits experienced during this early process. They were young, separated from friends and family, and they had no idea what White inspectors were examining them for. If they were cleared for service, officers marched them to regiment training depots for further drill. According to Richard Wyvill, who served as a major in the First West India Regiment at the turn of the nineteenth century, on arrival into the unit as fresh recruits, African soldiers were given a white piece of paper to hang around their necks and were taught to understand different command words as they drilled. This type of seasoning was probably just as traumatic as it was for enslaved people sent to work on plantations in the West Indies. From 1795 to 1808 the British government purchased 13,400 enslaved Africans for a total of £925,000 in this way. This group of slave soldiers represented 7 percent of all British slave imports during the period. Civilian magistrates were legally required to hear recruits' attestations of enlistment in the Caribbean per the 1694 Mutiny Act, but there is no record of enslaved soldiers testifying to do this in most places in the British Caribbean. Officers generally avoided the practice to ensure that magistrates would not block recruitment. Slave soldiers generally had to serve for life.[12]

The Problems of Language and Legal Status among Slave Soldiers

While it was clear that African slaves were purchased in the transatlantic slave trade for service in the West India Regiments, as Buckley has shown, the actual slave-free status of these soldiers was ambiguous and contested in the British Caribbean for many years. In part, their ambiguous status contributed to the mutiny in April 1802 when slave soldiers believed their privileged status was being reduced. Before the mutiny commanders and military officials were deeply concerned what the men in the regiments would think about their status and how they related to other enslaved people in the Caribbean. If the men did not think they were any better than plantation field slaves, then the regiments could be dangerous because slave soldiers would disobey White commands. Instead, officers wanted the men to think that they were "superior" to plantation slaves to ensure their loyalty and excellence in service. Thus, slave soldiers were treated in the same hospitals as White soldiers, they were paid the same wages as White soldiers, and they wore the same uniforms. They enjoyed many of the same allowances and privileges as well. These privileges were intended to ensure obedience and loyalty. But how slave soldiers could be punished differed somewhat from White soldiers. White British soldiers had long been subject to two different legal codes, both military and civilian, since they were both soldiers and citizens. In most cases commanders in the British army used the Mutiny Acts, a series of renewed acts passed by Parliament to regulate and fund the army, to discipline White soldiers. If any free White soldier disobeyed or refused orders, he could be punished under the acts, but once enslaved Africans enrolled in the army, officers were confused on how to handle any potential disciplinary actions. Black soldiers including enslaved Africans purchased in the transatlantic slave trade were not citizens. What to do with them, then? Should they be subject to military jurisdiction that regulated so many other British soldiers in the Caribbean? Or should they be treated in the slave courts just like thousands of other enslaved people in the British Atlantic? Moreover, what should they do with slave recruits once they retired or were released from military service and integrated with the rest of the enslaved community?[13]

Colonial authorities in the British Caribbean had always treated enslaved people in slave courts for their crimes or witness testimony, and many believed that WIR soldiers should be no different. In 1799 the attorney general of Saint Vincent declared that slave soldiers in the regiments were subject to colonial police regulations, which ensured that they would go to the petty sessions courts much like their plantation slave counterparts. While army officers sought to protect recruits from the slave courts, there was only so much they could do. They could try enslaved recruits in military courts while in service, but those who became too old or infirm and who absorbed into the rest of the enslaved community were somewhat beyond the reach of army officials.[14]

This issue of whether or not service in the West India Regiments made enslaved people free or free from colonial-slave jurisdiction was settled over a series of legal opinions that the law officers of the Crown rendered in the years shortly before the 1802 mutiny. In three opinions that were essentially reiterations of each other, the justices ruled that military service in the West India Regiments did not free Black soldiers from slave laws and slave court jurisdictions. Secondly, they ruled that enslaved soldiers could be manumitted only by the jurisdiction of colonial slave laws on each island where each slave soldier served. Cementing the opinion, the justices ruled in 1801 that West India Regiment soldiers did not become subject to the Mutiny Act like other soldiers because of their military service, and that "they remain to all intents and purposes slaves, and that their condition as slaves is in no respect altered in consequence of their being engaged in military service." These decisions were not amended until the 1807 Mutiny Act that made the enslaved soldiers free. Thus, on the eve of the Eighth WIR mutiny in 1802, soldiers in the regiment were clearly still legally slaves. Even if they were paid, clothed, and fed like White soldiers, if they ever so much as raised the ire of a planter, they could face the humility and terror of colonial slave courts anywhere they were stationed.[15]

Language barriers were also a substantial obstacle to how slave soldiers in the regiments understood themselves and their soldierly status leading up to the mutiny in 1802. Despite being conscripted into service and learning how to soldier per English customs, it was clear that many of the African slaves serving in the West India Regiments did not speak English or understand most of the orders that their officers gave. An army surgeon in the First WIR illustrated this problem clearly when he garnered the affection of new African recruits because of his demeanor and, more importantly, his ability to speak multiple West African languages. During inspections of the Sixth WIR in 1806, one officer observed that "Half these Men cannot speake an intelligible Language, and as their Ideas of time are different from ours, it is extremely difficult at present to make them comprehend what they have a right to in money matters." Another commented four years later in Guadeloupe that men in the Fourth WIR had "so slight a knowledge of the language of their officers" since so many were African-born and caught up in the transatlantic slave trade. Given the legal complications and the substantial language hurdle in the West India Regiments, enslaved African soldiers in the regiments, especially those who just survived the Middle Passage, probably did not fully understand their liminal status in the British army. If "New Negroes" understood they held a somewhat privileged status over plantation slaves, they probably did not initially know how long it would last. They at least knew the alternatives of field labor that they witnessed outside their garrisons every day. They were probably not aware of the apprehension among the highest officers in the army in how to legally discipline slave soldiers, but they likely understood colonial opposition to them as armed soldiers in slave societies. It was this understanding and this strange status that contributed to their mutiny in Dominica on April 9, 1802.[16]

Mutiny!

Enslaved soldiers in the Eighth WIR broke out in a rebellion of "the most serious and melancholy nature" on April 9, 1802, at Prince Rupert's Bluff in Dominica. The rebellion purportedly started around nine o'clock at night when mutineers approached the officers' barracks and shot through the window shutters. The gunfire was at first astonishing, and a second volley confirmed that the first was no accident. Something else was happening: a mutiny. The rebel soldiers immediately surrounded and killed several White commissioned and noncommissioned officers that they approached. As some officers lay dead or wounded, others scrambled in terror to save their lives but were cut off from escape by sentries posted at entrance and exit points. The rebels had thought their plan out well in advance, they understood the avenues and escape routes to Fort Shirley, and they knew how their commanding officers would react. As they shot at and chased the officers from the barracks, they bayoneted and mutilated those like Lieutenants Mackay and Westerneys whom they caught. The initial confrontation was chaotic and terrifying, but success appeared palpable. Only a faction of soldiers in the regiment remained loyal, but they tried to save the officers whom they liked. Men in Captain Allan Cameron's company were especially angered by the mutiny. They had tried to protect him from being taken captive, and when he was shot to death they reportedly executed the mutineer who killed him. But they were the minority, and the mutiny spread like wildfire. By the time commander Major John Gordon could bring some order to the situation, there were only approximately 120 men who remained loyal to him. Together they launched an immediate counterattack against the rebels at Fort Shirley, but the rebels were ready and fought back fiercely. The mutineers ambushed the loyal force and wounded several men, forcing them to retreat.[17]

As they took several officers captive, including Captains Barr and Cassin, the rebels told them they were angry about not being paid to drain a ninety-acre swamp next to the fort and they feared they were being turned into plantation slaves. Sergeant Dodds had reportedly spread the rumor among other mutineers that they were to be used on sugar estates and that "bill hooks were put into their hands for that purpose." Another unnamed mutineer, a grenadier, told Lieutenant Alexander Cameron that the men understood they were to be sold to work on Governor Johnstone's estate adjacent to the fort. As the fighting continued, the rest of the White soldiers inside the garrison fled to the hills to get help.[18]

By ten o'clock in the morning, Governor Johnstone learned of the mutiny. He immediately imposed martial law, and he summoned White soldiers in the Sixty-Eighth Regiment garrisoned at Morne Bruce and the St. George's Militia to march out and attack the rebels. The mutineers terrified the planters that they were trying to spread the rebellion to plantation slaves on the island and that together they would kill all the White people. Meanwhile in Prince Rupert's Bay, Commodore Stopford and Captain Giffard laid in wait aboard the *Excellent* and *Magnificent* as fighting on the island unfolded. Their presence was assuredly worrisome for the mutineers who did not have the ability to effectively engage the vessels at sea. From Fort Shirley nestled in the Cabrits, rebel soldiers fired at the men of war but did little damage. The fighting then came to a standstill temporarily. Later that evening Governor Johnstone departed from Prince Rupert's aboard a French ship and sailed to Point Round where he met with Commodore Stopford and the St. George's Militia. Together they devised a strategy to take down the mutinous slave soldiers.[19]

The following morning Johnstone informed Commander of the West Indies, General Sir Thomas Trigge, of the serious events. The mutineers were threatening to destroy slavery in the colony, and Johnstone supplicated Trigge to send reinforcements: "for God's sake send us every assistance you can, and all the Men of War possible to Prince Ruperts." Johnstone's tone underscored the terror and panic that the mutineers aroused and how deadly the rebellion was. If they could succeed, they would undermine the slave system in the colony. Indeed, they probably knew they were close, and Johnstone wrote that the rebels had "threatened the existence of this colony if longer allowed to continue." The mutineers were pushing White authorities to take extreme measures to suppress the rebellion. Later that morning Johnstone's forces sent an officer to Fort Shirley under truce to garner the rebels' surrender, but the mutineers refused such overtures and took the man captive. Subsequently, the rebels watched the militia maneuver through the swamp below the fort and began to engage the militiamen. While still defiant, the rebels must have known their situation was getting bleaker. They were now outnumbered and outsupplied, and Johnstone had placed the militia near the swamp to prevent the rebels from escaping. Still, they fought on and fired musket shot and artillery rounds into the swamp to dislodge the militiamen. Their volleys had little effect.[20]

As this fighting continued, the *Magnificent* returned to Johnstone with reinforcements. Major Paxley arrived with approximately 200 White men, who combined with the more than 350 soldiers in the Sixty-Eighth Regiment under Majors Scott and Hamilton, Johnstone's 150 marines, and 400 militiamen from St. George. In total, the four to five hundred mutineers faced more than a thousand White soldiers ready to attack. These staggering odds prompted the enslaved rebels to send a flag of truce with their captive, Lieutenant Alexander Cameron, to Johnstone in hopes they could prevent utter defeat. The rebels wanted Johnstone to enter the fort alone and unarmed, which was a proposal that Johnstone refused. In turn, he ordered them to come to the parade grounds for a meeting to "deliver up the perpetrators of the horrid murders," and he would "listen to them with attention and redress them." The rebels probably resented Johnstone's orders, but they accepted them in order to garner peace in a rebellion that increasingly grew bleaker. With a meeting set for later that evening, Johnstone started marching to Fort Shirley by two o'clock in the afternoon, and the rebels allowed him to enter the garrison at four o'clock. He ordered the rebels to meet him at the parade grounds and lay down their arms.[21]

At that moment the tension reached a peak. The rebels had agreed to meet Johnstone, and they allowed him to enter within their defense lines. While there was not total silence, the temporary truce certainly contrasted with the bursts of gunfire and artillery rounds that had characterized much of the mutiny thus far. Most of the rebel soldiers complied with Johnstone's orders and presented their arms to him. Still, they did not trust him as he approached to address them and convince the remaining holdouts to lay down their weapons. He then ordered the rebels to walk three feet toward him and away from their weapons so that he could speak to them without fear of being shot. His command was too much to tolerate. It was met by an unknown soldier's dread, reportedly a sergeant, who broke the tension with a loud yell. The man encouraged the rebels not to relinquish their arms and warned that Johnstone would "cheat them."[22]

The yell shattered the fragile truce, and White soldiers accompanying Johnstone fired at the rebels. Soldiers from the Sixty-Eighth and St. George's Militia followed suit. After just three volleys, chaos reigned, and the rebels scrambled to try to stay alive. From that point on, they certainly knew that the mutiny was a lost cause. At best now all they could do was shoot and run for their lives. Perhaps they could make it to the swamp and hide out for a few days to later disappear among plantation slaves. Maybe they could run as far as to the mountains and forests to the southeast and find asylum with Maroons. Some probably thought that they would at least fight to their deaths. Johnstone and his detachment chased the rebels into the Inner Cabrits, while Majors Scott and Hamilton pursued others to the Outer Cabrits. The rebels were probably afraid as they saw the White men approach with bayonets. The rebels fired back but also retreated in a panic. They had let the enemy come too close, and they knew there was little they could do to mount a successful defense. They returned fire, but some scrambled up to the Outer Cabrits, and perhaps as many as two or three hundred jumped down to the sea. A few died from this fall, but dozens more died in the gunfire on the parade grounds. Several men in Johnson's force were killed, including two or three officers, while at least a dozen were also wounded. Unfortunately for the mutineers, the battle was lopsided.[23]

Others continued to fire from their positions in Fort Shirley. They still commanded the artillery battery there and fired grapeshot on their enemies. Unfortunately for their cause, their actions did little damage to the oppos-

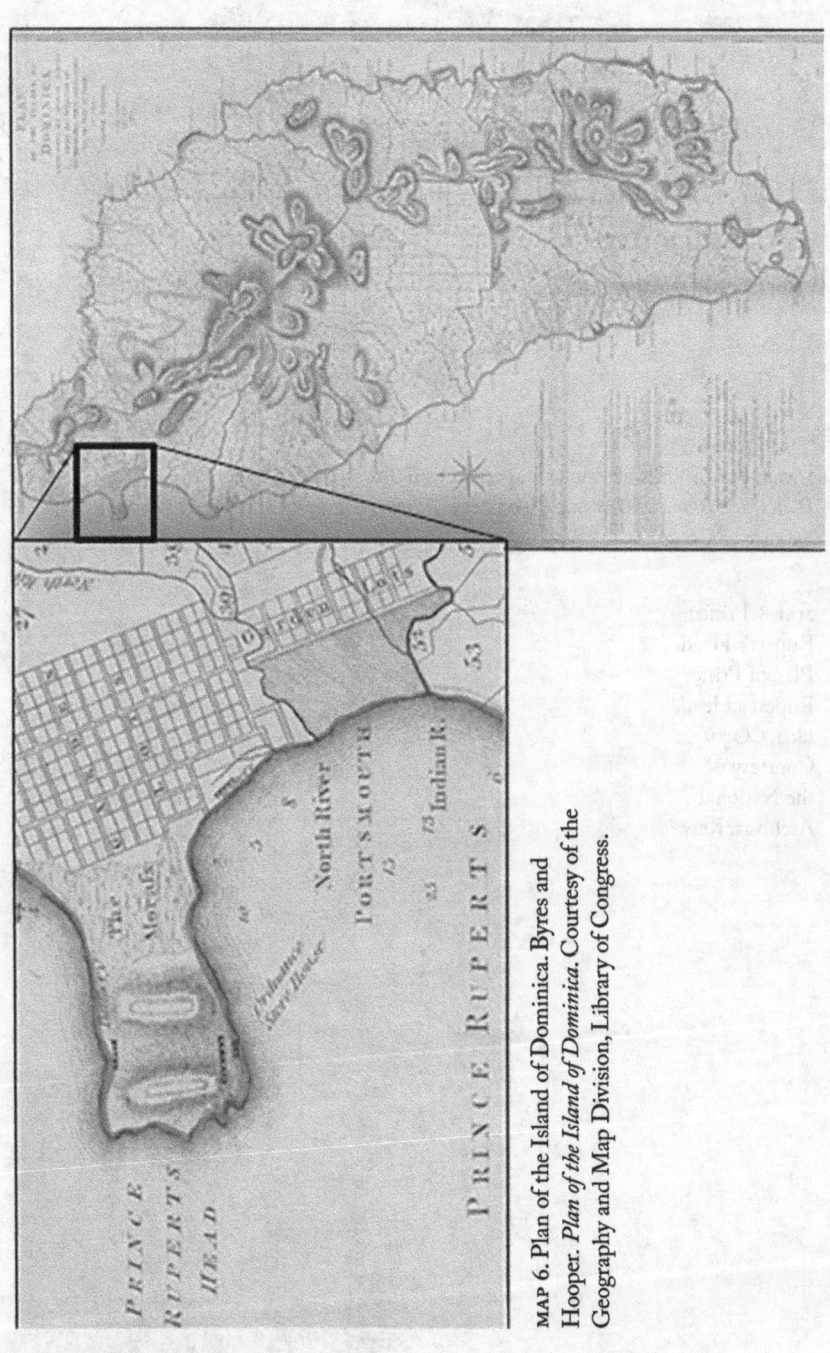

MAP 6. Plan of the Island of Dominica. Byres and Hooper. *Plan of the Island of Dominica*. Courtesy of the Geography and Map Division, Library of Congress.

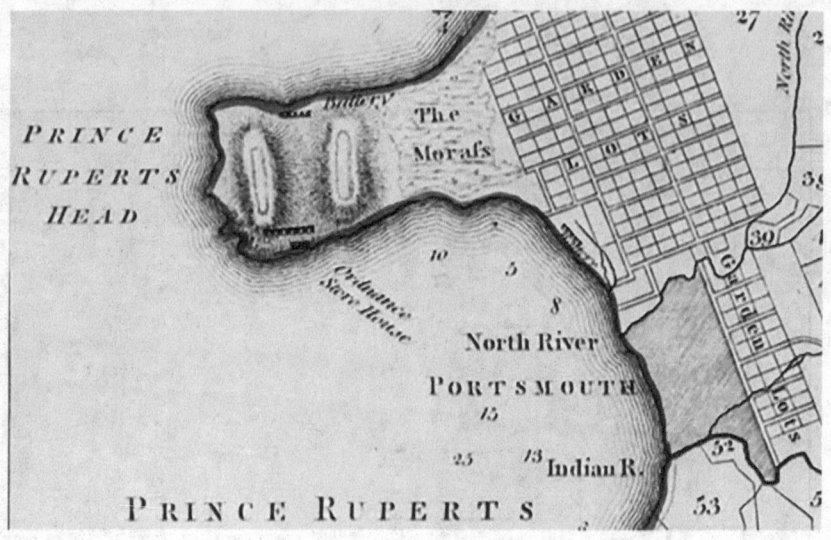

MAP 7. Fort Shirley at Prince Rupert's Head. Byres and Hooper. *Plan of the Island of Dominica*. Courtesy of the Geography and Map Division, Library of Congress.

MAP 8. Prince Rupert's Head. Plan of Prince Rupert's Head, 1802, CO 71/34. Courtesy of the National Archives, Kew.

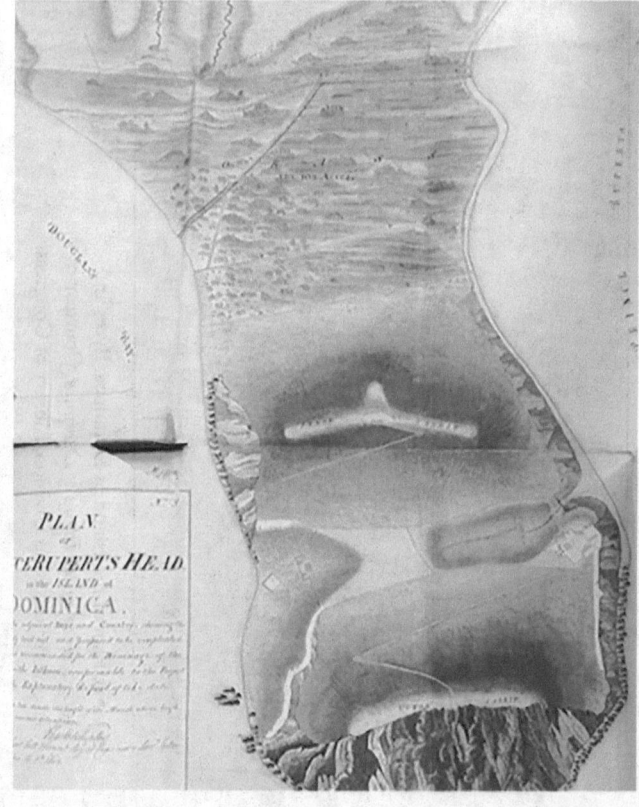

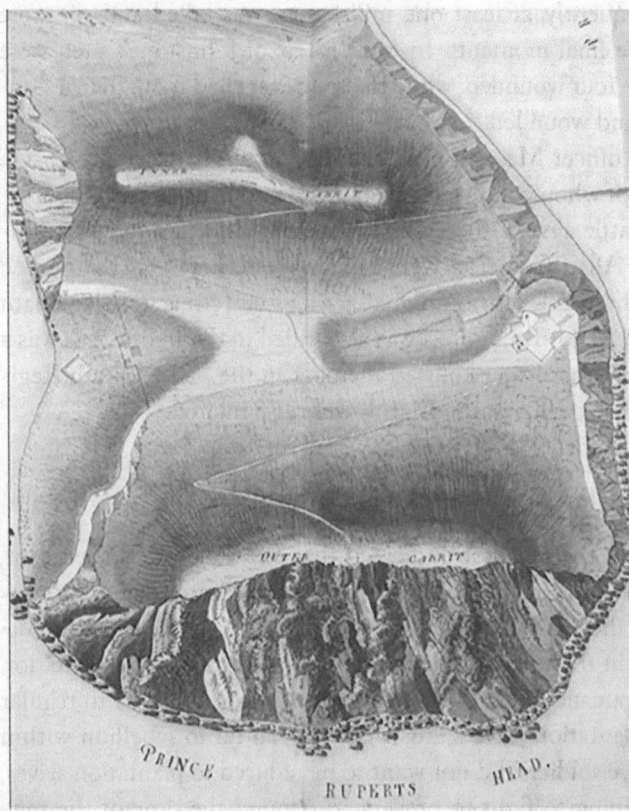

MAP 9. Cabrits at Prince Rupert's Head. Plan of Prince Rupert's Head, 1802, CO 71/34. Courtesy of the National Archives, Kew.

ing forces, and several were killed in the fighting. The rest retreated from the fort and fled across the adjoining swamp in hopes to escape capture. They were shot as they fled. Sergeant Curry, who was one of the "most violent mutineers," died as he ran. Still others not killed by the militia were taken prisoner. A few were able to abscond undetected into the countryside without their guns, including one private Hypolite, who disappeared into the foothills near Morne Diablotins and joined the Maroons living there.[24]

As the militia retook Fort Shirley, they uncovered one last act of defiance among the rebels. They had laid down a train of explosives to blow up the assaulting force. This ambush could have been suicidal if it had ever been carried out. The rebels were probably ready to accept that, but for whatever reason it did not happen. As the battle ended, Johnstone reinstalled his headquarters and established a plan to care for the wounded. According to him, the fighting was over in about a half hour. As the last mutineers scrambled past the militia in the adjacent swamp, they fought desperately to escape. Consequently, at least one militiaman was killed and six more wounded in those final moments. In total, a few of Johnstone's men were killed and twenty-four wounded, while the mutineers had more than a hundred men killed and wounded.²⁵

Commanding officer Major John Gordon, Captain Cassin, and Ensign Greenshields, all of whom who were taken prisoner during the rebellion, escaped the final battle alive. Others like Lieutenants Mackay and Westerneys and Captain Allan Cameron were killed. Westerneys was bayonetted to death, while the rebels also mutilated acting quartermaster Lieutenant Mackay. Sergeant Major Broughton was also killed in the fighting, as was a bombardier and another lower enlisted member in the Sixty-Eighth Regiment. Two White sergeants in the Eighth were also injured.²⁶

Aftermath: Causes and Consequences

Initial reports after the rebellion indicated that one ringleader, a sergeant, had been the cause of the mutiny. The unknown conspirator had reportedly ordered others in the regiment to fall in for duty before eight o'clock and inculcated the idea in the rest that they were going to be sold into plantation slavery to dig sugarcane holes. It was this fear of being returned to regular field work and plantation slave status that was central to rebellion within the regiment. Slave soldiers did not want to be reduced to plantation slaves, and they were willing to fight to prevent it. Around the time of the mutiny, General Trigge knew that employing the soldiers in such manual labor was dangerous, and he did not give Governor Johnstone his permission to do so. Trigge was also convinced that continued work draining the swamp, and without pay, had "immediately and understandably" produced the mutiny. Just a week before the rebellion broke out, Trigge predicted that a mutiny would occur if slave soldiers were used to drain the swamp and not paid like White soldiers performing the same task. He thought it would be "not only impolitic but hazardous" and that the distinction made by not paying the soldiers "would be invidious and could not fail to occasion great discontent if not desertion and very possibly mutiny." Trigge also reported that he stopped Johnstone from a similar scheme with the Ninth WIR in Dominica two years earlier, which he thought would have probably encouraged another rebellion.²⁷

The court-martial testimonies after the mutiny confirmed the idea that slave soldiers in the regiment were deeply concerned about the unit being disbanded, that they were to be reduced to plantation slaves, and about their continued work draining swamps for sugarcane cultivation without pay and rations. Initial fears about disbandment of the Eighth WIR surfaced when peace with France was reached with the Treaty of Amiens the year before. Now that war with France was over, slave soldiers in the regiment believed that the British officers no longer needed so many of them in their current capacity. While officials were still debating how to use these soldiers during peacetime, the Eighth WIR was indeed among the six corps slotted for disbandment that year, and it was unclear if commanding officers were ever able to assuage soldiers' fears of what would happen to them should the reduction occur. This fear was strongest among the African soldiers who had been born in freedom, and those who were recently purchased in the transatlantic slave trade for service in the unit. When White soldiers from the Sixty-Eighth Regiment visited the African soldiers in the swamp at Prince Rupert's the night before the mutiny, slave soldiers believed that the White soldiers were there to apprehend them and divide them up to work on sugar estates.[28]

If their fear of being reduced to harsher life of plantation slavery was not enough, a faction of the recently purchased African mutineers had also endured more austere conditions in the months leading up to the mutiny. Life at Fort Shirley was miserable for men in the Eighth WIR. The swamps near the Cabrits were the largest on the whole island, and the wetlands substantially inhibited colonial development in the nearby town of Portsmouth because of the difficult environmental conditions. People complained that there were too many mosquitos, and both civilians and soldiers in the area suffered from malaria and yellow fever. Underscoring how unhealthy Prince Rupert's was for soldiers in the Eighth WIR, commanders like Lieutenant General Henry Bowyer advocated draining the swamps nearby not only to ease evacuations if necessary but also because they produced stagnant water and a state of "putrefaction." Indeed, Governor Johnstone reported that Prince Rupert's Bay was the "most unhealthy part of the island." But draining the ninety-acre swamp was also grueling work for the soldiers, who did not like fatigue duties that were often done by field slaves. Thick brush and vegetation had to be cut. Trees had to be felled, dams built, and soldiers had to dig several trenches and ditches that could be as wide as twenty feet in order to properly drain the swamp. All this was to happen in a deadly environment at Prince Rupert's in which several soldiers had already died in the last two years before the mutiny.[29]

These conditions compounded the already hard life of a soldier in the British army during the period. Mortality rates were high for soldiers in the

British Caribbean, and service was tough. Service commitments generally were for life, while pay was also low and rations often insufficient. Regular soldiers needed permission to marry, and they were otherwise expected to be celibate. Officers also utilized severe corporal punishment to ensure discipline and obedience, to include sometimes fatal flogging.[30]

If their hard work was not enough, withholding pay was also an issue for the soldiers before the mutiny. According to Sergeant Pinkett in Captain Barr's company, the mutineers were also upset about irregular pay and that they had not received their pay for some time despite their grueling work in the swamp. Sergeant Ramsey reported that some men had not been paid for nearly five months. Similarly, Corporal Shova testified that once the men had cut brushwood in the swamp, they complained that they had not been paid for their hard duties. An enslaved soldier named Quash who served in Captain Arbuthnot's company and who did not mutiny also testified that he asked mutineers during the rebellion why they resisted. They told him that it was for money. Corporal Davey from Captain Cameron's company reported much of the same. The men "had complained of want of their subsistence," after working in the swamp for some time and not receiving recourse for their labor. They had "adopted an idea that they were to become field negroes." What further exacerbated their concern was that Governor Johnstone had purchased the swamp privately and with the intention to change it into a profitable sugar plantation. Many of the enslaved rebels were apparently concerned that they were to be used to build houses on the budding plantation and then plant sugarcane for Johnstone, a massive deviation from their soldierly backgrounds.[31]

Sergeant Gold in Captain Hammond's company testified that soldiers in the regiment had been working in the swamp for nearly three weeks before the mutiny. They worked from dinner to sunset daily, cutting down thick brushwood in the swamp that was also infested with mosquitos. According to Gold, the swamp, and the grueling work associated with it, "imbibed" the idea in the slave soldiers that they would join plantation slaves working next to the swamp very soon. Creole sergeant Romeo verified Gold's testimony that enslaved soldiers had worked in the swamp for nearly three weeks before the mutiny and that their pay and rations were irregular, which further reinforced the idea among them that they were soon to be sold into plantation slavery. One soldier named Stuart also testified that daily work in the swamp for at least two weeks had been a growing grievance among the soldiers in the regiment. They had complained that they had been "worked too much," which also reinforced the point that soldiers' material conditions immediately before the rebellion were deteriorating.³²

Lieutenant Allen Cameron also testified that the soldiers were apprehensive of Governor Johnstone's estate plans and that they "did too much work." Captain Barr echoed this sentiment and said that after he was captured by the rebels, Sergeant Church told him that the cause of the mutiny was "too much work." Captain Cassin also testified that the mutiny broke out because the soldiers had not been paid, and that cutting brushwood in the swamp adjacent to the fort compounded their understanding that Governor Johnstone had plans to create a new plantation. This reinforced the idea that their service would be a "prelude" to plantation slavery. They had reportedly observed that "bill hooks were put in their hands, hoes would soon after: that they had carried firelocks for some time, and would not now use hoes." These officers also confirmed that the enslaved soldiers had not received their pay, and that some were unaware if Johnstone or Major Gordon had any intentions of paying them at all. Major Gordon himself testified that he had "never" heard that the soldiers used to clear the swamp were paid and that no one kept a list to record the men's work. Instead, Gordon testified, Governor Johnstone ordered quartermaster Lieutenant Mackay to give the soldiers an extra ration of rum the week before the mutiny erupted. Paymaster Seward confirmed the mutineers' accounts that they were upset about their pay, which he noted they had not received in January, February, and most of March before the rebellion.³³

Dozens of other soldiers in the regiment testified and affirmed these ideas. Enslaved soldiers complained about working in the swamp, which was exhausting and dangerous. It was also humiliating working next to adjacent plantations and in view of plantation slaves performing the same work. They complained about not getting enough rations to do this work and not being paid for it either. They were also suspicious that they were working for Governor Johnstone's private side project. Why were they being used to clear land for sugar when the governor could just as easily buy plantation slaves or hire out others to do the dirty work? Who was going to work on the plantation right next to their garrison? Why weren't they being paid for their work? All these factors converged to create the idea that they might soon become regular plantation slaves and that they were to be sold into plantation slavery very soon.³⁴

The testimonies reveal how slave soldiers in the regiment perceived themselves. It was clear that they knew they were not free, but they also believed they were better than how other enslaved people were treated. They rejected any attempt to treat them as if they were regular plantation slaves, and the notion that they could be converted to do field work permanently terrified and angered them. Their belief that their status was under attack fueled an armed uprising.

At least seven of the mutineers, including Congo Jack, Cuffy, Manby, Liveley, James, Genius, and Pedro, were convicted and executed for their role in the mutiny. At least three hundred more waited for transport to Barbados, where General Trigge ordered another court-martial since so many more soldiers were implicated in the rebellion. Eleven were executed for their role, and seven were whipped for their participation. Five more were acquitted of the charges. Governor Johnstone was recalled back to England after the mutiny, while the Eighth WIR was disbanded. A total of 148 enslaved soldiers were transferred to the First, Third, and Fourth WIRs to continue serving as soldiers, while 206 more were reclassified as pioneers, split into smaller groups, and sent to work for Whites as laborers. They had lost their prestige as armed combatants.[35]

Major Gordon was also court-martialed in the aftermath of the rebellion as investigators learned more about the cause of the mutiny. For the most part the charges against Gordon related to one of the main grievances that the rebel soldiers expressed after the mutiny: not receiving pay. Gordon was charged with embezzling money designated for baking bread for the regiment and falsifying pay lists. Whereas he swore just days before the mutiny that the men had been paid up to Christmas Eve 1801, at least two companies had only been paid to October 24 and another two up until November 24. The total amounts Gordon was accused of falsifying amounted to more than £1,000. These charges were directly related to the deprived condition of enslaved soldiers in the regiment, which facilitated their rebellion. The remaining two charges were related to Gordon's conduct after the mutiny. He was accused of embezzling compensation funds for the officers killed in the mutiny, as well as fleeing to Barbados to escape punishment. Though he was acquitted of all charges, the court found Gordon negligent in his duty and ordered him to make full and accurate reports of the regiment's accounts.[36]

But there were other indications that Gordon and Johnstone were negligent officers in charge of the Eighth WIR in ways that further contributed to the mutiny. From January to July 1801 a detachment of about eighty men quartered at Governor Johnstone's residence were put to work performing manual labor and other works on his lands for his personal benefit, and he did not pay them for their work. These conditions set the precedent for Johnstone's order to have others cut wood and clear the swamp near Prince Rupert's months later, which was a tract of land he hoped to convert for his own profit. These reports showed that enslaved soldiers in the regiment had withstood more than just a few weeks of clearing a swamp but more than a year of manual labor in which they thought their work was only benefiting Governor Johnstone. Surely they thought by April 1802 that a renewed order to clear the swamp meant that their lives as soldiers were over. Despite these misgivings, Johnstone still wanted to use WIR soldiers to drain the swamp even after the mutiny. Trigge also admonished Johnstone that he did not have Trigge's permission to employ soldiers as he did and that he did not authorize continued work in the swamp after the mutiny with the Eighth WIR.[37]

General Trigge also issued a new general order at the end of April to allay men serving the West India Regiments who had similar fears like the men in the Eighth WIR. He informed his enslaved subordinates that the idea of them being "sold as slaves" was "entirely without foundation." Moreover, and to ensure that the rest of the slave soldiers in the other West India Regiments understood, he ordered commanding officers to read his order to the men at least three times so that they understood it clearly and fully. He wanted to make sure that no other soldiers would start another rebellion over this fear. It is not clear if enslaved soldiers received this order or if they understood it any better than before. Trigge also ordered the surviving rebels to be sequestered from the rest of the West India Regiments. He did not want them "contaminating the rest" or to make them feel like "victims as themselves." Trigge thought that the idea of Black rebellion might spread among the thousands of enslaved soldiers in the West Indies, so he wanted to ensure that the conspirators from Dominica did not get a chance to advance their cause to others in the British Caribbean. He also wanted the regiment to move to Barbados where there were far more White soldiers on the island than in Dominica. In case enslaved soldiers felt the need to rise up again, they would face even more soldiers against them and a White-Black population proportion unfavorable to slave rebellion. He also did not think that the rebels could ever again be trusted to handle firearms, which was a concern echoed by others. Nevertheless, although Trigge had lost faith in the Eighth WIR rebels, he did not lose confidence in the remaining regiments or in their ability to help defend the British Caribbean from foreign adversaries and slave revolts. Despite the rebellion, his view in their value was relatively unaltered. How slave soldiers in the regiment viewed these orders or moves remains unclear. They probably resented the move to Barbados and their sequestration from other regiments. The fact that they were taken from Fort

Shirley and isolated from other regiments probably only exacerbated their fear of being reduced to plantation slavery.[38]

Like Other Militarized Slave Revolts

The mutiny reports and court-martial testimony show that several men in the regiment mutinied because they were enduring harsher material conditions and that they expected those conditions to worsen in the immediate future. Like the Eighth WIR mutineers, rebels in other major slave insurrections in the British Caribbean near the time of the mutiny endured material deprivation. Rebels in Bussa's Rebellion in Barbados in 1816 were subjected to falling sugar prices and a general economic downturn tied to the end of the Napoleonic Wars in Europe. Meanwhile, when slaves rose up during Fédon's Rebellion in Grenada in 1795–1796, French privateering efforts led by Victor Hugues captured trading vessels attempting to reach the island. Supply lines were thereby cut off, which contributed to a provision scarcity among the slave population on the island. Moreover, there had been a drought in the early months in 1795 shortly before the rebellion broke out, which further strained the island's food and water supply. Enslaved people on the island were also experiencing a subsistence crisis brought on by the French Revolutionary Wars. Conflict rearranged trade patterns and led to sharp increases in the prices of food. In turn, enslaved people suffered malnutrition and starvation and increased mortality rates while planters were forced to reallocate land to produce more food and supplies. These shortages contributed to the insurrection, while rebels also laid waste to plantation crops, livestock, and homes. Aside from utterly wrecking the Grenadian economy, the destruction assuredly made conditions worse for enslaved people who had not already joined the months-long rebellion and primed more to rise up as it progressed.[39]

Similar conditions were also extant at the onset of two other mutinies of enslaved soldiers in the Anglo-Atlantic near the time of the Eighth WIR mutiny. In September 1805 Black chasseurs in Suriname rose up against British authority at a small outpost called Oranjebo along the rain forest frontier. The mutineers killed all the White soldiers in the area and marched to other nearby garrisons with the aim to kill all the White people inside them. By the time they were finished, plantation slaves and Maroons had joined them. As was the case with the Eighth WIR mutineers, the chasseur rebels were angered about irregular pay. They were also concerned about the recent British conquest of the colony, and some had believed they would be reduced to plantation slave status with the colonial changeover. Just three years later, recently emancipated slave soldiers in the Second WIR in Jamaica also mutinied after facing similar material circumstances. Like the mutineers of the Eighth WIR, the rebels in the Second WIR were stationed near a swamp at Fort Augusta in Jamaica. The swamp was also infested with mosquitos, and soldiers had also complained about illnesses the insects spread.[40]

In many ways Black experiences during the 1802 mutiny were also like how enslaved rebels fought in other militarized insurrections and mutinies during the period. For example, how enslaved rebels in Bussa's Rebellion in Barbados fought in 1816 paralleled how the soldiers in the Eighth WIR mutinied in many ways. Driven by a putative rumor of emancipation tied to the 1815 Registry Bill, rebels rose up on the island on the night of Sunday, April 14 in St. Philip Parish. As the rebels moved through the area to the neighboring parish of Christ Church, they were armed with firearms, pikes, hatchets, and other blunt force weapons. They destroyed sugarcane fields, houses, provision grounds, and workhouses on each plantation estate. They burned household furniture, crops, and rum. They too fought in open field engagements with the White militia, and the Black soldiers in the First WIR mustered to suppress the rebellion. These engagements paralleled the counterattacks on Fort Shirley in Dominica in 1802 led by White soldiers in the Sixty-Eighth Regiment and St. George's Militia participated, as well as those Black soldiers in the Eighth WIR who did not mutiny. Bussa's rebels were also well organized and coordinated, and they took control of half the island as separate factions challenged Whites in different parishes. At least a thousand rebels were killed in battle, while another 144 were executed in trials after the rebellion was suppressed. Like the WIR mutineers in Dominica who ambushed militia forces approaching Fort Shirley, Bussa's rebels utilized ambush tactics in sugarcane fields to attack the First WIR.[41]

The mutiny of the Eighth WIR mirrored developments in Grenada in 1795 and 1796 when thousands of enslaved people and free Blacks rose up against British control. The revolt began on the night of March 2, 1795, when free Blacks and slaves conspired at Julien Fédon's plantation, Belvidere. From there the rebels moved to Grenville and Gouyave and took control of the two towns. The rebels were armed with muskets, bayonets, and swords, and they took prisoner several White planters and authorities. As they plundered, the rebels also stocked up on ammunition, livestock, and provisions in order to advance their movement. When they approached the town of St. Georges, they reportedly wore helmets inscribed with "la mort ou la liberté" (death or liberty) on them. To achieve liberty, they fought fiercely in pitched battles against White soldiers and laid waste to the island, burning sugarcane fields, buildings, factories, and homes, thereby turning the island into fire and ash.[42]

But as the revolt matured, the rebels were beaten back and forced to flee to the woods and hilly terrain for refuge, similar to the mutineers who fled to the forests and hills of the Cabrits in Dominica. Though they had requested substantial arms and assistance from Governor Victor Hugues at Guadeloupe, French support was insufficient and the British navy was able to blockade the island. By July 1796 most of the insurgents were dead or captured. The uprising only came to an end when the last holdouts, including Fédon himself, jumped down the sides of Mount Quaco where they had hidden and refused to be taken prisoner.[43]

Both Bussa's and Fédon's rebellions also underscored a rise in militarized slave rebellions during the age of revolution also tied to the Eighth WIR mutiny. Although more peaceful rebellions occurred in which slave rebels promoted ideas of liberty and citizenship and rebels chose less violent means to further their agendas during the period, ideas of republicanism and liberty also promoted violence. It also created more opportunities for slaves to become soldiers and use military service and military tactics to effect their goals.

Bussa's and Fédon's rebellions also underscored how, like soldiers in the Eighth WIR, not every slave joined rebel causes during Atlantic slave insurrections. Not every enslaved person in Barbados joined Bussa's movement, while WIR soldiers fought to suppress the insurrection. Of the nearly twenty-five thousand slaves in Grenada at the time of Fédon's Rebellion, approximately eight thousand rose up with Fédon. But hundreds also helped defend British plantation owners. In the first week of the rebellion, Lieutenant Colonel McDonald and James Campbell had mustered "trusty" slaves to help defend the colony. Eventually five companies of sixty men each armed to defend the British on the island. At least two hundred Black Rangers fought for British authorities during the massive rebellion, and they were there for the final moments when Fédon finally surrendered at Mount Quaco (Saint Catherine). When the rebellion was over, more than seven thousand slaves and a thousand Whites were dead. More than three dozen ringleaders of the rebellion were executed, and hundreds more were banished to Honduras. While much larger in scale than the Eighth WIR mutiny, Fédon's Rebellion still engulfed an entire island like the 1802 mutiny, while enslaved people rose up and fought for freedom in a similar fashion. In both cases, loyal slave soldiers also pushed back. They understood that they had better chances at freedom by remaining loyal, or that they could gain more favor or privilege by remaining loyal. Others were probably unwilling to join what seemed like an unwinnable movement.[44]

The Eighth WIR mutiny also shared some general characteristics of a conspiracy and short-lived insurrection in Dominica that occurred approximately a decade earlier in 1791. Early that year African Maroons collaborated with free Blacks and Mulattos to attack the colonial administration and strike for freedom. While at first organized by plantation slaves and Maroon leaders like Pharcelle, the conspiracy evolved to include the participation of Creoles and eventually men like Jean Louis Polinaire who became the figurehead of the revolt and whom the revolt was named after. As early as December 1790, Maroons and plantation slaves learned of an alleged rumor to permit enslaved people to work three days a week on their own, which had not yet been allowed. Much like the soldiers in the Eighth WIR, Maroons and enslaved people in Dominica believed that they needed to take action to fight for a better life. Maroons in particular encouraged plantation slaves to fight for full emancipation instead, and rebels rose to the occasion. By then, it was estimated that as many as 250 conspirators had been involved, while at least dozens actually marched with firearms, swords, and other weapons toward Whites in the town of Rosalie. Their goal was to "kill all the white people." Just as slave soldiers rose up in 1802 on the island, Maroons and enslaved people in 1791 led a militarized revolt against White people in Dominica to fight for their freedom. They marched "in a warlike manner" with battle colors, and they fought open engagements with White soldiers garrisoned on the island. As the revolt began to unravel, the rebels fled into the woods for refuge, much like the mutineers in the Eighth WIR fled to the swamps and Cabrits after 1802. Just like the mutineers, they had wanted to kill the White people and take control of the island. They had wanted total emancipation. Unfortunately, and just like their successors in 1802, their rebellion did not succeed, and they were crushed within two weeks. Dozens were tried and executed in the ensuing months, including Polinaire, but many Maroon leaders survived the fracas to fight another day. They would still live in the woods of Dominica when soldiers in the Eighth mutinied in April 1802. How they may have influenced the mutineers' decision or assisted them during the rebellion is unclear.[45]

Aside from these conventional militarized slave insurrections that the Eighth WIR mutiny paralleled, the 1802 rebellion was also similar to several other mutinies of enslaved soldiers in the West India Regiments, some of which should also be analyzed as slave insurrections. Saltwater slave soldiers in the Fourth West India Regiment were implicated in a conspiracy to overthrow their officers in Saint Kitts in the summer of 1797. Details of the event are sparse, and unlike other mutinies, White authorities discovered the conspiracy at Saint Kitts and prevented the rebellion. It does not appear that there was an effort to kill all the Whites or return to Africa in the plot like other mutinies, and the regiment was transported from the island soon thereafter.[46]

The Eighth WIR mutiny also resembled the Black chasseurs in Suriname who revolted in early September 1805. The slave soldiers, who were first organized by the Dutch years before the British conquered Suriname, began their mutiny on September 6 at a small outpost in Oranjebo on the Upper Commewijne River when twenty enslaved rebels took control of the post. They killed all the White people inside the fort and moved on inside the frontier. As they maneuvered, the mutiny spread to other posts, and eighty more chasseurs joined the cause before fleeing into the forests with local Maroons. Several dozen plantation slaves also joined the soldiers in rebellion. At Imotapi north of Oranjebo, rebels shot a White sergeant and mutilated his corpse. The Black rangers then plundered the warehouses and moved on to the Marowijne River and attacked Post Armina, where they killed White colonists. At Armina the rebels were joined by even more enslaved soldiers inside, and together more than eighty rebels were involved. After Armina, the rebels moved to the forests and built their own village near an old Boni Maroon settlement called Ingi Pule Seton. In the course of their rebellion, the slave soldiers had become Maroons themselves, though some authorities suspected that Maroons had already infiltrated their ranks before the mutiny even began.[47]

After several months the rebels settled along the Lawa and Tapanhoni Rivers and closer to the Ndjuka Maroons living nearby. In a subsequent peace treaty with the British in 1809, the Ndjuka Maroons agreed to keep the Black soldiers turned Maroons under control. But the Ndjuka did not capture these new soldier Maroons, and in another decade they had grown in number to perhaps as many as eight hundred people. White officials who investigated the mutiny afterward concluded that the rebellion erupted due to the infiltration of Boni Maroons into the corps since the late eighteenth century. As noted above, the chasseurs were agitated about pay and what would happen to their status after the British conquest, and they understood they had a real chance to strike for freedom with so few White soldiers available to challenge them. Thus they joined with plantation slaves and Maroons to achieve that freedom.[48]

One of the most similar incidents to the Eighth WIR mutiny was the mutiny of the Second WIR at Fort Augusta, Jamaica, in 1808. As the rest of the regiment had gone to parade at sunrise on May 27, a detachment of twenty-eight recruits walked from the fort with fixed bayonets. They had together come from the same nation in Africa identified as "Rio Chambo," and they were the newest recruits purchased for service in the regiment. They approached their commander and the acting adjutant and fired at them. Their gunshots created "astonishment" among the rest of the soldiers, who responded to the gunfire to "avenge" the deaths of the men, much like the loyal soldiers did during the Eighth WIR mutiny. In the ensuing melee, fourteen mutineers were shot and killed and five more wounded while a few more ran away to the mangrove swamps for refuge. Twenty-four more were taken prisoner. Some would later confess that they had plotted the mutiny just three days after joining the regiment and that they believed if they could kill all the officers, they could "return to their own country."[49]

Like the Dominica mutineers, the Jamaican slave soldiers were angered about living conditions near a swamp at Fort Augusta. They also believed that if they were successful, they could return to their lives in Africa and avoid hardship in Jamaica. Unlike the previous mutinies and conspiracies, however, a significant difference with the Second WIR mutiny was that it occurred shortly after the 1807 Mutiny Act was passed. The act broke from previous precedent in which the law officers of the Crown ruled that soldiers in the West India Regiments were still slaves despite their service in the military. The 1807 act reversed course and declared all soldiers in the West India Regiments free so long as they continued to serve. Soldiers in the regiments were no longer slaves. Yet the fact that the newest recruits in the regiment were the culprits behind the Second WIR mutiny, and that they began plotting the uprising just days after their enlistment, provides some insight into how soldiers in the West India Regiments perceived their liminal status and how it related to mutinies in the ranks. By joining the Second WIR after the 1807 Mutiny Act, they had technically achieved their freedom from plantation chattel slavery so long as they stayed in active service. The fact that they still pushed for mutiny suggests that slave soldiers in the West India Regiments were not well informed about their status from high commanders and administrators in the metropole. It further suggests that slave soldiers in the West India Regiments during these early years considered mutiny as an act like conventional slave insurrection.[50]

It is likely that the lifelong and permanent nature of service in the West India Regiments encouraged slave soldiers to attempt mutiny or desertion more of than those who ran away to British lines and served in the British army in other conflicts during the period. Soldiers in the Carolina Corps or Ethiopian Regiment did not have a certain future like soldiers in the West India Regiments. They only knew that if they served they could escape their masters. But soldiers in the West India Regiments only knew that if they served they could escape the lowest rung on the ladder of plantation slavery, at least until they were too infirm to serve and retired.

Similar to the Second WIR mutiny that occurred after slave soldiers were emancipated, the mutiny of the Eighth WIR also paralleled a mutiny in 1836, when enslaved soldiers in the First WIR rose up in Trinidad. Like soldiers in the Eighth and Second WIR mutinies, those who decided to reject British military service were recently enslaved Africans, intercepted by British ships regulating the illegal transatlantic slave trade. In September of that year, approximately two hundred soldiers under their leader named Dâaga, supposedly a former prince who had helped enslave many of the men with whom he now sided, decided that they could return to their homes in Africa if they could attack all the White men in the regiment.[51]

The fact that the mutiny was generally confined to Africans who had just survived the Middle Passage and who did not speak English, and that they wanted to go back to Africa, paralleled other African slave mutinies in other regiments. What differed in this case but resembled the Second WIR mutiny was that these men had been legally free in the British military since the 1807 Mutiny Act, and that chattel slavery had been abolished in the British Caribbean since 1833 and the ban enforced in 1834. Although they were willing to use military violence, tactics, techniques, and procedures to fight for freedom, they technically did not need to do so since they were legally free. Notwithstanding this issue, both subsequent mutinies in the Second and First WIRs illustrate how slave soldiers in the West India Regiments did not necessarily view soldiering as an immediate act of emancipation. Instead, they would need to use their service as a vehicle to further fight for freedom, not unlike other plantation slaves.

Not only was the Eighth WIR mutiny similar to other slave revolts, but they were also linked to other enslaved people and Maroons who were resisting the chattel system at the time. When some of the mutineers in the Eighth WIR fled the final battle, they escaped into the woods and swamps of Dominica. At least one soldier named Hypolite found refuge with the island's Maroons for a time. Years later another private named Hypolite deserted from the Fourth WIR stationed in Dominica and fought with Maroons against the Royal Dominica Rangers and other Black soldiers during the Second Maroon War in 1814. Likewise, a peace treaty with the Djuka

Maroons in Suriname in 1837 required Maroons, some of whom were involved in the 1805 chasseur mutiny, to avoid combat against Whites. They also agreed to help White colonists fight the remaining mutineers who still lived in the rain forests. Additionally, after the Second WIR mutiny in 1808, plantation slaves in Kingston were apparently inspired by their attempts for freedom and conspired with surviving mutineers to rise up again. Mutineers Burgess, Watkins, and John were all implicated in the later conspiracy, and while Burgess was pardoned for his betrayal of the plot, Watkins and John were both executed. For them, their long history of resisting slavery inside and outside the British military came to an end in spring 1809. These incidents demonstrated how slave soldiers in the West India Regiments perceived mutiny as militarized slave insurrection.[52]

Conclusion

For mutineers of the Eighth West India Regiment, their movement was more than just a revolt against British military authority. Instead, it was an opportunity to fight for freedom and achieve Black liberation in Dominica. It resembled many militarized slave rebellions in the Atlantic world, in which plantation slaves rose up against their owners and ran away to woods, swamps, or mountains to fight for emancipation, to join existing Maroon communities free from White control, or to create their own societies where they could avoid chattel slavery. But their cause was also like the mutineers in the Black chasseurs and the Second and Fourth West India Regiments, in which enslaved soldiers rose up against their officers and fought to protect their status. They fought to guard against any possibility of them being reduced to plantation slavery. They had suffered conditions of slavery that often encouraged slave insurrection elsewhere in the Atlantic, and when they finally did rise up against those conditions, they fought like other militarized slave rebels in Dominica in 1791, in Grenada in 1795, and in Barbados in 1816. Militarized slave rebellions were on the rise during the period, and slave soldiers used their military experience to fight for some of the same goals as rebels elsewhere.

The liminal status of slave soldiers in the West India Regiments also reflected the changing nature of slavery and freedom as it related to military service in the British Atlantic during the age of revolution. Before the American Revolutionary War that led to the development of permanent peacetime slave armies, slave soldiers in the Anglo-Atlantic would never confront such an ambiguous state of bondage. Instead, they would have understood that they still faced unfreedom despite their military service in emergency situations. Only in a few cases could they expect their own personal manumission for exemplary conduct. The rebels in the West India Regiments confronted something else entirely. They served in peacetime, and revolution seemingly created a new kind of slave soldier. They were still slaves, but they were elevated and privileged compared to field slaves, and they expected to maintain this higher status. Revolution had also seemingly solidified the permanent professional militarization of slave soldiers in the British Atlantic. Slave soldiering was no longer predominantly a phenomenon involving colonial militia and professional armies caught up in exigent circumstances.

The case of the Eighth WIR mutiny is also one in which enslaved soldiers did not seize the opportunity produced by armed conflict to advance the cause of emancipation. Instead, it was a case in which they themselves initiated armed conflict in order to achieve these goals. True enough, the Caribbean had become a volatile region of military activity during the age of revolution, but Dominica in April 1802 was relatively peaceful. There were no large-scale military campaigns that made slavery particularly vulnerable, and there were no conflicts that produced chaos that enslaved people could easily take advantage of, as in Bacon's Rebellion in Virginia, the Yamasee War in South Carolina, or the southern colonies during the American Revolutionary War. Instead, Dominica was a relatively stable slave society with a large corps of enslaved soldiers serving to protect it. And still, slave soldiers found a way to challenge the Atlantic system.

The Eighth WIR's insurrection was also a case of armed resistance in which the rhetoric of the American, French, or Haitian Revolutions did not seemingly influence the rebellious soldiers. There were no reports of slave soldiers appropriating revolutionary rhetoric or any indication they were fighting for Republican ideas of citizenship or equality. More accurately, the African ringleaders of the mutiny were fearful they would be reduced to plantation slavery, and they were willing to risk everything to stop that from happening. At the very least, if they could take control of the island, they could prevent White officers from turning them into field slaves. Thus, it would appear that the influence of revolutionary rhetoric on slave soldiers may have been somewhat attenuated.

Lastly, this was a case that illuminated how even authoritarian military discipline and regimen could not contain disaffected people from below. No matter how well trained slave soldiers were to obey White officers, defer to White planters, and defend the British Empire, if the right incentives were not in place, or if the wrong policies were implemented, they were not afraid to push for what they thought was right. Slave soldiers had found another way to exploit White military and imperial ambitions in ways that could advance Black emancipation. They found a way to use their commanders' trust in them as loyal soldiers to attack the very system that made them slaves. They found a way to drive a wedge between the British army and chattel slavery in the British Caribbean colonies.

CHAPTER 5

Fugitives on the Front

Maroons in the Gulf Coast Borderlands War, 1812–1823

In September 1812 a "large body of Negroes and Indians" ambushed the provision lines of two companies of militiamen under the command of Lieutenant Colonel Thomas Adams Smith in northern East Florida. The Black–Native American force attacked the Georgia soldiers to drive them out of East Florida and prevent further American expansion into Florida during the Patriot War of 1812–1814. In October 1812 Colonel David Newnan, adjutant general of the Georgia militia, came to Smith's aid, and the Black and Indian soldiers attacked him and his 250-man force too. There were many Black warriors living in the area, and they fought for survival, since they were runaway plantation slaves from Georgia who had found refuge in Spanish Florida from American chattel slavery. They knew that if they let the Patriots, some of whom may have even been their former owners, take control of East Florida, they would be returned to the harsh life of plantation slavery again. About a year later and farther west in Mississippi Territory, runaway Black slaves fought with Creek Indians against U.S. soldiers in the Creek War. They fought U.S. soldiers on several occasions, and after the battle of Echanachaca, Lieutenant Joseph Morgan Willcox described them as "the most desperate foe." Willcox noted that approximately 120 Indians and runaway Black slaves defended the village. So many of these asylum seekers gathered in Echanachaca that a Creek agent called the place a "receptackle" for them. From there they fought fiercely alongside Indians to defend themselves and their homes "with the expectation of being free." But it was a losing effort as Americans took control of the region, which doomed the efforts of the Maroons to preserve their freedom, at least in this part of the borderlands.[1]

Runaway enslaved people continued to fight U.S. soldiers uninterruptedly in the Florida and Mississippi Territories as both British and Spanish authorities gave refuge to the slaves to counter American expansion in the region. The most notable instance of this occurred during the War of 1812, when hundreds of runaway slaves and Natives took up arms with British lieutenant colonel Edward Nicolls in the Florida Panhandle and helped him defend a fort on the Apalachicola River near present-day Tallahassee. Prospect Bluff, which Whites called Negro Fort because of the runaway Black slaves who occupied the position, was still a significant threat to White American merchants and frontier plantation owners even after the British defeat and their evacuation in the early months of 1815. So long as hundreds of these Maroons and their Native allies defended the Prospect Bluff stronghold, they could recruit more runaways on the border and stand up to American incursions into the area. The spectacular destruction of Negro Fort and the death of almost three hundred Maroon warriors at the hands of American soldiers under General Andrew Jackson on July 27, 1816, was celebrated as an important American victory, even though it did little to quell the Maroon violence that factored heavily in the First Seminole War. Indeed, the battle did not stop runaway slaves from fleeing into Florida to augment the large runaway Maroon communities existing both independently and attached to Seminole Indians living there (see map 11 below). Though the Maroon defeat in the battle at Prospect Bluff represented a significant setback for the runaway slave soldiers, it was still only one battle in what became a prolonged Maroon war for liberation that lasted another seven years.

Nearly a year after the battle at Prospect Bluff, Maroons continued their raids on plantations and attacked White planters on the border. American trading agent Edmund Doyle wrote to his partner, John Innerarity, that the Maroons still threatened their company's merchant house in Pensacola and that they "would put (and expect to do still) me to a cruel death if they dared." Others complained about Maroon raids and the enslaved exodus to Maroon and Indian villages in Florida. The persistent threat of Black Maroons and their Seminole allies in Florida in 1818 prompted General Jackson to invade the Spanish territory once again to destroy remaining Seminole Indian towns and capture or kill the Maroons living nearby. Pursuing Maroons was thus a central objective in the First Seminole War, much as it had been during Colonel Newnan's campaign six years earlier. Conversely, stopping American soldiers from destroying Maroon towns and capturing

Maroon soldiers had been the central Maroon objective during the same period.[2]

For many years, historians did not pay much attention to Maroon goals and perspectives in the Gulf Coast region, and only by the 1930s did historians more closely examine Black-Seminole relationships in Florida and how this group of Maroons (often named Black Seminoles) fit into broader narratives of Native American history, imperial warfare, slave resistance, and White-Native frontier conflict.[3] Thanks to more recent works by Jane Landers, Gene Allen Smith, James Cusick, and Nathaniel Millett, among others, we also now know more about how Maroons and Black soldiers fit into the imperial and Native-White frontier conflicts in the nineteenth century in the Gulf Coast region.[4] Moreover, other scholars are now beginning to understand the Black-Indian relationship in the region and how it paralleled typical Maroon societies elsewhere in the Atlantic world, recommending that the Black-Indian group should be known as the "Seminole Maroons." Indeed, the development of Seminole Maroon ethnogenesis was remarkably similar to a pattern of Maroon development elsewhere in the Atlantic world.[5]

But how did Maroon soldiers in Florida and the rest of the Gulf Coast borderlands interpret the various conflicts in the 1810s and early 1820s, or how did their role in the fighting compare to other Maroon wars in the Atlantic, which challenged colonial slave societies? From the perspectives of these Maroons, what exactly *were* they fighting for from 1812 to 1823? What exactly did the nearly constant conflict during this period actually mean to the Maroons involved, and what can it reveal about Maroon fighting in borderlands areas of the Atlantic world? What can it tell us about how Maroons became soldiers and how they interpreted armed conflict generally? How did it compare to other Atlantic conflicts in which Maroons also participated? How did the Seminole Maroons use armed resistance to stop chattel slavery, and how did slave and Maroon soldiers in the Lower South militarize resistance after the American Revolution? The borderlands area also offers a unique glimpse into Maroon warfare in the Atlantic world, in which three White/European imperial powers were competing for the same territory and vied for Maroon assistance. It can thus tell us more about how intense imperial conflict in borderlands areas affected armed resistance and slave militarization.[6]

Seen in greater Atlantic perspective, fugitive slaves and Seminole Indians in Florida comprised a typical Atlantic Maroon community, who were engaged in a "Gulf Coast borderlands Maroon war" against primarily White planters and their former owners in the region that lasted from 1812 to 1823. Instead of several discrete White-Indian and imperial conflicts, their fight was one long continuous war, similar to other Maroon wars in the Atlantic. They fought American slaveholders continuously for more than a decade in a struggle over slavery and freedom in their region. Ultimately, for some Seminole Maroons, it was a war for liberation. This Gulf Coast Borderlands Maroon War further demonstrated how militarized slave resistance had become in the Anglo-Atlantic. Plantation slaves became Maroon soldiers to fight a war against the expansion of slavery in Florida. In doing so, they also played on White and Native imperial rivals and allied with Native and White armies sympathetic to their cause, including British officers who promoted outright abolition. They were following their predecessors from the Yamasee War, and they had learned new strategies. They had learned how to build enduring relationships with Native Americans to form new Maroon bands. They had learned how to collaborate with an imperial army and its abolitionist agenda, and how to pit three competing imperial powers against each other to further their own ends. More than a century of learning how to militarize resistance played into the hands of enslaved people and Maroons in the Gulf Coast borderlands in the early nineteenth century.[7]

Freedom, Race, and Culture among Atlantic Maroons

Though Black slaves fought their former owners in Georgia and the Florida and Mississippi Territories, scholars have been reluctant to identify them as Maroons because of their affiliation and close relationship to the Seminoles and Creeks in the area who were also involved in the fighting. Indeed, race and identity are central to the problem of this interpretation of Maroon warfare from the Creek War through the First Seminole War, and historians cannot easily discount Native Americans involved in these conflicts. As Christina Snyder has shown, it is difficult to precisely label Africans and African Americans living among Seminole Indians in Florida in the eighteenth and nineteenth centuries. Those who lived on their own in Seminole territory still paid tributes to Seminole chiefs and were in effect vassal-like members of the Seminole chiefdoms in Florida.[8] In short, how can the fighting be Maroon warfare if belligerents were both Native American and African American? Were the runaway Black slaves who fought throughout this period in the region attached to the indigenous Seminole and Creek Indians? What was the true nature of this Black-Native alliance, how did the Maroons identify themselves, and how did their identity shape the fighting? Undeniably, the problems of race and identity complicate how scholars organize non-White people in the region and how to assess what they fought for. Yet analyzing who exactly the Seminole Maroons were in the Gulf Coast borderlands helps better explain their objectives and how they contributed to the longer militarization of slave resistance in the Anglo-Atlantic.

Scholars have long tried to understand Maroon race and identity in the Black Atlantic. African culture and ethnic identity were seemingly important for Maroon formation in some areas of the littoral, but ethnic affiliation was not always important to Africans in the Black Atlantic, especially Maroons. Native Americans were often part of developing Maroon communities, which highlights how Maroon groups were not entirely Black or African to begin with. Recent research has also shown that Seminole Maroon settlements in Florida showed high degrees of creolization as well. While the questions of Maroon race and ethnogenesis cannot be settled definitively here, this chapter does put Seminole Maroon demography into a broader perspective that can compare them to the Maroons elsewhere in the Atlantic. Such a comparison better explains Black-Indian relations within the Seminole Maroons during their development and how they resisted the Atlantic chattel system.[9]

Whereas identifying the Gulf Coast borderlands Maroons as "Black Seminoles" can conflate a racial distinction between African Americans and Native Americans, that distinction was not always clear in typical Atlantic Maroon societies and especially not so in their incipient stages. Instead, the name "Seminole Maroons" better addresses the Black-Native alliance in the area: they were both a group of runaway Black people evading enslavement and indigenous Seminole Indians. Over time some also formed new families. Notwithstanding their classification, and while both Native American and African American groups were part of the Maroon fighting from 1812 to 1823, Seminole and Creek Indian Nations existed independently of the Black slave presence in the southeastern United States, and at times they fought their own battles based on their own grievances against White planters, colonists, and even the Maroons themselves. Likewise, Black perspectives in the Gulf Coast borderlands were also diverse, and not all people who fled from slavery became a Seminole Maroon or fought exclusively against American planters. These variegated perspectives are perhaps best illustrated by fighting that broke out nearly a decade before 1812. At the turn of the century, Maryland Loyalist William Augustus Bowles embedded himself with the Muscogee and Seminole Indians in northern Florida, assumed a leadership position, and declared war against Spain in 1800. At the time, some slaves sided with Bowles, while others like Prince Witten continued to fight for the Spanish as their guarantor of freedom in Florida. Among the latter group were Haitian refugees led by General Jorge Biassou who were allied to Spain and people like Prince Witten, who would take up arms again in 1812 to protect Spanish Saint Augustine. There were also some slaves who accompanied their Patriot owners during campaigns, while General Andrew Jackson also recruited Louisianan slaves to fight for American forces leading up to the battle of New Orleans. Nevertheless, by 1812 a large and growing contingent of enslaved people became Maroons and allied with Native and European armies to prevent their re-enslavement in the borderlands. This chapter focuses on part of their story.[10]

By the time of the Gulf Coast Borderlands Maroon War in Florida, many White colonists in the Atlantic world held generalized racial views of Maroons. Any people who had non-White racial heritage, including Indians, were described as mulattos on censuses and tax records in the United States, while White planters around the Atlantic still believed that runaway African and African American slaves differed from the indigenous population based on predominant physical features. They also held this belief despite the fact that Black and Native American people often intermarried and had children together. French soldier Alexandre Moreau de Jonnès best illustrated White concepts of Maroon race during his travels in the Caribbean. When he arrived in Saint Vincent in 1795, he recalled meeting the Maroons there and identified them as two distinct Carib tribes, one "red" and one "black." He also noted that the Black Caribs were entirely different from the indigenous Caribs, writing, "Instead of a lanuginous hair, an enlarged nose, a gaping mouth, bordered with large lips turned away, they had the features of the Abyssinians: flat, long black hair, analogous to a mane; their nose was straight, starting from the forehead, slightly curved towards the point, and as one never seen from Cape Bon to the Gulf of Guinea."[11] Similarly, botanist Jean-Baptiste Thibault de Chanvalon highlighted racial differences among the Caribs during his travels to the Caribbean in the mid-eighteenth century as well. Chanvalon thought that although the Black Caribs had adopted indigenous mores, they still lived "confused with them." Jonnès's and Chanvalon's comments also reflected how White colonists used racial categories to classify Maroons as part of a larger project of determining who was not White in the Atlantic World.[12]

The problem of pinpointing Maroon identity is also complicated by the fact that White colonists and planters sometimes misidentified Indians and Black people too. Importantly, up until the late seventeenth century, Europeans often did not distinguish Africans living among Indians in the Caribbean. In Florida, traveler William Simmons noted how fugitive slaves in Seminole territory lived apart from the Indians, but that they dressed, carried firearms, and planted crops just like the Natives did. He also noted how they spoke Indian languages and sometimes appeared more like Indians than Black plantation slaves. Moreover, when a body of Patriot soldiers was attacked in 1812 at Twelve Mile Swamp near Saint Augustine, the soldiers reported that it was an Indian attack. However, after the assault Spanish military correspondence revealed that the Patriots were mistaken. Governor of East Florida Sebastian Kindelán y O'Regan wrote to Captain General Juan José Ruiz de Apodaca that the real attackers were runaway Black slaves whom the Spanish had armed. The Patriots only mistook the Black Maroons for Indians because "they wear the same clothing and go painted." At other times Maroons also wore moccasins, leggings, smocks, shirts, belts, turbans, and shawls per Seminole custom. In combat, the difference between fugitive slave and Native American was often hardly noticeable. Further complicating the matter, biracial Seminole Maroons also fought on the front, thereby challenging planters to identify them as either Black or Indian.[13]

Other contemporary accounts also differ as to how independent some Black fugitives were and whether or not they lived alone and separately from the Natives, who were sometimes both their allies and their enemies. By the end of the War of 1812, Seminole chief Kinache attempted to distance himself from the runaways at Negro Fort, not wanting to be any longer "the head of a band of rebellious rogues as blacks are." His son George Perryman would later describe hundreds of African Americans parading around Seminole villages, which suggested that the two groups lived with each other on somewhat equal ground. Likewise, Captain Hugh Young described several hundred runaway slaves living in villages on the Suwanee River. He claimed they had a form of government similar to that of the Seminole. William Simmons noted that some Black fugitives were still living freely and independently of their Seminole neighbors in 1823. Diplomat Horatio Dexter agreed and observed that even the Maroons "possessed" by the Natives still lived apart from them and had the liberty to do as they pleased.[14]

But while depictions of the Maroon towns suggested Black independence from Native oversight, other reports noted how many of the runaways appeared to have been owned as slaves by the Indians as well. General

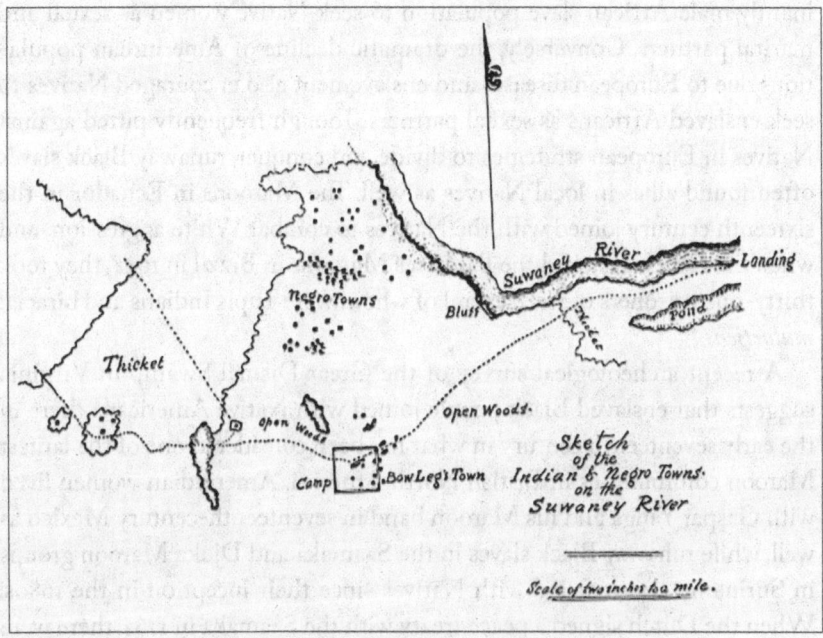

MAP 10. Sketch of Maroon Towns along the Suwannee River in North-Central Florida, 1818. From *Florida Historical Quarterly* 98, no. 2 (Fall 2019): 122; originally published as Alan Craig and Christopher Peebles, "Captain Young's Map, 1818," *Florida Historical Quarterly* 48, no. 2 (October 1977): 177.

Superintendent of Indian Affairs Benjamin Hawkins wrote to the Spanish governor of West Florida, Mauricio de Zuñiga, that many of the Black fugitives were slaves to the Natives and that Black Maroon commander Nero was reportedly a slave to Seminole Chief Bowlegs. Hawkins also reported how complex Black-Native relations were in Florida, noting that some Natives were willing to capture and recover Black fugitives to preserve their own autonomy from White aggression. Perfectly summing up how complex the role of slavery was inside the Seminole Maroon community, Hawkins wrote to Zuñiga in April 1816 that "if they [Natives] can take the negroes from among them and deliver them up to their masters, who are Americans, Indians, and Spaniards they will do an act of justice."[15]

Yet the presence of Native Americans and their connections to fugitive Black slaves were also in accordance with patterns of Maroon development throughout the Atlantic world. Since their inception, Maroons absorbed the local Native population as a challenge to White oppression. The sex imbalance of the Atlantic slave trade alone was enough to encourage the predominantly male African slave population to seek Native women as sexual and marital partners. Conversely, the dramatic decline of Amerindian populations due to European diseases and enslavement also encouraged Natives to seek enslaved Africans as sexual partners. Though frequently pitted against Natives in European strategies to divide and conquer, runaway Black slaves often found allies in local Natives as well. The Maroons in Ecuador in the sixteenth century joined with the Natives to combat White aggression, and when the Dutch attacked the Palmares Maroons in Brazil in 1644, they took thirty-one prisoners of war, several of whom were Tupis Indians and biracial *mulaetjens*.[16]

A recent archeological survey of the Great Dismal Swamp in Virginia suggests that enslaved Black people joined with Native Americans there in the early seventeenth century in what has been considered one of the largest Maroon communities in British North America. Amerindian women lived with Gaspar Yanga and his Maroon band in seventeenth-century Mexico as well, while runaway Black slaves in the Saamaka and Djuka Maroon groups in Suriname also married with Natives since their inception in the 1680s. When the Dutch signed a peace treaty with the Saamaka in 1762, there were still several Native American groups living among the Maroons, including the Arawak, Akurio, and Tunfinga. Runaway Africans also formed Maroon groups with the Kalingo Indians in Dominica in the late seventeenth century. New archeological evidence suggests that the Windward Maroons at Nanny Town in Jamaica also cohabitated with Taíno Indians throughout the seventeenth century and even into the start of the First Maroon War in the 1730s. Recent DNA analyses of the Accompong Town Maroons in Jamaica also show that the Leeward Maroons have Native American ancestry, which most likely came from indigenous women who partnered with enslaved Black men on the island in the late seventeenth to early eighteenth centuries. DNA analyses of the Garifuna have found similar results among these Maroon descendants in Belize, Saint Vincent, and Honduras. Even by the end of the eighteenth century in Cuba, one leader of a *palenque*, or Maroon village, near Jaruco was a Yucatecan Indian. Indeed, throughout the Atlantic, Native Americans helped found and were important constitutive members of Maroon groups. The Seminole Maroons fit this Atlantic pattern in the early eighteenth century and then again as they forged larger communities in Florida by the turn of the nineteenth century.[17]

Surviving Maroon groups throughout the Atlantic have also wavered on how they identified themselves in the past and how they continue to racially identify themselves to this day, making it difficult for scholars to assess Maroon history. Claudio Saunt has shown that a Black Maroon leader of a village near Columbus, Georgia, in 1790 identified as a Creek Indian. There is also some evidence that Seminole Maroons without any Native American ancestry still adopted Native American culture and identified as Seminole Indians once they arrived in Oklahoma after the Second Seminole War. Anthropologists have interviewed the descendants of Seminoles in Florida, Oklahoma, Texas, Mexico, and the Bahamas, as well as Maroon groups elsewhere in the Atlantic, with mixed results. Seminoles of both Black and indigenous Indian descent who now live in the Bahamas claim unconquered indigenous status casting aside their Black ancestry. Seminole descendants in the United States appear even more divided. Though an 1866 treaty with the U.S. federal government affirmed the right of Seminoles with African American ancestry to identify as full members of the Seminole Nation, they lived away from other Seminole and in their own separate towns in Indian Territory. Though a few elite Black leaders were included in the indigenous Seminole clans, most Black members were excluded and never participated in indigenous Seminole language, society, and culture.[18]

By the 1990s Seminole leaders voted to block anyone of African American ancestry from tribal membership to prevent them from receiving $56 billion in federal compensation. In the last two decades the Bureau of Indian Affairs has also questioned the idea that members of predominant African American descent were Seminole, first denying them certificates of degree of Indian blood cards in 2003, before changing course and issuing them later that year. But these issues are common to many Maroon communities in the Atlantic world too. As the descendants of the Black Caribs in Saint Vincent, the Garifuna in Honduras were accepted into the World Council of Indigenous Peoples in 1992, though recent interviews with members of the group show that they favor their African heritage when they self-identify. Moreover, DNA testing of various Garifuna communities in Belize, Honduras, and Saint Vincent show that several of these communities, descendants of the Black Carib Maroons in Saint Vincent, have significant Native American ancestry as well. Clearly modern concepts of scientific race and cultural identity have become important elements of Maroon identity, though it is unclear if Maroons abided by distinct racial notions that made Africans different from Native Americans. At the very least, Maroons have historically demonstrated the ability to navigate racial boundaries to their benefit, which may suggest that constructs of biological race may not be the only marker that they used and still use to identify themselves. The Seminole dispute also demonstrates how complicated racial identity has been for the descendants of the Seminole Maroons, and reiterates how scholars cannot simply apply current conceptions of race and identity to the past.[19]

The issue of slavery within the Seminole Maroon community also presents a number of difficulties for scholars identifying Maroons in the Gulf Coast borderlands. Were the Black fugitives actually Maroons since some accounts document them as slaves to the indigenous Seminole themselves? Moreover, can Maroons who resist slavery still be considered Maroons if they themselves owned slaves? Like many other Native groups in the Americas, the indigenous Seminole practiced a form of slavery independent of Black chattel bondage, but they also adopted Black chattel slavery by the end of the eighteenth century, and early reports document the rise of Black settlements affiliated with Seminole villages. Yet it was not uncommon for Maroons to own slaves elsewhere in the broader Atlantic. Like the indigenous Seminole and the Seminole Maroons, Palmarian Maroons in Brazil owned plantation slaves in their settlements in the seventeenth century, and the Leeward and Windward Maroons in Jamaica also owned plantation slaves until British emancipation in 1834. The Saamaka did in Suriname as well, and both Chatoyer and his brother Du Vallée personally owned slaves as leaders of the Black Caribs in Saint Vincent at the end of the eighteenth century. Palmarian Maroons in Brazil and Maroons in southern Mexico in the early seventeenth century prohibited their slaves from leaving their communities too. Seen in Atlantic context then, though Maroons were notorious for challenging European slaveholders, they frequently owned plantation slaves themselves, just like the Seminole Maroons did in Florida. In short, in Florida and much of the rest of the Atlantic world, Maroons owned slaves and intermarried with Native Americans.[20]

On Fighting in Florida:
Indians, Maroon Patterns, and Arming Slaves

While part of the Seminole Maroon story entails navigation through complicated webs of race, culture, identity, and slavery, much like other Maroon groups in the Atlantic, the rest of their tale shows that they also fought like other Maroons did in a continual struggle against their re-enslavement to White owners from 1812 to 1823. This prolonged period of violence that finally came to an end in 1823 marked what might be labeled as a "Gulf Coast borderlands Maroon war." This war demonstrated how plantation slaves became Maroons and used military violence and military service to attack the chattel system in the Gulf Coast borderlands. In many ways they were following in the footsteps of their predecessors in the Yamasee War one hundred years earlier.

It was clear that Maroons were heavily involved in the fighting in the Gulf Coast borderlands, but did they fight like other Maroons in the Atlantic world from 1812 to 1823? What was Maroon warfare, and how would we know when we, as historians, or contemporaries at the time saw it? At first glance, contemporaries did not easily define or demarcate Atlantic Maroon wars. During the First Maroon War in Jamaica in the 1730s, White planters and colonial authorities more often described the violence as a "rebellion" and called the Maroons "rebels." During the Second Maroon War in Jamaica in 1796, contemporaries described the conflict as a "maroon revolt" or a "dangerous rebellion," similar to how American planters and officials described the Seminole Maroons in Florida. During the First Carib War in Saint Vincent in 1773, newspapers and chronicler William Young described the fighting as a "war," but Young also called it an "insurrection of the Black Charaibs." Needless to say, scholars should not expect to find White records describing the fighting in the Gulf Coast borderlands as a "Maroon war," since Maroon wars were so often not described as such elsewhere in the Atlantic. More to the point, planters in the South rarely described Maroons in North America as such, instead referring to them more often as fugitives or rebels. Additionally, Maroon records of these events are scarce if they exist at all, and Maroon oral tradition sometimes differs from White records on when exactly these wars started. For example, some Jamaican Maroons believe the First Maroon War began when the British took possession of the island from Spain in the mid-seventeenth century.[21]

What then to make of Atlantic Maroon warfare generally, and how did it stack up against what the Seminole Maroons were doing in the Gulf Coast? As Wim Hoogbergen has shown, Maroon warfare could be typified by the intensification of plantation raids in which Maroons killed White planters and took supplies and slaves. These raids prompted Whites to raise military forces and send patrols to find and capture Maroons and to destroy their villages, which might attract more runaways.[22] In addition, Maroons used guerrilla tactics and the terrain to their advantage to stop White invasions. Finally, peace treaties between Maroons and colonial authorities formally ended these conflicts.

During the First Maroon War in Jamaica, Maroon raids on plantations were so successful that planters in Elizabeth, Hanover, and Cabarita Parishes stayed off roads to avoid ambushes, while others abandoned whole parts of the island entirely because they feared that more plantation slaves would join Maroon camps. The Jamaican response was similar to planters in Alabama like Thomas Powell, who removed his enslaved people from the Tombigbee River settlements in 1815, and Edmund Doyle, who refused to send his slaves to Pensacola because he thought that they would flee to the Seminole Maroons in 1817. Additionally, and like the Seminole Maroons who raided plantations for supplies and slaves, Maroons in Jamaica, Saint Vincent, and Suriname all raided plantations to capture slaves and gather supplies. The Black Caribs captured plantation slaves in 1777, as did the Trelawney Town Maroons in Jamaica in 1796. In 1789 nearly 150 Boni Maroons in Suriname surrounded and attacked the Clarenbeek plantation, and they killed several White workers before absconding with firearms, provisions, and thirty-three slaves to add to their community.[23]

After plantation raids and attacks, imperial authorities usually raised military forces to find and destroy Maroon settlements and kill and capture any Maroons they found. British forces attacked and burned provision grounds in Jamaica during the First Maroon War in the 1730s, and they destroyed several Maroon camps during the First Maroon War in Dominica in 1785–1786. White soldiers also destroyed the Baku Maroon town during the Boni Maroon War in Suriname in 1768. These attacks were similar to Patriot expeditions in Florida in 1812 and Jackson's campaign in 1818 in which American soldiers hoped to destroy Maroon camps to break up Maroon power.[24]

Like other Atlantic Maroons, the Seminole Maroons relied on their expertise in guerrilla warfare to fight their White enemies, while they also used terrain features to their advantage when they fought. The Jamaican Maroons were renowned for their use of mountainous terrain and thick rain forest to defend their communities, and only "steep, rocky, and difficult" paths could reach them. The Black Caribs in Saint Vincent also controlled "almost impenetrable woods," and so too did the Maroons in Dominica. In Suriname it took weeks for White soldiers to cut through forests to reach the Saamaka and Djuka, while the Boni Maroons lived so deep in the rain forest that they disappeared entirely for over a decade after the Second Boni Maroon War ended in 1793. In all these places, when Whites approached, Maroons ambushed them and used fire-and-withdraw tactics to escape. The use of terrain and guerrilla tactics that Atlantic Maroons used paralleled how the Seminole Maroons used swamps and thick pine forests to attack White invaders like Colonel Smith's forces in Florida and when they ambushed Captain John Williams's detachment of U.S. marines at Twelve Mile Swamp on September 12, 1812. They also used swamps, creeks, and thick forests surrounding Negro Fort to prevent American advances. When the first U.S.

troops did approach the Maroon bastion, the Seminole Maroons ambushed them on their approach and then retreated to safety within the fort's walls.[25] Thus it was clear that throughout the Gulf Coast Borderlands Maroon War, Seminole Maroons used terrain features much like other Maroons in the Atlantic.

Maroon fighting in the Gulf Coast borderlands intensified in 1812, which marked the start of the Maroon war. Patriot ambitions in Florida could be traced back to 1810 with the development of the Patriot War, when the Patriots, planters turned rebels who resented Spanish authority in Florida and who feared Spanish cession of Florida to France, first conspired against the Spanish Crown in Baton Rouge. Early plans to attack Spanish garrisons in East and West Florida were generally abandoned; however, former governor of Georgia General George Mathews became involved in the conspiracy, and he refused to give up on opportunities to seize East and West Florida for U.S. annexation. By March 12, 1812, Mathews had mustered enough fighters, along with U.S. Army gunboats, to invade East Florida and Patriot forces captured Fernandina and Amelia Islands, and they laid siege to Saint Augustine by the end of the month. War for the Maroons thus began in 1812 with the invasion. The Patriots destroyed several plantations in the area, razed crops, and released livestock. By May the Spanish counterattacked, and by June Spanish reinforcements arrived. That same month the United States declared war on Great Britain, a Spanish ally, thus linking the Patriot War to the larger War of 1812. By September the Spanish successfully broke the siege of Saint Augustine. Notwithstanding Patriot ambitions for more land in Florida, Maroons were heavily involved in the fighting, and from American planter perspectives in the area, Seminole Maroons were a significant threat and were key actors during the Patriot campaign.[26]

Though fugitive slaves poured into Florida in the aftermath of the American Revolution, hostilities between them and their former owners remained relatively unremarkable for several decades. Evidence points to the slaves being part of frontier conflicts against Whites in the Southeast during the Early Republic period, but significant and sustained violence between slaves and planters was somewhat limited. Slave flight from Georgia to Spanish Florida remained constant for decades, but Maroons also had to be cautious that the Spanish might comply with Pinckney's Treaty in 1795 in which the Spanish vowed to help protect Americans from Native attacks. Despite ostensible Spanish support, the growing Maroon population in Florida, along with their Amerindian allies, presented a greater challenge to increasing American concerns of tranquility on the border and expansion into Florida over the turn of the century. Georgians recognized that the state was not well defended against potential enemy attacks, while Maroons in Florida could incite a slave insurrection that might destroy American planter prosperity in Georgia. Governor Mitchell complained that the Spanish had armed too many Black men and runaway slaves, and that if they "suffered to remain in the province, our southern country will soon be in a state of insurrection." General Mathews even hoped that the Seminoles would invade Georgia on behalf of the Spanish government at Saint Augustine, as it would "afford a desirable pretext for the Georgians to penetrate their country, and Break up a Negroe Town: an important Evil growing under their patronage." Rumors also spread among the Patriots that the Maroons were taking up arms with the British and Spanish to attack the Patriots. Lieutenant Colonel Smith even believed that the English would send a detachment of Black troops to occupy East Florida and stop Patriot advances. When the Patriots finally invaded in 1812 to take over East Florida, defeating the Indians and hundreds of Black slaves in the territory was critical for their conquest. Thus the goal to destroy Maroon settlements was part of the decision to invade Florida and go to war with the Seminoles. Colonel Newnan's account of the expedition in 1812 also made these objectives clear, as well as how central Maroons were in the fighting, calling them the "best soldiers."[27]

Indeed, the Maroon soldiers on the border had wreaked havoc on the Patriots in 1812. Even before Newnan's expedition, Seminole Indians and Maroons made frequent raids in Florida and Georgia and attacked Patriot plantations. On July 25, 1812, they raided near the St. Johns River and killed eight or nine settlers before capturing a large amount of plantation slaves to add to their community. In August Archibald Clarke reported that the Seminole killed two Patriots in one skirmish, and on the same day they attacked Zephaniah L. Kingsley's plantation, killing three plantation slaves but also "carrying off" twenty-nine more. These attacks galvanized the support of 120 volunteers from St. Mary's to join Newnan's expedition. Combat seemed unavoidable, and on September 12, two dozen Seminole Maroons, along with free Black militiamen under the leadership of Prince Witten, ambushed Captain John Williams's detachment of U.S. marines at Twelve Mile Swamp near Saint Augustine and killed several, including Williams. One intelligence report from Newnan's forces noted that there was "serious alarm" as a "consequence of the conduct of the blacks" near Saint Augustine. In August, Lieutenant Colonel Smith reported that "the blacks assisted by the Indians have become very daring," and that the forces he sent out after them were always "unsuccessful." The Maroons were clearly still strong in northern Florida even after Newnan's expedition. They knew what was at stake if they were defeated.[28] Likewise, runaway slaves who joined the free Black militia at Saint Augustine, people like Prince Witten who fled from Georgia and who was also promoted to lieutenant after his role in the Twelve Mile Swamp ambush, continued to protect the Spanish fort because they knew it would help them keep their freedom. Witten was born Principe Huiten in 1756 in South Carolina and escaped to Saint Augustine from his owner Jacob Weed in Georgia in 1786. He was a skilled carpenter and "talkative," and he found refuge with the Spanish. Protecting Spanish interests would also help them protect their families, like Witten's wife, Judy Kenty, and their children, Glasgow and Rafaela (known as Polly). If Americans invaded, they would be re-enslaved.[29]

Haitian refugees living in Saint Augustine had also reinforced American runaways' connection to protecting Spanish interests. In 1796 Haitian revolutionary and then Spanish loyalist General Jorge Biassou fled the island with twenty-five followers and found asylum with the Spanish in Florida. Shortly thereafter they quickly built connections with the runaways that lived there. Biassou's own brother-in-law, Jorge Jacobo, married Prince Witten's daughter Rafaela (Polly), which may have been a marriage meant to consolidate the Haitian and American Black communities. Jacobo was the military successor to Biassou, and his marriage to the daughter of an American leader probably strengthened their ties. The two groups also sponsored each other's marriages and served as godparents to their progeny. Prince Witten was godfather to the children of Estévan Cheves, Bacas Camel, Andrés Camel, and Sayrus Thompson. Meanwhile, Francisco Witten and Rafaela sponsored Tomás Herrera's marriage. Aside from the familial connections, Biassou also helped train the runaways to serve in the Black militia attached to the Spanish fort before his death in 1801.[30]

Continued Maroon attacks instilled fear in planters along the border who also sought to retaliate against the Maroons. In September near Saint Augustine, Maroons and Natives killed at least ten Patriots under the command of Smith. In another incident, after Patriots destroyed Maroon farms near Saint Augustine, they also threatened to re-enslave Maroons living there who were once slaves in Georgia. This was the case for Thomas Primus and his wife and children, who sought to avoid being turned over to Primus's former owner, Lucia Braddock Fitzgerald. Another case was Tony Proctor, a man born in Jamaica in 1743 who served with the British during the American Revolutionary War. Proctor eventually arrived in Florida and became a slave for the Panton, Leslie and Company traders. He developed a reputation for being a skilled interpreter with the Seminole, and General Mathews and Creek Major William McIntosh kidnapped him to communicate with Chief Payne at Alachua. Unbeknownst to Mathews, Proctor surreptitiously told the Seminole leaders that the Patriots were lying to the Seminole and that they would attack the Seminole just as the Patriots were pursuing Maroons in Florida. Proctor later escaped from Mathews, and Governor Kindelán bought and freed Proctor for his actions, which also served Spanish interests since the Seminole took up arms against the American invaders.[31]

Benjamin Hawkins informed Governor Mitchell about the apprehension of fugitive slaves later in December 1812, indicating too that some runaways were captured while attempting to reach Seminole towns. Hawkins had also reported earlier to Judge Tomlin that the Seminole of Alachua had "a great number of negroes," including a handful of former slaves belonging to Patriot owners. Caught up in the conflict, enslaved people fled to reach potential allies who supported their freedom. Roger and his wife Phoebe fled from the Bethune plantation south to Cape Florida. Robin, from the Plummer plantation, fled west and would eventually reach Prospect Bluff. Sam, enslaved to Manuel Solana, fled to Seminole territory, as did Nancy of John Lofton who moved to live with the Seminole with her seven children. She was later recaptured after the war. But many were not captured, and runaway enslaved people continued to reach Maroon villages and take part in Maroon attacks. These attacks provoked fear of slave insurrection in 1812 and 1813, and Major McIntosh complained to Secretary of State James Monroe that Patriot slaves were "excited to rebel" and that "an army of Negroes raked up in this country" would "bring about a revolt of the Black population of the United States." By the end of the year Tennessee volunteer Willie Blount reiterated these concerns to William Eustis that there was "disaffection among the blacks, and incitement 'to commit murder and depredations.'" In early 1813 several plantation slaves had deserted their masters near the border and fled to Saint Augustine via the St. Johns River.[32] Maroons could hardly have failed to sense the growing fear among White planters and the threat they posed to the slave system in the region.

By spring 1813 Maroons in northern East Florida continued to attack Patriot fighters and raided plantations along the Georgia border. Buckner Harris, the president of the Georgia Legislative Council, complained to Governor Mitchell that American planters on the Florida border were still exposed "to the menaces of free negroes and the slaves" that the Spanish protected. The Seminole and the Seminole Maroons still attacked Patriot fighters, and Buckner appealed to Mitchell to loan the Patriots money to enable them to defend themselves against the Maroons, who had "the weapons of death placed in their hands for the destruction of the patriots." Underscoring how central the runaway slaves were in the fighting, Spanish planters threatened to reinvigorate the long-held Spanish policy that made Florida a safe haven for British slaves from Georgia. The threat came after a Patriot expedition in East Florida in November 1813 in which Patriot leader Charles Harris burned several Spanish plantations and stole several slaves. Jose Hibberson reminded Harris that if the Spanish retaliated, "half of the negroes of your sea coast" would cross the St. Marys River into Florida and supplement the existing Maroon population there. Even without Spanish help, by the end of the month Georgia slaves fled to East Florida en masse to join the burgeoning Maroon population there. The Maroons were gaining momentum in Florida, and plantation slaves sensed it too. If they kept up the pressure, they might possibly stop American expansion of slavery into Florida.[33]

Meanwhile, to the west in Mississippi Territory another group of Maroons fought U.S. soldiers from 1813 to 1814 in a conflict known as the Creek War. While also a civil war among the Creek, American planter expansion onto Creek lands along the Alabama and Tombigbee Rivers sparked Native-White hostilities. Like the Patriot War, the fighting spilled into the larger War of 1812, and Americans believed that both the British and Spanish were advising and arming the Creek and runaway slaves to attack U.S. outposts. Runaway slaves, mostly from Georgia, had both found refuge among the Creek and had been enslaved by others in the area for decades. Still others lived in their own camps independently in Creek territory. Initially these Maroons maintained separate communities along the Apalachicola River and farther south in Florida. There were minor skirmishes and frontier battles throughout 1812 and 1813, but the fighting escalated when the Creek and their Black allies attacked Major Daniel Beasley and a contingency of roughly 120 militiamen at Fort Mims on August 30, 1813.[34]

The attack at Fort Mims sparked widespread outrage and launched a wave of American reprisals against settlements in the Alabama and Tombigbee River watersheds. The American attack on the Creek town Echanachaca was part of this reprisal campaign. When soldiers surveyed the damage after the battle, they found letters from the Spanish governor of West Florida, Mateo González Manrique, congratulating the Creek and the Maroons on the massacre of Fort Mims. The correspondence eliminated any doubts that the Maroons in Spanish Florida were involved in the conflict in Alabama. It also reiterated to the Americans how serious a threat fugitive slaves were to their settlements in the region. Creek Indians posed a legitimate fear for Whites living near the Tombigbee and Alabama Rivers in 1813 too, but Maroons were also involved in the fighting and targeted White plantation owners. The Maroon-Creek alliance in the area prompted some planters to flee and others to remove their slaves from the region altogether, fearing that they might join the Maroons and destroy the planters. Planter Thomas Powell reportedly took his slaves from the Alabama and Tombigbee settlements in the summer of 1813 because of this fear. By November 1813 U.S. commanders near the Alabama River noted that Major Thomas Hinds had killed several Natives and Maroons in the skirmishing and taken several other runaway slaves as prisoners.[35]

The geographical separation of these Maroon groups involved in the Gulf Coast Borderlands War resembled Maroon warfare elsewhere in the Atlantic. Although the leaders of the Leeward and Windward Maroons in Jamaica may have been family members, the two groups lived on different sides of the island during the First Maroon War in the 1730s. Other smaller Maroon groups not affiliated with the Leewards or Windwards were also engaged in the First Maroon War. Similarly, there were at least three independent Maroon groups who fought in the Boni Maroon War in Suriname at the end of the eighteenth century. There were also several different Maroon camps, each with their own leader, during the First Maroon War in Dominica in 1785. Despite their geographical and political separation in each region, Maroons in these wars shared the same goals: to protect Maroon autonomy and stop White encroachment. To this same end, Maroons who first lived with the Creek or in Mississippi Territory during the Creek War demonstrated that they shared the same objectives as those who lived farther east and south in Florida. As they became enmeshed with the War of 1812, some of these Maroons also fled to Florida, where they joined existing Maroon groups or helped build Prospect Bluff. Still others probably became slaves to Lower Creek Indians who sided with Americans.[36]

Maroons found refuge in this western part of the borderlands, and they had the support of the Spanish in Florida and some Creek in the region. Other campaigns against the Seminole and Seminole Maroons in Florida in 1813 revealed how large the growing Maroon population was becoming. One expedition documented that American soldiers burned 386 houses and nearly 2,000 bushels of corn and destroyed hundreds of livestock animals. The Maroon population had swelled so much that Governor Mitchell wrote to Secretary of State Monroe that the Maroons threatened to incite a rebellion among plantation slaves in the United States. Additional military force

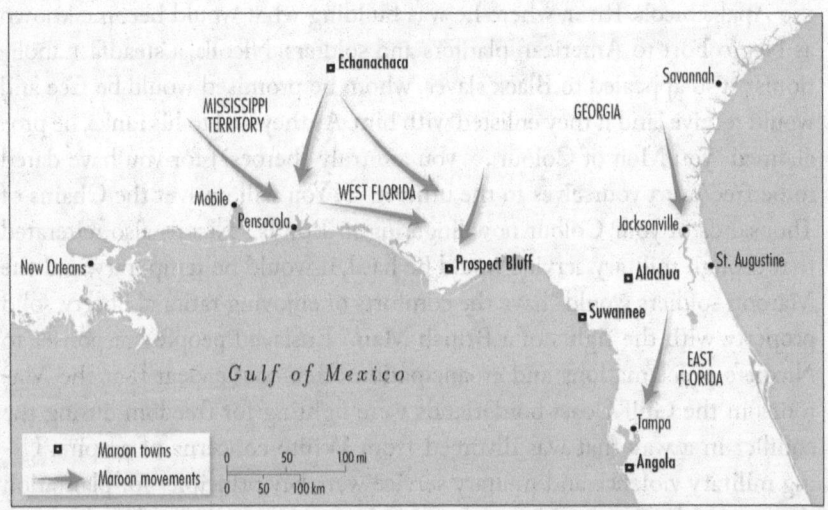

MAP 11. Gulf Coast Maroon Settlements, Movements, and Battles, 1812–1823. Map created by the author.

was needed to stop them, as they now took up arms and supplies from both British and Spanish officials.³⁷

American raids on Creek and Seminole villages pushed more fugitive slaves and their Indian allies farther south to the Gulf Coast and into the hands of British lieutenant colonel Edward Nicolls, where they became even more intertwined with imperial warfare during the War of 1812. Nicolls arrived in the borderlands under orders from Vice Admiral Alexander Leslie Cochrane, who looked to divert American forces from British operations to the north. Cochrane also ordered Rear Admiral George Cockburn to the Southeast during the summer of 1814; he landed along the Georgia coast and began raiding for enslaved refugees in the Sea Islands. While Cockburn operated in the Sea Islands, Nicolls sailed to West Florida. The British had started recruiting enslaved people in the Chesapeake in 1813, and on April 2, 1814, Cochrane issued an emancipation proclamation offering to evacuate enslaved people who fled to British lines during the war. Thousands of enslaved people answered his call, and Cochrane expected similar results along the Gulf Coast.³⁸

Nicolls continuously appealed to the Creek and to Black slaves in the area that the Americans had treated them unfairly with the Treaty at Fort Jackson, in which the Creek ceded a large swath of land to the United States to end the Creek War. Nicolls especially appealed to Creek anger involving the cession, and he welcomed them and runaway slaves to a post along the Apalachicola River, where he was building what would become known as Negro Fort to American planters and soldiers. Nicolls, a steadfast abolitionist, also appealed to Black slaves, whom he promised would be free and would receive land if they enlisted with him. As they fled to his ranks, he proclaimed "you Men of Colour ... you are truly [heroes?] for you have dared to be free/exert yourselves to the utmost.... You will unrivet the Chains of Thousands of your Colour now lingering in Bonds." Nicolls also reiterated that though military service would be hard, it would be temporary, and the Maroon soldiers would "have the comforts of enjoying rational liberty, solid property with the rights of a British Man." Enslaved people's responses to Nicolls's proclamations and emancipation offers made clear that the Maroons in the Gulf Coast borderlands were fighting for freedom during the conflict in a way that was divorced from White concerns of empire. Using military violence and military service were key principles for plantation slaves and Maroons in the area to resist chattel slavery. Before Nicolls eventually evacuated the continent and left the Maroons, he issued discharge papers that reiterated their freedom. Those who evacuated to the Bahamas and their descendants would also place great emphasis on these papers to show their free status within the British Empire. They also formed a new settlement in the Bahamas named after him, which underscored how their fight had been for their freedom.[39]

Nicolls originally arrived at Fort San Carlos de Barrancas in Pensacola in 1814, bringing only about sixty men and a few artillery pieces to help protect Spanish colonists there from American invasion. Recruiting Natives and Seminole Maroons would help Nicolls augment his small fighting force, and under Nicolls's command the multiracial group formed the Third Battalion of Royal Colonial Marines. The force would also help the British army prevent American expansion. Admiral Cochrane reiterated these strategic points in a letter to the Indian leaders in July 1814 in which he expressed a desire to "engage to arm" any warriors the chiefs might provide. He also told them to "encourage also by every means the emigration of Negroes from Georgia and the Carolinas." Cochrane believed that he could augment his forces with Native and Black soldiers, and that slave soldiers more specifically could help him force the surrender of valuable New Orleans. Abolitionist Nicolls was proud to support their flight from slavery. In addition to fugitive Black slaves, almost eight hundred Creek Indians joined Nicolls, and they were eager to have a strong ally help them fight their common American enemy. Nicolls was eager to take them on as he quickly offered a proclamation to provide security to anyone who would join him or for those who would not resist his presence in the area. White Americans understood Nicolls's proclamations in Pensacola to be invitations for runaway slaves, Native Americans, pirates, and "all traitors to their country" to wage war against the United States. By October approximately three hundred Black slaves had fled to Nicolls, including women and children who absconded on barges and canoes in Pensacola Bay. Importantly, the British Native American allies assisted in creating confusion to help enslaved people sneak away. Approximately two hundred Native warriors also fought to stop the American pursuit across the Perdido River.[40]

Though the British and their Native and Black allies would suffer a defeat at the hands of American soldiers north of Pensacola in 1814, their expedition did succeed in razing several American plantations, destroying scores of livestock and crops, and recruiting many more plantation slaves along the way who joined on the retreat back to Pensacola. Others followed British captain George Woodbine and Nicolls from the west near Mobile Bay, as they and their Native allies plundered plantations and readily took on new enslaved recruits, livestock, gunpowder, and provisions. Though Nicolls and Woodbine recruited American slaves to assist the Spanish in defending Florida from U.S. invasion, they also readily took on Black slaves who ran away from Spanish planters in the area as well. If any planters protested, Woodbine ordered his men to "shoot at anyone who should attempt to take them" as the slaves departed with British soldiers and Indian warriors from the wharf in Pensacola Bay.[41]

If the British officers could not entice slaves themselves with emancipation after six months of military service, it was not difficult for enslaved people to simply walk to the British garrison at Pensacola before they could be taken to Prospect Bluff on the Apalachicola River. Others simply absconded on small watercraft overnight and crossed Pensacola Bay to reach their new ally. The chaos that the fighting caused in the bay also made it easy for slaves to escape from their owners to join their British ally. At least a hundred more enslaved people joined Woodbine and Nicolls in Pensacola in this way, while many more fled to the British officers once rumors spread that General Jackson was marching en route to destroy the British garrison there. Pensacola slave owners enumerated 136 slaves who joined the British and who were still at Prospect Bluff in spring 1815, including thirty-eight of John Forbes's slaves. Others who fled from Pensacola to Prospect Bluff became leaders at Prospect Bluff, including Garçon, Prince, and Cyrus, all of whom were carpenters in the city before fleeing. Garçon had been owned by Don Antonio Montero, while Prince had belonged to the mayor of Pensacola. Prince and Cyrus were both twenty-six years old and Garçon was thirty. Cyrus, who was also literate, was a valuable refugee who could read and understand British objectives in the area. Pensacolans' lists of slaves also made clear that Black women and children became involved in the war and that joining the Seminole Maroon community was often a family endeavor. Several enslaved mothers belonging to Forbes fled with their young children, including Polly and her three children of unknown ages. Likewise, another enslaved woman named Nelly belonging to Eugenio Sierra fled with her daughter, while Saly of Pedro Senal departed with her two sons. Though not entirely clear if they were actually partners, at least six family groups with at least eleven children fled from Pensacola to become Maroons farther east in Florida. Much like the women and children who joined the Ethiopian Regiment decades earlier, the age of revolution opened military service and the militarization of resistance to more enslaved women and children.[42]

Residents in Pensacola claimed that two-thirds of their slave population had fled to join the growing Maroon body in 1814 and 1815, including women and children. Edmund Doyle also noted to British captain R. C. Spencer that Woodbine arrived at Prospect Bluff with at least twenty slaves of both sexes, indicating that couples ran away together. The planters' petition also documented how some enslaved families fled together. Men and women fled to them separately as well, but couples were also listed among those who ran to the Seminole Maroons. Like Polly and Saly, Elize fled with her two children, and two more enslaved women named Mary and Sophy ran with their sons, one named Sam (age unknown). At least forty-five of John Innerarity's slaves had joined the Maroons by 1814, including several enslaved families who escaped to Prospect Bluff, like Billy and his wife Lally with their children Cressy, Flora, Beck, Cynthia, and Nero. Stephen and his wife Cynthia also joined the Seminole Maroons together. At least ten women of unknown ages were among the group of Maroons at Prospect Bluff whom British captain Robert Henry returned to Spanish lieutenant José Urcullo as the British prepared to evacuate North America in 1815. Henry's decision to return the women was peculiar as it pertained to the Maroon community at Prospect Bluff. They represented less than a tenth of the fighters still there, and though Henry claimed that he could not identify all of the Spanish slaves whom Urcullo pursued until Colonel Nicolls returned to the garrison, he also feared that an attempt to return all of the fugitives would produce a Maroon uprising against British soldiers, whom the Maroons significantly outnumbered. Henry also asked Maroons who would return, and those who volunteered probably at least knew the Spanish had little power against the British to take them. Remarkably Mary, Elize, and Saly were among those who returned with Urcullo, though it is unclear if their children came back with them. Perhaps they had been separated from their children and no longer wished to continue fighting. Perhaps they returned as a sacrifice to protect their family members who were still living in refuge. Perhaps their family members had died in what was by all accounts a bloody war. British officers like Nicolls had also encouraged them to return as they prepared to evacuate, reiterating that it would be better to return than allow the Creek to capture them for bounties and rewards. In any case, most who volunteered at first reneged on their offer, and several more disappeared before they could reach their former owners.[43]

These Maroon families had endured significant hardships in their war of resistance, and some were rewarded as they evacuated North America with the British in 1815. At least forty-two Maroons arrived in Bermuda aboard the *Ruby* in November, the vast majority of them former slaves to American trader John Forbes from Pensacola. A list of slaves on the ship also indicated that several women and children participated in the Gulf Coast Borderlands Maroon War and that they successfully fled to safety as family units. Eight women and eleven children were among those who arrived, representing nearly half of the group on board. Just like soldiers reported finding women and children in Maroon villages during their raids to obliterate them, Maroons fought as families, and some evacuated from Florida with family units still intact. Some were fortunate enough to escape death or re-enslavement by migrating to the West Indies.[44]

After the British retreat from Pensacola, Captain Woodbine moved to Apalachicola and then to Saint Augustine by the end of 1814. Though Governor Kindelán informed Woodbine that the neutral Spanish government could not support a campaign against the Americans from Florida, Woodbine nonetheless recruited more plantation slaves in the area, leaving with at least eighty more people in his ranks. Woodbine denied encouraging Spanish plantation slaves to join his ranks, and he stated that he understood Spanish apprehensions that the Maroons might incite slaves to rebel against Spanish owners. But he also reiterated his authority to Kindelán to obtain deserters from the United States in the area to serve British military interests during the war. As he moved west and through several Seminole towns, at least seventy more Maroons "belonging" to Chief Bowlegs and other Seminole joined him on the Florida-Georgia border.[45]

But Woodbine also encouraged Bowlegs to take in more Maroons and to raid American plantations for even more enslaved people. Together, Woodbine and Bowlegs's campaign to capture more plantation slaves to augment the Seminole Maroon population became a major point of contention for Americans in the borderlands. Benjamin Hawkins even went so far as to order the Upper and Lower Creek to put an end to the practice. He commanded them to attack and kill all White and Black people in arms, and to take all Whites "encouraging the blacks to mischief" as prisoners and bring them to him. If anyone resisted, Hawkins wanted the Creek to kill them. Hawkins even tried to turn the Creek by stating that the Seminole and Maroons with Woodbine were stealing cattle intended as Creek provisions outlined in the Treaty at Fort Jackson. If these were not strong enough incentives, Hawkins informed the Creek that they would be paid bounties of fifty dollars for each Maroon captured who had a White owner, and that they could keep any Maroon without an owner. Despite these commands, the Maroon population continued to grow. Far to the west, as the British evacuated Louisiana in 1815 they also moved scores of plantation slaves east into Florida as well, adding even more fugitives to the burgeoning Florida Maroon population. By the end of the year, there were an estimated two thousand fugitive slave soldiers in central Florida. The officers' recruitment of fugitive slaves from New Orleans to Saint Augustine attested to how central the Maroons were in the fighting in that region in 1814 and early 1815 and that the Maroons were critical actors in the southern campaigns during the War of 1812.[46]

Giving Maroon soldiers arms had become a low-risk British strategy to challenge American expansion into the Gulf Coast region, which was also part of the larger British strategy to entice American plantation slaves to leave their owners throughout the continent. Doing so served British imperial interests in several ways: it reduced manpower and sowed unrest on the domestic front in the United States, and it could also be claimed as a small victory for the growing abolitionist movement in Britain. Cochrane's success recruiting slaves in the Chesapeake, and his ambitions for similar results in the borderlands, also withdrew American forces from British operations in Canada. In the north near Canada and in the Chesapeake, the British heavily relied on Native American and some Black soldiers to fight American forces. These kinds of provincial fighters enhanced British military power and allowed the commanders to divert forces elsewhere in the empire. If the British could expand their operations in the Gulf Coast and intensify the racial component of the war, they could capture and hold important American cities like New Orleans, which Cochrane believed was vulnerable if enslaved people joined his Regulars in large numbers. Cochrane also believed that enslaved soldiers could help the British harass American forces into submission. Plantation slaves near the Florida border accepted the offer and ran to British lines in hopes of freedom. The British were happy to oblige and take them into their lines. The British were also content with taking in Spanish fugitives in Florida, and they did little to return or recapture them despite Spanish requests.[47]

This was neither the first nor the last time in which Maroons allied with one imperial power to fight another in the Atlantic. When two imperial powers vied for control in a borderlands area in the Atlantic world, it enhanced Maroon diplomatic leverage and military position in the area. One of the first times Maroons collaborated with Europeans at their rivals' expense occurred in 1571 when they helped British privateer Sir Francis Drake invade the Isthmus of Panama. Maroons had been in hiding from their Spanish owners, and they happily led Drake and his men toward Spanish settlements to attack them. They were happy to "wreak their wrongs on the Spaniards." Their expertise in guerrilla warfare and their knowledge of the terrain in Panama was of great value to Drake, who wrote highly of them. Conversely in Jamaica, Maroons were happy to ally with the Spanish against the British shortly after the British conquest of the island in 1655 and for several decades after. There were reports as late as the First Maroon War in the 1730s that the Spanish were still supplying Maroons with arms and ammunition from Cuba as Maroons continued to fight British planters.[48]

Two centuries after Drake, after the British annexed Saint Vincent from the French in 1763, the Black Caribs sought the assistance of French officials in nearby Martinique and Saint Lucia. The first attempt at a peace treaty with the strong Maroons was thwarted when the Black Caribs met with the French governor of Martinique, who suggested that they reject it. Several years later in 1769 the British also intercepted Maroons at sea, as they attempted to bring back French supplies of firearms and kegs of ammunition. The Franco-Maroon alliance lasted for more than a decade, as the Black Caribs allowed French spies on the island to reconnoiter in the 1770s and fought with them during a British invasion in 1780. During the same period the French had also made peace with the Boni Maroons in Suriname, and they refused to let the neighboring Dutch venture into French Guiana and lead military expeditions against them. While there is no evidence that the French intervened with the Trelawney Town Maroons in Jamaica at the outbreak of the Second Maroon War in 1795, Jamaican officials feared that French officials were trying to help them, attesting to the fact that European colonists knew it was always a potential problem.[49]

Similarly, Europeans relied on Maroons to help suppress the Haitian Revolution. While insurgent Maroon camps sprouted once the revolution started, republicans sometimes struggled to recruit them on their side as some preferred to stay on the periphery and work White diplomacy and politics to their advantage. The Dokos Maroons attacked plantations belonging to *gens de couleur* in 1793 after White encouragement, and they also fought for Spanish and Napoleonic forces throughout the war. Spanish authorities in Santo Domingo armed and supplied Naranjo and Le Maniel Maroons on the border of Saint-Domingue to encourage French plantation slaves to run away. Francophobia and property rights on the island also encouraged the Spanish to support the Maroons as a way to weaken the French on the other side of the island.[50]

Seminole Maroons took up arms for European powers similar to how Maroons participated in imperial warfare elsewhere in the Atlantic, and they still survived when their imperial allies left them in Florida. The British were forced to evacuate Florida when it became clear their Spanish allies were not strong enough to help defend it. Even though most British soldiers departed the Gulf Coast, they left arms and ammunition with the Seminole Maroons, along with Negro Fort on the Apalachicola River. In spite of American petitions to restore runaway slaves who joined the Maroon community via British assistance during the fighting, it had become clear in 1815 that British officers had no intention of doing so. Indeed, Secretary of War William Crawford informed General Jackson that the Maroon presence at Negro Fort had gotten stronger by the end of March 1815, and Benjamin Hawkins suspected that the Maroon population at Prospect Bluff would even grow over the summer. Inside and around the fort, the Maroons were seemingly doing very well too. Aside from the supplies the British left, they farmed crops and were not in want of food. Jackson himself informed Governor Zuñiga that Prospect Bluff had been getting stronger and that the Maroons there threatened the peace on the border. Though the British had left, Americans complained that the Spanish in Florida were doing little to stop the Maroons or plantation slaves from Georgia from adding to their community. By February 1816 at least two dozen more Black slaves from Georgia crossed the border and fled to Prospect Bluff, which Americans estimated held more than three hundred Maroons by then. They knew they needed to maintain pressure on American planters if they were to keep their freedom, and they remained a significant threat in northern Florida throughout 1816.[51]

Further east near Jacksonville, Maroons had "openly declared their Independence," while more runaways found refuge among the Seminole to such a scale that Major General John Floyd thought their presence demanded "the adoption, of decisive, and energetic measures" to stop more slave flight. Floyd believed that the Maroon presence encouraged emancipation, and with the help of foreign enemies, the "banditti" were capable of jeopardizing "the tranquility of our frontier," let alone destroying property and land value. By then, American leaders like Andrew Jackson realized that the situation was no longer tenable and that the Maroons and their Native allies were forcing a confrontation. Jackson opined to General Edmund Gaines in spring 1816 that if Prospect Bluff harbored fugitive slaves from Georgia, and that if the Maroons there induced more slaves to desert their American owners, "the fort must be destroyed." Such was the threat of Prospect Bluff to American planters that Crawford believed it would continue to encourage plantation slaves to flee and "excite irritations" among the "neighbouring settlements" that "may ultimately endanger the peace of the nation." The Maroons at Prospect Bluff had become a national security issue. Months later, U.S. forces invaded Florida once again.[52]

It is unlikely that the Maroons in Florida wished to provoke a large-scale U.S. invasion into their territory. Raiding plantations for more supplies and more recruits was part of the Maroon survival strategy, as was the case with Maroon communities elsewhere in the Atlantic world, whose members also found themselves at war with colonial forces when they did so. Perhaps the Maroons at Prospect Bluff and in northern Florida thought they were strong enough or had enough support from their Spanish allies to withstand such an attack. Perhaps they thought that if they projected strength, they could avoid a large-scale U.S. invasion. According to Nathaniel Millett, some Maroons held the belief that they had become British subjects and that they thought they had strong British support to defend what was in their view British territory. Nicolls also promised to return to the fort in six months, and at that moment he lacked the means to transport a large number of Maroons who may have wanted to flee to the British Caribbean for safety. When Nicolls left, he also ensured they were well armed and supplied. Nevertheless, the withdrawal of one major imperial power in the region weakened their position, and when the Spanish proved unwilling to prevent a U.S. invasion, their position weakened still further. Jackson was well aware of these new circumstances when he led U.S. forces into Florida once again in pursuit of the Maroon menace. With Nicolls gone, the stage was set for another great confrontation between American and Maroon forces.[53]

By July 1816 Maroons continued to stay within their stronghold on the

Apalachicola River, and they continued to prepare for armed conflict in case American soldiers would attack. Their rectangular fort was reportedly 120 feet long on each side, 18 feet thick, and 15 feet high with a pine tree palisade surrounding it. It was certainly a formidable position. They were effective and experienced soldiers after years of fighting, and they knew they could not let their guard down. Later that month, General Edmund Gaines ordered Colonel Duncan Lamont Clinch to approach Prospect Bluff from the north from nearby Fort Scott to undermine Maroon power in the area. Prospect Bluff also blocked U.S. supply lines to Fort Scott on the Flint River, and it was important to destroy the fort if U.S. military operations in the area were to be successful. Clinch embarked with a force of 116 White soldiers, while Major McIntosh and another 150 Creek fighters joined Clinch on the approach. From the south, sailing master Louis J. Loomis reached the mouth of the Apalachicola with two gunboats by July 10 to resupply Clinch in preparation for the attack. Loomis sent a water party on shore near the fort seven days later, but forty Maroons and Indians from the fort ambushed them and killed five. The Maroons also made one sailor a prisoner. The detachment retreated after the attack, and Clinch did not arrive close to Prospect Bluff until two o'clock in the morning on July 20, but he delayed the assault since he believed the final approach was difficult. Indeed, the hundreds of Maroons there were protected by swamps and thick pine forests on their flanks, while they were also armed with several heavy artillery pieces and howitzers. The Maroon soldiers inside also reportedly held five hundred rifles, eight hundred pistols, five hundred swords, and hundreds of pounds of powder. Throughout the Atlantic, Maroons used mountainous terrain, thick forests, and expansive swamps to defend themselves, and the Maroons at Prospect Bluff were no exception. They too used the natural terrain to their advantage and to form a staunch defensive position. Swamps and thick forests prevented the American attackers from placing their own field artillery in position to counter the Maroons' twenty-four-inch pounders, and the Americans could only really approach the fort by sailing upriver on the Apalachicola in the face of Maroon artillery.[54]

The Maroons had also promised Nicolls to prevent any White person from passing the river, which ensured a fiery defense. The Maroons also waved the British flag at the fort in defiance of American and Spanish masters. Surgeon Marcus G. Buck and other U.S. soldiers later recalled that the Maroons refused peace terms on July 23 and that they wished to fight. An unsuccessful assault on the fort by Major McIntosh and several hundred Creek soldiers in September 1815 might have emboldened the Maroons inside. Surrendering was apparently not an option, likely because the Maroons suspected it would lead to their re-enslavement. U.S. soldiers were convinced that the Maroons were determined to fight to the death. American gunboats moved in under the cover of darkness on the night of July 26. The Maroons started receiving American artillery fire in the early morning of July 27. As the fighting ensued, one lucky American cannon shot hit the fort's magazine, detonating its stores of gunpowder and ammunition and causing a massive explosion. Disaster struck in an instant. The blast killed most of the soldiers inside, maiming almost everyone who survived. Now that the fort was thoroughly destroyed, Clinch's men moved in to sweep the area and assess the damage. His Creek allies found Garçon, who had survived the inferno, but they promptly executed him. The battle was over.[55]

The destruction of Prospect Bluff was a disaster for the Maroons. Approximately two hundred people died, while seventy more were seriously maimed and twenty-five more Maroons were taken prisoner. But some escaped, and their war was not yet over. Some fled farther south toward Tampa Bay and joined an existing Maroon community there known as Angola, until its destruction in 1821. Others scattered elsewhere in Florida and were aided by British agents, including Captain Woodbine. Still others fled to the Seminole towns along the Suwanee River and linked up with British traders Alexander George Arbuthnot and Robert Ambrister. They still posed a threat to American planters, and Governor Mitchell expressed his concern to President James Madison about what might be done to protect Georgians. Mitchell successfully convinced the Madison administration that the Maroons were still dangerous, and Madison and Secretary of War John Calhoun relayed back that instructions would be given immediately to move an armed force to the southern border to "keep the hostile Creeks, Seminoles, and Negroes in check." By February 1817 Woodbine had returned to the Apalachicola River to stir up the Seminole Maroons still in the area, while Arbuthnot and Ambrister enticed both Native and Black leaders to prepare for war against the Americans, as they continued to trade at the Seminole towns along the Suwanee River in north-central Florida. The presence of Woodbine and Ambrister in Florida in 1817 reassured the Maroons that the British were still interested in continuing Nicolls's abolitionist agenda in the borderlands. Ambrister had even served with Nicolls in Florida and maintained communication with him, spreading Nicolls's abolitionist message to Maroons in the borderlands. There was seemingly little military action for a few months after the fort's destruction, and U.S. soldiers evacuated several frontier forts nearby and on the Georgia border. However, the interlude was very short lived, and hostilities between Natives, their Maroon allies, and White planters in the area quickly resumed.⁵⁶

Maroons feared additional American attacks as they linked up with Seminole and Creek Indians who resisted American expansion. Despite the devastating blow at Prospect Bluff, they still instilled fear among U.S. Americans in the borderlands, especially slave holders. These fears underscored how central Maroons were to the fighting at the onset of the First Seminole War. In Georgia, several former slaves of planter Zephaniah L. Kingsley were among the Maroons at Negro Fort during its destruction, and more than forty of them had fled to the Seminole Maroon towns between the Suwanee River and Tampa afterward. Similarly, eight to ten of trader Timothy Barnard's slaves fled to Prospect Bluff, and more had fled to Saint Augustine. Other plantation slaves near St. Mary's also fled to Negro Fort before its destruction, while another forty-nine found refuge with the Seminole after the fort lay in ruins. In 1817 more than four hundred Maroons lived in the area.⁵⁷ The defeat at Prospect Bluff seemingly did little to stop Maroon resolve to keep fighting. They simply would not give up.

In spite of the defeat at Prospect Bluff, Maroon refusal to surrender or stop offering asylum to runaway slaves, as well as their continued raids on U.S. plantations, still influenced U.S. policy and military strategy in the region. In a speech in the U.S. House of Representatives, Virginia congressman Charles Fenton Mercer even traced the beginning of the First Seminole War to the U.S. invasion of East Florida in 1816 and the destruction of Prospect Bluff. Moreover, he believed that the United States could not tolerate enemy Amerindians harboring Maroons, many of whom had escaped from planters north of the border. Other congressmen proclaimed that military force was needed because the Spanish were assisting runaway slaves from Georgia and inviting them to insurrection. Even worse, they charged that Ambrister and Arbuthnot were organizing the Maroons to make the "horrors of a savage negro war." These problems required military intervention.⁵⁸

Edmund Doyle complained to John Innerarity in June 1817 about the plundering of their company's trading houses and how fearful he was for his life. Doyle was "surrounded with outlaws & murderers, runaway negroes, all of when [sic] would put (and expect to do still) me to a cruel death if they dared." Doyle also reported less than two weeks later that the Maroons living near the Suwanee River would have to be dealt with very soon, and they were ready to decamp from their position as soon as an American expedition entered the country. Doyle would later send Joseph Perryman as a messenger to the Seminole near the Suwanee to offer them a pardon and protection for the Black Maroons living among them. But Doyle was also unwilling to send his remaining plantation slaves to Pensacola to safeguard them. He suspected that the minute the opportunity presented itself they would flee to the Seminole, as had already happened to one of his female slaves and her brothers Isaac, Steel, and Chester, along with her sister and her children.[59]

Native Americans, with their Maroon allies, prompted yet another U.S. invasion of Spanish Florida. In late December 1817 John Calhoun ordered Jackson to march from Nashville to Fort Scott with five hundred regular soldiers, a thousand militiamen, and eighteen hundred Creek allies. Jackson's forces arrived on March 9, 1818, and quickly began attacking the Seminole Maroon towns. He also informed Governor Zuñiga that he had presidential orders to enter Florida to "chastise a savage foe who combined with a lawless band of Negro brigands, have for some time past been carrying on a cruel and unprovoked war against the citizens of the United States." Other accounts also stipulated that southern planters needed border security against the Maroons in Florida, which in part instigated the U.S. attacks. The hundreds of Maroons now living with the Seminole along the Suwanee River continued to raid their former owners, and Jackson had to break up the "hostile collections of Indians and negroes" to maintain border security in the area. To American planters the Seminole War was as much about eradicating Maroons as it was about removing the Seminole threat to Florida and Georgia. The fact that hundreds of Maroons living with the Seminole on the Suwanee kept up the pressure seemed to justify U.S. policy as officials hurried to raise more troops to stop them. Because the Maroons would not stop their raids and attacks on the borderlands, U.S. forces invaded.[60]

As fighting in 1818 raged on, Americans continued to charge British and Spanish officers with aiding the Maroon enemy. There were rumors that the British might invade Florida with the West India Regiments and fourteen thousand soldiers that would pay bounties for plantation slaves and Maroons who would join them, similar to how the Black regiments fought in Florida a few years earlier. Although Nicolls and Woodbine had left, British agents Arbuthnot and Ambrister stayed behind in Florida near the Seminole towns along the Suwanee River and provided the Seminole and Maroons with more arms and ammunition to keep fighting. They even helped plan an attack at St. Marks on the Florida Panhandle before American forces could arrive. Frustrated with the inability to quell the Maroons and their Seminole allies, President James Monroe told Congress in 1818 that the First Seminole War was due to the inability of Spain to honor Pinckney's Treaty in

1795 and to protect American vessels from attack. He was also frustrated that Spanish colonists would not stop arming Indians and Maroons in the territory, which enabled them to attack American planters to the north. Similarly, John Quincy Adams explained to diplomat George William Erving that Jackson's campaign in 1818 was geared toward attacking Seminole Indians "and the banditti of negroes combined with them." An anonymous officer involved in the Seminole campaign reiterated that these concerns drove the U.S. invasion of Florida during the First Seminole War. Indeed, he proclaimed that "the gauntlet was thron," and because British and Spanish authorities in Florida had recruited "disaffected Indians, absconding negroes, and vagabond adventurers" who "continued a predatory warfare on the borders of the U. States," the United States could not stand by. U.S. forces had to invade.[61]

General Jackson and the Committee of Military Affairs echoed similar sentiments after Jackson led expeditions into Florida against the Seminole Maroons and captured Arbuthnot and Ambrister. The committee first declared that Jackson's decision to invade Florida in 1816 reflected the "necessity" of destroying Maroon towns to protect American planters, while the committee also noted that the conflict ended only after Jackson had captured Pensacola, where the "Indians and fugitive negroes were effectually deprived of all possible means of continuing their depredations, or screening themselves from the arm of justice." Jackson himself was pleased about the executions of Ambrister and Arbuthnot in 1818 for inciting and supplying enemies of the United States. In his view they were "exciters of this Savage and Negro War," and he hoped that their punishment for "exciting Negroes & Indians in East Florida to war against the U States" would serve as a deterrent for American rivals in the future. Earlier that year, he made similar claims to the governor of West Florida, José Masot, that runaway slaves from the United States had found refuge among the Creek and Seminole living in Spanish-held Florida territory, and that they had all united and had "raised the Tomahawk & in the character of savage warfare have neither regarded sex or age helpless women have been massacred and the cradle crimsoned with the blood of innocence." Congressmen too went so far as to proclaim that Georgia militiamen "were, in fact suppressing an insurrection of slaves, aided by an Indian force, all assembled and armed for purposes hostile to the country," and that Arbuthnot and Ambrister were at the head of the rebellion. U.S. forces were needed to quash the rebels.[62]

Regardless of their alliances with Maroons, Seminole and Creek chiefs also believed that the Maroons played a large part in the reason why the

Americans attacked Indians in Florida from 1812 to 1818. General Edmund Gaines complained to Seminole chief Kenhagee that the Seminole were malicious and harbored his Black slaves along the Suwanee River in 1817. He promised the Seminole that if they would let him pass through their territory to attack the Maroons, he would not harm them. Kenhagee responded that he did not harbor any plantation slaves and that the Black Maroons who fled to the British during the War of 1812 were a matter for "white people to settle." Chief Bowlegs affirmed Kenhagee's view in a letter to the governor of Saint Augustine, José Coppinger, saying that the Americans had attacked him for no reason, as "we have none of their slaves, we have taken none of their property since the Americans made peace with our good father King George." Chief Cochean also believed these were matters for Whites to settle, and he refused to fight for them because his nation was "confused" about the proper policy regarding the Maroons. Some Creek chiefs expressed their grievances and kept on fighting after the fall of Negro Fort in 1816 because they were frustrated with American traders harassing and disturbing their brethren who were living with the Seminole Maroons, while they had also lost a significant amount of supplies and provisions inside Prospect Bluff when it exploded. Others sided with Jackson but still noted that Maroons were critical for their involvement in the fighting. Lower Creek Tustunnuggee Hopoy stated in April 1816 that Agent Hawkins had told him and his warriors to "go down to the fort of the blacks, and take them out of it, and give them to their masters." By 1818 Chief William McIntosh noted that even after attacking rival Creek factions fighting U.S. forces, he and his warriors continued to march with General Jackson to wipe out the Maroons in the Suwanee villages. It is unclear if Maroon leaders were aware of these diplomatic conversations, although they probably were given their prominence as skilled interpreters during the period. They probably appreciated statements from leaders like Kenhagee and Bowlegs that gave Maroons cover from White ambitions.[63]

For their part, the Spanish denied giving any assistance to the Maroons in Florida by that time and that they too feared rebellious Black slaves and Native Americans living there who threatened the safety of colonists living near Pensacola. Fort St. Marks was also weak due to supply demands that Maroons and Natives put on the commandant there. Perhaps in an attempt to save face with Jackson, Governor Zuñiga informed him that although the Maroons at Apalachicola were legitimate inhabitants of Florida and could become subjects to the Spanish king, Zuñiga declared them "insurgents, or rebels against the authority," and denounced them for their actions. He also blamed Nicolls and Woodbine for "seducing" plantation slaves to join the Maroons and for assisting them years earlier before the British withdrawal. Zuñiga's assurances made clear that although both the British and Spanish had assisted the Maroons, or at least neglected to attack them to serve their imperial ambitions against U.S. expansion, the Seminole Maroons also created diplomatic problems for European authorities in Florida, as the Maroons gave the stronger and larger U.S. forces in the region legitimate reasons to invade Spanish territory and drive out Spanish colonists still living there.[64]

In the end, the Maroons fought hard in a gradual withdrawal south to the Suwanee River, with U.S. American forces hot on their trail, destroying several settlements including Fowl Town. In November 1818, however, the Maroons regrouped and counterattacked. By the end of the month, Maroon, Red Stick Creek, and Seminole warriors attacked an American boat moving slowly down the Apalachicola River that carried forty U.S. soldiers, seven women, and four children. The Black-Native force ambushed the ship from a swamp and killed everyone on board except for four men and one woman. They also attacked five other boats shortly after and inflicted heavy casualties. Additionally, they captured traders William Hambly and Edmund Doyle to punish them for the destruction of Prospect Bluff. Despite avenging the loss of the fort, the Maroons were under pressure to scatter and evade U.S. soldiers still searching for them in Florida, and they moved farther south. By 1820 there were still at least sixty-five Black "gunmen" living with the Seminole in central Florida, but others had moved to West Florida and Tampa.[65] Imperial dynamics in the Gulf Coast borderlands had changed with the British withdrawal, and it was not a coincidence that Maroons began losing after the British left and Spanish strength weakened. They were no longer able to play on three imperial rivalries, which weakened Maroon diplomatic and military positioning.

Peace finally came for these Maroons in 1823 when Maroon, Seminole, and U.S. diplomats met at Moultrie Creek near Saint Augustine to formally end the violence. Peace with Spain came years earlier with the Adams-Onís Treaty in 1819, which was ratified in 1822. Spanish colonists were forced to evacuate Florida, and the United States formally annexed the territory. The Maroons' European allies were finally gone, and they now faced only Americans. Rumors that Spain was ceding Florida to the United States understandably provoked Seminole concerns about how their own lands would be treated. Although hostilities had effectively eased, General Jackson advocated for Seminole and Maroon removal from Florida to west of the Mississippi River. Governor Mitchell had also relayed to the Creek that the United States was not likely to buy land in Florida from the Seminole, since it cost "a very great expense" to subdue them. Instead, Mitchell told the Creek that according to Secretary Calhoun, the Seminole had forfeited their right to land claims, and Mitchell advised the Creek to help remove Seminoles onto Creek lands, promising them "liberal compensation" for their help. By April 1823 Secretary Calhoun appointed Colonel James Gadsden and Bernard Segui, among others, to make a peace treaty with the Seminole, which was to be done at a crossing over Moultrie Creek four miles from Saint Augustine. Reiterating how important securing Maroons in Florida was on the eve of peace, Florida governor William Duvall instructed diplomat Horatio Dexter to make note of and round up any of the runaways he encountered on his way to Moultrie Creek. At the time, Dexter also recorded how many remaining Maroons lived in the area and with Seminole Indians in north-central Florida. In all, Dexter counted 430 Black Maroons living among 1,395 Native Americans. Although the war was ending, the Maroons lived on and hoped to avoid re-enslavement to American planters.[66]

Peace at Moultrie Creek

The manner in which Maroons solidified peace with Whites in Florida followed the longer pattern of Maroon warfare and how White imperial and colonial forces fought and armed Maroons in the Black Atlantic. Though American plantation owners successfully rid themselves of the Spanish presence in Florida with the Adams-Onís Treaty in 1819, the treaty did not fully address the hostile Amerindian and Maroon populations in the territory. Formal peace with the Florida fugitives and the Seminole Nation would not come until September 18, 1823, when the United States came to terms with the signing of the Treaty of Moultrie Creek.

Approximately 425 Florida Natives were present at the signing of Moultrie Creek, and thirty-two Seminole leaders signed the 1823 treaty, seventeen of whom can be positively identified. Although the only known account of the treaty meeting does not make a reference to Seminole Maroons being present at the signing, at least a handful of Seminole chiefs who were present presided over communities that included the Black settlers, including Chief Philip, Chief Oponney, and Chief Emoteley. Even more importantly, at least one signatory of the treaty was a Black Seminole Maroon named Vacapachasie or Cow Driver, whom Americans called Mulatto King. King was once at Prospect Bluff before its destruction, and he was one of the "six principal chiefs of the Florida Indians" who also signed Article 11 of the treaty, which promised the six chiefs that they could stay on their lands instead of moving to a reservation. King was able to stay with his Maroon community near the Apalachicola River.[67]

Composed of eleven articles, the treaty reflected planter ambitions for more land in Florida and other boundary concerns. The treaty greatly extended the boundary for White settlement from what the Seminole and Creek previously agreed to in Georgia in a treaty in 1790. Articles 1 and 2 gave all of Florida to the United States except for land that was allotted to the Seminole, who would also receive livestock and farm implements to sustain their villages. Importantly, American diplomats forced the Seminole to agree to help capture Black Maroons and destroy the surviving communities, a point that further underscored how central the Maroons were to the fighting and peacemaking process. Article 7 stipulated that Seminole chiefs and warriors be "active and vigilant in the preventing the retreating to, or passing through, of the district of country assigned them, or any absconding slaves, or fugitives from justice; and further agree to use all necessary exertions to apprehend and deliver the same to the agent." It was this article that was most unique to the treaty.[68]

In contrast to Article 7 in the 1823 treaty, there was no provision in the 1790 agreement for the Natives to continue to capture and return Maroons still living in their midst or who might later join them, which matched treaties that the Seminole's predecessors and many other Native nations agreed to throughout American history. Instead, Natives in 1790 were obligated to restore enslaved people who fled to them or whom they captured during the fighting. This practice followed a general pattern of Indian treaties throughout early American history, in which Natives almost always agreed to return Whites and Black slaves whom they had captured in previous campaigns. The Creek agreed to restore runaway slaves and slaves captured in war in South Carolina in 1717 and in Georgia and Florida in a treaty in 1774, as did the Huron, Shawnee, and Delaware in 1764 in the Northeast. The Cherokee agreed to restore Black slaves in South Carolina in 1751 and again in 1762. So too did the Chickasaw and Wyandot Nations in the mid-eighteenth century. To be sure, several nations in the Southeast also agreed to return runaway slaves as a general policy to appease White colonists in the absence of armed conflict. This was the case for the first treaty James Oglethorpe made with the Creek in Georgia in 1733. In Oglethorpe's case, colonists and the Creek were not at war with each other, but Whites could not afford to have the Natives unite with Black slaves in South Carolina, so they offered to pay the Creek bounties for each Maroon captured and returned to White owners. Even earlier in Maryland, several tribes agreed to capture Maroons in an agreement in 1666. Successive settlements in that colony continued the practice as the Nanticoke agreed to return fugitive slaves in 1668 and in 1678, the Piscataway, Mattawoman, and Choptico in 1692, and Natives along the Indian River as late as 1742.[69]

But in other cases Natives were not required to continue to capture and return fugitive slaves still living with them or in their territory after armed conflict. Indeed, the runaway perpetuity clause in Article 7 of the Moultrie Creek treaty differed substantially from other Indian treaties previously secured by colonists in British North America and by the United States. To be clear, the presence of Maroons at Moultrie Creek and Article 7 do not mean that the treaty was not also an Indian treaty. However, the perpetuity clause in Article 7 did more closely resemble a long history of Maroon treaties in the Atlantic, and the fact that Maroons were present at the signing of the treaty suggests their interests were also reflected in its design. As early as 1608 Europeans recognized that they were not able to completely destroy Maroon groups in their American colonies. Maroon strength and power forced colonists to pursue peace so long as Maroons agreed to help them maintain the slave system. That year Spanish colonial officials came to peace terms with a large Maroon group in New Spain and its leader, Gaspar Yanga, whom they could not defeat. The treaty decided Maroon autonomy and territorial boundaries, and it obligated the Maroons to return Black slaves who fled from the Spanish ports. It also stipulated that the Maroons would be paid twelve pesos to track and return new runaways in the future. Farther south in Brazil, the Palmares Maroons briefly agreed with Portuguese authorities to return fugitive slaves in exchange for their own free state in 1663 and again in 1678.[70]

By the eighteenth century, Europeans continued the pattern to settle for Maroon autonomy in exchange for their assistance in returning runaway slaves and suppressing slave rebellions. Similar to the Seminole Maroons in the 1810s, by 1768 British colonists on Saint Vincent recognized how strong the Black Caribs on the island had become, and they pursued peace knowing they could not defeat them without substantial costs. The peace treaty comprised fifteen articles and allotted land on the island for permanent Maroon settlement. Moreover, the treaty promised that the Maroons would have five years to build new homes on their allotted territory and that the proceeds from the sale of their old lands would be paid to them in two equal payments. The Maroons also had to swear a loyalty oath to King George III, while the British also promised the indigenous Red Caribs that the colonists would help separate them from the Black Carib population if they so desired. The provision was an obvious attempt to sow division among the Maroon population, and not surprisingly the Maroons rejected the treaty. Continued Maroon raids on plantations on the island eventually led to a large Maroon war in 1772–1773 in which the Caribs secured another peace accord more to their liking. Like the other Maroon treaties in the Atlantic and the 1823 treaty at Moultrie Creek, the Caribs were allotted lands to protect their communities and were obligated to acknowledge a European king as their sovereign. Moreover, they agreed to return runaway plantation slaves living among them and to seek and apprehend others in the future. Those who refused and harbored runaways would forfeit their lands. Finally, they were obligated to defend the island against British enemies and help quell plantation slave rebellions.[71]

Perhaps the most notorious Maroon conflict in all of the Black Atlantic was the First Maroon War in Jamaica in the 1730s. While the British had fought several different bands of Jamaican Maroons intermittently since taking possession of the island in the mid-seventeenth century, the Maroons were not a large enough population to present a substantial threat to the colonial planters for most of the seventeenth century. However, Maroon numbers appeared to swell in the early eighteenth century with the addition of more plantation slaves, and the colonial government determined their presence was too much by 1731. Following the ensuing First Maroon War, the British secured peace treaties with the Leeward and Windward bands within three months of each other in 1738 and 1739. Among the articles of pacification included the stipulation that hostility would cease between the Maroons and colonial planters forever, and that the Maroons would live in a "perfect state of freedom and liberty, excepting those who have been taken by them, or fled to them." Like the earlier treaties and the one at Moultrie Creek, the Jamaican Maroons agreed to return runaway slaves who had fled to them within the previous two years and those who would run to them in the future.[72]

Probably the most similar Maroon treaty arrangements to the Moultrie Creek treaty in 1823 were those made by Maroons in Dutch Suriname in the seventeenth and eighteenth centuries. There, waves of Maroon wars in which Whites were largely unsuccessful in defeating Maroon power led to a series of peace treaties over almost a hundred years. In 1686 the Karboegers of Coppename, a mixed-race group of Indians and African Maroons, signed a peace treaty that obligated them to search for and return new runaway slaves, and the Saamaka first agreed to similar gestures when they signed a treaty in 1749. They were followed by the Djuka in 1760.[73]

But none of these treaties preserved peace for very long, and almost twenty years after the first attempt at peace with the Dutch, the Saamaka again agreed to help eradicate other Maroon bands in order to preserve their own group's autonomy. The Saamaka agreed in a new treaty in 1762 to never again commit hostilities against White planters or "free Indians" not living with them, and to identify all of their villages to Dutch colonial authorities. They also agreed to point out villages of Native Americans and other Maroon towns that they lived in or whom they had an alliance with, and to pressure those groups to take part in the treaty agreement or else help destroy them. Article 5 of the 1762 agreement also stipulated that planters would pay the Saamaka a fifty-guilder bounty for each runaway they returned, much like the bounty the Seminole were offered. Aside from trading provisions and land and tool allotments in the treaty that were also similar to what the Seminole Maroons gained in 1823, the Saamaka were also obligated to capture runaways when the colonial government informed them of mass slave desertions, to help defend the colony against foreign adversaries and slave rebellions, and to never ally with the nearby Djuka without informing Whites first. These same provisions would be reiterated to the Boni Maroon group in 1837 when they signed for peace in Suriname, agreeing to return runaway slaves for a small bounty. In addition and like the Seminole Maroons, at the time of the signing of the 1762 treaty, it was clear that groups of Natives were living with the Saamaka and joined in the accord too.[74] Importantly, these Suriname Maroon treaties demonstrate two remarkable points as they relate to the Seminole Maroons in 1823: Maroons were obligated to return runaway plantation slaves in the future to protect their own communities, and Native Americans were part of these groups and involved in the treaty-making process in Maroon wars fought over slavery.

Indeed, Maroon groups throughout the Atlantic signed peace treaties to ensure their survival as the Seminole Maroons had in Florida. Some did so despite also playing on European rivalries and calling on foreign intervention and aid, just as the Seminole Maroons at first relied on Spanish and British protection against their former masters. The fact that the Florida Maroons struck peace in the model of Atlantic Maroon treaties also attests to their strength as a community. Only when Maroon groups were too small and not considered more than a nuisance did White authorities pursue other options to eradicate them.[75] This was certainly not the case with the Seminole Maroons, who maintained their strength and forced three White empires to reckon with them and make them part of their imperial strategies in North America. Though their British and Spanish allies were eventually driven out of Florida, they were too strong to be removed themselves, and with their Indian allies they forced American planters to settle for peace that sought to perpetuate Maroon existence.

Ultimately the end of the Gulf Coast Borderlands Maroon War did not quell hostilities between Whites, Natives, and Maroons in Florida in the long term. Travelers to Florida in the 1820s reported that five to six hundred fugitive slaves still lived among more than 4,500 Amerindians in Florida, and that they lived in the Seminole towns. Some even tried moving closer to the coast so that they could attempt to flee farther to Caribbean islands. The Maroon towns affiliated with the Seminole prospered as their inhabitants continued to plant corn, melons, pumpkins, and vegetables, as well as tend to livestock. Though many had to abandon their fields near the Suwanee River, they simply moved farther south and established new towns, fields, and families.[76] Violence flared up again in 1835 during the Second Seminole War, and again in 1855 during the Third Seminole War, when Maroons allied with the Seminole Indians to stop White invasion and prevent Black re-enslavement. By then, most of the indigenous Seminole and Seminole Maroons were defeated and evicted to the Bahamas and to Indian Territory.

Conclusion

The fighting in the Gulf Coast borderlands from 1812 to 1823 was another Atlantic Maroon war in an expanding imperial colonial world dominated by Black chattel slavery, in which Maroons were concerned first and foremost with fighting their former owners to prevent re-enslavement and to limit the expansion of the slave system. Like other Atlantic Maroon wars, runaway Black slaves on the Gulf Coast created their own communities, in this case cooperating with Native Americans and some of the imperial rivals in the region, and they led a series of plantation raids that provoked American attempts to destroy Maroon villages in Florida. Their efforts were part of the long trajectory of armed Black resistance to slavery and the fight for emancipation, which did not come to the United States until 1865. It was also one of the last Maroon wars in the Atlantic world.[77]

But considering Maroon perspectives in the Gulf Coast borderlands from 1812 to 1823 also points toward an aspect of this Maroon war that was rare, if not unique in the Atlantic world, yet also reveals something about that world. Whereas Atlantic Maroons typically faced one or two imperial powers at a time, the Maroons in the Gulf Coast borderlands confronted three empires from 1812 to 1823. They had first allied with the Seminole and Creek Indians and Spanish in Florida against American ambitions, but as their war matured they both accepted and sought out British assistance before finally formalizing peace with the Americans. Their ability to do this in the Gulf Coast borderlands demonstrated how they could change alliances and transform competing imperial interests to serve Maroon ambitions. It was another case in which Maroons crossed racial divides to preserve their autonomy.

In another way, the fighting in the Gulf Coast borderlands also revealed how Maroons, often interracial communities made up of runaway Black slaves and Native Americans, could also continue to cooperate with established Native groups to preserve their own interests. Throughout Atlantic history, Whites tried to pit Natives against Black slaves and emerging Maroon societies as a way to divide and conquer. Yet Maroons and Natives often resisted these efforts and cooperated with each other to fight against White interests. Native Americans could often pit White empires against each other too, as could Maroons. In the Gulf Coast borderlands Natives and Maroons successfully cooperated with each other and did the same for entire generations against American imperial interests. They were successful until they began losing imperial allies, and eventually American military power overwhelmed them near the end of the first half of the nineteenth century.

The fighting in the borderlands during the period demonstrated that enslaved people still clung to militarized tactics and military service as an outlet to challenge chattel slavery in the Anglo-Atlantic. The militarization of resistance survived the American Revolution and continued to surge despite a growing abolition movement and increasing calls for nonviolence among some enslaved and free Black leaders in the Anglo-Atlantic. But soldiering was also something different for Maroons than it was for slaves. Enslaved people still rose to calls of emancipation during the period as they had done since 1676, yet Maroons also joined them even though they had already formed free and independent communities in thick forests and swamps in the Gulf Coast borderlands. War between Native Americans, Britain, and Spain seemingly intensified the military options for Maroons in the area, and as more plantation slaves fled to become Maroons or join others, they increasingly seized on these militarized options.

But by 1823 conditions also seemed to deteriorate for slave soldiers in the mainland Anglo-Atlantic. They were not free like their Caribbean counterparts in the West India Regiments, and they had lost the last European imperial rivals to ally with and resist slavery. Native Americans in the Southeast were on a sharp decline as well, and they too had lost the last European empires that could help them stop American expansion. By then, state militias prohibited enslaved people from serving, as did the U.S. Army in 1821. After 1823 enslaved people and Maroons would have to find other methods to militarize resistance and use military service to undermine slavery in the United States.[78]

The Gulf Coast Borderlands War also demonstrated how European imperial rivalries both supported and threatened Maroon communities in the Atlantic. Europeans needed Atlantic Maroons to support their imperial agendas, which in the borderlands area could mean undermining slavery among an imperial rival, when an empire's own slave interests were elsewhere. Maroons in the Gulf Coast borderlands assisted the Spanish in defending Florida, and they assisted the British in attacking American planters and taking in scores of plantation slaves. Their ability to play on multiple European imperial rivalries enabled them to negotiate for European support of their communities without signing a treaty that obligated them to suppress slave rebellions or return runaway slaves, which Maroon communities often did elsewhere in the Atlantic world. While Maroons in the Gulf Coast borderlands still used a hostile natural environment to take refuge, like their Atlantic counterparts in places like Jamaica, Suriname, and Brazil, they also found refuge in the complicated and shifting alliance systems of Native Americans and three imperial rivals in the region. Ultimately, all of the competing powers became enemies of the one slave power in the region, the United States, and this development favored the Maroons. But as the United States began to defeat its enemies one by one, the Maroon refuge deteriorated, and they too had to withdraw—ultimately to the point where they could no longer maintain distinct, autonomous communities.

In this case the multiple imperial rivalries that Maroons played on reinforced Maroon communities that challenged the Black chattel slave system. But multiple imperial rivalries at play in the Gulf Coast borderlands also threatened Maroon community formation and preservation. As the Maroons accepted Spanish and British help, they provoked American aggression. As they shifted from Spanish to Seminole and British assistance, they drew the ire of American and Spanish planters whose enslaved people ran away to join the Maroons. Throughout the Atlantic world, Maroons adopted various strategies to fight until they sooner or later could no longer hold out. In this Maroon war, they chose to fight with numerous allies in the region, and they lasted as long as those allies could or would fight against the growing U.S. slave power that ultimately overwhelmed them all.

Finally, the war was also another case in which slaves and then Maroons fought for a cause entirely different from Whites and Natives. Whereas Maroons took up arms for the British and Spanish to serve their imperial interests in Florida, the Maroons instead fought to challenge the Atlantic system and resist American expansion that would have certainly led to their demise. European allies certainly enabled the Maroons to fight for freedom in an environment in which White Americans aggressively pursued Black enslavement. In other words, the British and Spanish imperial authorities who sought Seminole and Maroon assistance could not control these groups, who pursued their own interests. The practice of arming the Seminole Maroons was as reliable a strategy as arming slaves throughout the Atlantic world, and it served broader and emerging British imperial ambitions, including abolition. But arming Maroons in the Atlantic may have also been something of a paradox, as European empires built on slavery continuously supported Maroons who challenged their rivals. European support for their Maroon allies ensured Maroon peace treaties that protected Maroon survival and autonomy throughout the Atlantic. European support had promoted the presence of powerful examples for plantation slaves to resist their enslavement. It promoted communities that were examples for millions of enslaved Africans to challenge the Atlantic system. It promoted communities that struck fear in Dutch, Portuguese, Spanish, British, and French slave societies, and it promoted Maroon peace treaties that could undermine empires built on slavery. Arming Maroons was clearly a double-edged sword. It both served some imperial interests and provided clear examples to other Maroons and slaves to undermine White empires elsewhere. Yet despite this challenge to the Atlantic system that Maroons represented, White imperial officials were always eager to arm them and support their survival so long as it targeted their imperial rivals and enemies. Maroon soldiers were eager to accept such support. This was the case in Florida, as it was throughout the Atlantic littoral, and the United States joined the fray as a republic.

CHAPTER 6

Resistance Militarized

Slave Soldiers in the First South Carolina Volunteers, 1862–1865

Runaway slave, Union soldier, U.S. congressman, and South Carolina state senator Robert Smalls is laid to rest in the Tabernacle Baptist Church Cemetery in Beaufort, South Carolina. Next to his resting place is a memorial bust, which has parts of his speech at the 1895 South Carolina Constitutional Convention: "My race needs no special defense for the past history of them and this country. It proves them to be equal of any people anywhere. All they need is an equal chance in the battle of life." On May 13, 1862, Smalls, who was enslaved at the time, left Charleston aboard the CSS *Planter* along with his family and several other unfree people in a daring escape to join Union forces. Smalls later proved himself an invaluable soldier as a skilled pilot and knew the meandering waterways throughout the Sea Islands scattered along the South Carolina and Georgia coasts. Officially, Smalls joined Company B of the First South Carolina South Carolina Volunteer Infantry Regiment, although he continued to serve as a pilot for the remainder of the war.[1]

Less than a mile from the Tabernacle Cemetery lie the remains of many of Smalls's comrades in arms at the Beaufort National Cemetery including Private William Verdier from Company G. Verdier was killed in action on July 10, 1863, after fighting Confederate soldiers at Willstown Bluff on the South Edisto River just north of Beaufort. Verdier was born in Pocotaligo, South Carolina, he was a waiter, and he had joined the First South Carolina Volunteers in late October 1862 in Beaufort. Like Verdier and Smalls, hundreds of enslaved men joined the First South Carolina and saw combat action in the Lowcountry from 1862 to 1865.[2]

For the hundreds of enslaved people who joined the First South Carolina Volunteers, running away to become a soldier had almost become an instinct. For more than 150 years in the Anglo-Atlantic, enslaved people had come to understand that massive war brought opportunity, and they knew that they could fight for freedom with an enemy army and occupying force nearby. They had learned for more than a century how military service might lead to emancipation, and in the spring of 1862 they began mobilizing for the final push to end the chattel system entirely.

Too often scholars and more recently the general public seem to believe that the story of Black people fighting for freedom, the end of slavery, and Union victory was in response to the Emancipation Proclamation and President Lincoln's leadership, with soldiers in the Fifty-Fourth Massachusetts Volunteer Infantry Regiment highlighted as some of the first people to respond to Lincoln's call to arms. In fact, slave soldiers were continuing their longer history of militarized resistance that reached a new phase in the Civil War, and it began in the Sea Islands, not in the parlors of Boston or Washington, D.C.[3]

Initial histories of the American Civil War excluded the exploits of Black regiments like the First South Carolina, and little was written about them except by abolitionists, civil rights advocates, and veterans of the regiments. In 1956 Dudley Taylor Cornish's *The Sable Arm* became the first comprehensive history of the more than 150 Black regiments that fought in the war, which paved the way for more research into the Black military experience. Since then many more historians have written about the Black regiments, classified as United States Colored Troops or USCTs later in the war, and nearly all comprehensive histories of the war at least mention the contributions of the USCTs and the 180,000 Black soldiers who served in the North's war effort. Likewise, histories focusing exclusively on the Black military experience during the war make note of the First South Carolina and its importance in helping mobilize enslaved people to fight in the Union army, although there is still no scholarly book-length history of the First South Carolina.[4]

The First South Carolina was the first Black unit in the Civil War to mobilize, and nearly all members in its ranks were former slaves from areas where the regiment fought. Like the cases in chapters 2 and 5, this chapter examines the final developments of slave soldiering in the same areas of northeastern Florida, Georgia, and South Carolina. Black experiences during the war were diverse, and the First South Carolina as a case study captures early moments of slave soldiering and armed resistance during the conflict. Like soldiers in the Ethiopian Regiment nearly a century before them, slave soldiers in the First South Carolina were not hermetically sealed from enslaved people elsewhere in the South, and they were not the only case of slave soldiering or armed resistance during the Civil War. But their case was localized to the Lowcountry, and the continuous Union occupation of some Sea Islands in the war where the regiment mobilized was also a unique experience for enslaved people in the South that offers a distinctive glimpse into how slaves ran away to become soldiers during the period. Finally soldiers in the First South illuminate how so many enslaved people ran away to become slave soldiers during the Civil War, which became the apex of the militarization of resistance in the Anglo-Atlantic. Their story illuminates how slave soldiers finally achieved their centuries-long goal to destroy the chattel system in the Anglo-Atlantic.

Opportunities to fight in large-scale armed conflicts had somewhat declined since the end of the Gulf Coast Borderlands Maroon War in 1823. While the age of revolution had more broadly expanded the opportunities for enslaved people to take up arms and serve as soldiers in the Anglo-Atlantic, besides soldiers tied to the British military, actual opportunities for slave soldiers to fight for liberation somewhat declined in mainland North America after 1821. In general, state militias excluded enslaved people from serving, while free and enslaved Black people were excluded from serving in the U.S. Army in 1821. More importantly, there were no opportunities to fight in large-scale war or armed conflict for nearly forty years in the U.S. South. Although some slaves and free Black people fought for Anglo and Mexican forces during the Texas Revolution and in the Mexican-American War, there were no large-scale attempts by enslaved people to run away to enemy forces and fight slaveholders, and nor were there consistent attempts or official policies to recruit slave soldiers and reward them with freedom for their service. Aside from Mexican campaigns into Texas in 1836 and borderlands skirmishes in Texas a decade later, the Civil War was the first time since the Gulf Coast Borderlands Maroon War that enemy forces invaded the U.S. South and deep into slave country.[5]

Unfortunately, most slave soldiers who served in the regiment were illiterate. Despite the construction of schools to educate freedmen and teachers who lived in army camps to teach soldiers basic literacy skills, there are only a handful of firsthand accounts regarding service in the First South Carolina by slave soldiers themselves. Yet it is clear from available accounts that runaway slaves joined the First South Carolina to attack chattel slavery and demand freedom for themselves and millions of other enslaved people. Ultimately, their fight became part of the apex of the militarization of resistance in the Anglo-Atlantic as hundreds of thousands of enslaved people took to military service to resist chattel slavery. Their efforts led to mass emancipation and finally abolition.

Slave Soldiering for the First South Carolina Volunteers

The idea among northern authorities that enslaved people could be valuable soldiers to help suppress the Confederate insurrection emerged in summer and fall 1861. On August 6, 1861, Congress passed the First Confiscation Act, which permitted the confiscation and seizure of Confederate property, including slaves, and declared that all people ordered to work for or provide services for Confederate military purposes were relieved of those obligations. According to the act, enslaved people who toiled away in support of the Rebel war effort were no longer obligated to do so. Southern slaveholders voided their claims to slaves who also worked on such projects. In many ways, the act was similar to Admiral Cochrane's proclamation that promised freedom to enslaved soldiers forty years earlier in the Gulf Coast borderlands, as well as Lord Dunmore's proclamation in Virginia in 1775. In 1814 Cochrane promised safe haven and free migration for unfree refugees in the borderlands if they reached British military lines. Lord Dunmore, meanwhile, declared martial law and freed all servants, convicts, and slaves who joined his forces to help restore "peace and good order." Enslaved people in South Carolina were following their predecessors in militarizing resistance to fight for freedom.[6]

The First Confiscation Act had little immediate impact on slaves in the South as the act could not be enforced in areas the federal army did not control. It did, however, lay the groundwork for new policies concerning how the Union army would confront Confederate plantations and the millions of enslaved people working on them during the war. By November, Union forces captured Hilton Head, South Carolina, along with hundreds of enslaved people still living on the island. Brigadier General Thomas Sherman had orders to use slaves as laborers and to ensure southerners still in the area that he would not disrupt daily life there. President Abraham Lincoln also ordered Treasury Department agents to prevent plantations from deteriorating and keep enslaved people working in the Sea Islands. Despite these policies, it was clear that plantation life had changed. Many Rebel masters had already abandoned the area and took slaves farther inland to safety. Those who stayed were under the constant guard of Union soldiers and northern agents. Enslaved people were also put to work building Union fortifications in the area. More enslaved people in nearby islands saw Hilton Head as a refuge and ran away to the Union camps there.[7]

The policy was an important step to further mobilize slaves as soldiers, and Frederick Douglass encouraged Union authorities to arm more slaves to defeat Rebel forces. In 1862 he wrote that Union forces "ought to be recruiting [troops] on the plantations of the south. We are striking the guilty rebels with ... [the] white hand, when we should be striking ... from the hand of the black man." Douglass knew that slave soldiers would be more easily mobilized than many northerners who did not support abolition or who were tepid to African American rights. If the Union would win the war and achieve emancipation, Douglass knew that northern White soldiers would not be enough to accomplish those goals.[8]

By March 1862 Major General David Hunter took command of the Department of the South and control of the Union-occupied Sea Islands. Hunter, an avid abolitionist, immediately sought to strengthen Union authority to undermine chattel slavery. At Hilton Head on May 9, 1862, he issued General Order No. 11, in which he declared all persons in South Carolina, Georgia, and Florida "heretofore held as slaves ... forever free." Hunter reasoned that since the three Rebel states were previously ordered under martial law in April, both slavery and martial law in a "free country" were "incompatible." Hunter's order built on the long history of militarized emancipation proclamations in the Anglo-Atlantic. Nathaniel Bacon in 1676, Lord Dunmore in 1775, and Admiral Cochrane in 1814 had all promised to free enslaved people who responded to their calls to fight for them. Hunter's order also served two purposes. As an abolitionist, the order was an emancipation proclamation and foremost struck a blow to slavery in the South where he commanded. As a commander, it weakened Confederate war efforts and further opened the door to recruit enslaved people to serve as laborers and soldiers for the Union army. In addition to Hunter's proclamation, he also ordered Union officers to immediately send all "abled-bodied Negroes capable of bearing arms" to his headquarters. He hoped to be able to raise two regiments with Captain Charles Trowbridge as the commander of the first company in nearby Beaufort, South Carolina.[9]

Hunter's order received immediate blowback in Washington from President Lincoln, who still worried about losing support from border states and northern Democrats. On May 19 Lincoln issued his own order, voiding Hunter's proclamation and reinforcing his authority as commander in chief as the only person authorized to give such instructions. While Lincoln admonished Hunter for his edict, he had also sent Congress a special message two months earlier stating that "the United States ought to co-operate with any State which may adopt a gradual abolition of slavery." In June congressmen also grew wary of what they heard about Hunter's operations in South Carolina. Kentucky representative Charles Wickliffe demanded that Secretary of War Edwin Stanton inform the legislature if Union forces were arming slaves. Stanton passed the message to Hunter who responded sarcastically and defiantly. He told Stanton that he had not formed a regiment composed of "fugitive slaves" but had in fact mobilized a regiment whose soldiers once belonged to "fugitive rebels." Hunter was unapologetic and happy that emancipation seemed looming. Just two months later Congress passed the Second Confiscation Act. The act declared that any enslaved person who deserted from a disloyal owner to join a Union garrison would be freed. Whether or not every Union officer was an abolitionist like Hunter, field officers appreciated the military value of hundreds of thousands of enslaved people in the South, and emancipation in exchange for their help seemed worthwhile. For would-be enslaved soldiers, freedom was palpable. They would capitalize on the largest conflict they had ever seen in North America.[10]

For many Union officers, abolitionists, northern politicians, free Blacks, and enslaved people, the spring and summer of 1862 seemed the right time to make slavery the sole focus of the war. They could use the massive conflict to finally free millions of people. But for many enslaved people on the front lines, however, the timing was not quite right. Although hundreds of slaves from the Sea Islands ran away to Union camps by the time Hunter issued his proclamation, many others refused to join Union forces. Instead they ran away and hid in nearby swamps and woods. Rumors abounded, especially those invented by slaveholders, that northern forces were preparing to send enslaved people to Cuba to help pay for the war. Some White recruiting officers who opposed enlisting slaves also spread the rumor. As a result, entire plantations were missing nearly all "able-bodied" men eligible to serve. According to plantation superintendent G. M. Wells, slaves had "'smelt a very large Rat,' and according to the expression of an old Man on the place had found it 'very necessary to go to the woods to split Rails.'" In bands of six to ten at a time, recruiters resorted to scouring adjacent woods and swamps to find the men, explaining to those they found that they were needed to serve in the army and that General Hunter wanted to see them. Recruiters told the slaves that they would be taken anyway if they did not volunteer, and they let potential recruits retrieve their clothes and supplies one or two at a time to prevent group flight. They also told women and children that they did not need to worry about being separated from their husbands and fathers. In other cases, the recruiters entered enslaved people's homes in the middle of the night and yelled at them to fall in for inspection. That tactic scared enslaved people even more, and many were "disheartened" by forcible recruiting techniques. Women "gave way to the wildest expressions of grief." Some clung to their male relatives and screamed in grief. Some had already lost friends and family members during the war and the migration of their former owners to the interior. For some, their husbands were their last surviving kin and their only source of income or support. They worried that if their husbands were taken, they would "die uncared for." It was clear that there was confusion and that practical impressment into military service was traumatic. Some enslaved people had already begun to lose what little "confidence" they had in northern White men. Thus it was no wonder that some emancipated people chose to run away from Union lines and avoid service.[11]

Special Agent Edward Pierce, charged with overseeing captured plantations in the Sea Islands, thought Hunter's initial techniques also caused trepidation among the formerly enslaved population there. Hunter's proclamation would take a majority of the people still cultivating crops in the area, and their departure to Hilton Head would effectively break up families. Men as soldiers would be reluctant to leave, and women and children would reject the men's departure.[12]

Hunter also relied on cooperative slaves to recruit even more people without resorting to coercive practices. In April 1862 Hunter approached Abram Murchison, a local slave minister who was very influential among Sea Island slaves. Hunter asked Murchison to get "the feeling of the blacks in regard to military organization," and at Hilton Head on April 7, Murchison held a meeting with Black men to determine their reception to military service. Murchison led the meeting in secret to prevent unwanted ears from listening, and only two White officials tied to the federal government were present. According to one newspaper report about the meeting, Murchison spoke to the potential recruits with "eloquence" and explained to them the potential advantages and disadvantages of military life. Murchison then asked all the men in the room who were willing to serve to stand up, and "every man sprang to his feet in an instant." By the end of the night, 105 men enlisted, and by the end of the week Murchison recruited 150 in total. Union authorities had to reject others who were infirm or too young to serve. Murchison was clearly an effective mobilizer of Sea Island slaves for Hunter's vi-

FIGURE 2. Sergeant William Bronson of Company A. From Higginson, "The First Black Regiment," 526.

sion of a large slave fighting force. Murchison himself never joined, probably due to his older age. He remained at Hilton Head during the war and continued to provide religious services to freed people and Black soldiers.[13]

Still other enslaved people fled to Union camps eagerly knowing that they would be free if they served. Between those eager to join and those pressed into service, Hunter was able to muster at least one company under the command of Sergeant (acting captain) Charles Trowbridge in 1862. Sergeant William Bronson was the first person to muster in the new unit. However, the first wave of slave soldiers in the First South Carolina was short lived. Many enslaved people resented their pay and equipment. The first recruits were not paid for several months, and their families were forced to support themselves. Morale was low and some men even deserted the ranks. Hunter was unable to issue commissions, and by August 9, 1862, he was forced to disband the regiment. Only Trowbridge and Company A, composed of thirty-eight men, survived the downsizing, and the detachment moved to St. Simons Island near Brunswick, Georgia, to protect free Blacks living there.[14]

FIGURE 3. Company A at Beaufort, South Carolina. From Higginson, "The First Black Regiment," 524.

Just as the regiment began to disband, the last remaining slave soldiers in Company A, along with a group of armed slaves, engaged Confederate forces for the first time. In August Union reports noted that Confederate guerrillas landed on St. Simons Island. Approximately five hundred Black people still lived on the island, and Union authorities wanted to ensure that the Rebel guerrillas did not harass, kill, or capture them to support the Confederate war effort. One Sunday, the guerrillas chased two contraband slaves named Adam Miller and Daniel Spaulding near the beach on the island. The men escaped and alerted other contrabands. Roughly ninety former slaves took up arms immediately, and the following day, under the leadership of Charles O'Neal, twenty-five went on patrol looking for the guerrillas. The detachment found and chased the Rebels into the woods and forced a Rebel retreat into an adjacent swamp. The guerrillas, led by local plantation owner Miles Hazard, took cover behind a felled tree and mounted a hasty defense. In the subsequent exchange on August 8, Black leader John Brown was shot and killed, as was O'Neal. Brown was the first Black soldier to die in the Civil War, and the small battle was the first encounter between slaveholders and slave soldiers in the massive conflagration. Shortly after, Trowbridge and his men arrived to assist the others, and together they searched for the guerrillas through woods and swamps for several days. At one point they discovered the Rebel camp in a thick palmetto forest and even destroyed one of their boats. The Rebels were effectively trapped on the island, and slave soldiers waited to exact their revenge. Before they were able to do so, a loyal slave came to the Rebels' aid and delivered them a canoe to secure their escape. The Rebels slipped away from the island without detection. Revenge would have to wait. There would be plenty of time to achieve it, however, and some slaves kept fighting, including Edward Gould, who stayed on to become a corporal when the regiment mustered into service again by the New Year. John Brown's father Uncle York also joined the unit later on, as did O'Neal's nephew Edward King.[15]

After the August skirmish, surviving members of the First South Carolina Volunteers remained in garrison duty on St. Simons Island until October. By November President Lincoln authorized the recruitment of slaves in the Sea Islands. By early November the soldiers had orders to conduct raids on the Florida-Georgia border, and on Monday, November 3, Company A departed St. Simons Island and headed south to St. Marys, Georgia, a coastal town on the St. Marys River, which ran along the Florida-Georgia border. In addition to Company A, White soldiers of the Forty-Eighth New York Volunteers under command of Colonel Oliver Beard boarded the steamer *Darlington* and headed south for the operation. Orders came from Brigadier General Rufus Saxton, who sent the men on the expedition to accomplish two objectives: "The first was to prove the fighting qualities of the negroes (which some have doubted), and the other was to bring away the people from the main-land, destroy all rebel salt-works, and to break up the rebel picket stations along the line of the coast." By then, President Lincoln had issued a preliminary Emancipation Proclamation, and slave soldiers probably knew that they could recruit more people to join their cause.[16]

The Black and White force first arrived on the Bell River in Florida and engaged Confederate picket lines. Shortly after they destroyed saltworks in the area, and then they sailed farther inland on the Jolly River and destroyed two more saltworks there. They also carried off provisions and rescued at least two enslaved families on their approach to St. Marys. The operation was a freedom raid. The next day the force sailed to King's Bay, Georgia, and gathered more provisions from Rebel plantations. While there, a detachment of approximately eighty Confederate soldiers engaged them, and the men killed at least two Rebel soldiers. Two days later they landed on Butler Island and acquired more provisions. They also approached Darien, Georgia, and captured at least three Rebel soldiers. Some of the Rebel prisoners were captured by their former slaves. Their capture was sweet vengeance for the bondsmen.[17]

By Friday, November 7, the men sailed up the Sapelo River, and another Confederate detachment of approximately eighty or ninety soldiers attacked them ten miles upriver. In the fighting at least one Black soldier was wounded, and after fending off the enemy, the men carried on and continued to target local saltworks. As they made their return downriver, yet another Rebel force engaged them, forcing the freedom-fighting soldiers to land on shore. At least five Rebels were killed and three Union soldiers wounded in the affair. According to Union accounts of the fighting, White officers were thoroughly impressed with the slave soldiers. They were excellent guerrilla tacticians, and as soon as the men rescued an enslaved recruit from the area, they put a "musket in his hand and he began to fight for the freedom of others." They had left St. Simons Island with sixty-two soldiers, but they returned after the week with 156 Black soldiers. They had freed another sixty-one women and children and destroyed nine saltworks. They killed nine Rebels in total and took three more as prisoners. They brought back more than $20,000 in horses, wagons, food, and other provisions. They had made thirteen different landings during the expedition, and according to General Saxton, the men had fought "with a coolness and bravery that would have done credit to veteran soldiers." The expedition was a "perfect success."[18]

The success of the first raiding expedition bred another before the end of November, and on November 13, three companies of the First South Carolina and men from the Forty-Eighth New York embarked again for the Florida-Georgia coast. On board the *Darlington* and the steamer *Ben Deford*, the men reached Doboy Sound on November 19. While conducting a reconnaissance patrol during the expedition, the former slave soldiers were attacked in dense woods and at least one man was wounded. Despite the surprise, the men rallied and drove back Rebel forces after firing more than fifteen volleys into the woods. At least three more men were wounded in the fighting. Yet again, Union officers were impressed with how their new soldiers fought, noting that they fought like true veterans even though some had never even held a musket just four days before the engagement. The men also carried away hundreds of thousands of boards and planks of lumber, as well as tools for the Union war effort.[19]

During fighting that fall, contraband slaves continued to flee to Union camps in the Sea Islands, while the early raiding expeditions led to the emancipation of others. By the end of November, 550 men had enrolled in the regiment, and Colonel Thomas Wentworth Higginson arrived by the end of the month to take command. At the time of Higginson's arrival, the First South was still too small to reach minimum strength as a regiment, and Higginson sent some of his officers to Florida to recruit more soldiers. Union camps in northeastern Florida provided a safe haven for more enslaved people to run away who could also be recruited to serve in the First

FIGURE 4. Engagement at the Doboy River, Georgia. From Higginson, "The First Black Regiment," 525.

South. By the end of the year there were enough men in the regiment to reach minimum strength. While still a small regiment, the *Chicago Daily Tribune* reported in mid-December that more than ten thousand enslaved people had been liberated near the Sea Islands. De facto freedom had come to many enslaved people in the area right before President Lincoln issued his Emancipation Proclamation. Still, soldiers in the regiment knew they could not stop. They knew they had to keep up the pressure to achieve their goal: freedom for themselves and for thousands of other enslaved people in their area of operations.[20]

News of Lincoln's proclamation had reached slave soldiers in the First South before the order even took effect. Nevertheless, officers like General Saxton and Colonel Higginson thought it was a good idea to boost morale and encourage more slaves to take up arms by celebrating the proclamation. On January 1, 1863, Saxton ordered soldiers to assemble for dress parade at Camp Saxton near Beaufort. More than three thousand soldiers and other plantation slaves assembled. They arrived at the parade grounds early in the morning, and many came alone, in pairs, or even as full squads. They assembled at an old oak grove that had once been part of a wealthy plantation. At the center of the grounds, Saxton, Higginson, Chaplain French, and the Reverend Peck sat at a stand. The ceremony began at 11:30 a.m., and after some music, Chaplain Fowler read the Emancipation Proclamation to the very large group. After Fowler, former slave owner William Brisbane read Saxton's remarks to the crowd, which Saxton wrote just a week earlier. In part he wrote, "It is your duty to carry this good news to your brethren who

FIGURE 5. Emancipation Day with the First South Carolina Volunteers. From *Frank Leslie's Illustrated Newspaper*, January 24, 1863, 276.

are still in slavery. Let all your voices, like merry bells, join loud and clear in the grand chorus of liberty—'We are free,' 'We are free.'—until listening, you shall hear its echoes coming back from every cabin in the land—'We are free,' 'We are free.'" The soldiers responded to the reading with twelve "deafening" hurrahs.[21] Then the group collectively sang J. C. Zachos's Ode for Emancipation Day, singing:

> Ye sons of burning afric's soil,
> Lift up your hands of hardened toil;
> Your shouts from every hill recoil—
> To-day you are free!
> A mighty aim has struck your chain,
> The same that broke a tyrant's reign,
> And took the Lion by beard and mane
> Beneath his knee.
> To-day you hear a nation's voice,
> To-day you have the glorious choice
> Forever, ever, to rejoice

> In freedom's reign;
> Or, ground to earth as fearful slaves,
> Your thirsting soul forever craves
> To find dishonorable graves
> From earthly pain.
> The sun of Liberty's first ray
> Reveals a shining throng's array;
> Millions unborn to hail this day—
> The day you are free!
> They spread their shadowy hands to you:
> O, fathers! to your sons be true;
> Snatch us the fruit that early grew
> On Liberty's tree!
> Oh! Abraham Lincoln, thanks to you,
> From every Christian heart you drew,
> The grand, the beautiful, the true,
> And sent it down
> To gladden, to uplift our hearts
> To give the life that hope imparts,
> The joy of dawn when night departs,
> And vails its frown.
> We hail this dawn of future days;
> And God's right arm that still upstays
> The cheering sun's perpetual rays,
> Now make us free.
> We thank the Lord, we thank the North,
> Whose breath hath sent the tidings forth;
> To-day a people's glorious birth—
> To-day we are free![22]

Following the ode, Chaplain French gave a short speech and soldiers again broke out in song, singing the patriotic song "America." Colonel Higginson then accepted the regimental colors from Corporal Robert Sutton and Sergeant Prince Rivers, and both men gave speeches. General Saxton also spoke, as did Francis Gage, who retold a story about a slave insurrection in the Danish West Indies. Gage told the audience that they had the power to make themselves free "in a single day" if they followed a similar course of action like the rebellious enslaved people in the Caribbean. Then the crowd sang "John Brown's Body" together. Once the parade ended, everyone on the grounds held a massive barbecue where they ate oxen and hard tack and drank water. Susie King Taylor, an enslaved woman who ran away from her owner months earlier and had married a soldier in the regiment, wrote that the ceremony "was a glorious day for us all, and we enjoyed every minute of it.... The soldiers had a good time. They sang or shouted 'Hurrah!' all through the camp, and seemed overflowing with fun and frolic until taps were sounded, when many, no doubt, dreamt of this memorable day." The celebration had exemplified their longer fight to turn war and armed conflict into opportunities to achieve Black freedom. They knew they might finally break the shackles of slavery if they did not stop. War and freedom had come together.[23]

Despite the jubilee of emancipation on January 1, 1863, soldiers in the First South quickly got back to work fighting for freedom. As had been the case for their predecessors in the Ethiopian Regiment nearly a century before them during the American Revolution, they would have to win the war to get their full freedom. The regiment officially mustered in on January 17, 1863, along with dozens of other Black regiments. The regiment had ten companies, each with sixty-four to eighty-two men. While the former slaves would compose the rank and file and could become noncommissioned officers, all commissioned officers were White men. Women and children could also serve as cooks, laundresses, nurses, and laborers in support of the regiment. It is unclear exactly how many enslaved women and children served in these capacities with the First South or with various USCTs during the war, but the scope and scale of their service far exceeded that of any other armed conflict in American history that preceded them. The Union army had thus opened more opportunities for enslaved people to serve and to militarize resistance even as they served in noncombatant roles. In short, the Civil War offered the greatest opportunity for enslaved people to serve in the military than ever before in the Anglo-Atlantic world.[24]

Just a week later, the regiment had orders to sail back to the St. Marys River again, once again to show their presence, capture supplies, and liberate slaves. With 462 men on board the steamers *Ben Deford*, *John Adams*, and CSS *Planter*, Colonel Higginson and the men left Beaufort for Georgia. When the men arrived at the St. Marys River shortly after, Rebel cavalry immediately engaged them overnight in a nearby patch of woods. At least one Black soldier was killed and seven more wounded, while twelve Rebels were also killed. Despite calls from soldiers in the unit to chase after the Rebels, Colonel Higginson refused to pursue them as he was unsure how many enemy soldiers they actually faced, and he thought it was not safe to chase them in the middle of the night. He later regretted his decision as they discovered the Rebel camp the next morning and realized they could have easily defeated the enemy had they kept up the pressure. Despite the setback, the men moved on and went farther inland to continue their raid.[25]

Approximately 250 soldiers onboard the *John Adams* moved nearly forty miles up the St. Marys River, where they encountered yet another Rebel cavalry force. From the banks of the river, Rebel soldiers fired heavily into the boat, riddling it with bullet holes. Higginson was amazed that so few of his men were seriously hurt despite the intense gunfire, and he attributed their safety to keeping most of the men below deck and behind armored plates. Still, the "men were wild to come on deck, and even implored to be landed on shore and charge the enemy." They had even fought each other for places to shoot through portholes that were open to engage the enemy. Similarly, regiment surgeon Dr. Seth Rogers detailed how eager the former slaves were to fight the Rebels. Corporal Robert Sutton, a former slave who grew up along the St. Marys River, fired two muskets from the pilothouse of the *John Adams*, giving a comrade his discharged weapon to reload after every shot. Sutton was wounded three times during the battle, including one wound to his skull, but he refused to give up fighting because this expedition was personal for him. Even when Dr. Rogers later ordered Sutton to stop and rest, Sutton refused, although he later "begged" Dr. Rogers to "forgive him" for disobeying his orders. Likewise, other soldiers on board fired back at the Rebels with great alacrity and rapidity, and they were heard shouting, "Neber gib it up!" They would not stop fighting for freedom. Captain Clifton, who had been on the deck during the engagement, was shot and killed. He remained the only Union fatality during the skirmish.[26]

Corporal Sutton was an invaluable asset for the expedition, as he grew up on the Alberti plantation in Woodstock, Florida, near the St. Marys River. He knew the geography of the area well, the plantations adjacent to it, and the local enslaved community there. He therefore helped pilot the *John Adams* as the men navigated the river in search of lumber, supplies, and slaves to recruit. At one point during the expedition, Sutton returned to the Alberti plantation and met his former owner, Mrs. Ernestine Alberti. Colonel Higginson arrived at the plantation and described their encounter. As told by Higginson, when he arrived at the plantation he addressed Alberti and called Sutton forward. Higginson asked Alberti if it were true that she had "previously been acquainted" with Corporal Sutton. When Sutton appeared, Higginson "never saw a finer bit of unutterable indignation than came over the face" of Mrs. Alberti. She recognized Sutton and replied that "we call him

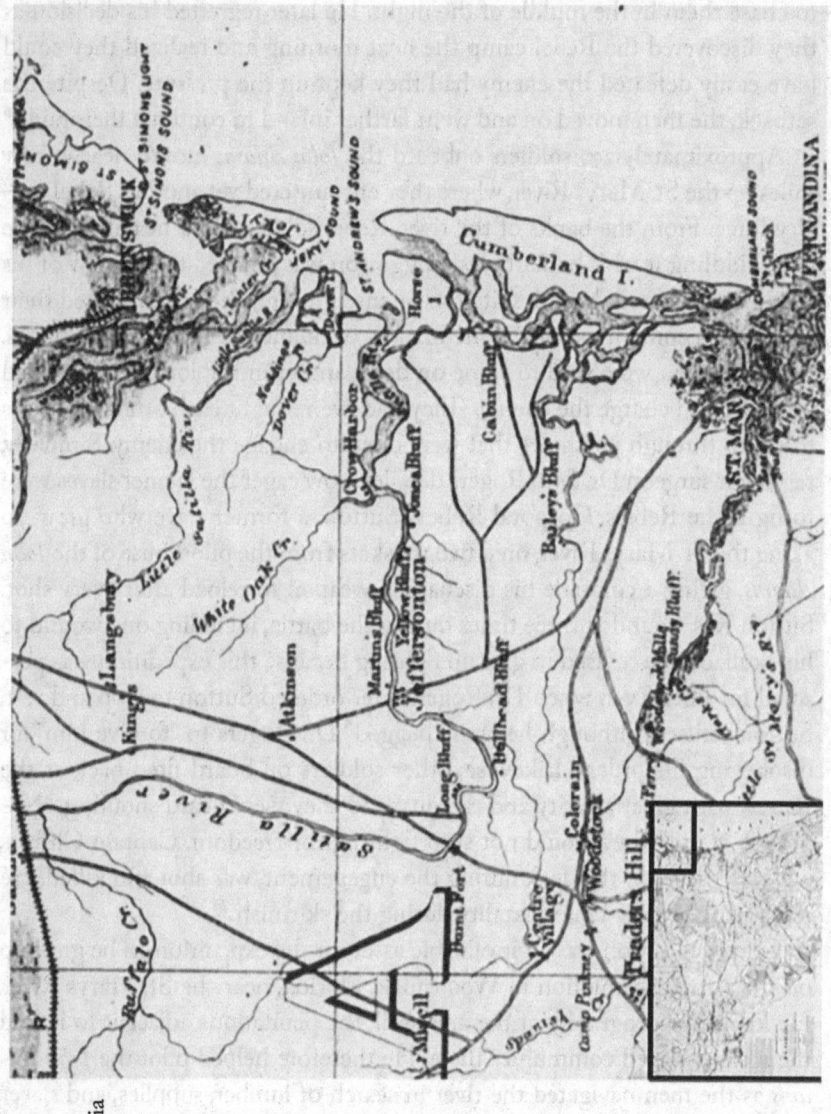

MAP 12. St. Marys River Area of Operations. Adapted from Wikimedia Commons.

bob!" Sutton did not speak to the woman, whose response undercut his authority as a soldier. Instead, he turned away from her, tipped his hat to Higginson, and asked him if he wanted to see the slave jail. Before they left, the soldiers took twenty-five sheep from the plantation. Sutton probably relished the opportunity to plunder his former owner's plantation. He probably also knew the encounter put his own safety at risk. If ever captured he would face severe treatment. He knew that if the Union would lose the war or abandon enslaved people like himself, he would face severe retribution for his service. He could not give up and he could not fail. His life depended on it.[27]

All told, the men succeeded in capturing more than 40,000 bricks, 250 iron bars, lumber, and more than two dozen sheep from St. Simons Island, Jekyll Island, and Woodstock, Florida, during the raid. Twelve Confederate soldiers were killed, and six more were taken prisoner. The raid was a "great success" in military terms. Higginson also reflected on its importance for his soldiers as liberated slaves more broadly. They ate the two dozen sheep they had captured from the Alberti plantation when they returned to their headquarters in South Carolina. Higginson wrote that the men enjoyed eating the "secesh sheep" and that "they frisked and fattened in the joy of their deliverance from the shadow of Mrs. A's slave-jail and gladly contemplated translation into mutton-broth for sick and wounded soldiers. The very slaves who once, perchance, were sold at auction with yon aged patriarch of the flock, had now asserted their humanity, and would devour him as hospital rations." The raid had not only resulted in the acquisition of vital military supplies but also enabled the men to exact revenge on their former owners, liberate even more enslaved people, and restore the humanity once stripped from them in chattel bondage.[28]

Less than two months later, the First South was sent into action again, this time on a larger operation to capture Jacksonville and recruit the thousands of enslaved people living nearby in its hinterland. While the men began loading supplies for the upcoming operation on March 3, formal orders came down from General Saxton on March 5. Higginson would lead the regiment along with Colonel David Montgomery and the Second South Carolina Volunteers. Significantly, the objectives for the mission included disseminating the Emancipation Proclamation to enslaved people in the area, to call on them to enlist in the Union army, to take control of as much of Florida as possible, and to "weaken, harass, and annoy" Confederates in the area. By March 10 the two regiments arrived in Jacksonville nearly unopposed.[29]

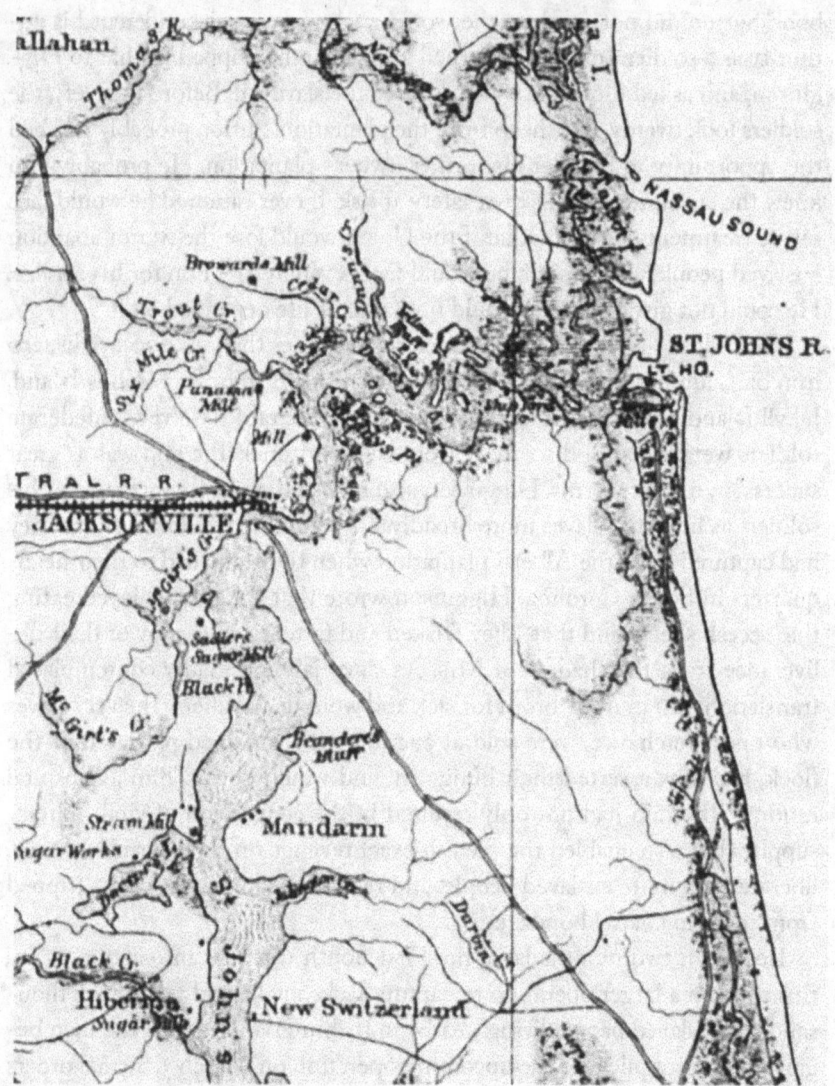

MAP 13. Jacksonville and St. Johns River Area of Operations. Adapted from Wikimedia Commons.

While the city was captured without much fanfare, the emancipated soldiers quickly chased and engaged Confederate picket lines in the outlying areas and on the St. Johns River. Even before the Union force began patrolling outside Jacksonville, there were reports of some Rebel guerrillas still in the city. They had reportedly put on blackface to disguise themselves, but once members of the First South discovered them and challenged them, the Rebels began firing and fled. From outside the city, Rebel soldiers shot at Union sentinels from a distance in the night. Rebel artillery also pounded the men inside city limits, delivering intense impacts that made some men fearful for their lives at every moment. Over the next week, companies of the First South participated in several raids up the St. Johns River and liberated dozens of slaves. While doing so, they also skirmished with local Confederate forces.[30]

As had happened months earlier along the St. Marys River, expeditions on the St. Johns River enabled emancipated soldiers to reunite with their families and meet their former owners. On one such mission to Palatka, Florida, Sergeant McIntyre met with his former owner, Governor William Mosely, who was a suspected Unionist. Since Mosely had been nice to him as an owner, Sergeant McIntyre wanted to persuade him to flee to the Union army and find refuge. Ultimately, the plea turned into a demand, and as Mosely refused to run away, McIntyre told him that he would take back his parents and sisters who were still held as slaves regardless if Mosely refused. Mosely consented and McIntyre took home his family except for his older mother, who decided to stay. Exactly why she chose not to reunite with her family is not known. Perhaps she did not want to risk capture and punishment. Perhaps she thought there would be another opportunity later. Maybe she did not think she could stay healthy enough to live in a Union camp. Regardless of her decision, she was at least able to see her son again and know that the rest of her family was reunited and living free with the army. In another case, Private John Quincy from Company G requested to join the expedition on the St. Johns to help liberate his enslaved family as well. His wife and two children were still held in bondage in Palatka, and he was motivated to reunite with them and take them back to freedom. He was not just seeking to free total strangers. Instead, he sought to emancipate his closest relatives, so the fighting was clearly personal. It is not clear if Quincy reached Palatka or reunited with his wife and children, but it was clear that riverine raids became liberating opportunities for members of the First South.[31]

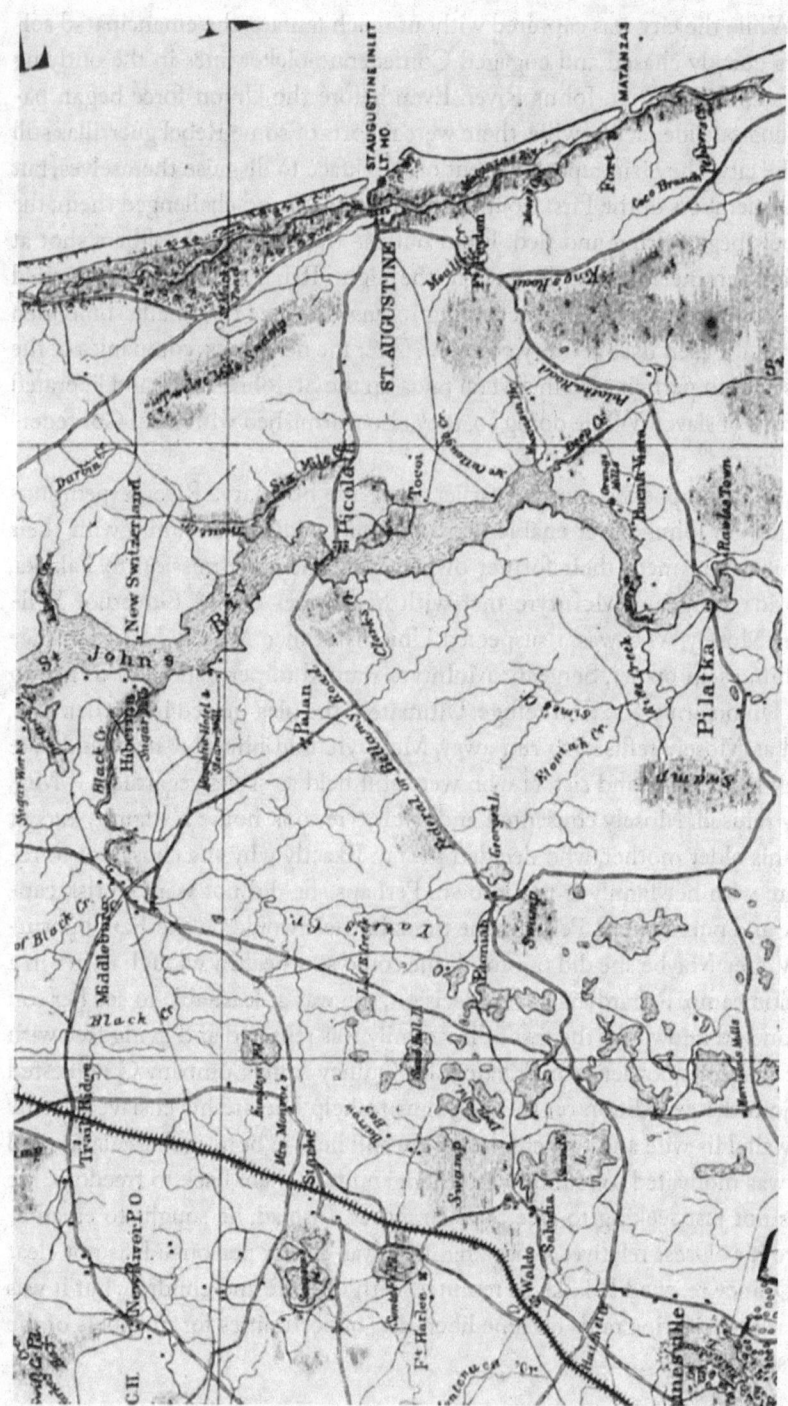

MAP 14. Palatka and St. Johns River Area of Operations. Adapted from Wikimedia Commons.

While the men were in uniform during their occupation of Jacksonville, Higginson authorized guerrilla activity on expeditions outside the city. On at least one occasion, Corporal Thomas Long from Company G received permission to set fire to a railroad trestle above a swamp to the west of the city. Long snuck out beyond the picket lines on March 25 and approached the trestle in civilian clothes. Seeing that the Rebels had guarded the location, Long realized he could not safely execute the plan and aborted the mission. He returned to his regiment three days later. The mission underscored the great lengths and risks that men in the First South took to fight for freedom for themselves and for others in the area. Had Long been spotted, he almost certainly would have been shot on sight.[32]

At the end of March, White soldiers from the Sixth Connecticut and Eighth Maine Infantry Regiments joined the First South on expeditions from Jacksonville. It was the first racially integrated force to go into action during the Civil War. Their action was short lived, however, as the force was recalled in April. While they had managed to occupy Jacksonville and successfully engage the Rebels on several occasions, recruiting new slave soldiers was not always as successful as they had hoped, and many plantation owners in the area had left with their slaves for the interior. The men moved north again to prepare for more fighting. In May soldiers in the First South served picket duty near the Coosaw River outside Charleston. Their comrades in the Second South Carolina Volunteers participated in more raids that also led to the liberation of hundreds of slaves on the Combahee River in June.[33]

While some enslaved people eagerly fled with soldiers in the First South during their emancipatory raids and expeditions, soldiers took others away by force. In one such case in 1863, Captain Alfred Sears complained in April that soldiers in the First South under Major J. D. Strong attacked contraband slave laborers under Sears's charge at Fort Clinch on Amelia Island in Florida. According to Sears, men from the First South seized Jeff Houston, Peter Williams, Jake Forrester, Sam Major, and John Wanton overnight in an apparent impressment raid. As a result, those still working at the fort were in a state of "panic," and Sears feared they might run away to the Rebels. Sears also believed that some of his men were complicit in the raid, including Reverend Kennedy, who sought revenge against Houston because he flirted with widows in the fort and whose actions were an "interference" with Kennedy's "pastoral duties."[34]

According to Forrester, Major Strong and Captain James approached his house in the evening and asked both him and John Wanton their names and where they worked. After their replies, Strong told the men that it did not make "any difference" where they worked and that he had orders to take the men. Strong then took the two outside and ordered them to fall in with fifteen to twenty guards, and they marched together to the impressment party's boat. Later the recruits reported to Colonel Higginson who asked them if they came to the regiment under their own volition. Forrester told Higginson that he had been "taken" against his will and that he did not wish to be a soldier as he had "plenty of chances before." Forrester asked for and received a pass to leave, and he returned to Fort Clinch a day later. Higginson later denied impressment strategies to his superiors, but Forrester's case illustrated how not everyone in the Sea Islands wanted to join the First South as a soldier to fight for freedom. Some people wished to farm or work for Union camps and probably wanted to avoid armed conflict altogether. Some probably wanted to avoid risking their lives any further by fighting in units like the First South Carolina. Impressment was needed to mobilize some soldiers during the conflict.[35]

In June Major General Quincy Gillmore replaced General Hunter as commander of the Department of the South, and he quickly developed a plan to attack Charleston with units like the First South. Gillmore believed that if Union forces captured Fort Wagner on Morris Island, Union artillery could bombard Fort Sumter, which protected the city's harbor. If Fort Sumter could be destroyed, Union gunboats could pound Charleston, which was of both important military and symbolic value in the war. Gillmore put Colonel Montgomery in charge of the main attacking force responsible for assaulting Fort Wagner, which consisted of both his Second South Carolina Volunteers and the Fifty-Fourth Massachusetts. Meanwhile, Colonel Higginson and men of the First South were charged with traveling up the Edisto River to the south and destroying a railroad bridge that connected Charleston to Savannah. They would help cut Rebel supply lines and prevent Confederate reinforcements from reaching Charleston.[36]

Higginson and the soldiers departed Beaufort on July 9 and first reached Confederate forces at Willstown at 3:00 p.m. the next day. With 260 men, two cannons, and three boats, the men routed the smaller Confederate detachment there, set fire to provisions and houses, and broke rice plantation sluices. They were using tactics just like thousands of militarized slave rebels before them on plantations in the area. Indeed, all across the Atlantic, militarized slave rebels frequently engaged slave owners and militiamen in open battle, and they routinely razed plantation homes and destroyed cash crops to undermine slaveholding power. Now it was happening again in South

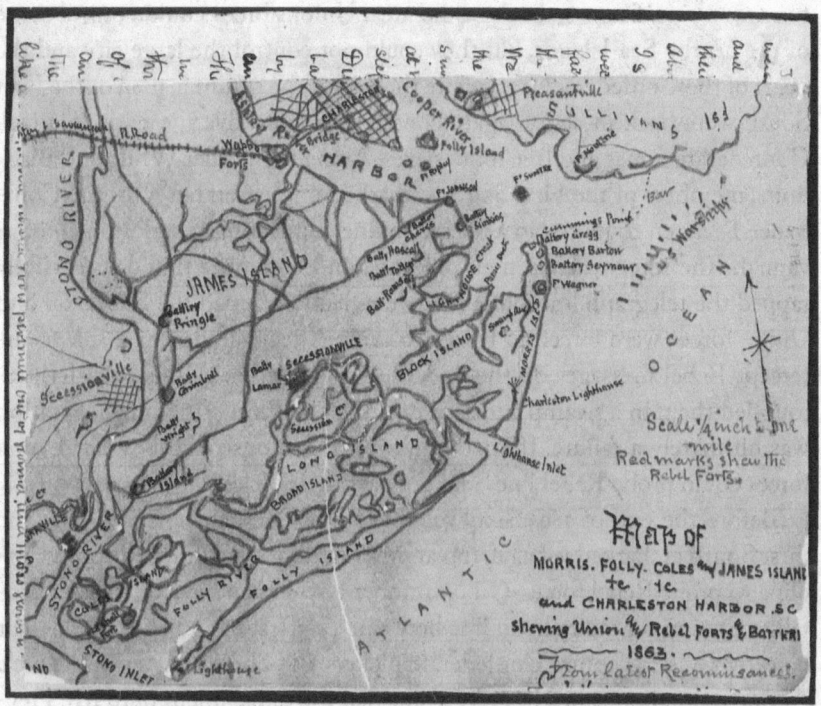

MAP 15. Map of Charleston Area Sea Islands. Adapted from Wikimedia Commons.

Carolina. The men continued up the river, but Confederate pilings and a low tide prevented their advance. Two ships ran aground, and by the time high tide returned, Rebels had placed an artillery battery near the First South's railroad objective, which prevented the men from successfully attacking. Before they could extricate themselves from the river, another ship ran aground and the men abandoned it and set it on fire. It was better to leave it than stay on and endure heavy Confederate fire. While they did not capture their objective, and while the remaining Union forces failed to capture Fort Wagner, the First South succeeded in liberating two hundred contraband slaves during the operation. They also destroyed several rice plantations and burned several houses. They had engaged Confederate artillery five times during the campaign. Private July Green from Company A was killed in action, as was Private William Verdier from Company G. They had died fighting for the freedom of others. One contraband slave was also killed, and another was severely injured. Higginson suspected that three Confederate soldiers had died in the action. Higginson himself was also wounded.[37]

The failure of Union forces to capture Fort Wagner and thereby Charleston was a significant setback in the area. Union forces could control some of the nearby Sea Islands, but they could not control the large city and the heart of the Confederacy. Yet before the end of the summer, men of the First South were back in action again conducting more riverine raids to attack Confederate forces and free more slaves. Along with other White and Black units, members of the First South embarked on September 9 for the Combahee River en route to tap a telegraph line connecting Charleston and Savannah. The force reached their objective on September 11 and successfully tapped the telegraph line, but a faulty connection tipped the Rebels off and Union forces were forced to return to camp. They would not be able to intercept Rebel messages on the line. On their way back, Rebel cavalry surrounded them in a swamp and captured several officers. The small operation was ultimately a failure. If anything, it only demonstrated how far Union forces could probe Rebel lines and get past their pickets.[38]

Before the end of 1863, sixty soldiers from Companies E and K in the First South embarked yet again on another raiding expedition in South Carolina to probe Rebel forces. On November 24 the men moved toward Pocotaligo Station on the railroad line between Charleston and Savannah. Their objective was to capture Confederate pickets and liberate slaves in the area. At one point, Sergeant Harry Williams led the detachment onto Mr. Heyward's plantation and liberated twenty-seven enslaved people before making their way back. As they headed home, dense fog set in and delayed their return. When the fog cleared, a Rebel cavalry detachment attacked the men. The Confederate soldiers, who also had five bloodhounds, sent the hounds after the Black soldiers. For the slave soldiers serving in the regiment, the bloodhounds assuredly reminded them of their enslaved past. Hounds were a frequent tool that slave owners and patrols used to track runaways and deter resistance. Now they were being used in combat. Soldiers in the First South must have been both angered and terrified by the tactic, but they knew they could not give in and fired back. They killed three of the dogs with bayonets as the dogs ran up to their lines. Another small detachment of ten men who guarded the flank killed the rest. At least two men drowned during the fighting, and several others were wounded. Two Rebel soldiers were taken prisoner. In an unusual battle that otherwise mimicked a White militia suppressing runaway slaves, the former slaves unleashed their wrath on the dogs. Slave soldier James R. reportedly skinned the dead body of one of the hounds to take to New York as a trophy. No doubt it was an act of revenge. The dogs had once prevented enslaved people from escaping slavery.

On that day in November 1863, escaped slave soldiers refused to let that happen again.[39]

By February 1864 northern strategists in the Department of the South were preparing for more campaigns in the region and possibly another assault on Charleston. They also decided to rename the First South to conform to Union standards. Almost a year before, on May 22, 1863, Secretary of War Edwin Stanton issued General Order no. 143, which created the Bureau for Colored Troops, thereby establishing the United States Colored Troops. In making the change in February, the First South Carolina Volunteers became the Thirty-Third United States Colored Troops. Despite the name change, many soldiers in the regiment still called themselves "De Fus' Souf," and they were proud of their military heritage throughout the war. They would not have to wait much longer for more combat action.[40]

In June Colonel Higginson left the regiment due to his earlier wounds. The men adored him and were saddened with his departure. Lieutenant Colonel Trowbridge assumed command. In early July 1864 the men were once again tasked with another assault in the Charleston area, including on Confederate batteries they had failed to capture just a year earlier with the assault on Fort Wagner. According to Susie King Taylor, a laundress and nurse attached to the regiment, when the men departed camp for the mission, the failure of Fort Wagner weighed heavily on them. Lieutenant Colonel Trowbridge told King, "Good-by Mrs. King, take care of yourself if you don't see us again." They were unsure of what would come next. The men left for James Island while other units involved in the multipronged offensive moved to the mainland, to Johns Island, and near Charleston's harbor. On July 2 they landed on James Island and became stuck in deep mud. Confederate cannons fired into the men as they strained to advance, and several men were wounded. In the end, Union forces involved in the assault failed to accomplish their objectives yet again. Charleston remained unattainable. After the failed attack, the Thirty-Third USCT went to nearby Cole Island for nearly a month.[41]

In November the regiment returned to Morris Island and skirmished with Rebels still there. By the end of the year, the Thirty-Third USCT returned once again on a mission to Pocotaligo Road. In the afternoon on December 20, Colonel Trowbridge sent a three-hundred-man reconnaissance team along the Tullifinny River and beyond the Union picket line. Within a mile of reaching the road, Rebel cavalry engaged the detachment. Despite a large fighting force well positioned in thick woods and a swamp, the Thirty-

Third USCT still made a strong charge against the Rebels and routed them. At least one Rebel soldier was killed, although Trowbridge suspected many more had been carried away in the hasty retreat. Seven Black soldiers had been wounded during the fighting, and Trowbridge noted that the area was too well fortified by felled trees and thick swamps to make another attack with regular troops. They would have to leave the area and let guerrillas fight. The men returned to their camp shortly after.[42]

As the war came to an end, the Thirty-Third USCT began occupation duty. At the end of February 1865, they entered Charleston as the Rebels evacuated it, and they helped save several buildings the retreating enemy had set on fire. On March 12 they marched to Savannah and then to Augusta, Georgia. Along the way they routinely encountered Rebel guerrillas who ambushed them from thick cover and concealment along the roads. Rebels even attacked the men at night in their camps when sentries were not vigilant. At least a handful of men died in these ways as the war came to an end. After a month in Augusta, the regiment marched back to Charleston and arrived there in November. They were officially mustered out of service in the Union army on February 9, 1866. Addressing the regiment on that day, Colonel Trowbridge reminded the men of their military heritage and the long journey they took part in since spring 1862 when he commanded Company A. He told them, "Soldiers, you have done your duty, and acquitted yourselves like men, who, actuated by such ennobling motives, *could* not fail; & as a result of your fidelity and obedience, you have won your *freedom*— And oh! How *great* the reward!" The former slaves, now free soldiers, had finally accomplished what they had set out to do nearly four years ago. They were free, and slavery was dead. The Thirteenth Amendment abolishing slavery had been ratified just two months earlier, on December 6, 1865.[43]

Reaching Union Lines

Despite the full mobilization of the First South in a matter of months, initial recruitment was mediocre. When General Hunter first ordered enslaved people to muster in, many rejected the order and ran away from Union recruiting officers. Many resented the coercive recruiting policies, and early recruits were also employed as military laborers, a condition that some believed did not substantially improve their livelihoods from slavery. Some were also scared to leave plantations because they feared reprisals from vindictive owners still living in the area, and they feared Rebel guerrillas who were eager to punish runaway slaves. On St. Simons Island in 1862, slaves were afraid to leave their owners during the day, and they were terrified that Rebels might kidnap them at night if they were caught off their plantations. Some people had probably even thought about what happened to enslaved people who ran away nearly a century before them during the Revolutionary War. Just as they had probably reflected on the thousands of enslaved people whom the British army largely abandoned in 1783, they knew that nothing was certain in 1862 and if the Confederacy would win the war they would face severe punishment for their actions.[44]

Recruitment was also mediocre because of low pay. There were reports that the first recruits were not paid at all, and when they did receive their pay, it was lower than what White soldiers earned. The July 17, 1862, Militia Act entitled Black privates to be paid ten dollars per month, but three dollars were deducted for clothing. In contrast, White privates received thirteen dollars per month and were given an additional clothing allowance. The differential was not resolved for most of the war, and pay was not equalized for Black soldiers until 1864.[45]

In addition, rumors that enslaved people were to be sold to new owners in Cuba also scared them and prevented some from joining the regiment. Union impressment efforts drove others to resist service as well. The fear that male relatives might die was also a mitigating factor. Sergeant Prince Rivers recalled how early recruitment caused consternation among family members. As Rivers helped recruit more soldiers, he said he still saw women "hold back" their husbands from fighting out of fear they might be killed. Some women stood in front of their husbands, and others helped hide them in the woods.[46]

Once it was clear that Union soldiers were not sending slaves to Cuba, enlistments increased. When some people also recognized that they did not have to be separated from their families or that any separation might not be permanent, enlistments improved. According to Clarence Mohr, among slaves who ran away from the Georgia Sea Islands, only six were recorded as having reached Union lines in 1861. The very next year, more than 150 did so, and eighty-one reached the Union army in 1863. More than 90 percent reached safety in groups of three or more, and the remainder at least ran away in pairs. Women and children especially fled to Union camps where they knew there would be refuge, like St. Simons Island. Following the camps was also a way to preserve families. Susie King Taylor was married to Private Ned King in Company E, and she had several more relatives in the regiment throughout the war. She had been in Savannah in April 1862 when the Union army attacked nearby Fort Pulaski, and she fled with her family to St. Catherines Island where Union soldiers protected them.[47]

Private Cato Wareing, or Uncle Cato, a nurse in Company F, amused his comrades with a campfire tale of how he escaped his owner and made it to Union lines safely. Wareing had been a driver, and he ran away the night before he was supposed to be punished for refusing to administer harder workloads to other slaves. He described how he approached his master's house in the middle of the night to steal food but instead encountered a dog that "flew" at him. The commotion woke up everyone in the house, and Wareing ran for his life. He crossed a fence to go to a nearby river. He waded through a nearby swamp the next morning to wash away his scent as he knew bloodhounds pursued him. He went days without eating and got lost on more than one occasion. At one point he snuck onto another plantation and entered the slave quarters to ask for food. Instead, he encountered another dog, which bit him. He "silenced" the canine with a hickory cane and traveled through more woods and swamps to avoid detection. He wandered for almost a month and a half, avoiding Rebel traps to catch runaways like him along local rivers. Finally, he hid on a river bank and watched passing boats so that he could approach them, show himself, and redeem his freedom. But Confederate ships also patrolled the waters, and Wareing had to be careful not to reveal himself to the wrong sailors. He slept in bushes as he waited for Union forces. Finally, he recognized a Union gunboat and presented himself with a white flag. He had found freedom. Wareing's story was a comic performance for slave soldiers in the regiment, but they could relate to his story, which in part made it amusing to them. His story was exemplary of several other soldiers who never recorded their own escape stories and how they reached the First South.[48]

In a similar way, Corporal Robert Sutton escaped from his plantation by floating down the St. Marys River. He hid on a dug-out canoe and navigated his way to Union lines. Once he found the correct way, he returned to his plantation to bring back his wife and his child named Jeff. While some soldiers might run back to their plantations to show their family members how to reach Union lines, there were reports that some of the soldiers in the First South also returned frequently to their former plantations to reunite with friends and family members throughout the war. They also used the trips as opportunities to hear gossip and news. They could also be opportunities to recruit more soldiers, although they did not always return to Union lines with more men to fight.[49]

Robert Smalls, an enslaved man working in Charleston, earned great fame for his escape from Charleston's harbor in 1862. His escape was also illustrative of how some enslaved people reached Union lines in the Sea Islands as the First South mobilized. Smalls began serving on the CSS *Planter* in the city's harbor in 1862, and the idea of escaping the area onboard the ship first developed as a joke among his companions. Over time Smalls and his friends began to think of the idea more seriously and held secret meetings to plan a course of action. When they were ready, they stockpiled three days' worth of rations in the ship's hold, and one Monday evening while on shore the men decided it was the right time. They also notified their family members that it was time to leave. At 3:00 a.m. on Tuesday, May 13, they set fire to the ship's boilers and began moving down the harbor. If they were caught, they would blow up the ship and kill themselves. They first moved to the wharf and picked up nine of the crew's family members who were hiding aboard the moored *Etowah*. The men picked up Robert's wife Hannah, their two children, four-year-old Elizabeth Lydia and toddler Robert Smalls Jr., and Hannah's eighteen-year-old daughter, Clara Jones. They also picked up W. William Morrison, who was a steward on the *Etowah*. Hannah's oldest daughter Charlotte decided to stay with her husband and did not escape with the group. The escape would separate the family. Crewman John Smalls's wife Susan and their child also came on board, as did Annie White and Lavina Wilson, who were both probably girlfriends of the other crew members.[50]

From the wharf, they moved out to sea. As they moved, they passed at least four Confederate checkpoints and gave the correct countersigns to Rebel sentinels at each stop. From the pilothouse of the *Planter*, Smalls passed each countersign as he wore captain's clothes and tried to impersonate the ship's Rebel commander, Captain Relyea, whom Smalls somewhat resembled. Once out of range of Fort Sumter's guns, Smalls and his crew lowered the Rebel flag, raised the U.S. flag, and approached the Union blockade. They had reached safety. In total, sixteen slaves escaped during the daring expedition, including Robert Smalls, John Smalls, Alfred Gradine, Abraham Jackson, Gabriel Turno, Samuel Chisholm, Abraham Allston, and David Jones. Though Smalls never officially served in the First South as an infantryman, he attempted to join the unit, and Union authorities instead thought he was of better use as a ship pilot throughout the war. Since he was illiterate he was also ineligible to attend naval training school, and thus he enrolled in Company B of the regiment. Although he did not serve as an infantryman, he did participate in several raids and engagements with the

First South as the pilot on the *Planter* for the rest of the war. Smalls's escape was daring, and the group risked exposing themselves to several Confederate soldiers along the way. Yet others who reached Union lines to join the First South risked similar odds and faced similar dangers as they hid from Rebel soldiers and their former owners in South Carolina, Georgia, and Florida.[51]

While it was clear that family groups and pairs were running away together in Georgia to reach federal forces, even more people were freed by coastal raids carried out by units like the First South. During one raid on the Combahee River, Union soldiers freed more than 725 people. The raid began overnight and in the early morning hours on June 3, 1862. Colonel Montgomery and three hundred soldiers from the Second South moved upstream under cover of darkness. Their guide was famed fugitive Harriet Tubman, who had led other escape efforts for years. Her renown among enslaved people in the region made her a perfect spy who could gather intelligence and help Union forces in the area. Together, the force passed several Confederate picket lines on the river and evaded sentries without firing a shot. Once they landed on the shores of the river, groups of slave soldiers marched directly to nearby plantations. From a distance, Rebel soldiers reported that they saw the slave soldiers set fire to plantation buildings as early as 6:00 or 6:30 a.m. At least fifty to sixty soldiers immediately approached Charles Lowndes's plantation and set fire to it. Another detachment approached the slave quarters to recruit bondsmen living there. Nearby on Colonel William Heyward's plantation, enslaved people informed the driver there that they saw Union gunboats on the river as early as 6:00 a.m. When the driver ordered them to disperse and hide in the woods, they "refused to obey, and scattered." Confederate reports of the mission repeatedly detailed how slave soldiers in the operation possessed the element of surprise and they had slipped out of the area before Rebel commanders could mount any semblance of an effective counterattack. Slave soldiers destroyed four plantations, six mills, and multiple outbuildings during the raid. The only structures left intact were slave quarters. The men did not shy away from Rebel soldiers and returned fire when shot at, but the expedition was somewhat covert, and Confederate soldiers did not know how to respond to the surprise "abolition raid." Slave soldiers suffered no casualties during the raid, and nearly all the men liberated during the operation became soldiers in the USCTs. Hunter reported to Secretary Stanton that he would send soldiers on more raids to free more people and bolster the ranks of the slave regiments serving in South Carolina.[52]

During emancipatory raids led by the First South, they carried off whole families at a time from plantations along rivers they patrolled. General Saxton also thought the first St. Marys expedition in November 1862 was a model for further recruitment. He proposed to Secretary Stanton to send more steamers up various coastal rivers and marshes to pick up more plantation slaves. He noted that once steamers would blow their whistle, slaves would "come in from every direction." He would have extra muskets and ammunition ready for the runaways, and they could start fighting as soon as they reached Union boats. If Rebel forces arrived, Saxton's forces would retreat and move to another area to recruit more enslaved people. He thought that if Union forces kept repeating this model, they "could very soon have complete occupation of the whole country."[53]

During the second St. Marys expedition in January 1863, Colonel Higginson reported how the spread of news further facilitated the willingness of enslaved people to help Union soldiers and join their ranks. Slaves who were "timid and distrustful" with the First South's presence in the area completely changed once soldiers informed them about Lincoln's Emancipation Proclamation. Once they were told they were free, they became eager guides and assisted the regiment's maneuvers.[54]

After the war, an anonymous soldier wrote to General Daniel Sickles in January 1866 and described the process of becoming a soldier and his motivations. He stated that most of the soldiers in the First South ran away in 1862 and 1863 to join Union forces and left behind most of their family members, including spouses, children, and parents. They ran away from slavery and "come Right in under the Bondage of Soldiers life." They had "Run Right out of Slavery in to Soldiery" under the agreement that they would be discharged at the end of the war and go back to their homes and find their relatives. They ran away without any possessions, and some lost touch with their relatives while in service. They had heard reports that their family members were suffering, and they were eager to return home and help. The man's plea revealed how rapid some decisions to join the regiment were. Caught up in the chaos and violence that armed conflict produced, some enslaved people had to make split-second decisions to run and join. They were often forced to separate from their families, even if they hoped they would eventually reunite. Some certainly believed their separation would be only for a short time, and some probably anticipated that they might not ever see their loved ones again. War made life too precarious, and the people who joined the First South could have no way of knowing what their situation would be just hours after they made the fateful choice to run away from slavery.[55]

Some soldiers later expressed that they knew military service was essential if they were ever to achieve a modicum of equality or respectability in a postwar society. They knew that they would have to enlist if a regiment like the First South arrived at their plantation, or if recruiting officers appeared nearby. The war might have achieved emancipation without slave soldiers fighting for it, but the men knew that they and their progeny would forever face racism and stigma if they had not served. On the first anniversary of the 1863 Jacksonville expedition, Corporal Thomas Long delivered a sermon to men at camp expressing these essential points and why it was necessary for slaves to enlist and fight:

> We can remember, when we first enlisted, it was hardly safe for we to pass by de camps to Beaufort & back, 'lest (unless) we went in a mob & carried our side arms. But we whipped down all dat. Not by going into de white camps for whip um; we didn't tote our bayonets for whip um; *but we lived it down by our naturally manhood*; and now de white sojers take us by de hand & say Broder sojer. Dat's what dis regiment did for de Epiopian (Ethiopian) race[.] If we hadn't become sojers, all might have gone back as it was before; our freedom might have slipped through de two houses of Congress & President Linkum's four years might have passed by & notin been done for we. But now tings can never go back, because we have showed our energy & our courage & our naturally manhood. Anoder ting is, suppose you had kept your freedom widout enlisting in dis army; your chilen might have grown up free, & been *well cultivated* so as to be equal to any business, but it would have been always flung in dere faces—'Your fader never fought for he own freedom'—and what could dey answer? *Neber can say that to dis African race any more*, (bringing down his hand with greatest emphasis on the table.) Tanks to dis regiment, never can say dat any more, because we first showed dem we could fight by dere side.[56]

Sergeant Rivers made similar sentiments earlier in 1863 when he spoke about how and why slaves took up arms in units like the First South. He stated that as soldiers, they were "men de first time in our lives. Now we can look our old masters in de face. They used to sell and whip us, and we did not dare say one word. Now we an't afraid, if they meet us, to run the bayonet through them." Moreover, Rivers stated he did not "intend to lay down my gun till the war is done, and our brethren all get their freedom—and then, if I be alive, I will come home and enjoy my family and my land." Fighting for the First South was a way for slaves to strike a final blow against chattel slavery and to liberate millions of unfree people.[57]

No matter how they joined or if they initially resisted military service, it appeared that many veterans held General Hunter in high esteem by war's end. They were appreciative of his efforts to promote abolition. Veteran of the Fourth USCT and Medal of Honor recipient Christian Fleetwood recalled that Hunter was an important figure for mobilizing slaves to fight in the war. He thought Hunter was due more credit than any other person for "the successful entry upon the stage of the Negro as a soldier in this war."[58]

Militarized Resistance

How slaves ran away to mobilize for the First South clearly showed how freedom was the impetus that urged them to join and fight. New recruits had an incredible opportunity to strike at chattel slavery and to free not only themselves but thousands of other slaves living in South Carolina, Georgia, and Florida. As the war progressed, perhaps they could extend their efforts to other states. While obtaining freedom for themselves and for others was crucial for how slaves took up arms and fought in the First South, to nearly everyone involved in the fighting it was clear how the slave soldiers were militarizing resistance and tying conventional rebelliousness to military service. The process of militarizing resistance was reaching its high point in 1862 in the Sea Islands.

Confederate soldiers and authorities made it clear early on that any slave who ran to Union lines and served in the Union army was participating in insurrection. Enslaved people caught off plantations were kidnapped or shot. Rebel Brigadier General Nathan Evans reported in January 1862 that he had captured fifty slaves on Edisto Island, many of whom had previously attacked his picket line. Evans recommended that the slaves be hanged "as an example. The negroes have evidently been incited to insurrection by the enemy." Slave insurrection had been a crime in every Confederate state, and many Rebels believed that Black Union soldiers should be punished accordingly.[59]

Lieutenant Charles C. Jones, who owned a plantation near the Georgia coast, wrote to his father in summer 1862 about what to do more generally with the slaves running to Union lines. He noted that if any White person was caught helping enslaved people run away to the enemy, they would be hanged immediately as if they were encouraging insurrection. Any slave caught inducing others to flee would be executed as well. His father replied and asked rhetorically about the slave soldiers. "Could they be taken up under the head of insurrection? Could their overt rebellion in the way of casting off all the authority of their masters be made by construction insurrection? They declare themselves enemies and at war with owners by going over to the enemy." By the end of the year, Confederate president Jefferson Davis also issued an order in which he proclaimed that all slave soldiers captured with the Union army would be delivered to the respective states where they once lived and treated in accordance of executive authority. They would not be treated as prisoners of war. Officers found "serving in company with armed slaves in insurrection" would be executed.[60]

Reporting on the First South's occupation of Jacksonville in March 1863, Confederate brigadier general Joseph Finegan also sounded the alarm about the effects of slave soldiers on the rest of the slave population. The Black troops were enticing slaves to run away and fight, and Finegan thought that "the entire negro population of East Florida" would "be lost and the country ruined there cannot be a doubt, unless the means of holding the Saint John's River are immediately supplied." Moreover, Finegan warned about "the danger of the permanent establishment of these posts of negro troops on the Saint John's River," as plantations in the area were connected to the river. Slave soldiers could easily maintain communication lines with plantation slaves along the watershed, and within a few weeks they could "corrupt the entire slave population of East Florida." It was clear that planters and Rebel soldiers equated slave soldiers as insurrectionaries, and as such they would be treated with the most severe punishments if captured.[61]

Likewise, Confederate battle reports of the June 1863 raid on the Combahee River expressed disdain for slave soldiers in the Carolina regiments. Captain John Lay called the expedition an "abolition raid" and thought that the Black soldiers were actually "negro wretches" who called themselves "soldiers." He also noted that they marched "with the incendiary torch to rob, destroy, and burn a large section of the country." By participating in the raid that was "designed only for plunder, robbery, and destruction of private property," slave soldiers "disregarded all rules of civilized war, and have acted more as fiends than human beings." Instead, he wrote, they were involved in the "fiendish work of destruction." In his view, they were not real soldiers or legitimate combatants.[62] His sentiment remarkably paralleled the tropes that White slave owners often employed when describing slave rebels, and it is not surprising that Lay applied the same language to slave soldiers tasked with freeing hundreds of people.

It was also noteworthy that many of the White officers in the First South and those who envisioned a large slave fighting force were abolitionists and tied to other acts of slave resistance before the war began. General Hunter was an ardent abolitionist and first ordered slaves to take up arms to undermine slavery at the start of the war. Colonel Higginson was also an avid abolitionist who had ties to radical John Brown. Higginson had previously traveled to Kansas Territory before the war to stop slaveholders from making the territory a slave state, and he helped fund John Brown's raid on Harpers Ferry in 1859. There was no doubt that when Higginson planned emancipatory raids in Georgia and Florida and led men into battle with objectives to liberate enslaved populations, Brown's raid weighed on his mind. He had, in fact, remarked after the war that he "had been an abolitionist too long, and had known and loved John Brown too well, not to feel a thrill of joy at last on finding myself in the position where he only wished to be." Likewise, Colonel Montgomery, commander of the Second South Carolina Volunteers, was a radical abolitionist as well. During one engagement, Montgomery reportedly ordered five Rebel prisoners shot to avenge the deaths of five of his own soldiers who were executed on capture. Dr. Seth Rogers thought that the order reflected Montgomery's ambitions and that he "seems to me one of the John Brown men of destiny." John Brown's resistance legacy was clearly influential among White leaders of the Carolina regiments.[63]

In February 1863 the *New York Tribune* reported news about Hunter's plans to conduct raids along the St. Johns River. The news was probably leaked to the press from Hunter's office, and the newspaper reported that the plan was to "surprise the Rebels, not with the phantom, but the reality of servile insurrection." Furthermore, the newspaper reported that slave soldiers had kept some lines of communication with bondspeople still living on plantations, and that the arrival of slave soldiers in the area would cause thousands of unfree people in northeastern Florida to rise up and "sweep both Rebellion and Slavery out of existence." Higginson later pushed back against the characterization that he was inciting slave insurrection during that expedition, but his orders were nonetheless to "carry" the Emancipation Proclamation to the enslaved population and recruit them into the Union army.[64]

Higginson, who had thought and written about slave resistance in the Atlantic world, once asked Sergeant Rivers why enslaved people in the United States did not rise in insurrection before the war. Rivers told Higginson, "What would be de use. What could dey do? No gun, no sword, no knowledge, no chance—no nothing." He told Higginson that slaves remembered the long tradition of betrayal and how revolts were rarely successful. But with the help of the federal government, Rivers knew that people would fight. As a recruiter he told fellow slaves that it might be their "last chance" to fight and that they had a "good chance" of being successful. Higginson believed that by waiting until they had the support of the Union army at their side, they ensured that Black emancipation would become a factor in the war. Had they rebelled too soon, Higginson thought, northern states would have been forced to help the South suppress slave insurrection, which would have also undermined support for emancipation by the end of the war. Waiting to join the Union army and to militarize resistance secured enslaved people their freedom.[65]

Like Higginson and Montgomery, former slaves in the First South routinely talked and sang about John Brown, and they clearly admired his radical efforts to use militarized methods to undermine slavery. They sang about him in camp and on marches, and they sang about him during the 1863 Emancipation Day dress parade. Higginson also noted that men in the regiment had a deep obligation to free those still in bondage. In January 1863 he proposed to the men to pledge themselves "to be faithful to those still in bondage," and they "heartily" agreed. Only one man initially refused the pledge, telling his comrades that his wife was with him and no longer living as a slave. According to Higginson, other soldiers were "indignant" with the man, and they "shoved" him around and called him a coward as they marched back to camp. The incident was emblematic of how soldiers in the First South viewed their mission and the extent to which they were committed to it. Now was their chance to strike a final blow to chattel slavery, and anyone in the ranks who was unwilling to help others was not tolerated.[66]

It was also noteworthy that Harriet Tubman, famed conductor of the Underground Railroad, also carried out expeditions with the Carolina regiments during the war. Tubman arrived in Beaufort in spring 1862 and at first served as a nurse for the slave soldiers serving in the area. Her work as a resister also made her a valuable operative, and Hunter employed her as a spy later on in the war. She could work with other runaway slaves in the area, gather intelligence, and help soldiers navigate various winding waterways. Importantly, she had led the Second South's raid on the Combahee River in 1863 to free hundreds more people, and she continued to lead Black rebels in South Carolina for several years. Tubman thought that Black people deserved more credit for the raid, which exemplified the final process of the militarization of resistance. She was a fugitive slave who led other armed fugitives, and they attacked their slave owners during a military operation to free more enslaved people. They were not loyal slaves who enlisted in an army to fight for a different cause in hopes that their loyal military service might grant them their individual freedom. They were not fighting for their owners. They were rebels attacking their owners, and they hoped that they could destroy chattel slavery once and for all.[67]

In some ways, the manner in which enslaved people joined the First South and how they fought for emancipation paralleled John Brown's emancipation raid. Brown, with twenty-one followers, had hoped to incite a massive slave insurrection with his attack at the Federal Arsenal at Harpers Ferry, which would eventually lead to abolition in the South. At midnight on Sunday, October 16, 1859, Brown and his followers crossed the Potomac Bridge and made an assault on the arsenal. They shot watchmen who refused to join them and all those who stood in their way. Among Brown's immediate followers were several free Black men and former slaves who wanted to free people in the area. By October 17 Brown's forces had engaged the local militia and proslavery forces, and they fortified the arsenal in preparation for future attacks. In the process they armed approximately twenty to fifty slaves in the area with pikes and firearms, and at least fourteen slaves helped guard prisoners, transport weapons, and defend the raiders' position. By October 18, U.S. Marines arrived to suppress the uprising and assaulted Brown's position in town. They shot and killed several of the rebels during the short engagement, while they shot at as many as three hundred armed slave rebels who were across the Potomac River in Maryland. The rebels scattered and hid in the woods once it was clear the rebellion had failed. Without a strong professional army to reinforce them like the First South, the rebels understood that their plan had faltered. In the end, seventeen to twenty-seven Black rebels died in the insurrection, which helped spark the Civil War. Many more continued to destroy property in its aftermath to avenge Brown's subsequent execution. Some ran away after the rebellion, while Brown's abolitionist friends and financial backers like Higginson carried on the cause during the Civil War.[68]

Conclusion

After the war, soldiers in the First South began work on occupation duty and set out to enjoy the fruits of their newfound freedom. They officially mustered out of service in the Union army in January 1866. Some probably joined one of the many Black militia units that developed during Reconstruction to protect freed people, and some probably joined the federal army to serve in campaigns elsewhere. At least a few men immediately sought political office to improve the lives and condition of emancipated people. Sergeant Prince Rivers became a delegate to South Carolina's Constitutional

Convention and served three terms in the state legislature. He also served as a judge in Aiken County northeast of Augusta, Georgia. Likewise, Robert Smalls attended the Constitutional Convention and served as a state senator and U.S. congressman before his death in 1915. Most others went to nearby towns in the Lowcountry such as Savannah to find work.[69]

Landownership was also a priority for veterans, who knew that they would be forced to work for their former owners and in similar conditions if they could not acquire their own plots. In 1863 Sergeant Rivers indicated that he did intended to enjoy his land once the war was over. He also discouraged soldiers from taking the best plots and to let the elderly, infirm, and women buy cleared land. Before the regiment mustered out in 1866, another veteran petitioned General Daniel Sickles to release men from service so that they could move back to their homes and acquire cheap land. He wanted to be able to buy land before others could take advantage of his absence. Likewise, Sergeant Rivers wrote to General Saxton about how veterans could acquire land. Rivers asked Saxton if it were true that the government was disbursing plots to veterans, and if he could acquire a piece of his former owner's plantation. Perhaps he believed he was avenging his bondage by taking his old master's land. It was at least some due compensation for a lifetime of unfreedom.[70]

By fighting in the Union army and against their former owners, slave soldiers in the First South were able to make a massive war *entirely* about emancipation and Black freedom. The long trajectory of militarizing resistance had changed from turning armed conflicts into incidents that raised the specter of Black emancipation, into the Civil War in which the outcome was dependent on Black freedom. The Civil War became a conflict in which Black freedom was at its core. Slave soldiers would not fight without their freedom, and the North would not win without their help. The South could not win with rebellious slaves who took up arms against slave owners. There would be no dispute about the future of chattel slavery once the war was over. In the end, the First South set the stage for the participation of hundreds of thousands of enslaved people and free Blacks to serve in the Union military, and to link their final acts of resistance to slavery to military service.

Slave soldiers in the First joined a professional army in a time of crisis, much like some of the slave soldiers who came before them in the seventeenth and eighteenth centuries. But they also nudged a large professional army further toward emancipation, and together with thousands of other slave soldiers in other USCT regiments, they made the Union army devoted to Black emancipation in order to win the war. This objective had not yet been achieved in the Anglo-Atlantic with rank-and-file slave soldiers. The British Empire had come close to achieving this objective decades before, but by the time the empire had devoted its military efforts toward abolition, all the soldiers in its military were free and did not face the prospect of re-enslavement if they were defeated in their energies.

There were also important differences between the soldiers in the First South and their predecessors in the Second West India Regiment, the Ethiopian Regiment, and the Gulf Coast borderlands Maroons who fought with the British army. European imperial rivals no longer exerted as much pressure or influence in mainland North America as they had decades before, and the Native American population in the Lowcountry had dwindled and could not match the influence it once had. Slave soldiers were thus left with two competing expansionist powers: the North and its commitment to preserve the Union and further free soil ideology, and the Confederacy and its aggressive policy to expand chattel slavery everywhere within its reach. In this environment, slave soldiers in the First South could not really pit imperial rivalries against each other as they once had, and their only real option to fight for freedom was to ally with a powerful Union army.

The Union army also gave more enslaved people an opportunity to use military service to challenge the chattel system. Women and children who were not allowed to be combatants could still serve as camp cooks, laundresses, nurses, and laborers. Some like Harriet Tubman found ways to serve as spies and guerrillas to free more people. If they did not choose these options, they faced separation from family members who did. Yet family ties could also be strengthened as relatives escaped slavery and served together in units devoted to ending chattel slavery. These had been options for enslaved people running to the British military in previous conflicts, but the scope and scale of these opportunities during the Civil War reached its peak in the broader Anglo-Atlantic.

Finally, while slave soldiers in the First South represented the apex of the militarization of resistance to slavery in the Anglo-Atlantic, they also represented the beginning of a shift to the militarization of resistance to discrimination, injustice, and civic inequality. They had earned legal freedom with their service and by winning the war, but they still faced an uphill battle in obtaining basic equality in a deeply segregated and racist postemancipation society. With these new obstacles, so began their turn to use military service to promote civil rights. In the immediate aftermath of the war, de facto freedom would come by organizing Black militia units to combat terrorist organizations like the Ku Klux Klan, and to gain control of farmland that White slaveholders had once owned. More would also come as former slave soldiers and their descendants exchanged military service for a greater stake in U.S. society, as Black soldiers would do in the last Indian Wars in the American West, during the Spanish-American War, in both world wars, Korea, Vietnam, and into the twenty-first century. Black soldiers, like earlier slave soldiers, would have to shed more blood to achieve their goals.

EPILOGUE

Enslaved people in the Anglo-Atlantic took up arms in several conflicts for more than two hundred years. They first fought for slaveholders and for the planter regime in the seventeenth century. They served as soldiers to protect imperial projects, including slavery, from the seventeenth to the nineteenth centuries. But while slave soldiers fought to protect imperial interests, including the plantation slave system, in the Anglo-Atlantic, they also turned armed conflict and war into something else. Often they turned their participation in imperial conflict into acts of resistance, in which slave soldiers fought for Black liberation. In other words, they turned war and armed conflict into struggles about slavery itself, at least from their own perspectives.

As early as 1676 in Virginia, enslaved soldiers took up arms in Bacon's Rebellion. They were among the last soldiers who kept fighting, and it was clear that they refused to surrender because they were in "distrest of their hoped for liberty."[1] So many slave soldiers took up arms in the colony that they raised the specter of emancipation and even forced King Charles II to issue a proclamation to promote it in order to protect this royal possession. Their fight for freedom revealed that the chattel system had already taken root in early America, and it had produced the first crisis to threaten that system.

Something similar was going on in the Carolina Lowcountry by the early eighteenth century. Slave soldiers took advantage of Indian warfare and the nearby presence of Spanish colonists in South Carolina, Georgia, and Florida to resist. During the Yamasee War in 1715 they made colonial warfare about Black liberation, as they took up arms with Native American and

Spanish allies and fled to Saint Augustine in groups. They fought their former owners and found refuge in Florida. Imperial and Native allies intensified slave soldiers' ability to mutate armed conflict compared to what could happen during internal imperial crises like what occurred in the Chesapeake decades earlier. Conversely, armed resistance could be mitigated with certain conditions and colonial policies that had also been in place in the Lowcountry that were also absent in the Chesapeake years earlier. By law, slave soldiers could use loyal military service for their owners to achieve personal manumission, which encouraged many to take up arms for their masters and for the defense of the English plantation system in the colony. Notwithstanding these policies, slave soldiers still threatened the slave system by fighting against English interests in the colony.

The age of revolution opened more opportunities for enslaved people to take up arms, become soldiers, and turn warfare into movements that supported emancipation and freedom. Revolution also led to an increase in the militarization of resistance. Throughout the Atlantic imperial and revolutionary armies became agents of mass emancipation, and enslaved people increasingly took up arms in conflicts in which offers of freedom and emancipation were vital for their mobilization. In British North America, a professional army gave more enslaved people, including women and children, an opportunity to use military service to challenge the slave system. Black rebels of the Ethiopian Regiment fought against their owners in Virginia for freedom at the start of the Revolutionary War, and some continued to fight elsewhere after they evacuated the Chesapeake and migrated north to New York. They had tied revolutionary rhetoric and ideology with their military service as they wore the words "liberty to slaves" inscribed on their uniforms. Many survived the conflict to find freedom in Canada and then Sierra Leone. With the success of the Black Loyalists like those who served in the Ethiopian Regiment, the age of revolution also led to the first permanent peacetime corps of professional enslaved soldiers in the Anglo-Atlantic and the establishment of the West India Regiments shortly after. Military service and armed resistance in the Anglo-Atlantic had thus changed as slave soldiers professionalized. While the ability to join a professional army and fight for freedom expanded in British North America after the American Revolution, actual opportunities to join were limited to European armies as White Americans increasingly excluded Black people from military service in the early Republic. Slave soldiers had become too great a threat to the American slaveocracy.

As permanent, peacetime, and professional soldiers, slaves in the West

India Regiments could not simply use military service to fight for freedom and emancipation like their predecessors. Stationed in the Caribbean in the early nineteenth century, they could not turn to potential Native American allies to alter armed conflict either. Instead, slave soldiers had to *create* armed conflict to achieve their goals, which they did in April 1802 when soldiers in the Eighth West India Regiment mutinied over concerns that they were going to be disbanded and sold into plantation slavery. Although these rebellious soldiers were defeated, they shook the plantation system in Dominica to its very core. Their actions ultimately contributed to the mass emancipation of all slave soldiers in the West India Regiments just a few years later, thus freeing thousands of enslaved people from the military-slave system in the Anglo-Atlantic.

By the nineteenth century thousands of slave soldiers were using professional military service as capital for emancipation. By 1812 enslaved people took up arms and became Maroons who allied with Native Americans and the British army to challenge American plantation expansion in the Gulf Coast borderlands. Nearly 150 years after they first challenged the plantation system in Bacon's army, they still fought against it. Yet Native, British, and Spanish allies all helped Seminole Maroons attack the plantation system and sustain armed conflict against American planters for more than a decade. Unlike their predecessors a century earlier in the Carolina Lowcountry in 1715–1717 and in the Chesapeake in 1676, the Seminole Maroons also joined professional armies to resist chattel slavery. Despite an expanding abolitionist movement in early America that was tied to rhetoric and ideology of the American Revolution, Maroon soldiers who fought American planters in the Gulf Coast borderlands proudly flew British flags at their fort at Prospect Bluff. They did not make appeals to Patriots of a generation before them. Much like the soldiers in the Eighth West India Regiment a decade before, the appropriation of revolutionary ideology among enslaved and Maroon soldiers was seemingly limited in the Anglo-Atlantic.

While revolution opened more opportunities for enslaved people to take up arms and serve as soldiers in the Anglo-Atlantic, the ability to fight for other European armies and Native Americans in mainland Anglo-America eroded in 1823 with peace at Moultrie Creek. The British and Spanish left the continent, and Native Americans in the Southeast had suffered a substantial defeat. Slave soldiers on the mainland could no longer play on European imperial rivalries to resist the chattel system, and potential Native American allies were increasingly becoming less reliable. After 1823, slave soldiers in the mainland would have to learn other ways to use military service and militarized methods to resist the chattel system. The next large-scale opportunity to do so came nearly forty years later during the American Civil War, when hundreds of thousands of enslaved people ran away to the Union army and fought their former owners.

The militarization of resistance reached its apex in the broader Anglo-Atlantic during the American Civil War when more than one hundred thousand enslaved people fled to the Union army and fought to end slavery. They formed all-Black units and led efforts not only to defeat Confederate forces but also to free and liberate scores more of unfree people from southern plantations. Soldiers in the First South were at the tip of the spear in these efforts, and they seized the initiative months before Union leaders warmed to the idea of slave soldiers. By 1865 slave soldiers finally earned what they had been fighting for centuries for: broad and widespread mass emancipation. No longer were their efforts limited to regional success, and after they were done fighting, millions of unfree people would benefit from the fruits of their labor.

Slave soldiers in Virginia in 1676 and 1775–1776, in South Carolina in 1715–1717, in Dominica in 1802, in the Gulf Coast borderlands in 1812–1823, and in the Sea Islands in 1862–1865 demonstrated that Black armed resistance against slavery in early America and the British Atlantic was more pervasive than historians have realized. Enslaved people and Maroons increasingly used military service to rebel against chattel slavery. The opportunity to do so emerged as a viable option in the seventeenth century with the rise of the Atlantic chattel slave system, and it increasingly became a stronger option as the chattel system matured. In various conflicts during the rise of the Atlantic chattel system, slave soldiers turned those conflicts into opportunities for freedom for themselves and others in the area. Historians often stress the danger and futility of slave revolts as a form of resistance, with the exception of the Haitian Revolution, but slave rebellion when part of war and armed conflict often became the best opportunity for freedom from chattel slavery. As the Atlantic chattel system became more developed and violent, enslaved people increasingly used military conflict to rebel against it. Their ability to do this in the eighteenth century peaked during the American Revolutionary War and continued well into the nineteenth century, as more conflicts erupted that opened opportunities for enslaved people to become soldiers. They ultimately set the stage for the absolute peak of militarized resistance in the Anglo-Atlantic during the American Civil War, when hundreds of thousands of slaves and free Blacks ran away or joined the Union army to help win the war and eventually abolish slavery in the United States.

By using military conflict to resist chattel slavery, enslaved soldiers helped militarize resistance in the Anglo-Atlantic. Military service became a viable option to attack chattel slavery, and slave soldiers seized on opportunities that military service offered. They did so alongside other slave rebels who relied on martial tactics, techniques, and procedures to achieve the same goals. They used military structure and military violence to achieve their goals.

The increasing militarization of resistance also reflected how enslaved people attempted to integrate into colonial society and that of the early U.S. Republic. Militarization offered competing rebel visions of slave societies: the ability to withdraw and isolate from them entirely, or to challenge, reform, and remake them. In the seventeenth and early eighteenth centuries, soldiering meant overturning slave societies and withdrawing from them altogether. By the age of revolution, it meant reform and change. Either way, slave soldiers used the same militarized methods to achieve these visions. Alongside the rise of Creole and White leaders and rebels who promoted more peaceful approaches to advancing emancipation and abolition, such as in Barbados in 1816, Demerara in 1823, and Jamaica in 1831, slave soldiers continued to rely on military methods and violence to fight for freedom. Like plantation and Maroon rebels, slave soldiers complemented other abolitionist approaches, and together they helped lay the groundwork for full emancipation that enslaved people finally achieved in the British Empire in 1838 and in the United States in 1865. Their actions were ultimately part of a longer military history of abolition in the Anglo-Atlantic.[2]

The connection between war and slavery for Black soldiers of the African diaspora in the Atlantic world also changed in the process of their enslavement in Africa, their forced migration to the Americas, and their participation in armed conflict in the western edges of the littoral. Whereas soldiers defeated in battle in Africa were often sold into the transatlantic slave trade, on the other side of the Atlantic enslaved people took to war and armed conflict to undermine that very same system at least in the localities where they lived.[3] In all of the above cases, they at least threatened that system regardless of their success. They threatened the chattel system in some places even if they represented only a tiny fraction of the millions of people caught up in the Atlantic slave trade. By the time of the American Civil War, they finally achieved broader success and helped free millions of enslaved people in the U.S. South. Slavery's soldiers were thus a double-edged sword: soldiering, rebellion, and *grand marronnage* often were or became the same thing. Slave soldiers both defended and challenged the Atlantic chattel slave system through military service. Those who chose the latter did so in ways that were similar to how plantation rebels and Maroons challenged the plantation regime. They used violence, military knowledge from Africa, North America, and Europe, and organizational structures to attack the plantation regime. As they did this, they transformed the slave societies in which they lived. Military forces, military discipline, and military surveillance increasingly defined slave societies and were tools that Whites used to control Black slaves and Maroons. But recruitment of enslaved soldiers by proponents of slave regimes to protect them from imperial rivals or Native Americans also gave enslaved people and Maroons an outlet to resist that same system. Slaves and Maroons turned the militarization of slave societies on its head, and they used military service, structure, and violence to undermine chattel slavery without destroying all of the societies that had so mistreated them. In the end, slavery's soldiers revealed how people from below could transform slavery, war, and freedom despite the intentions of people above.

NOTES

Abbreviations

ADM	Admiralty Papers, National Archives, Kew, United Kingdom
ADD. MSS	Additional Manuscripts, British Library, London
ASFR	*American State Papers Foreign Relations*
ASPMA	*American State Papers Military Affairs*
BL	British Library, London
CO	Colonial Office, National Archives, Kew, United Kingdom
CSP	*Calendar of State Papers*
FO	Foreign Office, National Archives, Kew, United Kingdom
HSP	Historical Society of Pennsylvania, Philadelphia
NBL	Newberry Library, Chicago
NDAR	Naval Documents of the American Revolution
OR	*The War of the Rebellion: A Compilation of the Official Records of the Union and Confederate Armies*, 128 volumes
PKY	P. K. Yonge Library of Florida History, Gainesville
SCBPRO	Records in the British Public Record Office Relating to South Carolina, Newberry Library, Chicago
WO	War Office, National Archives, Kew, United Kingdom

Introduction

1. *Report of the Proceedings of a Meeting*, 23; March 27, 1864, entry in Looby, *Complete Civil War Journal*, 209, 210.

2. Edmund Doyle to Captain R. C. Spencer [n.d.] and Doyle to John Innerarity, April 6, 1815, both in "Panton-Leslie Papers," 238; Honychurch, *Dominica Story*, 113.

3. James Johnson to Unknown, November 16, 1775, in Curle, "Intercepted Letters of Virginia Tories," 342; Edmund Pendleton to Richard Henry Lee, November 27, 1775, in Mays, *Letters and Papers of Edmund Pendleton*, 1:132; Colonel William Woodford to the President of the Convention at Williamsburg, Return of Prisoners Taken after Great Bridge, December 12, 1775, in Scribner and Tarter, *Revolutionary Virginia*, 5:118; *Book of Negroes*, book 1 [1783], Sir Guy Carleton Papers, Nova Scotia Archives Microfilm, no. 10149, http://novascotia.ca/archives/africanns /archives. For Menéndez, see Landers, "The Atlantic Transformation," 215–220, 227; Landers, "African-Yamasee Ties," 180; Memorial of Jospo in Manuel de Montiano to Philip V, March 3, 1738, AGI SD 844, reel 15, P. K. Yonge Library of Florida History, Gainesville (hereafter PKY).

4. Kupperman, *Providence Island*, 170n72; Handler, "Freedmen and Slaves," 1–25; Voelz, *Slave and Soldier*, 24, 437; S. C. Ukpabi, "West Indian Troops," 136.

5. Restall, "Black Conquistadors," 171–205; Thornton, "Armed Slaves," 79–94.

6. Nell, *Services of Colored Americans*; Hartgrove, "Negro Soldier," 110–131; Quarles, "Colonial Militia and Negro Manpower," 643–52; Quarles, *Negro in the American Revolution*; Kupperman, *Providence Island*, 170n72; Handler, "Freedmen and Slaves," 1–25; Altoff, *Amongst My Best Men*; Christopher Brown, "Arming Slaves in Comparative Perspective," 330–353; Buckley, *Slaves in Red Coats*; Buckley, *British Army*; Clifford, *From Slavery to Freetown*; Dyde, *Empty Sleeve*; Egerton, *Death or Liberty*; Horne, *Negro Comrades of the Crown*; Nash, *Forgotten Fifth*; Gene Allen Smith, *Slaves' Gamble*; Walker, *Black Loyalists*; Joseph Wilson, *Black Phalanx*.

7. Aptheker, *American Negro Slave Revolts*; Genovese, *Roll Jordan Roll*; Linebaugh and Rediker, *Many-Headed Hydra*; Bastide, *African Civilizations*; Mintz and Price, *Birth of African-American Culture*; Schwartz, "Cantos and Quilombos," 247–270; Mullin, *Flight and Rebellion*; Mullin, *Africa in America*; Sidbury, *Ploughshares into Swords*; Thornton, "African Dimensions," 1101–1113; Thornton, "I Am the Subject," 181–214; Rucker, *River Flows On*.

8. Millett, *Maroons of Prospect Bluff*; Leaming, *Hidden Americans*; Lockley, *Maroon Communities in South Carolina*; Diouf, *Slavery's Exiles*; Sayers, *Desolate Place*. See also Frey, *Water from the Rock*; Curtin, *Rise and Fall*; Paul Lovejoy, "Problems of Slave Control," 235–272; Lovejoy and Hogendorn, *Slow Death for Slavery*; Paul Lovejoy, "Fugitive Slaves," 71–95; Klein and Roberts, "Banamba Slave Exodus," 375–394. See also Rivers, *Rebels and Runaways*; Rivers and Brown, "Indispensable Man," 1–23; Hahn, *Political Worlds of Slavery*; Hahn, *Nation under Our Feet*; Barcia, *West African Warfare*; Thornton, "African Dimensions"; Childs, *1812 Aponte Rebellion*; Vincent Brown, *Tacky's Revolt*; Henry Lovejoy, *Prieto*.

9. For typologies of resistance, see Kilson, "Towards Freedom," 175–187; Twyman, *Black Seminole Legacy*; Genovese, *From Rebellion to Revolution*; Mullin, *Flight and Rebellion*, 36–38, 93, 162; Patterson, *Sociology of Slavery*; Thornton, *Africa and Africans*, 273; Craton, *Empire, Enslavement, and Freedom*, 179.

10. For differing contemporary definitions of slave rebellion, see United States Adjutant General's Office, *Federal Aid in Domestic Disturbances*, 258nA; Saunders,

Colonial and State Records, 23:202; Mattoso, *To Be a Slave in Brazil*, 142; Aptheker, *Slave Revolts*; Geggus, "Slavery, War, and Revolution," 6. For participation rates in various rebellions, see Pannet, *Report on the Execrable Conspiracy*, 2; Wood, *Black Majority*, 146, 302; Dormon, "Persistent Specter," 402; Allmendinger, *Nat Turner*, 183, 197.

11. Scholars who express this opinion in these systems of slavery include Worden, "Revolt in Cape Colony Slave Society," 11; Stilwell, *Slavery and Slaving*, 173; Genovese, *From Rebellion to Revolution*; Toledano, *As If Silent and Absent*; Paul Lovejoy, *Transformations in Slavery*, 34. See also Miers and Kopytoff, "African 'Slavery,'" 1–81; Sears, *American Slaves*. For material deprivation, see Grouse, *French Pioneers*, 100; see also *Continuation of the State of New-England*, 19; Oldmixon, *British Empire in America*, 50, 51, 52; Kea, "When I Die," 172; Thompson, "Berbice Revolt," 79; Mullin, *Flight and Rebellion*, 126; Viotti da Costa, *Crowns of Glory*, 28; Aptheker, *Nat Turner's Slave Rebellion*, 9, 15, 16; Geggus, *Haitian Revolutionary Studies*, 60; Reis, *Slave Rebellion in Brazil*, 11, 18, 20; for more on this theory, see Craton, *Empire, Enslavement, and Freedom*, 187.

12. For cases in which rebel leaders were personally motivated, see Sidbury, *Ploughshares into Swords*, 56; Allmendinger, *Nat Turner*, 67.

13. Rucker, *River Flows On*, 102; Egerton, *Gabriel's Rebellion*, 53; Genovese, *From Rebellion to Revolution*, xiv; Viotti da Costa, *Crowns of Glory*, 21, 101, 239.

14. For oaths, see Aboagye, *Indigenous African Warfare*, 433; Reindorf, *History of the Gold Coast*, 116; Rucker, *Gold Coast Diasporas*, 181, 183. See also Hanserd, "Gold Coast," and Hanserd, "Okomfo Anokye," 531–535.

15. Voelz, *Slave and Soldier*; Christopher Brown, "Arming Slaves in Comparative Perspective," 335; Restall, "Black Conquistadors," 197; Landers, "Transforming Bondsmen into Vassals," 121, 122, 123, 125; Mattos, "Black Troops," 8, 10; Schwartz, *Slaves, Peasants, and Rebels*, 107; Kraay, "Arming Slaves in Brazil," 152; Morgan and O'Shaughnessy, "Arming Slaves," 181, 183; Klooster and Oostindie, *Realm between Empires*, 181; Price and Price, *Stedman's Suriname*, lxxn8; Manuel, "Slavery, Coffee, and Family," 20, 21; Garrigus, *Before Haiti*, 104; Hanger, *Bounded Lives, Bounded Places*, 118; Westergaard, *Danish West Indies*, 246n6.

16. Handler, "Freedmen and Slaves," 19; Kupperman, *Providence Island*, 170n72; Philip Wright, "War and Peace," 12, 20; Bollettino, "Of Equal or More Service," 510–533; Bollettino, "Slavery, War, and Britain's Atlantic Empire"; Quarles, "Colonial Militia and Negro Manpower," 643–652; Morgan and O'Shaughnessy, "Arming Slaves," 180; Voelz, *Slave and Soldier*, 17, 18, 24, 30, 112, 113, 114. Resistance strategies among enslaved Black people differed in other systems of slavery. For example, see Alpers et al., *Resisting Bondage*, 2.

17. Christopher, *Slave Ship Sailors*, 62; Costello, *Black Salt*, xx, 9.

18. Edmund Morgan long ago argued that the rebellion transformed Virginia by promoting White unity at the expense of Black slavery. The rebellion thus facilitated the rise of the Black chattel system in the colony. See Edmund Morgan, *American Slavery, American Freedom*, 345, 368–369, 386.

19. For the thousands of slave soldiers who served in the age of revolution and in

wars of independence in the Iberian Atlantic, see Blanchard, *Under the Flags of Freedom*; Rebecca Scott, *Degrees of Freedom*; Kraay, "Arming Slaves in Brazil," 159–164, Escheverri, *Indian and Slave Royalists*; Higgins, *"Licentious Liberty"*; Lyman Johnson, *Workshop of Revolution*.

20. Morgan and O'Shaughnessy, "Arming Slaves," 180.

21. Cornish, *Sable Arm*, 92; Trudeau, *Like Men of War*, xx.

22. Anonymous to General Daniel Sickles, January 13, 1866, in Berlin et al., *Freedom's Soldiers*, 777.

Chapter 1. Enslaved Rebels Fight for Freedom

1. William Berkeley, Proclamation to Pardon Rebels, September 7, 1676, in Billings, *Papers of Sir William Berkeley*, 543; The Royal Commissioners' Narrative, in Michael Oberg, *Samuel Wiseman's Book of Record*, 167, 168; George Chalmers Collection, Virginia 1. Digital Collections, 189, New York Public Library, http://digitial collections.nypl.org.items.

2. Thomas Grantham to Henry Coventry, November 21, 1677, Henry Coventry Papers, 77:302, microfilm, reel 901, Virginia Colonial Records Project, Virginia State Library, Richmond.

3. Linebaugh and Rediker, *Many-Headed Hydra*, 136; Webb, *1676*, 21; Rice, *Tales from a Revolution*, 216; Breen, "Changing Labor Force," 3–25; Edmund Morgan, *American Slavery, American Freedom*, 369; Russo and Russo, *Planting an Empire*, 117; Wertenbaker, *Torchbearer of Revolution*, 31; Washburn, *The Governor and the Rebel*; Coombs, "Beyond the 'Origins Debate,'" 239–278; Kruer, "Bloody Minds and Peoples Undone," 405; April Hatfield, *Atlantic Virginia*.

4. Heywood and Thornton, *Central Africans*, 6, 7, 236, 237, 238, 275, 276; Thornton, "African Experience," 421, 434; Deal, "Race and Class," 194, 224; Parent, *Foul Means*, 64; Knight, *Working the Diaspora*, 66–70; Edmund Morgan, *American Slavery, American Freedom*, 327; the Trans-Atlantic Slave Trade database, Slave Voyages, https://www.slavevoyages.org/voyage/database; Gomez, *Exchanging Our Country Marks*, 107; O'Malley, *Final Passages*, 132, 151, 160. For Africans in Virginia, see Berkeley's estimate in Billings, *Old Dominion*, 118.

5. Sprinkle, "Loyalists and Baconians," 29, 67, 137, 229; Thomas Holden to Williamson, February 1, 1677, in Blackburne Daniell, *Calendar of State Papers*, 18:530 (hereafter *CSP*); Hening, *Statutes at Large*, 2:395; Philip Ludwell to Joseph Williamson, June 28, 1676, in Fortescue, *CSP*, 9:414–415; Samuel Wiseman's Book of Record, in Neville, *Bacon's Rebellion*, 319–323.

6. William Berkeley, Proclamation, September 7, 1676, in Billings, *Papers of Sir William Berkeley*, 543; Mathew, "The Beginning, Progress, and Conclusion," in Andrews, *Narratives of the Insurrections*, 35; "Bacon's and Ingram's Rebellion," in Andrews, *Narratives of the Insurrections*, 60, 65, 67–68; Cotton, "An Account of Our Late Troubles in Virginia," in Force, *Tracts and Other Papers*, 1:7–8, 24; "Personall Grievances," in Michael Oberg, *Samuel Wiseman's Book of Record*, 284, 286; Al-

NOTES TO CHAPTER ONE   217

len, *Invention of the White Race*, 2:213; Commissioner's Resolve, in Michael Oberg, *Samuel Wiseman's Book of Record*, 192; Washburn, "Sir William Berkeley's 'History,'" 411; "*A true narrative*" (Speech, National Archives, Kew, Colonial Office [hereafter CO] 5/1371, part 2, 1676/10/17), accessed October 28, 2018, http://www.colonial america.amdigital.co.uk, 394, 395; Chalmers Collection, Virginia 1, 189; Klooster, "Slave Revolts," 402, 413; Webb, *1676*, 121; "Bacon's and Ingram's Rebellion," in Andrews, *Narratives of the Insurrections*, 94. For more on the kidnapped Loyalist wives, see Kathleen Brown, *Good Wives*, 166; Commissioners' Narrative, in Andrews, *Narratives of the Insurrections*, 122.

7. The destruction is best exemplified by petitions and personal grievances submitted after the rebellion, including a complaint by Otto Throp in Michael Oberg, *Samuel Wiseman's Book of Record*, 258. The rebels also destroyed Charles Roane's estate after Bacon's untimely death. See Webb, *1676*, 110; Ludwell to Williamson, June 28, 1676, in Fortescue, *CSP*, 9:414–415.

8. Journal of the Ship Young Prince, Robert Morris, Commander, in Fortescue, *CSP*, 9:450–455.

9. "Character of the Severall Commanders," in Michael Oberg, *Samuel Wiseman's Book of Record*, 276; Grantham to Coventry, November 21, 1677, 77:301–302.

10. Grantham to Coventry, November 21, 1677, 77:302; "The History of Bacon's and Ingram's Rebellion," in Andrews, *Narratives of the Insurrections*, 94.

11. Grantham to Coventry, November 21, 1677, 77:301; "Personall Grievances," in Michael Oberg, *Samuel Wiseman's Book of Record*, 268, 271, 272; King Charles II, "Proclamation against Nathaniel Bacon," February 1, 1677, in Billings, *Papers of Sir William Berkeley*, 552.

12. Ligon, *True & Exact History*, 46; *Great Newes from the Barbadoes*, 9–10, 45, 46; Report of the Commissioners, in Fortescue, *CSP*, 13:733–34; Handler et al., *Plantation Slavery in Barbados*, 45; "Personall Grievances," in Michael Oberg, *Samuel Wiseman's Book of Record*, 286. For St. John, see Kea, "When I Die," 168, 172; Thornton, "African Dimensions," 1101–1113; "The Commissioners' Narrative," in Michael Oberg, *Samuel Wiseman's Book of Record*, 164; Pannet, *Report on the Execrable Conspiracy*, 17.

13. Beckles, *Black Rebellion in Barbados*, 37, 44, 45; *Great Newes from the Barbadoes*, 9–10; Report of the Commissioners, *CSP*, 13:733–34; Handler, "Slave Revolts and Conspiracies," 15, 16, 25, 26.

14. Pannet, *Report on the Execrable Conspiracy*, 13, 17; Kea, "When I Die," 160, 176; Craton, *Testing the Chains*, 75–77; Thornton, "War, the State, and Religious Norms," 197, 198; Governor Hender Molesworth to William Blathwayt, August 29, 1685, in Fortescue, *CSP*, 12:82, 83; Knight, "Natural, Moral and Political History of Jamaica . . . 1742," British Library (hereafter BL), ADD. MSS. 12415, 136, 145, 146; Knight, "Natural, Moral and Political History of Jamaica . . . 1746," BL, ADD. MSS. 12419, 49; Oldmixon, *British Empire in America*, 2:53, 287; Patterson, "Slavery and Slave Revolts" (1970), 297, 298.

15. April Hatfield, *Atlantic Virginia*, 159; Gerbner, *Christian Slavery*, 50, 66; The

Commissioners' Resolve, in Michael Oberg, *Samuel Wiseman's Book of Record*, 193; An Act Concerning Servants who were out in rebellion, in Hening, *Statutes at Large*, 2:395; Grand Assembly of 20 February 1677, Act 1, in Hening, *Statutes at Large*, 2:373; Act 5, in Hening, *Statutes at Large*, 2:381; Act 20, in Hening, *Statutes at Large*, 2:404; An Act for Preventing Negroes Insurrections, in Hening, *Statutes at Large*, 1:481, 482; Aptheker, *American Negro Slave Revolts*, 165–66; Att a Councell, October 24, 1687, in McIllwaine, *Executive Journals*, 1:86; Handler, "Slave Revolts and Conspiracies," 19; Act for the Better Ordering and Governing, May 1740, in Mark Smith, *Stono*, 20. While Aptheker partially attributes this law to runaway slaves, Parent interprets it as a response to a conspiracy in 1680 in *Foul Means*, 127.

16. Rice, *Tales from a Revolution*, 15; Michael Oberg, *Samuel Wiseman's Book of Record*, 11; Webb, *1676*, xv; John Atkins to Joseph Williamson, October 3, 1675, in Fortescue, *CSP*, 9:294; Richard Watts to Joseph Williamson, October 10, 1675, in Blackburne Daniell, *CSP*, 14:342, 360; Nathaniel Osborne to Joseph Williamson, April 15, 1676, in Neville, *Bacon's Rebellion*, 204; Sir Joseph Williamson Memorandum, April 23, 1677, in Fortescue, *CSP*, 10:64; Washburn, "Sir William Berkeley's 'History,'" 403; Berkeley Address to Charles II, March 24, 1675, in Billings, *Papers of Sir William Berkeley*, 505; Billings, "Causes of Bacon's Rebellion," 421–423.

17. See Act X, All persons to be armed except negroes, in Hening, *Statutes at Large*, 2:26; Act CII and CV in Hening, *Statutes at Large*, 2:117–119; Act CXXXVII, in Hening, *Statutes at Large*, 2:143; Act XII, in Hening, *Statutes at Large*, 2:170; Billings, "Law of Servants and Slaves," 58.

18. Coombs, "Beyond the 'Origins Debate,'" 239–278.

Chapter 2. "Negroes Plundered by the Indians from Carolina"

1. Crane, *Southern Frontier*, 162; Gallay, *Indian Slave Trade*, 7, 346; Oatis, *Colonial Complex*, 2, 170; Ivers, *This Torrent of Indians*, xii; Worth, *Timucuan Chiefdoms*, 2:149; Ramsey, *Yamasee War*, 3, 223; Ramsey, "Coat for 'Indian Cuffy,'" 57; Hahn, *Invention of the Creek Nation*, 83; also see all contributors in Bossy, *Yamasee Indians*.

2. Hewatt, *Historical Account*, 1:228; Milling, *Red Carolinians*, 146; Crane, *Southern Frontier*, 173; Porter, "Negroes on the Southern Frontier," 58, 62; Wood, *Black Majority*, 127, 129, 130; Tepaske, "Fugitive Slave," 12; Ramsey, *Yamasee War*, 163; Riordan, "Finding Freedom in Florida," 29; Landers, "Atlantic Transformation," 216; Landers, "African-Yamasee Ties," 163. Others have speculated about such an alliance; see Braund, "Creek Indians, Blacks, and Slavery," 606; Worth, "Razing Florida," 296, 297, 298, 305.

3. Extract of Letter, September 17, 1708, in Rivers, *Sketch of the History of South Carolina*, 232; Ivers, *This Torrent of Indians*, 6; Governor and Council of Proprietors to Board of Trade, September 17, 1708, in Merrens, *Colonial South Carolina Scene*, 32–33; The Intra-American Slave Trade Database, Slave Voyages, https://www.slavevoyages.org/american/database.

4. Governor Johnson to Council of Trade and Plantations, January 12, 1720, in Sainsbury et al., *CSP*, 31:302–303; Robert Johnson Letter from Charlestown, January 12, 1719, Parish Jr. Transcripts on Slavery, no. 133, 25, New-York Historical Society; Ivers, *This Torrent of Indians*, 25, 30.

5. Worth, *Timucuan Chiefdoms*, 1:xv, 121, 2:133, 134, 140, 148; Hoffman, *Florida Frontiers*, 183.

6. George Rodd to Lords of trade, May 8, 1715, in Records in the British Public Record Office Relating to South Carolina (hereafter SCBPRO), 6:74–75; Ivers, *This Torrent of Indians*, 2, 3, 51; Charles Rodd to his employer, May 8, 1715, in Sainsbury et al., *CSP*, 28:167.

7. Journal of George Chicken, 1714, in Cheves, *Yearbook*, 334, 335; Salley, *Journal of the Commissioners*, 13, 36, 46, 86.

8. Governor Francisco de Córcoles y Martínez and Salvador Garcia de Villegas, Autos regarding the Arrival of the Yamasees, May 28–29, 1715, in Worth, "Razing Florida," 305; Landers, "Yamasee-African Ties," 173, 174; Testimony of Four Caciques attached in Governor Córcoles y Martínez to the King, January 26, 1716, Archivo de Indios 58-1-30, Stetson Collection, PKY; Amanda Hall, "San Antonio de Pocotalaca," 46.

9. Ivers, *This Torrent of Indians*, 56, 63, 64; Klingberg, *Carolina Chronicle*, 154, 156; Charles Rodd to his employer, May 8, 1715, in Sainsbury et al., *CSP*, 28:168; Governor Charles Craven to Lord Townshend, May 23, 1715, in Sainsbury et al., *CSP*, 28:227.

10. Ivers, *This Torrent of Indians*, 86, 87, 88; Letter to Carolina Agents, July 19, 1715, in Cheves, *Yearbook*, 319; Klingberg, *Carolina Chronicle*, 159.

11. Ivers, *This Torrent of Indians*, 90, 91; Klingberg, *Carolina Chronicle*, 161; Corkran, *Carolina Indian Frontier*, 21.

12. Samuel Eveleigh to Messrs Boone and Beresford, October 7, 1715, in Sainsbury et al., *CSP*, 28:296–302; Porter, "Negroes on the Southern Frontier," 57; Crane, *Southern Frontier*, 181; Willis, "Divide and Rule," 167.

13. Ivers, *This Torrent of Indians*, 91, 92, 93; Letter to Carolina Agents, July 19, 1715, in Cheves, *Yearbook*, 319, 320; Klingberg, *Carolina Chronicle*, 155, 159, 161.

14. General Assembly of South Carolina to King George, May 1, 1715, SCBPRO, 6:86; Klingberg, *Gideon Johnstone*, 176; McIlwaine, *Executive Journals*, 3:405; Letter to Carolina Agents, July 19, 1715, in Cheves, *Yearbook*, 320; Klingberg, *Carolina Chronicle*, 155, 159, 161; Samuel Eveleigh to Gentleman, October 1715, SCBPRO, 6:118; Commissioners of Commons House Assembly to Boone and Beresford, August 20, 1715, SCBPRO, 6:132.

15. Letter to Carolina Agents, July 19, 1715, in Cheves, *Yearbook*, 321, 322; Klingberg, "Mystery," 24; Samuel Eveleigh to Messrs Boon and Beresford, July 19, 1715, in Sainsbury et al., *CSP*, 28:298, 299; Ivers, *This Torrent of Indians*, 109, 121; Samuel Eveleigh to Messrs Boone and Beresford, October 7, 1715, in Sainsbury et al., *CSP*, 28:296–302.

16. Humphreys, *Historical Account*, 93, 94, 98.

17. Commissioners to Boon and Beresford, August 25, 1715, in Sainsbury et al., *CSP*, 28:299; Letter to Carolina Agents, July 19, 1715, in Cheves, *Yearbook*, 323; Mr. Molyneux to Mr. Popple, November 30, 1715, in Sainsbury et al., *CSP*, 29:251.

18. Ivers, *This Torrent of Indians*, 141; Crane, *Southern Frontier*, 184; Assembly of South Carolina to Boone and Beresford, March 15, 1716, in Sainsbury et al., *CSP*, 29:50.

19. Ivers, *This Torrent of Indians*, 143, 151; Extract of Letter from South Carolina, March 29, 1717, in Sainsbury et al., *CSP*, 29:50; Addison to Council of Trade and Plantations, April 30, 1717, in Sainsbury et al., *CSP*, 29:291.

20. Hahn, *Creek Nation*, 83, 87; Governor Johnson to Council of Trade and Plantations, January 12, 1720, in Sainsbury et al., *CSP*, 31:302–303; Reigelsperger, "Interethnic Relations," 66–69.

21. Governor Johnson to Council of Trade and Plantations, January 12, 1720, in Sainsbury et al., *CSP*, 31:301–302.

22. A Governor Answers a Questionnaire, January 12, 1720, [Gov. Johnson] in Merrens, *Colonial South Carolina*, 59, 62, 63.

23. Boyd, "Documents," 115, 116, 125.

24. Robert Johnson to Lords Commissioners of Trade and Plantations, July 24, 1716, SCBPRO, 6:230–231; Oatis, *Colonial Complex*, 170; Ivers, *This Torrent of Indians*, 90, 119, 123, 151, 152.

25. Cooper and McCord, *Statutes at Large*, 7:347–351.

26. Cooper and McCord, *Statutes at Large*, 7:350, 351; Ivers, *This Torrent of Indians*, 20; Milling, *Red Carolinians*, 146; Extract of Letter, September 17, 1708, in Rivers, *Sketch of the History of South Carolina*, 232; Governor and Council of Proprietors to Board of Trade, September 17, 1708, in Merrens, *Colonial South Carolina*, 32–33.

27. Governor Craven to Lord Townshend, May 23, 1715, in Sainsbury et al., *CSP*, 28:228; Lords Proprietors to King George I, 1715, in Sainsbury et al., *CSP*, 28:361; "An Act for the Enlisting," in Trott, *Laws of the Province*, 1:336.

28. Oatis, *Colonial Complex*, 172; Society for the Propagation of Gospel, as quoted in Pennington, "South Carolina Indian War," 263.

29. Lt. Gov. Alexander Spotswood to Mr. Secretary Stanhope, May 27, 1715, in Sainsbury et al., *CSP*, 28:226; Governor Hunter to the Council of Trade and Plantations, April 30, 1716, in Sainsbury et al., *CSP*, 29:65; Board of Trade to Secretary Stanhope, September 16, 1715, CO 5/1335; Anonymous letter, August 6, 1716, SCBPRO, 6:239; Landers, "African-Yamasee Ties," 167.

30. Ramsey, "Coat for 'Indian Cuffy,'" 59.

31. Anonymous letter, August 6, 1716, SCBPRO, 6:239; Committee of the Assembly of Carolina to Messrs. Boone and Beresford, August 6, 1716, in Sainsbury et al., *CSP*, 29:218; Governor Johnson to Council of Trade and Plantations, January 12, 1720, in Sainsbury et al., *CSP*, 31:304; McDowell, *Journals of the Commissioners*, 36.

32. Landers, "Atlantic Transformation," 215, 216, 217, 218, 220, 227; Landers, "African-Yamasee Ties," 180; Memorial of Jospo in Manuel de Montiano to Philip V, March 3, 1738, AGI SD 844, reel 15, PKY.

NOTES TO CHAPTER TWO   221

33. Joseph Boone and Richard Beresford to the Council of Trade and Plantations, December 5, 1716, in Sainsbury et al., *CSP*, 29:215–226; William Pulteney to Council of Trade and Plantations, July 18, 1715, in Sainsbury et al., *CSP*, 28:236, 237.

34. McIlwaine, *Executive Journals*, 3:405–406; At a Council, February 22, 1715, in McIlwaine, *Executive Journals*, 3:421; Journal of George Chicken, 1715, in Cheves, *Yearbook*, 344; Ivers, *This Torrent of Indians*, 92; "Tobias Fitch's Journal," in Mereness, *Travels in the American Colonies*, 184–86.

35. Deposition of George Duckett, enclosed in Certificate of Robert Daniel, August 13, 1716, in Sainsbury et al., *CSP*, 29:225; Oatis, *Colonial Complex*, 173; A List of the Negro and Indian Slaves Taken in the Year 1715 and Carryed to St. Augustin, 1723, SCBPRO, 10:39; Hewatt, *Historical Account*, 1:241.

36. Lt. Gov. Bennett to Mr. Popple, February 16, 1718, in Sainsbury et al., *CSP*, 30:186; Littlefield, *Africans and Creeks*, 9; Law to Reclaim Slaves and Horses from Western Indians, December 11, 1717, in Vaughan, *Early American Indian Documents*, 16:204; Ashley and Colleton to Craven, June 14, 1717, SCBPRO 7:53–55; Saunt, "The English," 165, 167; Braund, "Creek Indians," 601–636.

37. Ramsey, *Yamasee War*, 169.

38. Yonge, *Narrative of the Proceedings*, 7.

39. Landers, "Black-Indian Interaction," 148, 149; Landers, "Atlantic Transformation," 209; Landers, "Slavery in the Lower South," 25.

40. Robert Johnson Letter from Charlestown, June 18, 1718; Wood, *Black Majority*, 305; Rodd, Relation, SCBPRO, 6:81; Governor Craven to Lord Townshend, May 23, 1715, in Sainsbury et al., *CSP*, 28:228; Journal of Chicken, 1715, in Cheves, *Yearbook*, 336; Joseph Boone and Richard Beresford to Council of Trade and Plantations, December 5, 1716, in Sainsbury et al., *CSP*, 29:215–226.

41. Governor Bienville to Count of Pontchartrain, September 1, 1715, in Rowland and Godfrey, *Mississippi Provincial Archives*, 3:187–188; Governor Bienville to Count of Pontchartrain, October 12, 1708, in Rowland and Godfrey, *Mississippi Provincial Archives*, 2:39; "Tobias Fitch's Journal," in Mereness, *Travels in the American Colonies*, 184.

42. Córcoles y Martínez to Spotswood, May 30, 1716, enclosed in Addison to Council of Trade, in Sainsbury et al., *CSP*, 29:292–293; J. Leitch Wright, *Anglo-Spanish Rivalry*, 70; Ivers, *This Torrent of Indians*, 186; Antonio Benavides to the King, 1722, in Brooks, *Unwritten History*, 168–170.

43. Governor Antonio de Benavides to the King, August 25, 1718, Buckingham Smith Papers, reel 141J, PKY; Hoffman, *Florida's Frontiers*, 182; Rugemer, *Slave Law and Politics*, 100; Landers, "Yamasee-African Ties," 170, 180.

44. McDowell, *Journals of the Commissioners*, 177.

45. Humphreys, *Historical Account*, 104; Ramsey, "Coat for 'Indian Cuffy,'" 48; Boone to Unknown, June 24, 1720, SCBPRO, 8:24–26; Letter to Mr. Boone, June 24, 1720, in Sainsbury et al., *CSP*, 32:57.

46. Deposition of John Gray and William Gray, January 16, 1727, SCBPRO, 19:127–128.

47. Kenneth Scott, "Slave Insurrection," 2, 5, 7, 9, 10, 12, 15; Coroner's Inquisition on William Asht and on Augustus Grasset, New-York Historical Society, New York.

48. Aptheker, *Slave Revolts*, 172.

49. Sayre and Zecher, *Jean François-Benjamin du Montigny*, 227, 229, 230, 231.

50. de Ville, *Massacre at Natchez*, 9; Sayre and Zecher, *Jean François-Benjamin du Montigny*, 232, 233, 236; Balvay, *La Révolte des Natchez*, 129, 130; Delaye, *Relation du Massacre*, 2; Périer to Maurepas, March 18, 1730, in Rowland and Godfrey, *Mississippi Provincial Archives*, 1:62.

51. de Ville, *Massacre at Natchez*, 11, 16; Sayre and Zecher, *Jean François-Benjamin du Montigny*, 245; Périer to Maurepas, December 5, 1729, in Rowland and Godfrey, *Mississippi Provincial Archives*, 1:54; Diron d'Artaguette to Maurepas, February 9, 1730, in Rowland and Godfrey, *Mississippi Provincial Archives*, 1:58; Le Petit, *Natchez Massacre*, 26, 27.

52. Balvay, *La Révolte des Natchez*, 204; Usner, *Indians, Settlers, and Slaves*, 73; Delaye, *Relation du Massacre*, 50; Charlevoix in Gold Thwaites, *Jesuit Relations and Allied Documents*, 6:104.

53. Charlevoix in Gold Thwaites, *Jesuit Relations and Allied Documents*, 6:101–102; Le Petit, *Natchez Massacre*, 30; Gwendolyn Midlo Hall, *Africans in Colonial Louisiana*, 104.

54. Sayre and Zecher, *Jean François-Benjamin du Montigny*, 250; Charlevoix in Gold Thwaites, *Jesuit Relations and Allied Documents*, 6:90; Balvay, *La Révolte des Natchez*, 135; Périer to Maurepas, March 18, 1730, in Rowland and Godfrey, *Mississippi Provincial Archives*, 1:63.

55. Charlevoix in Gold Thwaites, *Jesuit Relations and Allied Documents*, 6:108; Périer to Maurepas, August 1, 1730, in Rowland and Godfrey, *Mississippi Provincial Archives*, 4:37; de Ville, *Massacre at Natchez*, 11, 12, 13.

56. Klingberg, *Carolina Chronicle*, 136–137; Lt. Gov. Drysdale to the Council of Trade and Plantations, December 20, 1722, in Sainsbury et al., *CSP*, 33:191–193.

57. Examination of John Pearson, October 28, 1727, SCBPRO 19:127, 128; Arthur Middleton, June 13, 1728, SCBPRO 13:61–67; An Account of the Negro Insurrection in South Carolina, October 1739, in Sainsbury et al., *CSP*, 45:200.

58. An Account of the Negro Insurrection in South Carolina, October 1739, in Sainsbury et al., *CSP*, 45:200.

59. Foy, "Seeking Freedom," 46, 47; Waller, "New York's Role," 47; Willson, *History of the United States*, 133; Genovese, *Roll Jordan Roll*, 591, 594; Carter, *Historical Statistics*.

60. Gwendolyn Midlo Hall, *Africans in Colonial Louisiana*, 60, 86; Usner, "The Frontier Exchange Economy," 172; Genovese, *From Rebellion to Revolution*, 12; Barnett, *Natchez Indians*, 99, 100.

61. Wood, *Black Majority*, 309, 313, 314.

62. Klingberg, *Carolina Chronicle*, 121; Cooper and McCord, *Statutes at Large*, 7:352, 353; Carter, *Historical Statistics*.

63. Cooper and McCord, *Statutes at Large*, 7:354–359.

64. Cooper and McCord, *Statutes at Large*, 7:362, 363; Roper, "1701 'Act,'" 407, 416; Rugemer, *Slave Law and Politics*, 90; Wood, *Black Majority*, 52.

65. Cooper and McCord, *Statutes at Large*, 7:364; Roper, "1701 'Act,'" 407.

66. Cooper and McCord, *Statutes at Large*, 7:367–68.

67. Cooper and McCord, *Statutes at Large*, 7:370; Rugemer, *Slave Law and Politics*, 102.

68. Klingberg, *Carolina Chronicle*, 150, 153.

69. Lt. James Fellow to Mr. Burchett, August 3, 1716, in Sainsbury et al., *CSP*, 29:160–161; Hewatt, *Historical Account*, 1:225; Aptheker, *Slave Revolts*, 169; Proceedings in the Case, in Palmer, *Calendar of Virginia State Papers*, 1:129.

Chapter 3. Liberty to Slaves

1. *Book of Negroes*, book 1 [1783], Sir Guy Carleton Papers, Nova Scotia Archives Microfilm no. 10149; Whitehead and Robertson, *Life of Boston King*, 21.

2. Frey, "Between Slavery and Freedom," 375–398; Frey, *Water from the Rock*, 4, 48, 87, 127; Egerton, *Death or Liberty*, 13, 260; Holton, "Rebel against Rebel," 190; Mullin, "British Caribbean," 235; Walker, *Black Loyalists*, 1, 8; Nash, *Forgotten Fifth*; Hodges, "Black Revolt," 21; Hodges, *Slavery, Freedom, and Culture*, 66; Carey, "Lord Dunmore's Ethiopian Regiment."

3. Whitehead, *Black Loyalists*, 83.

4. Captain Squire to Committee of Hampton, September 10, 1775, in Force, *American Archives, Fourth Series*, 3:679; Squire to Committee, September 10, 1775, Force, *American Archives, Fourth Series*, 3:680; Holton, "'Rebel Against Rebel,'" 158; Hampton Committee to Captain Squire, September 16, 1775, Force, *American Archives, Fourth Series*, 3:722–723; Captain Montague to Captain Squire, *Virginia Gazette* (Purdie), Williamsburg, September 15, 1775.

5. Holton, "Rebel against Rebel," 158; John Page to Thomas Jefferson, November 11, 1775, in McClure and Looney, *Papers of Thomas Jefferson*, 257; *Fresh Intelligence* (J. Dunlap), Philadelphia, November 6, 1775; Gilbert, *Black Patriots and Loyalists*, 22; *Virginia Gazette* (Dixon and Hunter), Williamsburg, September 23, 1775; Committee of Elizabeth City County and Town of Hampton to Mathew Squire, September 16, 1775, in William Well Clark, *Naval Documents of the American Revolution* (hereafter NDAR), 2:123; *Virginia Gazette* (Pinkney), Williamsburg, October 19, 1775, supplement.

6. James Johnson to Unknown, November 16, 1775, in Curle, "Intercepted Letters of Virginia Tories," 342; Edmund Pendleton to Richard Henry Lee, November 27, 1775, in Mays, *Letters and Papers of Edmund Pendleton*, 1:132; Colonel William Woodford to the President of the Convention at Williamsburg, Return of Prisoners Taken After Great Bridge, December 12, 1775, in Scribner and Tarter, *Revolutionary Virginia*, 5:118; James Brown to William Brown, November 21, 1775, in "Loyalist Letters," 135; Unknown to Jack, November 20, 1775, in Curle, "Intercepted Letters of Virginia Tories," 345.

7. Robert Carter Nicholas to the Virginia Delegates in Congress, November 25, 1775, in McClure and Looney, *Papers of Thomas Jefferson*, 267; *Virginia Gazette* (Pinkney), Williamsburg, December 20, 1775; Lt. Col. Scott to Friend, December 4, 1775, in Force, *American Archives, Fourth Series*, 4:183; Captain Leslie to General Gage, December 1, 1775, in Force, *American Archives, Fourth Series*, 4:349; Frey, "Between Slavery and Freedom," 388; Fuss, "Billy Flora"; *Virginia Gazette* (Pinkney), Williamsburg, December 20, 1775; J. H. Norton Jr. to J. H. Norton Sr., December 9, 1775, NDAR, 3:25; *Virginia Gazette* (Purdie), December 15, 1775.

8. Deposition of Ralph and John Grissoll, April 2, 1776, in Scribner and Tarter, *Revolutionary Virginia*, 6:305, 317; Fifth Virginia Convention Proceedings, May 29, 1776, in Scribner and Tarter, *Revolutionary Virginia*, 7, part 1: 300.

9. Fifth Virginia Convention Proceedings, May 9, 1776, in Scribner and Tarter, *Revolutionary Virginia*, 7, part 1: 79; Thomas Parramore and John Bowdoin Jr. to the Honorable, the Committee of Safety in Williamsburg, April 23, 1776, in Scribner and Tarter, *Revolutionary Virginia*, 6:449; Schwarz, *Twice Condemned*, 188; Kaplan and Nogrady Kaplan, *Black Presence*, 76; Franklin and Schwenninger, *Runaway Slaves*, 242, 244.

10. John Johnson to James Balantine, November 17, 1775, in Scribner and Tarter, *Revolutionary Virginia*, 4:426; William Woodford to Edmund Pendleton, December 5, 1775, in Rhodehamel, *American Revolution*, 87; Fourth Virginia Convention Proceedings, January 17, 1776, in Scribner and Tarter, *Revolutionary Virginia*, 5:423; Frey, "Between Slavery and Freedom," 384; Macveagh, *Journal of Nicholas Creswell*, 128; Harrell, *Loyalism in Virginia*, 46–48.

11. William Bradford to James Madison, January 4, 1775, Bradford Family Papers, series 2, vol. 10, Historical Society of Pennsylvania (hereafter HSP); Madison to Bradford, June 19, 1775, Bradford Family Papers, series 2, vol. 10, HSP; James Johnson to Unknown, November 16, 1775, in Curle, "Intercepted Letters of Virginia Tories," 342; *Virginia Gazette* (Pinkney), Williamsburg, July 13, 1775.

12. Greene, *Diary of Landon Carter*, 2:1051, 1052, 1093, 1109, 1128; A Declaration in Mays, *Letters and Papers of Edmund Pendleton*, 1:138; Virginia Committee of Safety (undated) in Scribner and Tarter, *Revolutionary Virginia*, 4:282; *Virginia Gazette* (Pinkney), Williamsburg, July 13, 1775.

13. Holton, "Rebel against Rebel," 168, 173, 176; Frey, "Between Slavery and Freedom," 389; Kaplan, "Domestic Insurrections," 243–255.

14. Hannum, "Norfolk, Virginia"; Extract of a Letter from Colonels Howe and Woodford to the Virginia Convention, January 1, 1776, in Force, *American Archives, Fourth Series*, 4:358; Robert Howe to the President of the Convention, January 2, 1776, in Dice Robins Anderson, *Richmond College Historical Papers*, 1:1 (June 1915), 148–150.

15. Cecere, "Battle of Gwynn's Island"; Narrative of Captain Hamond, June 8, 1776, NDAR, 5:840.

16. Narrative of Captain Andrew Snape Hamond, May 19, 1776, NDAR, 5:321; *Pennsylvania Evening Post*, June 27, 1776, NDAR, 5:773; Narrative of Captain

Hamond, June 10, 1776, NDAR, 5:840; Narrative of Captain Hamond, June 8, 1776, NDAR, 5:840; *Virginia Gazette* (Dixon and Hunter), Williamsburg, June 15, 1776, NDAR, 5:554.

17. Posey, *General Thomas Posey*, 31, 32; Cecere, "Battle of Gwynn's Island"; *Pennsylvania Packet*, July 22, 1776, NDAR, 5:1068; Dunmore to Lord George Germain, July 31, 1776, NDAR, 5:1312; Revolutionary War Journal of Captain Thomas Posey, July 8–10, 1776, Thomas Posey Collection, Indiana Historical Society, Indianapolis, 1:10.

18. Andrew Lewis to Richard Henry Lee, July 15, 1776, NDAR, 5:1094; Posey Journal, July 8–10, 1776, 1:10.

19. Extract of Letter from Williamsburg, July 18, 1776, printed in *Pennsylvania Packet*, July 22, 1776, NDAR, 5:1068; Cecere, "Battle of Gwynn's Island"; Posey Journal, July 8–10, 1776, 1:10; *Virginia Gazette* (Dixon and Hunter), Williamsburg, July 20, 1776; *Virginia Gazette* (Purdie), Williamsburg, July 19, 1776; "Memoirs of the Life of Boston King," in Brooks and Saillant, "*Face Zion Forward*," 212; Andrew Lewis to Richard Henry Lee, July 15, 1776, NDAR, 5:1094.

20. Allard, "Potomac Navy of 1776," 419, 420, 426; Captain George Montagu, Journal of H.M.S. *Fowey*, July 1776, NDAR, 5:1316; Dunmore to Germain, August 31, 1776, NDAR, 5:1312, 1313; Narrative of Captain Andrew Snape Hamond, July 23, 1776, NDAR, 6:173.

21. Dunmore to Germain, August 31, 1776, NDAR, 5:1313; Master's Log on HMS *Roebuck*, August 1776, NDAR, 6:68.

22. Narrative of Captain Andrew Snape Hamond, July 23, 1776, NDAR, 6:173, 174; Captain Hamond to Hass Stanley, August 5, 1776, NDAR, 6:68; Dunmore to Dartmouth, February 18, 1776, in Davies, *Documents of the American Revolution*, 12:62; Robert Howe to the President of the Convention, January 2, 1776, in Dice Robins Anderson, *Richmond College Historical Papers*, 1:148; Colonel William Woodford to the Virginia Convention, January 21, 1776, in Dice Robins Anderson, *Richmond College Historical Papers*, 1:154; Edmund Pendleton to James Mercer, March 19, 1776, in Mays, *Letters and Papers of Edmund Pendleton*, 1:160; Edmund Pendleton to Thomas Jefferson, July 29, 1776, in Mays, *Letters and Papers of Edmund Pendleton*, 1:189; Diary of Miguel Antonio Eduardo, July 15, 1776, NDAR, 5:1346; Dunmore to Germain, February 25, 1776, CO 5/1373, 25; Dunmore to Howe, September 4, 1776, CO 5/1373, 31.

23. Hodges, *Slavery and Freedom*, 97; *New Jersey Gazette* (Isaac Collins), Trenton, April 4, 1782.

24. William Woodford to Edmund Pendleton, December 5, 1775, in Rhodehamel, *American Revolution*, 89, 90; Pybus, *Epic Journeys of Freedom*, 20; Virginia Committee of Safety to Virginia Delegates in Congress, November 11, 1775, in Scribner and Tarter, *Revolutionary Virginia*, 4:379–380; Dunmore to Dartmouth, February 18, 1775, in Davies, *Documents of the American Revolution*, 12:59; Deposition of William Barry, June 11, 1776, in Force, *American Archives, Fourth Series*, 6:811. Landon Carter also describes a typical attempt to reach the British by boat when Patriot militia discovered ten slaves near the Middlesex Shore on June 29, 1776, in Greene, *Diary of Landon Carter*, 2:1052; Carey, "Lord Dunmore's Ethiopian Regiment," 2, 81. By my count, al-

most all of the slaves were from Norfolk city, while Portsmouth featured heavily in the *Book of Negroes* as well.

25. "Memoirs of the Life of Boston King," in Brooks and Saillant, *"Face Zion Forward,"* 212.

26. *Virginia Gazette*, (Dixon and Hunter), Williamsburg, August 31, 1776; "An Account of the Life of Mr. David George," in Brooks and Saillant, *"Face Zion Forward,"* 182, 183.

27. Pybus, *Epic Journeys*, 20; Holton, "Rebel against Rebel," 182. Holton appears to base this figure on Sarah Stroud's "Tracing Runaway Slaves from Norfolk County, Virginia, during the American Revolutionary War" (seminar paper, Randolph-Macon Woman's College, fall 1995), which I have not been able to obtain. See also *Book of Negroes*, book 1, Carleton Papers, Nova Scotia Archives no. 10149, http://novascotia.ca/archives/africans/archives.

28. Franklin and Schwenninger, *Runaway Slaves*, 210.

29. Deposition of Archibald Campbell, Angus Fisher, and George Gray, September 4, 1775, in Scribner and Tarter, *Revolutionary Virginia*, 4:69–70; Selby, *Revolution in Virginia*, 58. Tom was a runaway from Carolina for nearly two years before he joined Dunmore. See Woodford to Pendleton, December 5, 1775, in Scribner and Tarter, *Revolutionary Virginia*, 5:57–58; Gilbert, *Black Patriots and Loyalists*, 24; Malcolm, *Peter's War*, 123; *Virginia Gazette* (Purdie), Williamsburg, November 17, 1775; *Pennsylvania Gazette* (Benjamin Franklin), November 22, 1775.

30. Mullin, *Africa in America*, 88n34–35; population figures are from Carter, *Historical Statistics*; Estimates Database, 2016, Slave Voyages, https://www.slavevoyages.org/assessment/estimates; O'Malley, *Final Passages*, 132; Fourth Virginia Convention, January 17, 1776, in Scribner and Tarter, *Revolutionary Virginia*, 5:423; "List of the Blacks in Birchtown who gave in their names for Sierra Leone in November 1791," Black Loyalist Database, http://www.blackloyalist.info/source-image-display/display/109; Egerton, *Death or Liberty*, 195; Sanneh, *Abolitionists Abroad*, 50; quotation from Dunmore to Dartmouth, February 18, 1776, in Davies, *Documents of the American Revolution*, 12:59.

31. *Virginia Gazette* (Dixon and Hunter), Williamsburg, August 31, 1776; Gilbert, *Black Patriots and Loyalists*, 31; Windley, *Runaway Slave Advertisements*.

32. Hodges, *Black Loyalist Directory*, 112; Pybus, *Epic Journeys*, 15, 31, 34, 219; Walker, *Black Loyalists*, 73–78, 386.

33. Long, *History of Jamaica*, 2:446, 447, 448, 452, 453; Lt. Gov. Henry Moore to Lords of Trade, June 9, 1760, CO 137/32, 7; Minutes of Jamaica Council, April 10, 17, 1760, enclosed in Lt. Gov. Moore to Board of Trade, April 19, 1760, CO 137/60, 296–299; Rear Admiral Charles Holmes to John Cleveland, June 11, 1760, Admiralty Papers, National Archives (hereafter ADM), 1/236, 41, 42; Holmes to Cleveland, July 25, 1760, ADM 1/236, 51, 52; List of White People Kill'd Since the Commencement of the Rebellion in Westmoreland, May 25, 1760, enclosed in Holmes to Cleveland, July 25, 1760, ADM 1/236; Vincent Brown, "Slave Revolt in Jamaica."

34. I believe that Jeremiah's plot was real and that he was principally involved in it. William Campbell to Earl of Dartmouth, August 19, 1775, in Ryan, *World of Thomas Jeremiah*, 50, 162; Campbell to Dartmouth, August 31, 1775, SCBPRO, 35:198; Campbell to Dartmouth, August 31, 1775, SCBPRO, 35:202; Arthur Middleton to Henry Drayton, August 4, 1775, in "Correspondence of Hon. Arthur Middleton and Joseph Barnwell," 121; Harris, *Hanging of Thomas Jeremiah*, 97; Campbell to Dartmouth, August 3, 1775, SCBPRO 25:191–216; Drayton, *Memoirs of the American Revolution*, 62; Magistrates Letter, CO 137/71, 276.

35. Gilbert, *Black Patriots and Loyalists*, 123; Piecuch, *Three Peoples, One King*, 170; Long, *History of Jamaica*, 2:453; Bernard Moitt, "Slave Women and Resistance," 240–242, 245; Abstract of those victualed at Gibb's Landing, April 7–9, 1780, Frederick Mackenzie Papers, Clements Library, box 1, vol. c; List of Negroes Employed in the Royal Artillery Department, October 1781, George Wray Papers, Clements Library, vol. 7; Abstract of the numbers of men, women, and children and wagoneers victualled at Commissary General's provision stores, July 20, 1778, Clinton Papers, Clements Library, vol. 37, series 1, nos. 18, 37, 39. For the role of women and children in other slave rebellions, see Kars, "Dodging Rebellion"; Holden, "Generation, Resistance, and Survival."

36. Antoine Dalmas, "Histoire de la Revolution de Saint-Domingue" (1814), in Dubois and Garrigus, *Slave Revolution in the Caribbean*, 89–93; Thornton, "African Soldiers"; Buckley, *Haitian Journal of Lieutenant Howard*, 47, 50. There were also key differences between the Ethiopian rebels and slave soldiers in the Haitian Revolution. Those who rose to the call of French commissioners Étienne Polverel and Léger Félicité Sonthonax fought against insurgents. Others also fought for the British and for pro-slavery forces during the conflict. See Stein, *Léger Félicité Sonthonax*, 75; Geggus, *Slavery, War, and Revolution*, 303, 314, 315, 316, 415n98; Geggus, "Arming of Slaves," 209–232.

37. Charles Stedman, *History of the Origin*, 146.

38. Ehmert Clark, *Journal and Letters of Francis Asbury*, 1:163; Extract of Letter from Jamaica, July 24, 1776, *Public Advertiser* (Henry Sampson Woodfall), London, October 25, 1776; Proclamation of Sir Basil Keith, July 24, 1776, CO 137/71; Extract of a letter from Jamaica, July 30, 1776, *General Evening Post* (Richard Nutt), October 24–26, 1776; Fuller to Germain, October 27, 1776, CO 5/154 part 2, 81; Basil Keith to Lord George Germain, July 13, 1776, CO 137/71, 202; Sheridan, "Jamaican Slave Insurrection Scare," 26, 33, 34, 36.

39. "An account of the life of Mr. David George from Sierra Leone in Africa / given by himself in a conversation with Brother Rippon of London and Brother Pearce of Birmingham," in Brooks and Saillant, *"Face Zion Forward,"* 187, 188; Settlers' Petition to Directors of Sierra Leone Company, 1793, in Fyfe, *"Our Children Free and Happy,"* 37, 38; Petition to John Clarkson, November 19, 1794, in Fyfe, *"Our Children Free and Happy,"* 44; Petition to Governor and Counsil of Sierra Leone, April 22, 1795, in Fyfe, *"Our Children Free and Happy,"* 48.

40. Trial of Gabriel, October 6, 1800, in Schwarz, *Gabriel's Conspiracy*, 271.
41. *Virginia Gazette* (Dixon & Hunter), August 31, 1776; "List of the Blacks in Birchtown"; Walker, *Black Loyalists*, 22.

Chapter 4. Mutiny in the Caribbean

1. Discover Dominica Authority, http://discoverdominica.com/en/places/78/fort-shirley (accessed March 28, 2019); UNESCO World Heritage site on Fort Shirley, http://whc.unesco.org/en/tentativelists/6020/ (accessed March 28, 2019).
2. Honychurch, *In the Forests of Freedom*, 143, 146; Honychurch, *Dominica Story*, 113; Geggus, "Slavery, War, and Revolution," 6; Craton, *Testing the Chains*, 171, 14, 17, 228; Voelz, *Slave and Soldier*, 264; Buckley, *Slaves in Red Coats*, 142n5; Dyde, *Empty Sleeve*, 26; Lambert and Lockley, "Introduction," 453; Barcia, "Weapons from Their Land," 485; Lockley, "Mutiny!"
3. Kupperman, *Providence Island*, 170n72; Handler, "Freedmen and Slaves," 19; Joseph Wilson, *Black Phalanx*, 26; Quarles, "Colonial Militia and Negro Manpower," 644, 645, 646, 647; Bollettino, "Slavery, War, and Britain's Atlantic Empire," 31, 43, 44, 45; Morgan and O'Shaughnessy, "Arming Slaves," 180.
4. Buckley, *Slaves in Red Coats*, 1, 4; Remarks on the Establishment of the West India Regiments, 1801, enclosed in General Thomas Hislop to the Duke of York, July 22, 1804, UK National Archives, War Office Records (hereafter WO), WO 1/95, 194, 195; Henry Dundas to Sir John Vaughan, no. 14, April 17, 1795, WO 1/83, 118.
5. Buckley, *Slaves in Red Coats*, 24, 25; "West India Committee, Standing Committee Minutes," June 27, 1795, BL.
6. Buckley, *British Army*, 87; Duffy, *Soldiers, Sugar, and Seapower*, 364, 366; Vaughan to Dundas, 25 December 1794, quoted in Buckley, "Early History," 376; Andrew James Cochrane Johnstone to Sir Ralph Abercromby, April 14, 1796, WO 1/82, 352.
7. Buckley, "Black Man," 54; Buckley, *Slaves in Red Coats*, 30; Lockley, "Mutiny!," BL; Honychurch, *Dominica Story*, 112.
8. Buckley, *Slaves in Red Coats*, 20, 23, 30; Dundas to Vaughan, no. 14, April 17, 1795, WO 1/83, 122; "Remarks on the Establishment of the West India Regiments," 1801, enclosed in Hislop to the Duke of York, July 22, 1804, WO 1/95, 194, 196, 197; General Cornelius Cuyler to Henry Dundas, March 8, 1798, WO 1/86.
9. Buckley, *Slaves in Red Coats*, 54; Governor Andrew Johnstone to Committee of Gentlemen in Dominica, June 28, 1798, WO 1/86; Buckley, "Slave or Freedman," 92, 94; Chartrand, "Black Corps," 248–254.
10. "Remarks on the Establishment of the West India Regiments," 197, 198. According to Dyde, only six out of every one hundred men were actually allowed to marry. See Dyde, *Empty Sleeve*, 44–45.
11. "Remarks on the Establishment of the West India Regiments," 200, 201, 203.
12. Handler, "Memoirs," 27; Buckley, *Slaves in Red Coats*, 54, 55; Richard McNully

to Lieutenant Colonel Henry Darling, May 9, 1798, WO 1/86; Buckley, "Slave or Freedman," 90, 91; Fergus, "Emancipation and 'Military Necessity,'" 32.

13. General Bowyer to Dundas, September 6, 1798, War Office, WO 1/86, 731; Buckley, *Slaves in Red Coats*, 70; Bowyer to Colonel Robert Brownrigg, September 6, 1798, enclosed in Duke of Portland to Attorney and Solicitor General, November 12, 1798, WO 1/86; Buckley, *Slaves in Red Coats*, 65; Buckley, "Slave or Freedman," 87.

14. Buckley, "Slave or Freedman," 97.

15. Buckley, "Slave or Freedman," 98, 99, 100, 101, 113.

16. One occasion that illuminates this understanding best was when soldiers in the First WIR were required to carry a dying runaway slave back to his quarters. The man, "in the agonies of death," died along the way. See Handler, "Memoirs," 25, 27; Buckley, *Slaves in Red Coats*, 113.

17. Quote in Thomas Trigge to Robert Brownrigg, April 16, 1802, WO 1/95, 25; Buckley, "Black Man," 52; "Mutiny of the 8th West India Regiment," 207, 208; *Sketches and Recollections*, 113, 114.

18. Proceedings of a Court of Inquiry, CO 318/19, 26, 27, 28, retrieved from the British Library; Johnstone to Lord Hobart, no. 14, April 4, 1802, CO 71/34; Lockley, "Mutiny!"

19. *Sketches and Recollections*, 105, 106, 107; Johnstone to Hobart, April 17, 1802, no. 15, CO 71/34.

20. Johnstone to Trigge, April 10, 1802, enclosed in Trigge to Brownrigg, April 16, 1802, WO 1/95, 29; Johnstone to Trigge, April 16, 1802, WO 1/95, 36; *Sketches and Recollections*, 107; Johnstone to Trigge, April 16, 1802, WO 1/95, 33.

21. *Sketches and Recollections*, 108, 109; Johnstone to Trigge, April 16, 1802, WO 1/95, 33, 34; Gott, *Britain's Empire*, 150; Johnstone to Hobart, April 17, 1802, no. 15, CO 71/34.

22. *Sketches and Recollections*, 109–110; Johnstone to Trigge, April 16, 1802, WO 1/95, 34; Johnstone to Hobart, April 17, 1802, no. 15, CO 71/34.

23. *Sketches and Recollections*, 110, 111; "Mutiny of the 8th West India Regiment," part 3, 209; Johnstone to Trigge, April 16, 1802, WO 1/95, 34; Johnstone to Trigge, April 12, 1802, WO 1/95, 31.

24. Proceedings of a Court of Inquiry, CO 318/19, 25; *Sketches and Recollections*, 111, 112; Honychurch, *Dominica Story*, 113.

25. *Sketches and Recollections*, 112; Johnstone to Trigge, April 16, 1802, WO 1/95, 34, 35.

26. *Sketches and Recollections*, 113, 114; Andrew Johnstone and Henry Dundas, *To the Right Honourable Lord Viscount Melville*, 43; Lockley, "Mutiny!"; Johnstone to Hobart, no. 15, April 17, 1802, CO 71/34.

27. Johnstone to Trigge, April 16, 1802, WO 1/95, 35; Trigge to Brownrigg, April 23, 1802, WO 1/95, 37, 38; Extract of letter Trigge to Lord Hobart, April 2, 1802, WO 1/95, 43; Trigge to Brownrigg, May 4, 1802, WO 1/95, 57.

28. Buckley, "Black Man," 61, 62, 63; Trigge to Brownrigg, April 23, 1802, WO 1/95,

37; Corporal Balisle Testimony, in Proceedings of the Court of Inquiry, April 28, 1802, WO 1/95, 65; Stuart's Testimony, in Proceedings of the Court of Inquiry, April 28, 1802, WO 1/95, 66.

29. Johnstone to Trigge, April 22, 1802, WO 1/95, 47; James, *Freshwater Swamps*, 4, 7; Bowyer to Dundas, July 13, 1798, WO 1/86, 411, 412; Johnstone to Abercromby, April 14, 1796, WO 1/82, 350; Enclosure in Johnstone to Hobart, no. 14, April 4, 1802, CO 71/34; "The Method for Draining Lands," CO 71/34.

30. Buckley, *British Army*, 94, 99, 159, 160, 206.

31. Johnstone to Trigge, April 22, 1802, WO 1/95, 47, 48; Sergeant Pinkett Testimony, In Proceedings of the Court of Inquiry, April 28, 1802, WO 1/95, 64; Sergeant Ramey Testimony, in Proceedings of the Court of Inquiry, April 28, 1802, WO 1/95, 64; Corporal Shova Testimony, in Proceedings of the Court of Inquiry, April 28, 1802, WO 1/95, 65; Quash Testimony, in Proceedings of the Court of Inquiry, April 28, 1802, WO 1/95, 66; Corporal Davey Testimony, in Proceedings of the Court of Inquiry, April 28, 1802, WO 1/95, 65; Corporal Domingue Testimony, in Proceedings of the Court of Inquiry, April 28, 1802, WO 1/95, 64.

32. Sergeant Gold Testimony, in Proceedings of the Court of Inquiry, April 28, 1802, WO 1/95, 63; Sergeant Romeo Testimony in Proceedings of the Court of Inquiry, April 28, 1802, WO 1/95, 64; Stuart Testimony, in Proceedings of the Court of Inquiry, April 28, 1802, WO 1/95, 66.

33. Lieutenant Allen Cameron Testimony, in Proceedings of the Court of Inquiry, April 28, 1802, WO 1/95, 76; Proceedings of a Court of Inquiry, CO 318/19, 25–31, retrieved from the British Library.

34. Testimonies of King, Burke, Shell, Essex, Bestonian, James chattel, in Proceedings of the Court of Inquiry, WO 1/95, 66, 67, 68, 73; Proceedings Summary Conclusion, WO 1/95, 81.

35. Trigge to Brownrigg, April 30, 1802, WO 1/95, 51; Adjutant Council Report, CO 71/34; Lockley, "Mutiny!"

36. Johnstone and Dundas, *To the Right Honourable Lord Viscount Melville*, 20, 21, 22, 74; *Proceedings of the General Court Martial*, 2, 298.

37. Johnstone and Dundas, *To the Right Honourable Lord Viscount Melville*, 75, 76, 188; Trigge to Brownrigg, April 30, 1802, WO 1/95, 51; Extract of letter, Trigge to Johnstone, April 25, 1802, WO 1/95, 53; Trigge to Johnstone, April 17, 1802, CO 71/34.

38. New General Orders by General Thomas Trigge, April 27, 1802, WO 1/95, 55, 56; Trigge to Brownrigg, April 16, 1802, WO 1/95, 25, 26; Trigge to Brownrigg, April 23, 1802, WO 1/95, 41, 42; McCallum, *Travels in Trinidad*, 26.

39. Kenneth Morgan, *Slavery and the British Empire*, 144; Geggus, *Haitian Revolutionary Studies*, 60; Jacobs, "Fedon's Rebellion in Grenada," 11; Woodville Marshall, "Provision Ground," 471; Behrendt, "Annual Volume," 200; Cox, "Fedon's Rebellion," 15.

40. Governor William Hughes to Lieutenant General Sir George Beckwith, November 31, 1805, CO 318/28; Hughes to Secretary John Windham, WO 1/150, 190; Hughes to Beckwith, November 2, 1805, WO 1/149; Buckley, *British Army*, 74.

41. Governor James Leith to Earl Bathurst, April 30, 1816, CO 28/85; Colonel Edward Codd to Governor Leith, April 25, 1816, CO 28/85, 11, 12, 13, 14, 15; Minutes of the Barbados Assembly, August 6, 1816, CO 31/47, 18; Beckles, *Black Rebellion in Barbados*, 87, 88, 89, 93, 103; Beckles, "Slave-Drivers' War," 87.

42. Turnball, *Narrative of the Revolt*, 15, 17; Francis McKenzie to Duke of Portland, March 28, 1795, CO 101/34, 22–36; Hay, *Narrative of the Insurrection*, 23, 24, 32, 34, 42, 126; Candlin, *Last Caribbean Frontier*, 1, 2, 3, 6.

43. Alexander Houston to Duke of Portland, July 30, 1796, CO 101/34, 245; Hay, *Narrative of the Insurrection*, 14, 125, 142.

44. Candlin, *Last Caribbean Frontier*, 6, 8; Ellis, *History of the First West India Regiment*, 97; Address of Council to President, May 12, 1795, CO 101/34, 81; Turnball, *Narrative of the Revolt*, 52, 56, 114; Act of August 1, 1795, CO 103/9, 227; Candlin, "Role of the Enslaved," 685.

45. Vaz, "Dominica's Neg Mawon," 122–143; Honychurch, *In the Forests of Freedom*, 101.

46. Minutes of the Privy Council, enclosed in King to William Huskisson, December 11, 1797, WO 1/769.

47. Chartrand, "Black Corps," 253; Hoogbergen, *Boni Maroon Wars*, 184, 185; General Hughes to Windham, September 25, 1806, WO 1/150, 301; Court of Inquiry Proceedings, WO 1/150, 167.

48. Hoogbergen, *Boni Maroon Wars*, 185, 186; Hughes to Beckwith, November 11, 1805, CO 318/28, 354; Hughes to Beckwith, November 31, 1805, CO 318/28; Hughes to Windham, WO 1/150, 190; Hughes to Beckwith, November 2, 1805, WO 1/149.

49. General William Villettes to Lord Castlereagh, June 15, 1808, CO 137/123, 61; General Hugh Carmichael to Castlereagh, August 12, 1808, CO 137/123; *Savannah (Ga.) Republican*, July 23, 1808; Dyde, *Empty Sleeve*, 82, 83.

50. Villettes to Castlereagh, June 15, 1808, CO 137/123, 61; Buckley, *British Army*, 74.

51. Ellis, *History of the First West India Regiment*, 188, 189, 192, 195, 197, 201; Kingsley, *At Last*, 14:207, 208.

52. Gott, *Britain's Empire*, 151, 154, 155; *Dominica Journal or Weekly Intelligencer*, March 19, 1814, vol. 10, no. 480, CO 71/49; de Groot, *From Isolation Towards Integration*, 69.

Chapter 5. Fugitives on the Front

1. *Niles Weekly Register* (Hezekiah Niles), Baltimore, November 5, 1812, December 12, 1812; Cusick, *Other War of 1812*, 11; Joseph Willcox to Father, January 1, 1814, in *Narrative of the Life*, 5; Nunez, "Creek Nativism," 170, 171, 172.

2. Edmund Doyle to John Innerarity, 5 June 1817, Mary Taylor Greenslade Papers, box 2, folder 4, PKY; Niles W*eekly Register* (Hezekiah Niles), Baltimore, January 16, 1819.

3. Porter, "Negroes and the Seminole War," 249–280; Porter, *Black Seminoles*; Canter Brown Jr., "Tales of Angola," 5–21; Horne, *Negro Comrades of the Crown*, 58;

Landers, *Black Society in Spanish Florida*; Altoff, *Amongst My Best Men*; Owsley, *Struggle for the Gulf Borderlands*; Twyman, *Black Seminole Legacy*; Stampp, *Peculiar Institution*, 138.

4. See Millett, "Britain's 1814 Occupation," 235, 236; Millett, "Defining Freedom," 367–394; Millett, "Radicalism," 164–201; Cusick, *Other War of 1812*, 234; Gene Allen Smith, *Slaves' Gamble*, 25; Landers, *Atlantic Creoles*, 111–192; Milligan, "Slave Rebelliousness," 4–18. For other interpretations, see Mulroy, *Freedom on the Border*; Mulroy, *Seminole Freedmen*; Howard, "Black Towns," 107–121; Howard, *Black Seminoles in the Bahamas*; Rivers and Brown, "Indispensable Man," 1–23; Klos, "Blacks and the Seminole Removal Debate," 128–156; Gill, "Mascogo/Black Seminole Diaspora," 23–43.

5. Mulroy, "Ethnogenesis and Ethnohistory," 290; Clavin, "It Is a Negro," 185; Mulroy, *Freedom on the Border*, Mulroy, *Seminole Freedmen*; Kai, "Black Seminoles," 146–157; Christina Snyder, *Slavery in Indian Country*, 232; Sturtevant, review of *Africans and Seminoles*, 916–917.

6. Millett, *Maroons of Prospect Bluff*; Bateman, "Africans and Indians," 1–24; see all contributions in Belko, *America's Hundred Years' War*. While the contributors to this collection reperiodize the Seminole Wars, most of the essays focus on the Second Seminole War. See also J. Leitch Wright, "Note on the First Seminole War," 565–575; Kly, "Gullah War," 50–100.

7. Millett, "Radicalism," 165, 170, 175.

8. Christina Snyder, *Slavery in Indian Country*, 232; Adams, "Race, Kinship, and Belonging," 144–161; Schwaller, "Contested Conquests," 609–618, 637.

9. Bastide, *African Civilizations*, 49, 51; Thornton, "Les États de l'Angola," 796; Schwartz, *Slaves, Peasants, and Rebels*, 118, 116, 124–128. Counterarguments include Sidbury, *Becoming African in America*; Mintz and Price, *Birth of African-American Culture*, 1, 2; Price, *To Slay the Hydra*, 85; Mulroy, *Freedom on the Border*, 2; Bateman, "Naming Patterns," 239; Weik, "Role of Ethnogenesis," 232, 233; Braund, "Creek Indians," 632–634.

10. Sturtevant, review of *Africans and Seminoles*, 916–917; Mulroy, "Ethnogenesis and Ethnohistory," 290; Clavin, "It Is a Negro," 185; Gene Allen Smith, *Slaves' Gamble*, 25, 60, 61, 64, 164; Cusick, *Other War of 1812*, 207; Landers, *Black Society in Spanish Florida*, 220.

11. Moreau de Jonnès, *Aventures de Guerre*, 246.

12. Forbes, *Africans and Native Americans*; Chanvalon, *Voyage à la Martinique*, 39.

13. Buker, *Notices of East Florida*, 76; Kindelán to Apodaca, August 2, 1812, as quoted in Landers, "Africans and Native Americans," 67; Porter, "Negroes and the East Florida Annexation Plot," 15; Jose Urcullo to Henry, December 30, 1814, Heloise Cruzat Papers, 2:7, PKY; Whitehead, "Black Read as Red," 234.

14. Howard, "Black Towns," 111; Felipe Prieto to Edmund Doyle, September 17, 1815, Cruzat Papers, 2:8, PKY. See also Hugh Young, "Topographical Memoir," 100; Dexter, *Observations on the Seminole Indians*, in Boyd, "Horatio Dexter," 84.

15. George Perryman to Lieutenant Sands, February 24, 1817, in Lowrie and

Franklin, *American State Papers Foreign Relations* (hereafter *ASFR*) 4:596; Buker, *Notices of East Florida*, 41, 76; Benjamin Hawkins to Governor Mauricio de Zuñiga, May 24, 1816, in Grant, *Letters*, 2:789; Power of Attorney from Indian Chiefs to Alexander Arbuthnot in Lowrie and St. Clair Clarke, *American State Papers: Military Affairs* (hereafter *ASPMA*), 1:727.

16. Forbes, *Africans and Native Americans*, 63, 182; Medina, "Alonso de Ellescas," 16; Orser, *Historical Archeology*, 50.

17. Sayers, *Desolate Place*, 4, 89; Goucher and Agorsah, "Excavating the Roots of Resistance," 148; Rodriguez, "Negro Slavery," 82; Price, "Uneasy Neighbors," 9; Journal of J. C. Dörig, October 2, 1762, in Price, *To Slay the Hydra*, 174; Pérez de la Riva, "Cuban Palenques," 57; Honychurch, *In the Forests of Freedom*, 21; Madrilejo et al., "Origins of Marronage," 436; Fuller and Benn Torres, "Investigating the 'Taíno' Ancestry," 58, 65, 67; Crawford, "Origin and Maintenance," 157–180; Salas et al., "Shipwrecks and Founder Effects," 855–860; Monsalve and Hagelberg, "Mitochondrial DNA Polymorphisms," 1217–1224. Jamaican Maroons also have White ancestry, likely from the post-Emancipation period. See Besson, *Transformations of Freedom*, 269.

18. See Little Black Factor in Saunt, "The English," 167; Miles and Naylor-Ojurongbe, "African-Americans in Indian Societies," 14:756; Howard, *Black Seminoles in the Bahamas*, 28; Mulroy, *Seminole Freedmen*, 267, 269, 292, 318, 320; Mock, *Dreaming with the Ancestors*, 4, 295; Kappler, *Indian Affairs*, 2:911.

19. Glaberson, "Who Is a Seminole"; Christopher Taylor, *Black Carib Wars*, 158; Crawford et al., "Black Caribs," 87; Crawford, "Anthropological Genetics," 161.

20. Mulroy, *Freedom on the Border*, 8, 11; Mulroy, *Seminole Freedmen*, 7, 11; Kent, "Palmares," 180; Campbell, *Maroons of Jamaica*, 202; Kwasi's Intelligence Coup [1754] in Price, *To Slay the Hydra*, 87; Christopher Taylor, *Black Carib Wars*, 104; McKnight, "Elder, Slave, and Soldier," 71; Thornton, "Les États de l'Angola," 780; Amy Johnson, "Captivity among the Maroons," 1–16.

21. Lockley and Doddington, "Maroon and Slave Communities," 129; Long, *History of Jamaica*, 1:155; Extract of Letter from M. R. Hals to Earl of Westmoreland, October 13, 1733, in Sainsbury et al., *CSP*, 40:216; Governor Robert Hunter to Lords Commissioners, September 20, 1732, CO 137/20, 104; Chopra, *Almost Home*, 26; *Providence Gazette*, January, 30, 1773; William Young, *Account of the Black Charaibs*, 6, 51. Some Jamaican Maroons mark the start of the First Maroon War in 1655. See Dunkley, *Agency of the Enslaved*, 126n13. For ambiguity in Maroon-White conflicts, see also McKee, "From Violence to Alliance," 27–52; de Groot, "Boni Maroon War," 31.

22. Hoogbergen, *Boni Maroon Wars in Suriname*, 15.

23. Council of Trade and Plantations to Committee of Privy Council, December 12, 1734, in Sainsbury et al., *CSP*, 41:334; Doyle to John Innerarity, July 11, 1817, Greenslade Papers, 2:4, PKY; Dallas, *History of the Maroons*, 1:245; William Young, *Account of the Black Charaibs*, 55; Hoogbergen, *Boni Maroon Wars in Suriname*, 129.

24. Governor Hunter to Duke of Newcastle, October 20, 1733, in Sainsbury et al.,

CSP, 40:222; Hunter to Lords Commissioners, September 20, 1732, CO 137/20, 104; Captain Lambe's Journal, September 22, 1732, CO 137/20, 112–114; Honychurch, *In the Forests of Freedom*, 88; Hoogbergen, *Boni Maroon Wars in Suriname*, 52; Porter, "Negroes and the East Florida Annexation Plot," 17; *Niles Weekly Register*, January 16, 1819.

25. Captain Lambe's Journal, September 22, 1732, CO 137/20, 112; Edwards, *History, Civil and Commercial*, 1:525; William Young, *Account of the Black Charaibs*, 92; Journal of Captain Ernst Godfried Hentschel, 1755, in Price, *To Slay the Hydra*, 87–113; Hoogbergen, *Boni Maroon Wars in Suriname*, 129, 185; John Gabriel Stedman, *Narrative of Five Year's Expedition*, 2:99; Porter, "Negroes and the East Florida Annexation Plot, 1811–1813," 19, 20; Forbes, *Sketches, Historical and Topographical*, 204; Thompson Smith, *Letter from the Secretary*, 15.

26. Cusick, *Other War of 1812*, 2, 3, 4; Alexander, "Ambush of Captain John Williams," 282; Sterkx and Thompson, "Philemon Thomas," 378–386; Coker and Parker, "Second Spanish Period," 163.

27. Kappler, *Indian Affairs*, 2:26; Cusick, *Other War of 1812*, 11; Saunt, *New Order of Things*, 237; *Niles Weekly Register*, December 12, 1812; Porter, "Negroes and the East Florida Annexation Plot," 17, 18; Lieutenant Colonel Thomas Adams Smith to Secretary of War, March 18, 1812, and Smith to David Mitchell, May 14, 1812, in T. Frederick Davis, "United States Troops," 5, 12; Gov. Mitchell to General Edmund Gaines, February 5, 1817, *ASFR*, 4:595; Testimony of John Lewis Phenix, *ASFR*, 4:593; John Cumming to David Brydie Mitchell, April 9, 1812, Digital Library of Georgia, http://dlg.galileo.usg.edu.

28. Alexander, "Ambush of Captain John Williams," 293; Porter, "Negroes and the East Florida Annexation Plot," 19, 20; Archibald Clarke to David Brydie Mitchell, August 8, 1812, David Brydie Mitchell Papers, Newberry Library (hereafter NBL), 2:49; Clarke to Mitchell, September 7, 1812, Mitchell Papers, 2:49, NBL; Landers, *Atlantic Creoles*, 114; Gene Allen Smith, *Slaves' Gamble*, 77.

29. Gene Allen Smith, *Slaves' Gamble*, 59, 60, 62, 77.

30. Landers, *Black Society*, 81, 128, 216; Owsley and Smith, *Filibusters and Expansionists*, 79.

31. Patrick, "Letters of the Invaders," 62; Marotti, *Heaven's Soldiers*, 28; Cusick, *Other War of 1812*, 205, 206, 216; Landers, *Black Society in Spanish Florida*, 225.

32. Benjamin Hawkins to David Brydie Mitchell, December 7, 1812, Digital Library of Georgia, http://dlg.galileo.usg.edu; Hawkins to Judge Tomlin, September 12, 1812, Benjamin Hawkins Letters, NBL, 1:8; Porter, "Negroes and the East Florida Annexation Plot," 24, 25; Porter, "Freedom Over Me," unpublished manuscript, Kenneth Wiggins Porter Papers, Schomburg Center, New York Public Library, box 23, folder 5, 18; Smith to General Flournoy, January 3, 1813, in *State Papers and Publick Documents*, 9:268.

33. Buckner Harris to David Mitchell, May 24, 1813, in "East Florida Documents," 154–155; Jose Hibberson to Charles Harris, November 19, 1813, in "East Florida Doc-

uments," 156–157; Charles Harris to Governor Peter Early, November 29, 1813, in "East Florida Documents," 158.

34. Halbert and Ball, *Creek War*, 38; J. Leitch Wright, "Note on the First Seminole War," 566; Doster, "Letters," 269; Lieutenant Montgomery to Samuel Montgomery, September 4, 1813, in Doster, "Letters," 284.

35. Certificate of William Hambly, July 24, 1818, *ASFR*, 4:577; Willcox to Father, January 1, 1814, in *Narrative of the Life*, 6; McAfee, *History of the Late War*, 510; David Brydie Mitchell to Major General Allend Daniel, October 10, 1813, Digital Library of Georgia, http://dlg.galileo.usg.edu; Deposition of Thomas Powell, December 3, 1815, in Lackey, *Frontier Claims*, 30; George Smith to Andrew Jackson, November 22, 1813, in Bassett, *Correspondence of Andrew Jackson*, 1:358.

36. Ridley, *Cudjoe of Jamaica*, 52; Hoogbergen, *Boni Maroon Wars in Suriname*, 50; Honychurch, *In the Forests of Freedom*, 88; Honychurch, *Dominica Story*, 94, 97; Knight, "Natural, Moral and Political History of Jamaica . . . 1742," 50, 278, 283; Hunter to Lords Commissioners, November 13, 1731, CO 137/19, 111; Hunter to Lords, September 20, 1732, CO 137/20, 104; Governor Edward Trelawny to Duke of Newcastle, December 4, 1738, CO 137/56, 158, 159; Trelawny to Board of Trade, November 21, 1741, CO 137/23, 149.

37. Mulroy, *Freedom on the Border*, 13; David Mitchell to James Monroe, January 1813, as quoted in Saunt, *New Order of Things*, 245.

38. Alan Taylor, *Internal Enemy*, 205, 211, 271, 328, 331; Gene Allen Smith, *Slaves' Gamble*, 155; Alexander Inglis Cochrane Proclamation, April 2, 1813, Bermuda, Lockey Collection, 16:1, PKY.

39. Perkins, *Historical Sketches*, 91; Nicolls quoted in Millett, "Britain's 1814 Occupation," 239; Millett, "Radicalism," 181, 182; Millett, *Maroons of Prospect Bluff*, 252.

40. Millett, "Britain's 1814 Occupation," 235, 236; Cochrane to Chiefs of Indian Nations, July 1, 1814, Panton, Leslie, & Company Papers, Microfilm (reel 19), NBL; John Quincy Adams to George William Erving, November 28, 1818, in Ford, *Writings of John Quincy Adams*, 6:476; Narrative of the Operations of the British in the Floridas, 1815, Cruzat Papers, 2:8, PKY; John Innerarity to James Innerarity, October 11, 1814, Greenslade Papers, 2:2, PKY; Latour, *Historical Memoir*, 29, 45, 136; Diary of William Ellis, September 22, 1814, Panton, Leslie, & Company Papers (reel 19), NBL; Captain Robert Henry to Edward Nicolls, September 20, 1814, Foreign Office, National Archives (hereafter FO) 72/219, 40; Gene Allen Smith, *Slaves' Gamble*, 101, 159, 172.

41. Inhabitants of Pensacola to Governor of West Florida, March 1815, Greenslade Papers, 5:1, PKY; Deposition of Mayor in Relation to Deportation of Slaves in Pensacola 1854, Greenslade Papers, 2:2, PKY; File of Witnesses, Juan Galguera, Cruzat Papers, 2:8, PKY; Edmund Doyle to John Innerarity, June 5, 1817, Greenslade Papers, 2:4, PKY; File of Witnesses, Peter Gilchrist, Cruzat Papers, 2:8, PKY; File of Witnesses, Joseph Urcullo, Cruzat Papers, 2:8, PKY; File of Witnesses, Antonio Collins, Cruzat Papers, 2:8, PKY.

42. Narrative of the Operations of the British in the Floridas, 1815, Cruzat Papers, 2:8, PKY; File of Witnesses, Pedro Suarez, Cruzat Papers, 2:8, PKY; File of Witnesses, Don Pedro and Don Joseph Noriega, Cruzat Papers, 2:8, PKY; Pintado to Soto, April 29, 1815, and Petition of Slave Owners from Pensacola, May 6, 1815, Papeles de Cuba, PC file 1796, reel 117, 586–624, PKY; Gene Allen Smith, *Slave's Gamble*, 181.

43. Inhabitants of Pensacola to Governor of West Florida, March 1815, Greenslade Papers, 5:1, PKY; Jose Urcullo to Robert Henry, December 30, 1814, and Henry to Urcullo, January 7 and 8, 1815, Cruzat Papers, 2:7, PKY; Relación de los negros pertenecientes, Papeles de Cuba, May 6, 1815, file 1796, reel 117, 602, PKY; Report of Jose Urcullo, January 23, 1815, Forbes Innerarity Papers in Greenslade Papers, 2:3, PKY; Henry to Manrique, January 12, 1815, Cruzat Papers, 2:7, PKY. See also Doyle to Capt. R. C. Spencer (n.d.), cited in "Panton, Leslie Papers," 237; Doyle to John Innerarity, April 6, 1815, "Panton, Leslie Papers," 238; John Innerarity to Mateo González Manrique, May 16, 1814, cited in "Documents Relating to Colonel Edward Nicolls," 53; Millett, "Radicalism," 175–177.

44. List of Florida Refugee Negroes on board the *Ruby*, Lockey Collection of Documents Related to the History of Florida, PKY, 1:17; Andrew Evans to J. W. Croker, November 24, 1815, Panton, Leslie, & Company Papers (reel 20), NBL.

45. Woodbine to Kindelán, December 30, 1814, *ASFR*, 4:493.

46. Enclosure to Tustunnuggee Hopoie and Tustunnuggee Thlucco in Hawkins to Andrew Jackson, August 30, 1814, in Grant, *Letters*, 2:694; Perkins, *Historical Sketches*, 98.

47. Manrique to Cochrane, January 25, 1815, and Cochrane to Manrique, February 10, 1815, Cruzat Papers, 2:7, PKY; John Greves to John Innerarity, May 5, 1815, Cruzat Papers, 2:7, PKY; Narrative of the Operations of the British in the Floridas, 1815, Cruzat Papers, 2:8, PKY; Cochrane to Henry Bathurst, February 27, 1816, Lockey Collection 17:1, PKY; Cochrane to Lambert, February 17, 1815, ADM 1/508, 24; Gene Allen Smith, *Slaves' Gamble*, 35, 87, 98, 159, 172.

48. Hampden, *Francis Drake Privateer*, 72, 82; Knight, "Natural, Moral and Political History of Jamaica . . . 1746," 47; Knight, "Natural, Moral and Political History of Jamaica . . . 1742," 51, 303. French privateer Jacques de Sores may have armed Spanish slaves or Maroons in his 1555 attack on Havana. See Horne, *Dawning of the Apocalypse*, 96.

49. William Young, *Account of the Black Charaibs*, 48, 60, 105, 106; *Philadelphia Daily Evening Advertiser*, April 13, 1795 (John Frenno); *Charleston City Gazette*, August 23, 1796 (Peter Freneau and Seth Paine); Hoogbergen, *Boni Maroon Wars in Suriname*, 105, 116; Dallas, *History of the Maroons*, 1:168; Lt. Gov. Morris to Earl of Dartmouth, May 24, 1775, CO 101/18, 141, 142.

50. Debbash, "Le Maniel," 144; Daniels, "Marronage in Saint Domingue"; Geggus, "Marronage," 26, 27, 39, 43; Fick, *Making of Haiti*, 156–158.

51. Cusick, *Other War of 1812*, 303; James Innerarity to John Forbes, August 12, 1815, in "The Panton, Leslie Papers: James Innerarity to John Forbes," 128; Hawkins

to Edward Nicolls, March 19, 1815, in Grant, *Letters*, 2:723; Hawkins to Peter Early, April 21, 1815, in Grant, *Letters*, 2:724; Hawkins to Andrew Jackson, August 12, 1815, in Grant, *Letters*, 2:748; Poe, "Archaeological Excavations," 15; Jackson to Mauricio de Zuñiga, April 23, 1816, in Bassett, *Correspondence of Andrew Jackson*, 2:241; Benjamin Hawkins to William Crawford, February 9, 1816, in Grant, *Letters*, 2:773; Hawkins to Crawford, February 16, 1816, in Grant, *Letters*, 2:724; Doyle to Unknown, 1817, Greenslade Papers, 2:4, PKY.

52. John Floyd to David Brydie Mitchell, April 12, 1816, Digital Library of Georgia, http://dlg.galileo.usg.edu; Andrew Jackson to Edmund Gaines, April 8, 1816, in Bassett, *Correspondence of Andrew Jackson*, 2:239; William Crawford to Andrew Jackson, March 15, 1816, in Bassett, *Correspondence of Andrew Jackson*, 2:236.

53. Millett, *Maroons of Prospect Bluff*, 216, 117; Alan Taylor, *Internal Enemy*, 340.

54. Alan Taylor, *Internal Enemy*, 340; Mahon, "First Seminole War," 63; Perkins, *Historical Sketches*, 92; Extract, Letter to the Editor, *Niles Weekly Register*, September 14, 1816; Boyd, "Events at Prospect Bluff," 78, 79; Millett, *Maroons of Prospect Bluff*, 223; Owsley and Smith, *Filibusters and Expansionists*, 109–110.

55. Porter, "Freedom Over Me," 23:5; Colonel Duncan Clinch to Colonel Butler, August 2, 1816, in Forbes, *Sketches, Historical and Topographical*, 200–203; *Niles Weekly Register*, August 31, 1816; *Niles Weekly Register*, September 14, 1816; Thompson Smith, *Letter from the Secretary*, 15; Report of Colonel Cinch as quoted in Katz, *Black West*, 19; Boyd, "Events at Prospect Bluff," 80; Owsley and Smith, *Filibusters and Expansionists*, 107, 110.

56. Woodbine to Nicolls, quoted in *Annals of Congress*, House of Representatives, 15th Congress, 2nd Session, 1040; Canter Brown Jr., "Tales of Angola," 8, 9, 11, 12, 16; William Crawford to David Mitchell, January 27, 1817, Mitchell Papers, 2:78, NBL; Niles *Weekly Register*, January 16, 1819; *Concise Narrative*, 12, 13; Millett, *Maroons of Prospect Bluff*, 237, 238; Owsley and Smith, *Filibusters and Expansionists*, 112.

57. [Zephaniah] L. Kingsley to David Brydie Mitchell, September 13, 1816, Digital Library of Georgia, http://dlg.galileo.usg.edu; Mitchell to José Coppinger, August 7, 1820, Mitchell Papers, 1:12, NBL; William Gibson to David Brydie Mitchell, September 7, 1816, Digital Library of Georgia, http://dlg.galileo.usg.edu; Mahon, "First Seminole War," 64; Jackson to Edmund Gaines, November 21, 1817, in Moser et al., *Papers of Andrew Jackson*, 4:151.

58. *Speech of the Honorable Mr. Mercer*, 836, 1039.

59. Doyle to John Innerarity, June 17, 1817, Greenslade Papers, 2:4, PKY; Doyle to John Innerarity, July 11, 1817, Greenslade Papers, 2:4, PKY.

60. Perkins, *Historical Sketches*, 98, 102, 104; Mahon, "First Seminole War," 64, 65.

61. Millett, "Defining Freedom," 382; William Crawford to Mitchell, December 18, 1818, Mitchell Papers, 2:67, NBL; Perkins, *Historical Sketches*, 107, 155; Testimony of John Lewis Phenix, *ASFR*, 4:593; Benjamin Hawkins to John Armstrong, September 21, 1813, enclosure, in Grant, *Letters*, 2:664–65; James Monroe to Congress, May 25, 1818, *ASPMA*, 1:748; John Quincy Adams to George William Erving, November 28, 1818, in Ford, *Writings of John Quincy Adams*, 6:474; *Concise Narrative*, 6.

62. *Niles Weekly Register*, January 16, 1819; Andrew Jackson to John C. Calhoun, May 5, 1818, in Moser et al., *Papers of Andrew Jackson*, 4:198; Jackson to Jose Masot, May 23, 1818, in Moser et al., *Papers of Andrew Jackson*, 4:206; Annals of Congress, House of Representatives, 15th Congress, 2nd Session, 1040, 1113.

63. Porter, "Freedom over Me," 23:5; Edmund Gaines to Kenhagee, 1817, and Kenhagee to Gaines (n.d.), *ASFR*, 4:586; Forbes to Zuñiga, August 11, 1816, Panton, Leslie, & Company Papers, Microfilm (reel 20), NBL; Bowlegs to Don José Coppinger (n.d.), in *Message from the President of the United States* (1819), 152; Creek Chiefs to Governor Charles Cameron (n.d.), in *Message from the President of the United States* (1819), 138; Little Prince to Commander of U.S. Forces in the Indian Nation, April 26, 1816, Panton, Leslie, & Company Papers (reel 20), NBL; William McIntosh to David Brydie Mitchell, April 12, 1818, Digital Library of Georgia, http://galileo.usg.edu.

64. *Concise Narrative*, 27; Congressman Bassett, *Annals of Congress*, House of Representatives, 15th Congress, 2nd Session, 1109; Mauricio de Zuñiga to Andrew Jackson, May 26, 1818, in *Message from the President of the United States* (1819), 57.

65. Hugh Young, "Topographical Memoir," 97; George Perryman to Lieutenant Sands, February 24, 1817, *ASFR*, 4:596; Porter, "Negroes and the Seminole War," 268, 269; "Description, Strength, and Situation of the Seminoles," 1820, Mitchell Papers, 3:137, NBL; "Defenses of the Floridas," 248.

66. Mitchell to Creek Chiefs, October 22, 1819, Mitchell Papers, 1:20, NBL; Boyd, "Horatio S. Dexter," 66, 73, 75, 76, 77; Dexter, *Observations on the Seminole Indians*, in Boyd, "Horatio S. Dexter," 81–83.

67. Mahon, "Treaty at Moultrie Creek," 364, 370; Kappler, *Indian Affairs*, 2:205, 207.

68. Kappler, *Indian Affairs*, 2:204.

69. Vaughan, *Early American Indian Documents*, 2:676; vols. 10, 12, and 14 in their entirety; 11:16; 6:95, 204, 224; 13:243; Littlefield, *Africans and Creeks*, 9; Kappler, *Indian Affairs*, 2:3, 6, 7, 14, 25, 26.

70. Landers, "Cimarron and Citizen," 134; Thornton, "Les États de l'Angola," 778; Thompson, *Flight to Freedom*, 291.

71. Hugh Young, *Account of the Black Charaibs*, 39–42, 95, 97, 98.

72. Dallas, *History of the Maroons*, 1:28; Edwards, *History, Civil and Commercial*, 1:525, 532, 533; Trelawny to Board of Trade, October 12, 1738, CO 137/23.

73. Price, "Uneasy Neighbors," 1; John Gabriel Stedman, *Narrative of Five Year's Expedition*, 56; de Groot, *From Isolation Towards Integration*, 11.

74. Journal of Louis Nepveu [1762], in Price, *To Slay the Hydra*, 159–163; Price, "Uneasy Neighbors," 9; De Groot, *From Isolation Towards Integration*, 69, 99.

75. It took decades before the Boni Maroons were considered a significant enough of a threat for Whites to call for peace with them, while Spanish authorities in the 1780s in New Orleans launched sizable campaigns against the Maroons of Bas-du-Fleuve and their leader Saint Malo. Unlike the Seminole Maroons and others in the Atlantic, the Bas-du-Fleuve Maroons never secured a peace treaty after Spanish militias defeated them and executed Malo. See *Acts and Deliberations of the Cabildo*, 28 May–4 June 1784, New Orleans Public Library, MF reel 91–14, 195; Gwendolyn Midlo Hall, *Africans in Colonial Louisiana*, 236.

76. Morse, *Report to the Secretary of War*, 308, 309, 311; McCall, *Letters from the Frontiers*, 160; Buker, *Notices of East Florida*, 45, 84.

77. Hoogbergen, *Boni Maroon Wars in Suriname*, 15.

78. May, "Invisible Men," 464.

Chapter 6. Resistance Militarized

1. *Journal of the Constitutional Convention*, 476; Billingsley, *Yearning to Breathe Free*, 61.

2. Report of Higginson in *Official Records of the Union and Confederate Armies*, ser. 1, 28, pt 1: 195 (hereafter *OR*); Burial Ledgers, National Cemetery Administration, Washington, D.C. (Original records transferred to NARA: Burial Registers, compiled 1867–2006, documenting the period 1831–2006. ARC ID: *5928352*. Records of the Department of Veterans Affairs, 1773–2007, Record Group 15. National Archives at Washington, D.C.; *Compiled Military Service Records*; Microfilm Serial: M1992; Microfilm Roll: *46*.

3. There is still some dispute as to which Black regiments mobilized or fought in combat first. See Massachusetts Historical Society, "54th Regiment!," https://www.masshist.org/online/54thregiment/; Walton, "54th Massachusetts Infantry Regiment"; Egon Hatfield, "Black History Month"; Terry Jones, "Free Men of Color."

4. Among the important works include Cornish, *Sable Arm*; Dobak, *Freedom by the Sword*; James McPherson, *Marching toward Freedom*; Glatthaar, *Forged in Battle*; Berlin et al., *Freedom's Soldiers*; Wesley and Romero, *Negro Americans*; Quarles, *Negro in the Civil War*; Trudeau, *Like Men of War*; Dillon, *Slavery Attacked*; Hahn, *Nation under Our Feet*, Hahn, *Political Worlds of Slavery*; Egerton, *Thunder at the Gates*; Ash, *Firebrand of Liberty*.

5. May, "Invisible Men," 464; Carrigan, "Slavery on the Frontier," 66, 67; Tyler, "Fugitive Slaves in Mexico," 1–12; Kelley, "Mexico in His Head," 716; Alwyn Barr, *Black Texans*, 6, 32.

6. Dobak, *Freedom by the Sword*, 8; *Virginia Gazette* (Dixon and Hunter), Williamsburg, November 25, 1775, 2; Alexander Inglis Cochrane Proclamation, Lockey Collection, 16:1, PKY.

7. Berlin et al., *Freedom's Soldiers*, 37; Dobak, *Freedom by the Sword*, 28, 30; Edward Pierce to Major General David Hunter, May 11, 1862, enclosed in Treasury Secretary Salmon Chase to Secretary of War Edwin Stanton, May 21, 1862, in Berlin et al., *Freedom's Soldiers*, 46.

8. *Christian Recorder*, January 18, 1862.

9. Berlin et al., *Freedom's Soldiers*, 37; Dobak, *Freedom by the Sword*, 30; Abraham Lincoln, General order no. 11, Declaring order of General Hunter Emancipating Slaves void, etc. Washington, D.C., 1862, https://www.loc.gov/item/scsm000579/; Benham to de la Croix, May 7, 1862, 30, and Ed. W. Smith to Benham, May 9, 1862, *OR*, ser. 3, 2:31; Hunter to General Isaac Stevens, May 8, 1862, *OR*, ser. 3, 2:30.

10. Lincoln, General order no. 11; Dobak, *Freedom by the Sword*, 8, 33.

11. Robbins, "Recruiting and Arming of Negroes," 151; Pierce to Hunter, May 11,

1862, in Berlin et al., *Freedom's Soldiers*, 48; G. M. Wells to Edward Pierce, May 13 and 18, 1862, enclosed in Salmon Chase to Edwin Stanton, May 21, 1862, in Berlin et al., *Freedom's Soldiers*, 49; May 13, 1862, letter in Holland, *Letters and Diary of Laura M. Towne*, 48–52; Letter from Harriet Ware, May 11, 1862, in Ware, *Letters from Port Royal*, 38.

12. Pierce to Hunter, May 11, 1862, enclosed in Chase to Stanton, May 21, 1862, 46.

13. *New York Times*, May 1, 1862, 2; Quarles, *Negro in the Civil War*, 110; Mohr, "Before Sherman," 349.

14. McRae et al., *Nineteenth Century Freedom Fighters*, ix; Higginson, "First Black Regiment," 522; Susie King Taylor, *Reminiscences of My Life*, 15; Trudeau, *Like Men of War*, 16; Dobak, *Freedom by the Sword*, 33; Mohr, "Before Sherman," 344.

15. Higginson, "First Black Regiment," 522, 524; Susie King Taylor, *Reminiscences of My Life*, 12, 13"; "Letters of Dr. Seth Rogers, 1862, 1863," 394.

16. James McPherson, *Marching toward Freedom*, 53; Dobak, *Freedom by the Sword*, 34; Report of Saxton, November 12, 1862, OR, Ser. 1, 14:189; Lincoln, *First edition of Abraham Lincoln's preliminary emancipation proclamation*.

17. Report of Col. Beard, November 10, 1862, OR, ser. 1, 14:190, 191; J. H. Fowler to Higginson, November 10, 1862, in Looby, *Complete Civil War Journal*, 245.

18. Beard, OR, ser. 1, 14: 191, 192; Cornish, *Sable Arm*, 85; Report of Saxton, November 12, 1862, OR, ser. 1, 14:189, 190.

19. Report of Saxton, November 25, 1862, OR, ser. 1, 14: 192; Report of Beard, November 22, 1862, OR, ser. 1, 14:193; *Chicago Daily Tribune*, December 2, 1862, 1.

20. Dobak, *Freedom by the Sword*, 35, 36, 37; *Chicago Tribune*, December 16, 1862, 2.

21. Higginson, *Army Life*, 40, 41; Ash, *Firebrand of Liberty*, 19; *New York Herald*, January 7, 1863; *New York Daily Tribune*, January 14, 1863, 8.

22. *New York Herald*, January 7, 1863.

23. *New York Herald*, January 7, 1863; *New York Daily Tribune*, January 14, 1863, 8; Susie King Taylor, *Reminiscences of My Life*, 18.

24. Dobak, *Freedom by the Sword*, 11; Ash, *Firebrand of Liberty*, 55.

25. Dobak, *Freedom by the Sword*, 39; Report of Higginson, February 1, 1863, OR, ser. 1, 14:195.

26. Report of Higginson, OR, ser. 1, 14:195; Report of Higginson, February 1, 1863, in Berlin et al., *Freedom's Soldiers*, 522, 523, 524; "Letters of Dr. Seth Rogers," 350, 353; Higginson, *Army Life*, 90.

27. Cornish, *Sable Arm*, 135; Dobak, *Freedom by the Sword*, 39; Higginson, *Army Life*, 86, 96.

28. Report of Higginson, February 1, 1863, OR, ser. 1, 14:196; Report of General Saxton, February 2, 1863, OR, ser. 1, 14:194; Higginson, *Army Life*, 96.

29. Ash, *Firebrand of Liberty*, 96, 97; Report of Brigadier General Joseph Finegan, March 14, 1863, OR, ser. 1, 14:228.

30. Finegan, OR, ser. 1, 14:228; Looby, *Civil War Journal of Higginson*, 109; Susie King Taylor, *Reminiscences of My Life*, 22, 24; "Letters of Rogers," 373; Ash, *Firebrand of Liberty*, 124, 128.

31. "Letters of Dr. Seth Rogers," 361; Ash, *Firebrand of Liberty*, 97.

32. Ash, *Firebrand of Liberty*, 153; "Letters of Dr. Seth Rogers," 380, 382.

33. Ash, *Firebrand of Liberty*, 148; Susie King Taylor, *Reminiscences of My Life*, 25; "Letters of Rogers," 376, 377, 378; Dobak, *Freedom by the Sword*, 43.

34. Captain Alfred Sears to Lt. Colonel Chas. G. Halpine, April 3, 1863, enclosed in Colonel Jos. Hawley to Lt. Col. Halpine, April 29, 1863, in Berlin et al., *Freedom's Soldiers*, 55, 56.

35. Affidavit of Jacob Forrester, April 28, 1863, in Berlin et al., *Freedom's Soldiers*, 57, 58.

36. Dobak, *Freedom by the Sword*, 47; Report of Higginson, July 11, 1863, *OR*, ser. 1, 28 pt 1:194.

37. Dobak, *Freedom by the Sword*, 48. Report of Higginson, July 11, 1863, *OR*, ser. 1, 28 pt 1:194, 195; Susie King Taylor, *Reminiscences of My Life*, 26.

38. Dobak, *Freedom by the Sword*, 59, 60.

39. "Letters of Dr. Seth Rogers," 396, 397; Dobak, *Freedom by the Sword*, 61; Report of Saxton, November 30, 1863, *OR*, ser. 1, 28 pt 1:745, 746; Looby, *Civil War Journal of Higginson*, 329.

40. Egerton, *Thunder at the Gates*, 90; Dobak, *Freedom by the Sword*, 70; McRae et al., *Nineteenth Century Freedom Fighters*, 25; Higginson, "First Black Regiment," 531.

41. Susie King Taylor, *Reminiscences of My Life*, 32, 33, 34; Dobak, *Freedom by the Sword*, 75, 76.

42. Susie King Taylor, *Reminiscences of My Life*, 35; Dobak, *Freedom by the Sword*, 80; Trowbridge Report, December 21, 1864, in Mcrae et al., *Nineteenth Century Freedom Fighters*, 27, 28; Report of Trowbridge, December 21, *OR*, ser. 1, 44:451.

43. Susie King Taylor, *Reminiscences of My Life*, 42, 43, 45; General Order No. 1, 33rd USCT, February 9, 1866, in Berlin et al., *Freedom's Soldiers*, 786.

44. Dobak, *Freedom by the Sword*, 32; Susie King Taylor, *Reminiscences of My Life*, 14.

45. James McPherson, *Marching toward Freedom*, 91; Dobak, *Freedom by the Sword*, 423.

46. November 4, 1863, Speech by Prince Rivers, *Report of the Proceedings of a Meeting*, 22.

47. Ash, *Firebrand of Liberty*, 98; Susie King Taylor, *Reminiscences of My Life*, 16, 8.

48. Looby, *Civil War Journal*, 48, 49; Ash, *Firebrand of Liberty*, 38; "Letters of Dr. Seth Rogers," 363, 364.

49. Higginson, *Army Life*, 63; Higginson, "First Black Regiment," 524.

50. *Harper's Weekly*, June 14, 1862, 372; Billingsley, *Yearning to Breathe Free*, 54, 55, 56, 57, 58, 59, 61.

51. *Harper's Weekly*, June 14, 1862, 372; Billingsley, *Yearning to Breathe Free*, 54, 55, 56, 57, 58, 59, 61.

52. *Boston Commonwealth*, July 10, 1863, vol. 1, no. 45; Sernett, *Harriet Tubman*, 87; Report of Captain John Lay, June 24, 1863, *OR*, ser. 1, 14:299–308; Report of Hunter, June 3, 1862, *OR*, ser. 1, 14:463; Letter from Tubman, June 30, 1863, in Bradford, *Scenes in the Life*, 86.

53. Report of Saxton, November 12, 1862, *OR*, ser. 1, 14:190.
54. Report of Higginson, February 1, 1863, in Berlin et al., *Freedom's Soldiers*, 526.
55. Anonymous to General Daniel Sickles, January 13, 1866, in Berlin et al., *Freedom's Soldiers*, 777.
56. Looby, *Civil War Journal*, 209, 210.
57. *Report of the Proceedings of a Meeting*, 23.
58. Fleetwood, *Negro as a Soldier*, 6.
59. Egerton, *Thunder at the Gates*, 64, 169; Report of Nathan Evans, January 25, 1862, *OR*, ser. 1, 6:77–78; Howard Westwood, "Captive Black Union Soldiers," 28.
60. Hunter to Davis, April 23, 1863, in Berlin et al., *Freedom's Soldiers*, 573; Davis Order no. III, December 24, 1862, *OR*, ser. 2, 5:795–97; Lt. Charles C. Jones to Rev. C. C. Jones, July 19, 1862, in Myers, *Children of Pride*, 934, 935; C. C. Jones to Charles Jones, July 21, 1862, in Myers, *Children of Pride*, 935.
61. Report of Finegan, March 14, 1863, *OR*, ser. 1, 14:228.
62. Report of John Lay, June 24, 1863, *OR*, ser.1, 14:304, 306.
63. Ash, *Firebrand of Liberty*, 9, 85; Higginson, *Army Life*, 4; "Letters of Dr. Seth Rogers," 367.
64. Ash, *Firebrand of Liberty*, 87, 97; Higginson, *Army Life*, 99.
65. Higginson, *Army Life*, 248. Parts of this conversation were also reported in *The Liberator*, August 8, 1862.
66. Pierce, "Freedmen at Port Royal," 291–315; *New York Daily Tribune*, January 14, 1863, 8; Higginson, *Army Life*, 48.
67. Sernett, *Scenes in the Life*, 86; Saxton to Bradford, March 21, 1868, in Bradford, *Scenes in the Life*, 64; Letter from Tubman, June 30, 1863, in Bradford, *Scenes in the Life*, 86, 87.
68. *Independent Democrat*, October 25, 1859; Geffert, "John Brown," 591–610.
69. Dobak, *Freedom by the Sword*, 474, 502, 503.
70. "Letters of Dr. Seth Rogers," 396; *Report of the Proceedings of a Meeting*, 23; Anonymous to General Sickles, January 13, 1866, in Berlin et al., *Freedom's Soldiers*, 778; Rivers to Saxton, November 26, 1865, in Sterling, *Trouble They Seen*, 37.

Epilogue

1. Grantham to Coventry, November 21, 1677, Henry Coventry Papers, Virginia State Library, 77:301–302.
2. For a longer history of the abolition movement, see Sinha, *Slave's Cause*.
3. This does not discredit strategies used in Africa to avoid enslavement. See Diouf, *Fighting the Slave Trade*.

BIBLIOGRAPHY

Primary Sources
MANUSCRIPTS

Ann Arbor

CLEMENTS LIBRARY, UNIVERSITY OF MICHIGAN, ANN ARBOR

Henry Clinton Papers
Frederick Mackenzie Papers
George Wray Papers

Chicago

NEWBERRY LIBRARY

Collection of Transcripts of documents from the Archivo Nacional de Cuba concerning politics, defense, and administration of the Spanish colonies of Cuba, Florida
Benjamin Hawkins Letters
David Brydie Mitchell Papers
Letters Received from the Office of Indian Affairs
Louisiana from 1770 to 1830
Panton, Leslie & Company Papers, Reels 19, 20, Microfilm
Proceedings of the general court-martial in the trial of Major John Gordon of the late Eighth West India Regiment, 1804
Records in the British Public Record Office Relating to South Carolina, Microfilm
The Despatches of the Spanish Governors of Louisiana to the captains-general of Cuba, 1766–1791

Gainesville

P. K. YONGE LIBRARY OF FLORIDA HISTORY, GAINESVILLE

Alexander Cochrane Papers
Buckingham Smith Papers, Microfilm, reel 141J.
Heloise Cruzat Papers
Marie Taylor Greenslade Papers
Forbes-Innerarity Papers
Joseph Byrne Lockey Collection
Papeles de Cuba
John Batterson Stetson Collection

Indianapolis

INDIANA HISTORICAL SOCIETY LIBRARY

Thomas Posey Collection
Captain Thomas Posey's Revolutionary War Journal

British Library, London

ADDITIONAL MANUSCRIPTS

ADD MSS. 12415. James Knight. "The Natural, Moral and Political History of Jamaica, and the territories thereon depending, from the earliest account of time to the year 1742."

ADD. MSS. 12419. James Knight. "The Natural, Moral, and Political History of Jamaica, and the Territories thereon depending, in America, from the first discovery of the island by Christopher Columbus to the year 1746. By a Gentle-man, who resided above 20 years in Jamaica."

NATIONAL ARCHIVES, KEW, UNITED KINGDOM

Admiralty Office

ADM 1/236—Jamaica, Letters from Senior Officers, 1759–1761
ADM 1/508—North America, Original Correspondence, Letters from Admirals, 1815
ADM 51/717—Captains' Logs, Port Antonio, 1757–1763
ADM 51/1082—Captains' Logs, Wager, 1740–1748
ADM 52/892—Masters' Logs, Harwich, 1757–1760
ADM 52/1493—Masters' Logs, Viper, 1760–1765

Colonial Office

CO 1/123—America and the West Indies, Colonial Papers (General Series)
CO 1/137—America and the West Indies, Colonial Papers (General Series)
CO 5/154—America and the West Indies, Board of Trade and Secretaries of State, 1771–1776

CO 5/1335—America and the West Indies, Colonial Papers (Original Correspondence) Board of Trade and Secretaries of State, 1702–1752
CO 5/1371—Proceedings and Reports of the Commissioners for Enquiring into Virginia Affairs and Settling Virginian Grievances
CO 5/1373—America and the West Indies, Colonial Papers (Original Correspondence) Letters to Secretary of State, 1774–1777
CO 528/1—Barbados, Original Correspondence to Board of Trade, 1689–1692
CO 28/85—Barbados, Original Correspondence to Secretary of State, 1816
CO 31/47—Barbados, Sessional Papers, 1816–1818
CO 71/33–34—Dominica, Original Correspondence to Secretary of State, 1793, 1802
CO 101/16–18—Grenada, Original Correspondence to Secretary of State, 1771–1775
CO 101/34—Grenada, Original Correspondence to Secretary of State, 1795
CO 103/9—Grenada, Acts, 1789–1795
CO 103/9—Grenada, Acts, 1796–1810
CO 111/39–46—British Guiana, formerly Berbice, Demerara, and Essequibo, Original Correspondence, 1823–1824
CO 137/18–23—Jamaica, Original Correspondence to Board of Trade, 1729–1743
CO 137/54—Jamaica, Original Correspondence to Secretary of State, 1732–1733
CO 137/56—Jamaica, Original Correspondence to Secretary of State, 1736–1740
CO 137/60—Jamaica, Original Correspondence to Secretary of State, 1753–1761
CO 137/71—Jamaica, Original Correspondence to Secretary of State, 1775–1776
CO 137/95–96—Jamaica, Original Correspondence to Secretary of State, 1795–1796
CO 137/123—Jamaica, Original Correspondence to Secretary of State, 1808
CO 137/179–85—Jamaica, Original Correspondence to Secretary of State, 1831–1832
CO 140/29—Jamaica, Sessional Papers, Council in Assembly, 1737–1739
CO 140/43—Jamaica, Sessional Papers, Council in Assembly, 1760–1767
CO 318/18–20—West Indies, Original Correspondence to Secretary of State, 1795–1802
CO 318/18–28—West Indies, Original Correspondence to Secretary of State, 1805
CO 318/18–29—West Indies, Original Correspondence to Secretary of State, 1806
CO 318/18–33—West Indies, Original Correspondence to Secretary of State, 1808
CO 700/24—Florida, Map of the New Governments of East and West Florida, 1765

Foreign Office

FO 72/219—Foreign Office and predecessor: Political and Other Departments: General Correspondence before 1906, Spain, 01 April 1818–31 May 1818

War Office

WO 1/82—Dispatches from commanders in Guadeloupe, Jamaica, Martinique, Santo Domingo, St. Croix, Trinidad, Paramaribo, Newfoundland to Secretary at War, 1793–1797
WO 1/83—Windward and Leeward Islands, Miscellaneous Dispatches to Secretary at War, 1794–1795

WO 1/86—Windward and Leeward Islands, Miscellaneous Dispatches to Secretary at War, 1796–1798
WO 1/88—Windward and Leeward Islands, Miscellaneous Dispatches to Secretary at War, 1798–1800
WO 1/89—Windward and Leeward Islands, Miscellaneous Dispatches to Secretary at War, 1800–1801
WO 1/90—Windward and Leeward Islands, Miscellaneous Dispatches to Secretary at War, 1801
WO 1/95—Dispatches from commanders in Guadeloupe, Jamaica, Martinique, Santo Domingo, St. Croix, Trinidad, Paramaribo, Newfoundland, 1800–1810
WO 1/96—Dispatches from commanders in North and South America and the West Indies, 1800–1813
WO 1/149—Surinam, Governor's Original Dispatches, Letters, and Papers to Secretary at War, 1805
WO 1/150—Surinam, Governor's Original Dispatches, Letters, and Papers to Secretary at War, 1806
WO 1/623—Miscellaneous Dispatches to Secretary at War, 1801
WO 1/630—Miscellaneous Dispatches to Secretary at War, 1805
WO 1/769—Miscellaneous Letters to Secretary at War, 1797–1798
WO 4/339—Secretary at War out letters, 1684–1861
WO 17/251—Monthly Returns, 1st West India Regiment, 1795–1808
WO 25/644—Description and Succession Books, 2 West India Regiment, 1810–1829
WO 25/650—Description and Succession Books, 3 West India Regiment, 1861–1869
WO 25/662—Description and Succession Books, 7 West India Regiment, 1813–1817
WO 27/191—Office of Commander-in-Chief and War Office, Inspection Returns, 1829
WO 40/20—Letters to Secretary at War, 1804
WO 90/1—Judge Advocate General's Office: General Courts Martial Registers, abroad, 1796–1823

New Orleans and Louisiana
AMISTAD RESEARCH CENTER, TULANE UNIVERSITY
Gwendolyn Midlo Hall Papers

LOUISIANA STATE MUSEUM HISTORICAL CENTER
Spanish Judicial Records, 1781, 1784

NEW ORLEANS PUBLIC LIBRARY
Acts and Deliberations of the Cabildo

SAINT CHARLES PARISH COURTHOUSE, HAHNVILLE
Saint Charles Parish Original Acts Book 41

New York

NEW-YORK HISTORICAL SOCIETY

Daniel Parish Jr. Transcripts of Material on Slavery in the Public Record Office
"Coroner's Inquisition and Jury Finding on the Death of William Asht"
"Coroner's Inquisition and Jury Finding on the Death of Augustus Grasset"

NEW YORK MUNICIPAL ARCHIVES

Minute Book of the Court of General Sessions, 1705–1714
Minutes of the Court of Quarter and General Sessions, begun August 7th Anno. 1694

NEW YORK PUBLIC LIBRARY

An Account of the Late Negro Insurrection which took place in the Island of Barbados on Easter Sunday 14 April 1816
David Brydie Mitchell Papers
East Florida Papers, 1783–1821
George Chalmers Collection, Virginia 1. Digital Collections
Kenneth Wiggins Porter Papers
Personal Narratives of the Haitian Revolution
U.S. States and Territories, Virginia
U.S. State and Territories, Florida

Philadelphia

AMERICAN PHILOSOPHICAL SOCIETY

Peale-Sellers Papers

HISTORICAL SOCIETY OF PENNSYLVANIA

Birch Family Papers
Borie Papers
William Bradford Papers
Dillwyn and Emlen Family Correspondence
Dreer Collection
Elizabeth Drinker Diaries
McCall Family Papers
William Redwood Account Books

LIBRARY COMPANY OF PHILADELPHIA

Benjamin Rush Family Papers
Deborah Norris Logan Family Papers

Other

HARGRETT RARE BOOK AND MANUSCRIPT LIBRARY, ATHENS, GEORGIA

David Brydie Mitchell Letters, presented by Digital Library of Georgia, http://dlg.galileo.usg.edu/

HILTON HEAD HERITAGE LIBRARY AND ANCESTRY RESEARCH CENTER, HILTON HEAD, SOUTH CAROLINA

Index of Selected Soldiers of the 33rd USCT Regiment

LIBRARY OF CONGRESS, WASHINGTON, D.C.

Abraham Lincoln, General order no. 11, Declaring order of General Hunter Emancipating Slaves void, etc. Washington, D.C., 1862, https://www.loc.gov/item/scsm000579/

Map of Morris, Folly, Coles and James Islands etc., and Charleston Harbor S.C. shewing sic Union and Rebel forts and batteries

Abraham Lincoln, First edition of Abraham Lincoln's preliminary emancipation proclamation, Washington, D.C., 1862, Photograph, https://www.loc.gov/item/scsm001017/

Part of the Province of Virginia

Robert Smalls Photograph

NATIONAL ARCHIVES AT WASHINGTON, D.C.

Compiled Military Service Records of Volunteer Union Soldiers Who Served with the United States Colored Troops: 1st U.S. Colored Infantry, 1st South Carolina Volunteers (Colored) Company A, 1st U.S. Colored Infantry (1 Year); Microfilm Serial: M1819; Microfilm Roll: *18*

STATE LIBRARY AND ARCHIVES OF FLORIDA, TALLAHASSEE

Historical Maps Collection, *www.floridamemory.com*

UNIVERSITY OF SOUTH FLORIDA, TAMPA

Educational Technology Clearinghouse

VIRGINIA STATE LIBRARY, RICHMOND

Coventry Papers

Thomas Grantham to Henry Coventry, Coventry Papers 77:301–302, Virginia Colonial Records Project Reel 901, Microfilm

NEWSPAPERS

Antigua Herald and Gazette, St. Johns, 1798
Antigua Observer, St. Johns, 1848
Army and Navy Chronicle (T. Bernard), Washington D.C., 1836

Boston Commonwealth, 1863
Charleston City Gazette (Peter Freneau and Seth Paine), 1795, 1796
Chicago Tribune, Chicago, 1862
Christian Recorder, Philadelphia, 1862
Congressional Globe, Washington, D.C., 1862–1864
Connecticut Gazette (Timothy and Samuel Green), New London, 1796
Cornwall Chronicle, Montego Bay, 1791
Diario de la Habana, Havana, 1845
Dominica Journal or Weekly Intelligencer, 1814
Frank Leslie's Illustrated Newspaper, New York, 1863
Fresh Intelligence (J. Dunlap), Philadelphia, 1775
Gentleman's Magazine (E. Cave), London, 1740
General Evening Post (Richard Nutt), London, 1776
Grenada Free Press, St. Georges, 1832
Harper's Weekly, New York, 1862
The Herald (Noah Webster Jr.), New York, 1797
Independent Democrat, Charles Town, 1859
Independent Democrat, Elyria, Ohio, 1859
Jamaica Journal, Kingston, 1824
Jamaica Watchman, Kingston, 1831, 1832
The Liberator, Boston, 1859, 1862
New Jersey Gazette (Isaac Collins), Trenton, 1782
New York Daily Tribune, 1863
New York Gazette (James Parker), 1773
New York Herald, 1863
New York Semi-Weekly Tribune, 1859.
New York Times, 1862.
Newport Mercury, New Orleans, 1827
Niles Weekly Register (Hezekiah Niles), Baltimore, 1812, 1816, 1819.
Pennsylvania Gazette (Benjamin Franklin), Philadelphia, 1775.
Philadelphia Daily Evening Advertiser (John Frenno), 1795.
Philadelphia Gazette (Andrew Brown Jr.), 1798.
Providence Gazette (John Carter), 1773.
Public Advertiser (Henry Sampson Woodfall), London, 1776.
Royal Gazette, Kingston, 1816.
Savannah Republican: And Evening Ledger, 1808.
St. Georges Chronicle and Grenada Gazette, 1790.
Virginia Gazette (Alexander Purdie), Williamsburg, 1775–1776.
Virginia Gazette (John Dixon & William Hunter), Williamsburg, 1775–1776.
Virginia Gazette (John Pinkney), Williamsburg, 1775–1776.

OTHER PUBLISHED PRIMARY SOURCES

Anderson, Dice Robins, ed. *Richmond College Historical Papers*. Richmond: Richmond College, 1915.

Anderson, Osborne. *A Voice from Harper's Ferry: A Narrative of Events at Harper's Ferry: with Incidents Prior and Subsequent to Its Capture by Captain Brown and His Men*. Boston: Osborne Anderson, 1861.

Andrews, Charles Mclean, ed. *Narratives of the Insurrections, 1675–1690*. New York: C. Scribner's Sons, 1915.

Annual Report of the Board of Managers of the Mass. Anti-Slavery Society, 22 Jan 1840. Boston: Dow & Jackson, 1840.

Ardouin, B. (Beaubrun). *Etudes sur L'Histoire d'Haiti: Suivies de la Vie du General J.-M. Borgella*. Paris: Tome, 1853.

Authentic Papers Relative to the Expedition against the Charibbs, and the Sale of Lands in the Island of St. Vincent. London: J. Almon, 1773.

Barber, John Warner. *A History of the Amistad Captives*. New Haven, Conn.: E. L. and J. W. Barber, 1840.

Barr, James. *Correct and Authentic Narrative of the Indian War in Florida: With a Description of Major Dade's Massacre, and an Account of the Extreme Suffering, for Want of Provision, of the Army—Having Been Obliged to Eat Horse's and Dogs' Flesh, &c, &c*. New York: J. Narne, 1836.

Bassett, John Spencer, ed. *Correspondence of Andrew Jackson*. Vols. 1–2. Washington, D.C.: Carnegie Institution of Washington, 1926.

Berkeley, William. *A List of Those That Have Been Executed for the Late Rebellion in Virginia*. Reprint ed. Washington, D.C.: Peter Force, 1835.

Berlin, Ira, Joseph Reidy, and Leslie Rowland, eds. *Freedom: A Documentary History of Emancipation, 1861–1867*. 2nd series, vol. 1. New York: Cambridge University Press, 1982.

———. *Freedom's Soldiers: The Black Military Experience in the Civil War*. New York: Cambridge University Press, 1998.

Beverley, Robert. *The History and Present State of Virginia, in Four Parts . . .* London: R. Parker, 1705.

Billings, Warren, ed. *The Old Dominion in the Seventeenth Century: A Documentary History of Virginia, 1606–1689*. Chapel Hill: University of North Carolina Press, 1975.

———, ed. *The Papers of Sir William Berkeley, 1605–1677*. Richmond: Library of Virginia, 2007.

Bingham, Luther. *The Young Quartermaster: The Life and Death of Lieut. L. M. Bingham of the First South Carolina Volunteers*. New York: Board of Publication of the Reformed Protestant Dutch Church, 1863.

Blackburne Daniell, Francis Henry ed. *Calendar of State Papers Domestic Series, of the Reign of Charles II*, vol. 14. London: Mackie, 1907.

———. *Calendar of State Papers Domestic Series, of the Reign of Charles II*, vol. 18. London: Mackie, 1909.

Bleby, Henry. *Death Struggles of Slavery: Being a Narrative of Facts and Incidents in a British Colony, during the Two Years Immediately Preceding Negro Emancipation*. London: Hamilton, Adams, 1853.

Book of Negroes [1783]. Sir Guy Carleton Papers. Nova Scotia Archives Microfilm no. 10149. http://novascotia.ca/archives/africans/archives.

Booth, William. Personal Diary. Acadia University Archives. Canada's Digital Collections. https://blackloyalist.com/cdc/documents/diaries/booth_diary.htm, March 14, 1789.

Bossard, Johan ed. *C. G. A. Oldendorp's History of the Mission of the Evangelical Bretheren on the Caribbean Islands of St. Thomas, St. Croix, and St. John*. Translated by Arnold Highfield and Vladimir Barac. Ann Arbor, Mich.: Karoma, 1987.

Boyd, Mark. "Horatio Dexter and Events Leading to the Treaty of Moultrie Creek with the Seminole Indians." *Florida Anthropologist* 11, no. 3 (September 1958): 65–95.

Brooks, A. M., ed. *The Unwritten History of Old St. Augustine Copied from the Spanish Archives in Seville, Spain*. Translated by Annie Averette. St. Augustine, Fla.: The Record Co., 1909.

Brooks, Joanna, and John Saillant, eds. *"Face Zion Forward": First Writers of the Black Atlantic, 1785–1798*. Boston: Northeastern University Press, 2002.

Buckley, Roger Norman, ed. *The Haitian Journal of Lieutenant Howard, York Hussars, 1796–1798*. Knoxville: University of Tennessee Press, 1985.

Buker, George, ed. *Notices of East Florida with an Account of the Seminole Nation of Indians: A Facsimile Reproduction of the 1822 Edition by William Simmons*. Gainesville: University of Florida Press, 1973.

Butler, R., and D. L. Clinch. D. L. Clinch to R. Butler, August 2, 1816. Includes an inventory of captured stores from a fort in East Florida. August 2, 1816. Manuscript/Mixed Material. Retrieved from the Library of Congress, https://www.loc.gov/item/mjmo18225/.

Carter, Susan, ed. *Historical Statistics of the United States*. Millennial ed. Cambridge: Cambridge University Press, 2006.

Chanvalon, Jean-Baptiste de. *Voyage à la Martinique: Contenant Diverses Observations sur la Physique, l'histoire naturelle, l'agriculture, les moeurs, & les usages de cette isle, faites en 1751 & dans les années suivantes lu à l'Académie Royale des Sciences de Paris en 1761*. Paris: J. B. Bauche, 1763.

Chesnutt, David, James Taylor, Peggy Clark, David Fischer, Jean Mustain, and George Rogers Jr., eds. *The Papers of Henry Laurens*. Vol. 10. Columbia: University of South Carolina Press, 1985.

Cheves, Langdon, ed. *Yearbook... City of Charleston, South Carolina 1894*. Charleston: Walker Evans & Cogswell, 1894.

Clark, Ehmert, ed. *The Journal and Letters of Francis Asbury*. Vol. 1. London: Epworth Press, 1958.

Clark, William Well, ed. *Naval Documents of the American Revolution*. Vols. 1–2. Washington, D.C.: Government Printing Office, 1964–1966.

Coke, Thomas. *The Case of the Caribbs in St. Vincent's*. N.P. 1788.

A Concise Narrative of the Seminole Campaign by an Officer, Attached to the Expedition. Nashville: M'Lean & Tunstall, 1819.

Conrad, Glenn. *The German Coast: Abstracts of the Civil Records of St. Charles and St. John the Baptist Parishes, 1804–1812.* Lafayette: University of Southwestern Louisiana, 1981.

Conrad, Robert Edgar, ed. *Children of God's Fire: A Documentary History of Black Slavery in Brazil.* Princeton, N.J.: Princeton University Press, 1983.

A Continuation of the State of New-England; Being a Farther Account of the Indian Warr, and of the Engagement betwixt the Joynt Forces of the United English Colonies and the Indians . . . Together with an Account of the Intended Rebellion of the Negroes in Barbadoes. London: T. M., 1676.

Cooper, Thomas, and David McCord, eds. *The Statutes at Large of South Carolina.* 10 vols. Columbia: A. S. Johnston, 1836–1873.

Cooper, Willyams. *An Account of the Campaign in the West Indies in the Year 1794.* London: T. Bensely, 1796.

"Correspondence of Hon. Arthur Middleton and Joseph Barnwell." *South Carolina Historical and Genealogical Magazine* 27, no. 3 (July 1926): 107–157.

Craig, Alan, and Christopher Peebles. "Captain Young's Sketch Map, 1818." *Florida Historical Quarterly* 48, no. 2 (October 1969): 176–179.

Crawford, Michael, ed. *The Naval War of 1812: A Documentary History.* Vol. 3. Washington, D.C.: Naval Historical Center, 2002.

Curle, H. W. R. "Intercepted Letters of Virginia Tories, 1775." *American Historical Review* 12, no. 2 (January 1907): 341–346.

Dallas, Robert Charles. *The History of the Maroons: From Their Origin to the Establishment of Their Chief Tribe at Sierra Leone: Including the Expedition to Cuba, for the Purpose of Procuring Spanish Chasseurs, and the State of the Island of Jamaica for the Last Ten Years: With a Succinct History of the Island Previous to That Period.* Vol. 1. London: T. N. Londman and O. Rees, 1803.

Davies, K. G., ed. *Documents of the American Revolution, 1770–1783.* Colonial Office Series. Vol. 11. Dublin: Irish University Press, 1976.

"The Defenses of the Floridas: A Report of Captain James Gadsden, Aide-de-Camp to General Jackson" [August 1, 1818]. *Florida Historical Quarterly* 15, no. 4 (January 1937): 242–248.

de Groot, Silvia w., ed. *From Isolation Towards Integration: The Suriname Maroons and Their Colonial Rulers, Officials Documents Relating to the Djukas (1845–1863).* The Hague: Nijohh, 1977.

Delaye, Jean-Baptiste. *Relation du Massacre des François aux Natchez et de la guerre contre ces sauvages 1er juin 1730.* Translated by Gordon Sayre. http://darking.uoregon.edu.

de Ville, Winston, ed. *Massacre at Natchez in 1729: The Rheims Manuscript.* Platte: Louisiana Provincial Press, 2003.

DeWitt, Robert, ed. *The Life, Trial and Execution of Captain John Brown, Known as "Old Brown of Ossawatomie": with a Full Account of the Attempted Insurrection at*

Harper's Ferry; Compiled from Official and Authentic Sources. New York: Robert Dewitt, 1859.

Dexter, Horatio. *Observations on the Seminole Indians.* In Boyd, "Horatio Dexter," 65–95.

Distribution of Indian Tribes in the Southeast about the Year 1715. South Carolina Historical Center. Detroit Public Library reprint. 1960. Newberry Library.

"Documents Relating to Colonel Edward Nicolls and Captain George Woodbine in Pensacola, 1814." *Florida Historical Quarterly* 10, no. 1 (July 1931): 51–54.

Donnan, Elizabeth, ed. *Documents Illustrative of the History of the Slave Trade to America.* 4 vols. New York: Octagon, 1965.

Doster, James. "Letters Relating to the Tragedy of Fort Mims: August–September 1813." *Alabama Review* 14, no. 4 (October 1961): 269–285.

Drayton, John. *Memoirs of the American Revolution: From Its Commencement to the Year 1776, Inclusive, as Relating to the State of South-Carolina and Occasionally Referring to the States of North-Carolina and Georgia.* Charleston: A. E. Miller, 1821.

Dubois, Laurent, and John Garrigus, eds. *Slave Revolution in the Caribbean, 1789–1804: A Brief History with Documents.* Boston: Bedford/St. Martin's, 2006.

Dubroca, Louis. *La Vie de J. J. Dessalines: chef des noirs révoltés de Saint Domingue, avec des notes trés-détaillées sur l'origine, le caractère, la vie et les atrocities des principaux ches des noirs, depuis l'insurrection de 1791.* Paris: Dubcroca et Rondonneau, 1804.

"East Florida Documents." *Georgia Historical Quarterly* 13, no. 2 (June 1929): 154–158.

Edwards, Bryan. *The History, Civil and Commercial, of the British West Indies.* Vol. 1. London: G. and W. B. Whittaker, 1818–1819.

———. *The Proceedings of the Governor and Assembly of Jamaica, in Regard to the Maroon Negroes.* London: J. Stockdale, 1796.

Egerton, Douglas, and Robert Paquette, eds. *The Denmark Vesey Affair: A Documentary History.* Gainesville: University Press of Florida, 2017.

Ellis, A. B. *The History of the First West India Regiment.* London: Chapman & Hall, 1885.

Flournoy, H. W., ed. *Calendar of Virginia State Papers and Other Manuscripts.* 11 vols. Richmond, 1892.

Forbes, James Grant. *Sketches, Historical and Topographical of the Floridas: More Particularly of East Florida.* New York: C. S. Van Winkle, 1821.

Force, Peter, ed. *American Archives, Fifth Series: Containing a Documentary History of the United States of America, from the Declaration of Independence, July 4, 1776, to the Definitive Treaty of Peace with Great Britain, September 3, 1783.* 3 vols. [incomplete, through 1776 only]. Washington, D.C.: M. St. Clair Clarke and P. Force, 1848–1853.

———, ed. *American Archives, Fourth Series: Containing a Documentary History of the English Colonies in North America, from the King's Message to Parliament, of March 7, 1774, to the Declaration of Independence by the United States.* 6 vols. Washington, D.C.: M. St. Clair Clarke and P. Force, 1837–1846.

———, ed. *Tracts and Other Papers Relating Principally to the Origin, Settlement, and Progress of the Colonies in North America: From the Discovery of the Country to the Year 1776*. Vol. 1. Gloucester, Mass.: Peter Smith, 1963.

Fortescue, J. W., ed. *Calendar of State Papers Colonial Series: America and West Indies, 1689–1692*. Vols. 9, 10, 12, 13. Vaduz: Kraus, 1964.

Frantz, John, ed. *Bacon's Rebellion: Prologue to the Revolution*. Lexington, Mass.: D. C. Heath, 1969.

Fyfe, Christopher, ed. *"Our Children Free and Happy": Letters from Black Settlers in Africa in the 1790s*. Edinburgh: Edinburgh University Press, 1991.

Gold Thwaites, Reuben, ed. *Jesuit Relations and Allied Documents*. 71 vols. Cleveland: Burrows Brothers, 1901.

Grant, C. L., ed. *Letters, Journals, and Writings of Benjamin Hawkins*. Vol. 2, 1802–1816. Savannah: Beehive Press, 1980.

Grantham, Thomas. *An Historical Account of Some Memorable Actions, Particularly in Virginia; Also Against the Admiral of Algier* . . . London: J. Roberts, 1716.

Great Newes from the Barbadoes, or, A True and Faithful Account of the Grand Conspiracy of the Negroes against the English . . . London: L. Curtis, 1676.

Greenberg, Kenneth, ed. *The Confessions of Nat Turner and Related Documents*. Boston: Bedford/St. Martin's, 1996.

Greene, Jack, ed. *The Diary of Landon Carter of Sabine Hall, 1752–1778*. Vol. 2. Charlottesville: University Press of Virginia, 1965.

Hall, Douglas, ed. *In Miserable Slavery: Thomas Thistlewood in Jamaica. 1750–1786*. Kingston: University of the West Indies Press, 1999.

Hamilton, James. *Negro Plot: An Account of the Late Intended Insurrection among a Portion of the Blacks of the City of Charleston 1822*. Edited by Jill Kuhn. Chapel Hill: University of North Carolina Press, 1999.

Hampden, John, ed. *Francis Drake Privateer: Contemporary Narratives and Documents*. Tuscaloosa: University of Alabama Press, 1972.

Handler, Jerome, ed. "'Memoirs of an Old Army Officer': Richard A. Wyvill's Visits to Barbados in 1796 and 1806–7." *Journal of the Barbados Museum and Historical Society* 35, no. 1 (March 1975): 21–30.

Hay, John. *A Narrative of the Insurrection in the Island of Grenada Which Took Place in 1795*. London: J. Ridgway, 1823.

Hemphill, Edwin, ed. *The Papers of John C. Calhoun*. Vol. 2, 1817–1818. Columbia: University of South Carolina Press, 1963.

Hening, William Waller, ed. *The Statutes at Large: Being a Collection of all the Laws of Virginia, from the First Session of the Legislature, in the Year 1619 Published Pursuant to an Act of the General Assembly of Virginia, Passed on the Fifth Day of February, One Thousand Eight Hundred and Eight*. Vols. 1 and 2. New York: William Hening, R. & W. & G. Bartow, 1823.

Higginson, Thomas Wentworth. *Army Life in a Black Regiment*. Boston: Fields, Osgood, 1870.

———. "The First Black Regiment." *Outlook* 59 (July 1898): 521–531.

Hodges, Graham Russell, ed. *The Black Loyalist Directory: African Americans in Exile after the American Revolution*. New York: Garland in Association with the New England Historic Genealogical Society, 1996.

Holland, Rupert Sergeant, ed. *Letters and Diary of Laura M. Towne: Written from the Sea Islands of South Carolina, 1862–1864*. Cambridge: Riverside Press, 1912.

Horsmanden, Daniel. *A Journal of the Proceedings in the Detection of the Conspiracy Formed by Some White People, in Conjunction with Negro and other Slaves, For Burning the City of New-york in America, and Murdering the Inhabitants*. 2nd ed. New York: Southwick & Pelsue, 1810.

Hulme, Peter, and Neil Whitehead, eds. *Wild Majesty: Encounters with Caribs from Columbus to the Present Day*. Oxford: Clarendon Press, 1992.

Humphreys, David. *An Historical Account of the Incorporated Society for the Propagation of the Gospel in Foreign Parts: Containing Their Foundation, Proceedings, and the Success of Their Missionaries in the British Colonies, to the Year 1728*. London: Joseph Downing, 1730.

An Inquiry into the Causes of the Insurrection of the Negroes in the Island of St. Domingo. London: J. Johnson, 1792.

Jay, William. *The Creole Case, and Mr. Webster's Dispatch: with the Comments of the N.Y. American*. New York: New York American, 1842.

Johnstone, Andrew James Cochrane, and Henry Dundas Melville. *To the Right Honourable Lord Viscount Melville, First Lord Commissioner of the Admiralty*. London: Barfield, 1805.

Jones, Adam, ed. *German Sources for West African History, 1599–1669*. Wiesbaden: Steiner, 1983.

Journal of the Constitutional Convention of the State of South Carolina. Columbia: C. A. Calvo Jr., 1895.

Kappler, Charles, ed. *Indian Affairs: Laws and Treaties*. Vol. 2. Washington, D.C.: Government Printing Office, 1904.

Kingsley, Charles. *At Last, a Christmas in the West Indies*. Vol. 14. London: Macmillan, 1880.

Klingberg, Frank, ed. *The Carolina Chronicle of Dr. Francis Le Jau, 1706–1717*. Berkeley: University of California Press, 1956.

———, ed. *Gideon Johnstone, Carolina Chronicle: The Papers of Commissary Gideon Johnstone, 1707–1716*. Berkeley: University of California Press, 1946.

Knibb, William. *Facts and Documents Connected with the Late Insurrection in Jamaica, and the Violations of Civil and Religious Liberty Arising Out of It*. London, 1832.

Lackey, Richard, ed. *Frontier Claims in the Lower South: Records of Claims Filed by Citizens of the Alabama and Tombigbee River Settlements in the Mississippi Territory for Depredations by the Creek Indians during the War of 1812*. New Orleans: Polyanthus, 1977.

Latour, Arsene LaCarriere. *Historical Memoir of the War in West Florida and Louisiana in 1814–1815 with an Atlas*. Edited by Gene Smith. Gainesville: University Press of Florida, 1999.

Leslie, Charles. *A New and Exact Account of Jamaica: Wherein the Antient and Present State of That Colony, Its Importance to Great Britain, Laws, Trade, Manners and Religion, Together with the Most Remarkable and Curious Animals, Plants, Trees, &c. Are Described*... Edinburgh: R. Fleming, 1740.

"Letters of Dr. Seth Rogers, 1862, 1863." *Massachusetts Historical Society Proceedings* 43 (1910): 338–398.

Ligon, Richard. *A True and Exact History of the Island of Barbados*. London: Humphrey Moseley, 1657.

Lockley, Timothy James, ed. *Maroon Communities in South Carolina: A Documentary Record*. Columbia: University of South Carolina Press, 2009.

The London Missionary Society's Report of the Proceedings against the Late Rev. J. Smith, of Demerara... Who Was Tried under Martial Law, and Condemned to Death, on a Charge of Aiding and Assisting in a Rebellion of the Negro Slaves: with an Appendix. London: F. Westley, 1824.

Long, Edward. *The History of Jamaica or, General Survey of the Ancient and Modern State of That Island with Reflections on Its Situation, Settlements, Inhabitants, Climate, Products, Commerce, Laws, and Government in Three Volumes*. London: T. Lowndes, 1774.

Looby, Christopher, ed. *The Complete Civil War Journal and Selected Letters of Thomas Wentworth Higginson*. Chicago: University of Chicago Press, 2000.

Lowrie, Walter, and Walter Franklin, eds. *American State Papers: Foreign Relations*. Vol. 4. Washington, D.C.: Gales & Seaton, 1834.

Lowrie, Walter, and Mathew St. Clair Clarke, eds. *American State Papers: Military Affairs*. Vol. 1. Washington, D.C.: Gales & Seaton, 1832.

"Loyalist Letters in Virginia Legislative Papers." *Virginia Magazine of History and Biography* 14, no. 1 (July 1906): 126–136.

Luttrell, Narcissus, George Croom, and Louis Silver. *A Brief, but most true relation of the late barbarous and bloody plot of the Negro's in the Island of Barbado's on Friday the 21. of October, 1692. To Kill the governour and all the planters, and to destroy the government there established, and to set up a new governour and government of their own. In a letter to a friend*. London: G. Croom, 1692.

Macveagh, Lincoln, ed. *The Journal of Nicholas Creswell, 1774–1777*. New York: Dial, 1924.

Martson, Benjamin. Personal Diary. MG H2, vols. 2–22. New Brunswick Archives. Canada's Digital Collections. https://blackloyalist.com/cdc/documents/diaries/marston_journal.htm.

Mays, David John, ed. *The Letters and Papers of Edmund Pendleton, 1734–1803*. Vol. 1. Charlottesville: University Press of Virginia, 1967.

McAfee, Robert. *History of the Late War in the Western Country* [1816]. Bowling Green, Ohio: Bowling Green Historical Publications Company, 1919.

McCall, George. *Letters from the Frontiers: Written during a Period of Thirty Years' Service in the Army of the United States*. Philadelphia: J. B. Lippincott, 1868.

McCallum, Pierre Franc. *Travels in Trinidad: During the Months of February, March and April 1803*. Liverpool: W. Jones, 1805.

McClure, James, and J. Jefferson Looney, eds. *The Papers of Thomas Jefferson*. Digital ed. Charlottesville: University of Virginia Press, Rotunda, 2008–2016.

McDowell, W. L., ed. *Journals of the Commissioners of the Indian Trade, September 20, 1710–August 29, 1718*. Columbia: South Carolina Archives Department, 1955.

McIllwaine, H. R., ed. *Executive Journals of the Council of Colonial Virginia*. 6 vols. 1680–1699. Richmond: Virginia State Library, 1925–1928.

Mercer, Charles Fenton. *Speech of the Hon. Mr. Mercer, in the House of Representatives, on the Seminole War*. Washington, D.C., 1819.

Mereness, Newton, ed. *Travels in the American Colonies*. New York: Macmillan, 1916.

Merrens, Roy, ed. *The Colonial South Carolina Scene: Contemporary Views, 1697–1774*. Columbia: University of South Carolina Press, 1977.

Message from the President of the United States, Communication, in Compliance with a Resolution of the Senate, Copies of Correspondence in Relation to the Mutiny on Board the Brig Creole, and the Liberation of Slaves Who Were Passengers in the Said Vessal. Washington, D.C.: John Tyler, 1842.

Message from the President of the United States, Transmitting in Pursuance of a Resolution of the House of Representatives Such Further Information in Relation to Our Affairs with Spain. Washington, D.C.: E. de Krafft, 1819.

Meyer, Howard, ed. *The Magnificent Activist: The Writings of Thomas Wentworth Higginson (1823–1911)*. Cambridge, Mass.: Da Capo Press, 2000.

Millet, J. B. *A Particular Account of the Insurrection of the Negroes of St. Domingo, Begun in August 1791*. London, 1792.

Moore, John, Sir, 1761–1809, and John Frederick Maurice, ed. *The Diary of Sir John Moore*. London: E. Arnold, 1904.

Moreau de Jonnés, Alexandre. *Aventures de Guerre au Temps de la République et du Consulat*. Vol. 1. Paris: Pagnere, 1858.

Morgan, William. *Naval Documents of the American Revolution*. Vol. 5. Washington, D.C.: Government Printing Office, 1970.

Morse, Jedidiah. *Report to the Secretary of War of the United States on Indian Affairs: Comprising a Narrative of a Tour Performed in the Summer of 1820 . . .* New Haven, Conn.: S. Converse, 1822.

Moser, Harold, David Hoth, and George Hoemann, eds. *The Papers of Andrew Jackson*. Vol. 4, 1816–1820. Knoxville: University of Tennessee Press, 1994.

"The Mutiny of the 8th West India Regiment from the Papers of a Veteran Officer." *United Service Magazine*, October 1851, part 3, 207–309.

Myers, Robert Manson, ed. *The Children of Pride: A True Story of Georgia and the Civil War*. New Haven, Conn.: Yale University Press, 1972.

Narrative of a Voyage to the Spanish Main: In the Ship "Two Friends"; the Occupation of Amelia Island, by McGregor, & c.—Sketches of the Province of East Florida; and Anecdotes Illustrative of the Habits and Manners of the Seminole Indians: with an Ap-

pendix, Containing a Detail of the Seminole War, and the Execution of Arbuthnot and Ambrister. London: John Miller, 1819.

A Narrative of the Life and Death of Lieut. Joseph Morgan Willcox: Who Was Massacred by the Creek Indians, on the Alabama River, Miss. Ter., on the 15th of January, 1814. Marietta, Ohio: R. Prentiss, 1816.

Neville, John Davenport, ed. *Bacon's Rebellion: Abstracts of Materials in the Colonial Records Project.* Jamestown, Va.: Jamestown Foundation, 1976.

Northrup, Solomon. *Twelve Years a Slave: Narrative of Solomon Northrup, a Citizen of New York, Kidnapped in Washington City in 1841, and Rescued in 1853 from a Cotton Plantation Near the Red River in Louisiana.* New York: Miller, Orton & Mulligan, 1866.

Nunez, Theron A., Jr. "Creek Nativism and the Creek War of 1813–1814 Part 2 (Stiggins Narrative Continued)." *Ethnohistory* 5, no. 2 (Spring 1958): 131–175.

Oberg, Barbara B., ed. *The Papers of Thomas Jefferson*, vol. 32, 1 June 1800–16 February 1801. Princeton, N.J.: Princeton University Press, 2005.

Oberg, Michael, ed. *Samuel Wiseman's Book of Record: The Official Account of Bacon's Rebellion in Virginia.* Lanham, Md.: Lexington Books, 2005.

Oldmixon, John. *The British Empire in America: Containing the History of the Discovery, settlement, Progress, and Present State of All the British Colonies on the Continent and Islands of America.* 2 vols. London: John Nicholson, 1708.

Palmer, William Pitt, ed. *Calendar of Virginia State Papers and Other Manuscripts.* 11 vols. Richmond: WH Wade, 1875.

Pannet, Pierre J. *Report on the Execrable Conspiracy Carried Out by the Amina Negroes on the Danish Island of St. Jan in America 1733.* Translated by Aimery P. Caron and Arnold Highfield. Christiansted, St. Croix: Antilles Press, 1984.

"The Panton-Leslie Papers." *Florida Historical Quarterly* 17, no. 3 (January 1939): 237–242.

"The Panton-Leslie Papers: James Innerarity to John Forbes" [1815]. In the *Florida Historical Quarterly* 12, no. 3 (January 1934): 123–134.

"The Panton-Leslie Papers: Letters of John Innerarity and A. H. Gordon" [1816]. *Florida Historical Quarterly* 12, no. 1 (July 1933): 37–41.

Patrick, Robert. "Letters of the Invaders of East Florida, 1812." *Florida Historical Quarterly* 28, no. 1 (July 1949): 53–65.

Pearson, Edward, ed. *Designs against Charleston: The Trial Record of the Denmark Vesey Slave Conspiracy.* Chapel Hill: University of North Carolina Press, 1999.

Perkins, Samuel. *Historical Sketches of the United States from the Peace of 1815 to 1830.* New York: S. Converse, 1830.

———. *Reminiscences of the Insurrection in Santo Domingo.* Cambridge, 1886.

Predisposing Causes to Insurrection in Demerara. London: Ellerton & Henderson, 1824.

Price, Richard, ed. *To Slay the Hydra: Dutch Colonial Perspectives on the Saramaka Wars.* Ann Arbor: Karoma, 1983.

Price, Richard, and Sally Price, eds. *Stedman's Suriname: Life in an Eighteenth-Century Slave Society.* Baltimore: Johns Hopkins University Press, 1992.

Proceedings of the General Court Martial in the Trial of Major John Gordon of the Late 8th West India Regiment. London: E. Lloyd, 1804.

Rainsford, Marcus. *An Historical Account of the Black Empire of Hayti: Comprehending a View of the Principal Transactions in the Revolution of Saint-Domingo; with its Ancient and Modern State.* London: J. Cundee, 1805.

Redkey, Edwin, ed. *A Grand Army of Black Men: Letters from African American Soldiers in the Union Army, 1861–1865.* Cambridge: Cambridge University Press, 1992.

Reginald, Jeffrey, ed. *Dyott's Diary 1781–1845: A Selection from the Journal of William Dyott, Sometime General in the British Army and Aide-de-Camp to His Majesty King George II*, vol. 1. London: Archibald Constable, 1907.

Relation d'une conspiration tramé par les negres: dans l'Isle de S. Domingue, défense que fait le Jésuite donfesseur, aux negres qu'on suplicie, de reveler leur fauteurs & complices. 1759.

Remarks on the Insurrection in Barbadoes, and the Bill for the Registration of Slaves. London: Ellerton & Henderson, 1816.

Report of the Proceedings of a Meeting Held at Concert Hall Philadelphia, on Tuesday Evening, November 3, 1863, to Take into Consideration the Condition of the Freed People of the South. Philadelphia: Merrihew & Thompson, 1863.

Rhodehamel, John, ed. *The American Revolution: Writings from the War of Independence.* New York: Library Classics of the United States, 2001.

Rivers, William, ed. *A Sketch of the History of South Carolina: To the Close of the Proprietary Government by the Revolution of 1719, with an Appendix Containing Many Valuable Records hitherto Unpublished.* Charleston: McCarter, 1856.

Robey, Richard, ed. *A Genuine Narrative of the Intended Conspiracy of the Negroes in Antigua.* New York: Arno Press, 1972.

Rowland, Dunbar, ed. *Official Letter Books of W. C. C. Claiborne, 1801–1816.* Jackson, Miss.: State Department of Archives and History, 1917.

Rowland, Dunbar, and Albert Godfrey, eds. *Mississippi Provincial Archives 1701–1729 French Dominion.* 5 vols. Jackson: Press of the Mississippi Department of Archives and History, 1929.

Sainsbury, William, Cecil Headlam, Arthur Newton, and J. W. Fortescue, eds. *Calendar of State Papers Colonial Series: America and West Indies.* Vols. 28, 29, 30, 32, 32, 33, 40, 41, 45. Vaduz: Kraus, 1964.

Sainsbury, William, and A. S. Salley, eds. *Records in the British Public Record Office Relating to South Carolina, 1663–1782.* 36 vols. Columbia: Historical Commission of South Carolina, 1928–1947.

Salley, A.S., Jr. ed. *Journal of the Commissioners of the Indian Trade of South Carolina, September 20, 1710–April 12, 1715.* Columbia: Historical Commission of South Carolina, 1926.

Saunders, William. *The Colonial and State Records of North Carolina*. Vol. 23. Raleigh, N.C.: Hale, 1886.
Sayre, Gordon, and Carla Zecher, eds. *Jean François-Benjamin du Montigny, The Memoir of Lieutenant Dumont, 1715–1747: A Sojourner in the French Atlantic*. Chapel Hill: University of North Carolina Press, 2012.
Schwarz, Philip, ed. *Gabriel's Conspiracy: A Documentary History*. Charlottesville: University of Virginia Press, 2012.
Scott, Robert N. *The War of the Rebellion: A Compilation of the Official Records of the Union and Confederate Armies*, 1st ser. vols. 6, 14, 28 part 1, 44, 47 part 1, 2nd ser. vols 1, 5, 3rd ser. vol. 2. 1838–1887. Harrisburg, Pa.: National Historical Society; distributed by Broadfoot / Historical Times / Morningside House, 1985.
Scribner, Robert, and Brent Tarter, eds. *Revolutionary Virginia: The Road to Independence*. Vols. 4–7. Charlottesville: University Press of Virginia, 1978–1981.
Sketches and Recollections of the West Indies by a Resident. London: Smith, Elder, 1828.
Smith, Gene, ed. *Historical Memoir of the War in West Florida and Louisiana in 1814–1815, with an Atlas by Arsene LaCarriere Latour*. Gainesville: University Press of Florida, 1999.
Smith, John. *Insurrections in the West Indies: St. Lucia, Trinidad, Dominica, Jamaica, Demerara*. 1824.
Smith, Mark, ed. *Stono: Documenting and Interpreting a Southern Slave Revolt*. Columbia: University of South Carolina Press, 2005.
Smith, Thompson. *Letter from the Secretary of the Navy, Transmitting, in Obedience to a Resolution of the House of Representatives, of the Twenty-Sixth Ultimo, Sundry Documents Relating to the Destruction of the Negro Fort in East Florida, in the Month of July, 1816*. Washington, D.C.: E. DeKrafft, 1819.
Smyth, Alexander. *Speech of the Hon. Alexander Smyth in the House of Representatives on the Seminole War*. Washington, D.C., 1819.
Speech of the Honorable Mr. Mercer in the House of Representatives on the Seminole War, 25 January 1819. Washington, D.C., 1819. https://www.loc.gov/item/09019754/.
Sprague, J. T. *The Origin, Progress, and Conclusions of the Florida War: to Which Is Appended a Record of Officers, Non-commissioned Officers, Musicians, and Privates of the U.S. Army, Navy, and Marine Corps, Who Were Killed in Battle or Died of Disease as Also the Names of Officers Who Were Distinguished by Brevets, and the Names of Others Recommended; Together with the Orders for Collecting the Remains of the Dead in Florida, and the Ceremony of Interment at St. Augustine, East Florida, on the Fourteenth Day of August, 1842*. New York: D. Appleton, 1848.
State Papers and Publick Documents of the United States, from the Accession of George Washington to the Presidency, Exhibiting a Complete View of Our Foreign Relations since That Time. Vol. 9. Boston: TB Wait and Sons, 1817.
Stedman, Charles. *The History of the Origin, Progress, and Termination of the American War*. London: Printed for the Author, 1794.
Stedman, John Gabriel. *The History of the Origin, Progress, and Termination of the American War*. London: Printed for the Author, 1794.

———. *Narrative of Five Year's Expedition against the Revolted Negroes of Suriname, in Guiana, on the Wild Coast of South America, from the Year 1772, to 1777; Elucidating the History of That Country, and Describing Its Productions.* London: J. Johnson, 1796.

Stephen, James. *The History of Toussaint Louverture, A New Ed. with a Dedication to His Imperial Majesty the Emperor of All the Russias.* London, 1814.

Sterling, Dorothy, ed. *The Trouble They Seen: The Story of Reconstruction in the Words of African Americans.* New York: Doubleday, 1976.

Strange News from Virginia: Being a Full and True Account of the Life and Death of Nathanael Bacon Esquire . . . London: William Harris, 1677.

Taylor, Susie King. *Reminiscences of My Life in Camp with the 33d United States Colored Troops Late 1st S.C. Volunteers.* Boston: Taylor, 1902.

Thorndike, Israel. *Letter to a Member of the General Assembly of Virginia, on Subject of the Late Conspiracy of the Slaves: with a Proposal for Their Colonization.* Baltimore: Bonsal & Niles, 1801.

Trott, Nicholas, ed. *Laws of the province of south Carolina: in two parts: the first part containing all the perpetual acts in force and use, with the titles of such acts as are repealed, expired or obsolete, placed in the order of time in which they passed: the second part containing all the temporary acts in force and use, to which is added the titles of all the private acts and the two charters granted by King Charles II to the Lords Proprietors of Carolina and also the act of Parliament for establishing an agreement with seven of the said Lords Proprietors for the surrender of their life and interest to His Majesty.* 2 vols. Charlestown: L. Timothy, 1736.

Trowbridge, Charles. "Six Months in the Freedman's Bureau with a Colored Regiment." In *Glimpses of the Nation's Struggle: A Series of Papers Read Before the Minnesota Commandery of the Military Order of the Loyal Legion of the United States.* Minneapolis: Davis, 1909.

Turnball, Gordon. *A Narrative of the Revolt and Insurrection of the French Inhabitants of Grenada.* Edinburgh: Constable, 1795.

Vaughan, Alden T., ed. *Early American Indian Documents: Treaties and Laws, 1607–1789.* Vols. 2, 4, 6, 11, 12, 13, 14, 16. Washington, D.C.: University Publications of America, 1979–2002.

Vignoles, Charles Blacker. *Observations upon the Floridas.* New York: E. Bliss & E. White, 1823.

Walker, W. *The Report of a Select Committee of the House of Assembly, Appointed to Inquire into the Origin, Causes, and Progress of the Late Insurrection.* Barbados, 1816.

Wallbridge, Edwin Angel, ed. *The Demerara Martyr: Memoirs of the Rev. John Smith, Missionary to Demerara.* London: C. Gilpin, 1848.

Ware, Elizabeth Pearson, ed. *Letters from Port Royal, 1862–1868.* New York: Arno Press, 1969.

Warner, Samuel. *Authentic and Impartial Narrative of the Tragical Scene Which Was Witnessed in Southampton County (Virginia) on Monday the 22d of Aug. Last, When Fifty-Five of Its Inhabitants Mostly Women* . . . New York, 1831.

Whitehead, Ruth Holmes, and Carmelita Robertson, eds. *The Life of Boston King: Black Loyalist, Minister, and Carpenter*. Halifax, N.S.: Nimbus, 2003.

Windley, Lathan, ed. *Runaway Slave Advertisements: A Documentary History from the 1730s to 1790*. Vols. 1–2. Westport, Conn.: Greenwood, 1983.

Worthington, Chauncy Ford, ed. *The Writings of John Quincy Adams*. Vol. 6. New York: Macmillan, 1916.

Wylly, William. *A Short Account of the Bahama Islands, Their Climate, Productions, &c.: To Which Are Added, Some Strictures upon Their Relative and Political Situation, the Defects of Their Present Government, &c., &c.* London, 1789.

Yerrington, J. M. W. "Speech of Rev. Henry Bleby, Missionary from Barbados, on the Results of Emancipation in the British West Indies Colonies." Digital Library of the Caribbean. National Library of Jamaica (NLJ), 1858. http://ufdc.ufl.edu/CA01099989/00001/4j.

Yonge, Francis. *A Narrative of the Proceedings of the People of South-Carolina in the Year 1719; and of the True Causes and Motives That Induced Them to Renounce Their Obedience to the Lords Proprietors, as Their Governors, and to Put Themselves under the Immediate Government of the Crown*. London, 1726.

Young, Hugh. "A Topographical Memoir on East and West Florida with Itineraries of General Jackson's Army, 1818." *Florida Historical Quarterly* 13, no. 2 (October 1934): 82–104.

Young, William. *An Account of the Black Charaibs in the Island of St. Vincent's, with the Charaib Treaty of 1773, and Other Original Documents*. London: J. Sewell, 1795.

Zabin, Serena, ed. *The New York Conspiracy Trials of 1741: Daniel Horsmanden's Journal of the Proceedings with Related Documents*. New York: Bedford/St. Martin's, 2004.

Secondary Sources

Aboagye, Festus. *Indigenous African Warfare: Its Concept and Art in the Gold Coast, Asante, and the Northern Territories up to Early 1900s*. Pretoria: Africa Publishing Solutions, 2010.

Adams, Michaela. "Race, Kinship, and Belonging among the Florida Seminoles." In *The New South: New Histories and Enduring Legacies*, edited by Tim Alan Garrison, 144–161. Lincoln: University of Nebraska Press, 2017.

Alexander, J. H. "The Ambush of Captain John Williams, U.S.M.C.: Failure of the East Florida Invasion, 1812–1813." *Florida Historical Quarterly* 56, no. 3 (January 1978): 280–296.

Allard, Dean. "The Potomac Navy of 1776." *Virginia Magazine of History and Biography* 84, no. 4 (October 1976): 411–430.

Allen, Theodore. *The Invention of the White Race: The Origin of Racial Oppression in Anglo-America*. Vol. 2. New York: Verso, 1992.

Allmendinger, David, Jr. *Nat Turner and the Rising in Southampton County.* Baltimore: Johns Hopkins University Press, 2014.

Alpern, Stanley. "The European Introduction of Crops into West Africa in Precolonial Times." *History in Africa* 19 (1992): 13–43.

Alpers, Edward A., Gwyn Campbell, and Michael Salman, eds. *Resisting Bondage in Indian Ocean Africa and Asia.* New York: Routledge, 2007.

Altoff, Gerard. *Amongst My Best Men: African-Americans and the War of 1812.* Put-in-Bay, Ohio: Perry Group, 1996.

Anderson, Robert Nelson. "The Quilombo of Palmares: A New Overview of a Maroon State in Seventeenth-Century Brazil." *Journal of Latin American Studies* 28, no. 3 (October 1996): 545–566.

Anti, A. A. *Akwamu, Denkyira, Akuapem, and Ashanti in the Lives of Osei Tutu and Okomfo Anokye.* Accra: Ghana Publishing, 1971.

Aptheker, Herbert. "American Negro Slave Revolts." *Science and Society* 1, no. 4 (Summer 1937): 512–538.

———. *American Negro Slave Revolts.* 5th ed. New York: International Publishers, 1983.

———. *Nat Turner's Slave Rebellion.* New York: Humanities Press, 1966.

Ash, Stephen. *Firebrand of Liberty: The Story of Two Black Regiments That Changed the Course of the Civil War.* New York: Norton, 2008.

Austen, Ralph. "The Mediterranean Islamic Slave Trade out of Africa: A Tentative Census." In *The Human Commodity: Perspectives on the Trans-Saharan Slave Trade,* edited by Elizabeth Savage, 214–248. London: Frank Cass, 1992.

Balvay, Arnaud. *La Révolte des Natchez.* Paris: Félin, 2008.

Barber, John Warner, and Henry Howe. *Our Whole Country, or, The Past and Present of the United States, Historical and Descriptive: in Two Volumes.* Vol. 2. Cincinnati: Henry Howe, 1861.

Barcia, Manuel. *The Great African Slave Revolt of 1825: Cuba and the Fight for Freedom in Matanzas.* Baton Rouge: Louisiana State University Press, 2012.

———. *Seeds of Insurrection: Domination and Resistance on Western Cuban Plantations, 1808–1848.* Baton Rouge: Louisiana State University Press, 2008.

———. "Weapons from Their Land: Arming Strategies and Practices among West African-Born Soldiers in Early Nineteenth Century Bahia and Cuba." *Slavery and Abolition* 39, no. 3 (August 2018): 479–496.

———. *West African Warfare in Bahia and Cuba: Soldier Slaves in the Atlantic World, 1807–1844.* New York: Oxford University Press, 2014.

Barnett, James. *The Natchez Indians: A History to 1735.* Jackson: University Press of Mississippi, 2007.

Barr, Alwyn. *Black Texans: A History of African Americans in Texas, 1528–1995.* 2nd ed. Norman: University of Oklahoma Press, 1996.

Bastide, Roger. *African Civilizations in the New World.* Translated by Peter Green. London: C. Hurst, 1971.

Bateman, Rebecca. "Africans and Indians: A Comparative Study of the Black Carib and Black Seminole." *Ethnohistory* 37, no. 1 (Winter 1990): 1–24.

———. "Naming Patterns in Black Seminole Ethnogenesis." *Ethnohistory* 49, no. 2 (Spring 2002): 227–257.

Beckles, Hilary McD. *Black Rebellion in Barbados: The Struggle against Slavery, 1627–1838.* Bridgetown, Barbados: Antilles Publications, 1984.

———. "The Slave-Drivers' War: Bussa and the 1816 Barbados Slave Rebellion." *Boletin de Estudios Latinoamericanos y del Caribe* 39 (December 1985): 85–110.

———. *White Servitude and Black Slavery in Barbados, 1627–1715.* Knoxville: University of Tennessee Press, 1989.

Behrendt, Stephen. "The Annual Volume and Regional Distribution of the British Slave Trade, 1780–1807." *Journal of African History* 38, no. 2 (1997): 187–211.

Belko, William, ed. *America's Hundred Years' War: U.S. Expansion to the Gulf Coast and the Fate of the Seminole, 1763–1858.* Gainesville: University Press of Florida, 2011.

Besson, Jean. *Transformations of Freedom in the Land of the Maroons: Creolization in the Cockpits, Jamaica.* Kingston: Ian Randle, 2016.

Bilby, Kenneth. *True-Born Maroons.* Gainesville: University Press of Florida, 2005.

Billings, Warren. "The Causes of Bacon's Rebellion: Some Suggestions." *Virginia Magazine of History and Biography* 78, no. 4 (1970): 409–435.

———. "The Law of Servants and Slaves in Seventeenth-Century Virginia." *Virginia Magazine of History and Biography* 99, no. 1 (January 1991): 45–62.

Billings, Warren, John Selby, and Thad Tate. *Colonial Virginia: A History.* White Plains: KTO Press, 1986.

Billingsley, Andrew. *Yearning to Breathe Free: Robert Smalls of South Carolina and His Families.* Columbia: University of South Carolina Press, 2007.

Black, Jeremy. *Introduction to Global Military History, 1775 to the Present Day.* 3rd ed. New York: Routledge, 2019.

Blanchard, Peter. *Under the Flags of Freedom: Slave Soldiers and the Wars of Independence in Spanish South America.* Pittsburgh: University of Pittsburgh Press, 2008.

Blight, David. *Beyond the Battlefield: Race, Memory, and the American Civil War.* Amherst: University of Massachusetts Press, 2002.

Bollettino, Maria Alessandra. "'Of Equal or More Service': Black Soldiers and the British Empire in the Mid-Eighteenth Century Caribbean." *Slavery and Abolition* 38, no. 13 (2017): 510–533.

———. "Slavery, War, and Britain's Atlantic Empire: Black Soldiers, Sailors, and Rebels in the Seven Years' War." PhD diss., University of Texas, 2009.

Bossy, Denise, ed. *The Yamasee Indians: From Florida to South Carolina.* Lincoln: University of Nebraska Press, 2018.

Bowman, Larry. "Virginia's Use of Blacks in the French and Indian War." *Pennsylvania Historical Magazine* 53, no. 1 (January 1970): 57–63.

Boyd, Mark. "Documents Describing the Second and Third Expeditions of Lieutenant Diego Peña to Apalachee and Apalachicolo in 1717 and 1718." *Florida Historical Quarterly* 31, no. 2 (October 1952): 1–27.

———. "Events at Prospect Bluff." *Florida Historical Quarterly* 16, no. 2 (October 1937): 55–96.

Boyd, Mark, and Joseph Harris. "The Seminole War: Its Background and Onset." *Florida Historical Quarterly* 30, no. 1 (July 1951): 3–115.

Bradford, Sarah Hopkins. *Scenes in the Life of Harriet Tubman*. Auburn, N.Y.: W. J. Moses, 1869.

Braund, Kathryn Holland. "The Creek Indians, Blacks, and Slavery." *Journal of Southern History* 57, no. 4 (1991): 601–636.

Breen, T. H. "A Changing Labor Force and Race Relations in Virginia 1660–1710." *Journal of Social History* 7, no. 1 (Autumn 1973): 3–25.

Brown, Canter, Jr. "The Florida Crisis of 1826–7 and the Second Seminole War." *Florida Historical Quarterly* 73, no. 4 (April 1995): 419–442.

———. "Tales of Angola: Free Blacks, Red Stick Creeks, and International Intrigue in Spanish Southwest Florida, 1812–1821." In *Go Sound the Trumpet! Selections in Florida's African American History*, edited by David Jackson Jr. and Canter Brown Jr., 5–21. Tampa: University of Tampa Press, 2005.

Brown, Christopher L. "Arming Slaves in Comparative Perspective." In Brown and Morgan, *Arming Slaves*, 330–353.

Brown, Christopher L., and Philip Morgan, eds. *Arming Slaves: From Classical Times to the Modern Age*. New Haven, Conn.: Yale University Press, 2006.

Brown, Kathleen. *Good Wives, Nasty Wenches, and Anxious Patriarchs: Gender, Race, and Power in Colonial Virginia*. Chapel Hill: University of North Carolina Press, 1996.

Brown, Vincent. "Slave Revolt in Jamaica, 1760–1761: A Cartographic Narrative." 2012. http://revolt.axismaps.com.

———. *Tacky's Revolt: The Story of an Atlantic Slave War*. Cambridge, Mass.: Harvard University Press, 2020.

Brown, William Wells. *The Negro in the American Rebellion: His Heroism and His Fidelity*. Boston: Lee & Shephard, 1867.

Buckley, Roger. "The Admission of Slave Testimony at British Military Courts in the West Indies, 1800–1809." In Gaspar and Geggus, *Turbulent Time*, 226–250.

———. "'Black Man': The Mutiny of the 8th West India Regiment—A Microcosm of War and Slavery in the Caribbean." *Jamaican Historical Review* xii (1980): 52–76.

———. *The British Army in the West Indies: Society and the Military in the Revolutionary Age*. Gainesville: University Press of Florida, 1998.

———. "The Early History of the West India Regiments 1795–1815: A Study in British Colonial Military History." PhD diss., McGill University, 1975.

———. "Slave or Freedman: The Question of the Legal Status of the British West India Soldier, 1795–1807." *Caribbean Studies* 17, nos. 3/4 (October 1977–January 1978): 83–113.

———. *Slaves in Red Coats: The British West India Regiments, 1795–1815*. New Haven, Conn.: Yale University Press, 1979.

Buckmaster, Henrietta. *The Seminole Wars*. New York: Collier Books, 1966.

Bunn, Mike, and Clay Williams. *Battle for the Southern Frontier: The Creek War and the War of 1812*. Charleston, S.C.: History Press, 2008.

Campbell, Mavis. *The Maroons of Jamaica, 1655–1796: A History of Resistance, Collaboration, and Betrayal*. South Hadley, Mass.: Bergin & Garvey, 1988.

Candlin, Kit. *The Last Caribbean Frontier, 1795–1815*. New York: Palgrave Macmillan, 2012.

———. "The Role of the Enslaved in the 'Fedon Rebellion' of 1795." *Slavery and Abolition* 39, no. 4 (2018): 685–707.

Carey, Charles, Jr. "Lord Dunmore's Ethiopian Regiment." MA thesis, Virginia Polytechnic Institute and State University, 1995.

Carrigan, William. "Slavery on the Frontier: The Peculiar Institution in Central Texas." *Slavery and Abolition* 20, no. 2 (August 1999): 63–86.

Carroll, Patrick. *Blacks in Colonial Veracruz: Race, Ethnicity, and Regional Development*. Austin: University of Texas Press, 1991.

Carson, Jane. *Bacon's Rebellion 1676–1976*. Jamestown, Va.: Jamestown Foundation, 1976.

Cecere, Michael. "Battle of Gwynn's Island: Lord Dunmore's Last Stand in Virginia." *Journal of the American Revolution*, May 26, 2016. https://allthingsliberty.com/2016/05/battle-of-gwynns-island-lord-dunmores-last-stand-in-virginia/.

Chartrand, René. "Black Corps in the British West Indies, 1793–1815." *Journal of the Society for Army Historical Research* 76, no. 308 (Winter 1998): 248–254.

Cheney, Glenn Alan. *Quilombo dos Palmares: Brazil's Lost Nation of Fugitive Slaves*. Hanover, Conn.: New London Librarium, 2014.

Childs, Matt. *The 1812 Aponte Rebellion in Cuba and the Struggle against Atlantic Slavery*. Chapel Hill: University of North Carolina Press, 2006.

———. "'A Black French General Arrived to Conquer the Island': Images of the Haitian Revolution in Cuba's 1812 Aponte Rebellion." In *The Impact of the Haitian Revolution in the Atlantic World*, edited by David Geggus, 135–156. Columbia: University of South Carolina Press, 2001.

Chopra, Ruma. *Almost Home: Maroons between Slavery and Freedom in Jamaica, Nova Scotia, and Sierra Leone*. New Haven, Conn.: Yale University Press, 2018.

Christopher, Emma. *Slave Ship Sailors and Their Captive Cargoes, 1730–1809*. Cambridge: Cambridge University Press, 2006.

Clavin, Mathew. "'It Is a Negro, not an Indian War': Southampton, St. Domingo, and the Second Seminole War." In *America's Hundred Years' War: U.S. Expansion to the Gulf Coast and the Fate of the Seminole, 1763–1858*, edited by William Belko, 181–208. Gainesville: University Press of Florida, 2011.

Clifford, Mary Louise. *From Slavery to Freetown: Black Loyalists after the American Revolution*. Jefferson: McFarland, 1999.

Coker, William, and Susan Parker. "The Second Spanish Period in the Two Floridas." In *The New History of Florida*, edited by Michael Gannon, 150–166. Gainesville: University Press of Florida, 1996.

Coker, William, and Thomas Watson. *Indian Traders of the Southeastern Spanish Borderlands: Panton, Leslie, & Company and John Forbes & Company, 1783–1847*. Pensacola: University of West Florida Press, 1986.

Coombs, John. "Beyond the 'Origins Debate': Rethinking the Rise of Virginia Slavery." In *Early Modern Virginia: Reconsidering the Old Dominion*, edited by Douglas Bradburn and John Coombs, 239–278. Charlottesville: University of Virginia Press, 2011.

Corkran, David. *The Carolina Indian Frontier, Tricentennial Booklet no. 6*. Columbia: University of South Carolina Press, 1970.

Cornish, Dudley Taylor. *The Sable Arm: Negro Troops in the Union Army, 1861–1865*. New York: Norton, 1956.

Costello, Ray. *Black Salt: Seafarers of African Descent on British Ships*. Liverpool: Liverpool University Press, 2012.

Covington, James. *The Seminoles of Florida*. Gainesville: University Press of Florida, 1993.

Cox, Edward. "Fedon's Rebellion 1795–96: Causes and Consequences." *Journal of Negro History* 67, no. 1 (Spring 1982): 7–19.

Crane, Verner. *The Southern Frontier, 1670–1732*. Reprint. New York: Norton, 1981.

Craton, Michael. "The Black Caribs of St. Vincent: A Reevaluation." In *The Lesser Antilles in the Age of European Expansion*, edited by Robert Paquette and Stanley Engerman, 71–85. Gainesville: University Press of Florida, 1996.

———. *Empire, Enslavement, and Freedom in the Caribbean*. Princeton, N.J.: Markus Weiner, 1997.

———. *Testing the Chains: Resistance to Slavery in the British West Indies*. Ithaca, N.Y.: Cornell University Press, 1982.

Craven, Wesley Frank. *The Southern Colonies in the Seventeenth Century, 1607–1689*. Baton Rouge: Louisiana University Press, 1949.

Crawford, M. H. "The Anthropological Genetics of the Black Caribs (Garifuna) of Central America and the Caribbean." *Yearbook of Physical Anthropology* 26 (1983): 161–192.

———. "Origin and Maintenance of Genetic Variation on Black Carib Populations of St. Vincent and Central America." In *Genetic Variation and Its Maintenance in Tropical Populations*, edited by D. F. Roberts and G. De Stefano, 157–180. Cambridge: Cambridge University Press, 1986.

Crawford, Michael, et al. "The Black Caribs (Garifuna) of Livingston, Guatemala: Genetic Markers and Admixture Estimates." *Human Biology* 53, no. 1 (February 1981): 87–103.

Curtin, Philip. *The Rise and Fall of the Plantation Complex: Essays in Atlantic History*. 2nd ed. New York: Cambridge University Press, 1998.

Cusick, James. *The Other War of 1812: The Patriot War and the American Invasion of Spanish East Florida*. Gainesville: University Press of Florida, 2003.

Daaku, K. Y. *Trade and Politics on the Gold Coast, 1600–1720: A Study of the African Reaction to European Trade.* Oxford: Oxford University Press, 1970.

Dallas, Robert. *The History of the Maroons: From Their Origin to the Establishment of Their Chief Tribe at Sierra Leone: Including the Expedition to Cuba, for the Purpose of Procuring Spanish Chasseurs, and the State of the Island of Jamaica for the Last Yen Years: With a Succinct History of the Island to That Period.* 2 vols. London: T. N. Londman and O. Rees, 1803.

Daniels, Jason. "Marronage in Saint Domingue: Approaching the Revolution, 1770–1791." MA thesis, University of Florida, 2008.

Davis, David Brion. *Inhuman Bondage: The Rise and Fall of Slavery in the New World.* Oxford: Oxford University Press, 2006.

Davis, Robert. *Christian Slaves, Muslim Masters: White Slavery in the Mediterranean, the Barbary Coast, and Italy, 1500–1800.* New York: Palgrave Macmillan, 2003.

Davis, T. Frederick. "United States Troops in Spanish East Florida, 1812–13." *Florida Historical Quarterly* 9, no. 1 (1 July 1930): 3–23.

Deal, Douglas. "Race and Class in Colonial Virginia: Indians, Englishmen, and Africans on the Eastern Shore during the Seventeenth Century." PhD diss., University of Rochester, 1981.

Debbasch, Yvan. "Le Maniel: Further Notes." In *Maroon Societies: Rebel Slave Communities in the Americas*, edited by Richard Price, 143–148. Baltimore: Johns Hopkins University Press, 1996.

Debien, Gabriel. "Le Marronage aux Antilles Françaises au XVIIIe siècle." *Caribbean Studies* 6, no. 3 (October 1966): 3–43.

de Groot, Silvia W. "The Boni Maroon War 1765–1793, Surinam and French Guyana." *Boletín de Estudios Latinoamericanos y del Caribe* 18 (1975): 30–48.

———. "A Comparison between the History of Maroon Communities in Surinam and Jamaica." *Slavery and Abolition* 6, no. 3 (June 2008): 173–184.

———. *From Isolation towards Integration: The Surinam Maroons and Their Colonial Rulers. Official Documents Relating to the Djukas (1845–1863).* Leiden: Brill, 1977.

Diggs, Irene. "Zumbi and the Republic of Os Palmares." *Phylon* 14, no. 1 (1953): 62–70.

Dillon, Merton. *Slavery Attacked: Southern Slaves and Their Allies, 1619–1865.* Baton Rouge: Louisiana State University Press, 1990.

Diouf, Sylviane, ed. *Fighting the Slave Trade: West African Strategies.* Athens: Ohio University Press, 2003.

———. *Slavery's Exiles: The Story of American Maroons.* New York: New York University Press, 2014.

Dobak, William. *Freedom by the Sword: The U.S. Colored Troops, 1862–1867.* Washington, D.C.: U.S. Army Center of Military History, 2011.

Dormon, James. "The Persistent Specter: Slave Rebellion in Territorial Louisiana." *Journal of the Louisiana Historical Association* 18, no. 4 (Autumn 1977): 389–404.

Dubois, Laurent. *Avengers of the New World: The Story of the Haitian Revolution.* Cambridge, Mass.: Harvard University Press, 2004.

———. *A Colony of Citizens: Revolution and Slave Emancipation in the French Caribbean, 1787–1804*. Chapel Hill: University of North Carolina Press, 2004.

Dubois, Laurent, and Julius Scott, eds. *Origins of the Black Atlantic*. New York: Routledge, 2010.

Duffy, Michael. *Soldiers, Sugar, and Seapower: The British Expeditions to the West Indies and the War against Revolutionary France*. Oxford: Clarendon Press, 1987.

Dunkley, D. A. *Agency of the Enslaved: Jamaica and the Culture of Freedom in the Atlantic World*. New York: Lexington Books, 2013.

Dyde, Brian. *The Empty Sleeve: The Story of the West India Regiments of the British Army*. St. John's Antigua: Hansib Caribbean, 1997.

Egerton, Douglas. *Death or Liberty: African Americans and Revolutionary America*. New York: Oxford University Press, 2009.

———. *Gabriel's Rebellion: The Virginia Slave Conspiracies of 1800 and 1802*. Chapel Hill: University of North Carolina Press, 1993.

———. *Thunder at the Gates: The Black Civil War Regiments That Redeemed America*. New York: Basic Books, 2016.

Eltis, David. *The Rise of African Slavery in the Americas*. Cambridge: Cambridge University Press, 2000.

Engs, Robert. *Freedom's First Generation: Black Hampton, Virginia, 1861–1890*. New York: Fordham University Press, 2004.

Escalante, Aquiles. "Palenques in Colombia." In *Maroon Societies: Rebel Slave Communities in the Americas*, edited by Richard Price, 74–81. 3rd ed. Baltimore: Johns Hopkins University Press, 1996.

Escheverri, Marcela. *Indian and Slave Royalists in the Age of Revolution: Reform, Revolution, and Royalism in the Northern Andes, 1780–1825*. New York: Cambridge University Press, 2016.

Fergus, Claudius. "Emancipation and 'Military Necessity' during the Haitian Revolution: Challenging the Hegemonic Paradigms of Slavery and Freedom." In *Free at Last? Reflections on Freedom and the Abolition of the British Transatlantic Slave Trade*, edited by Amar Wahab and Cecily Jones, 19–38. Newcastle upon Tyne: Cambridge Scholars Publishing, 2011.

Fick, Carolyn. *The Making of Haiti: The Saint Domingue Revolution from Below*. Knoxville: University of Tennessee Press, 1990.

Finch, Aisha. "Insurgency at the Crossroads: Cuban Slaves and the Conspiracy of La Escalera, 1841–44." PhD diss., New York University, 2007.

Fisher, Humphrey. *Slavery in the History of Muslim Black Africa*. New York: New York University Press, 2001.

Fleetwood, Christian. *The Negro as a Soldier*. Washington, D.C.: Atlanta Exposition, 1895.

Forbes, Jack. *Africans and Native Americans: The Language of Race and the Evolution of Red-Black Peoples*. 2nd ed. Urbana: University of Illinois Press, 1993.

Foy, Charles. "Seeking Freedom in the Atlantic World, 1713–1783." *Early American Studies* 4, no. 1 (Spring 2006): 46–77.

Franklin, John Hope, and Loren Schwenninger. *Runaway Slaves: Rebels on the Plantation*. New York: Oxford University Press, 1999.

Frey, Sylvia. "Between Slavery and Freedom: Virginia Blacks in the American Revolution." *Journal of Southern History* 49, no. 3 (August 1983): 375–398.

———. *Water from the Rock: Black Resistance in a Revolutionary Age*. Princeton, N.J.: Princeton University Press, 1991.

Fuller, Harcourt, and Jada Benn Torres. "Investigating the 'Taíno' Ancestry of the Jamaican Maroons: A New Genetic (DNA), Historical, and Multidisciplinary Analysis and Case Study of the Accompong Town Maroons." *Canadian Journal of Latin American and Caribbean Studies* 43, no. 1 (2018): 47–78.

Fuss, Norman. "Billy Flora at the Battle of Great Bridge." *Journal of the American Revolution*, October 14, 2014. https://allthingsliberty.com/2014/10/billy-flora-at-the-battle-of-great-bridge/.

Gallay, Alan. *The Indian Slave Trade: The Rise of the English Empire in the American South, 1670–1717*. New Haven, Conn.: Yale University Press, 2002.

Garrigus, John. *Before Haiti: Race and Citizenship in French Saint-Domingue*. New York: Palgrave Macmillan, 2006.

Gaspar, David Barry. *Bondmen and Rebels: A Study of Master-Slave Relations in Antigua, with Implications for Colonial British America*. Baltimore: Johns Hopkins University Press, 1985.

Gaspar, David Barry, and David Patrick Geggus, eds. *A Turbulent Time: The French Revolution and the Greater Caribbean*. Bloomington: Indiana University Press, 1997.

Geffert, Hannah. "John Brown and His Black Allies: An Ignored Alliance." *Pennsylvania Magazine of History and Biography* 126, no. 4 (2002): 591–610.

Geggus, David. "The Arming of Slaves in the Haitian Revolution." In Brown and Morgan, *Arming Slaves*, 209–232.

———. "The Enigma of Jamaica in the 1790s: New Light on the Causes of Slave Rebellions." *William and Mary Quarterly* 44, no. 2 (April 1987): 274–299.

———. *Haitian Revolutionary Studies*. Bloomington: Indiana University Press, 2002.

———. "Marronage, Voodoo, and the Saint Domingue Slave Revolt of 1791." *Proceedings of the Meeting of the French Colonial Historical Society* 15 (1992): 22–35.

———. "Slave Rebellion during the Age of Revolution." In Klooster and Oostindie, *Curaçao in the Age of Revolutions*, 23–56.

———. *Slavery, War, and Revolution: The British Occupation of Saint Domingue, 1793–1798*. Oxford: Clarendon Press, 1982.

———. "Slavery, War, and Revolution in the Greater Caribbean, 1789–1815." In Gaspar and Geggus, *Turbulent Time*, 1–150.

Genovese, Eugene. *From Rebellion to Revolution: Afro-American Slave Revolts in the Making of the Modern World*. Baton Rouge: Louisiana State University Press, 1979.

———. *Roll Jordan Roll: The World the Slaves Made*. New York: Vintage Books, 1976.

Gerbner, Katherine. *Christian Slavery: Conversion and Race in the Protestant Atlantic World*. Philadelphia: University of Pennsylvania Press, 2018.

Gilbert, Alan. *Black Patriots and Loyalists: Fighting for Emancipation in the War for Independence*. Chicago: University of Chicago Press, 2012.

Gill, Rocío. "The Mascogo/Black Seminole Diaspora: The Intertwining Borders of Citizenship, Race, and Ethnicity." *Latin American and Caribbean Ethnic Studies* 9, no. 1 (December 2013): 23–43.

Girard, Philippe. *The Slaves Who Defeated Napoléon: Toussaint Louverture and the Haitian War of Independence, 1801–1804*. Tuscaloosa: University of Alabama Press, 2011.

Glaberson, William. "Who Is a Seminole, and Who Gets to Decide." *New York Times*, 29 January 2001.

Glatthaar, Joseph. *Forged in Battle: The Civil War Alliance of Black Soldiers and White Officers*. Baton Rouge: Louisiana State University Press, 1990.

Gomes, Flavio dos Santos. "A 'Safe Haven': Runaway Slaves, Mocambos, and Borders in Colonial Amazonia, Brazil." *Hispanic American Historical Review* 82, no. 3 (August 2002): 469–498.

Gomez, Michael. *Exchanging Our Country Marks: The Transformations of African Identities in the Colonial and Antebellum South*. Chapel Hill: University of North Carolina Press, 1998.

———. *Reversing Sail: A History of the African Diaspora*. Cambridge: Cambridge University Press, 2005.

Gott, Richard. *Britain's Empire: Resistance, Repression, and Revolt*. New York: Verso, 2011.

Gottlieb, Karla Lewis. *"The Mother of Us All": A History of Queen Nanny Leader of the Windward Jamaican Maroons*. Trenton, N.J.: Africa World Press, 2000.

Goucher, Candice, and Kofi Agorsah. "Excavating the Roots of Resistance: The Significance of Maroons in Jamaican Archaeology." In *Out of Many, One People: The Historical Archaeology of Colonial Jamaica*, edited by James Delle, Mark Hauser, and Douglas Armstrong, 144–162. Tuscaloosa: University of Alabama Press, 2011.

Grouse, Nellis. *French Pioneers in the West Indies, 1624–1664*. New York: Columbia University Press, 1940.

Guinn, Jeff. *Our Land Before We Die: The Proud Story of the Seminole Negro*. New York: Jeremy Tarcher/Putnam, 2002.

Hahn, Steven. *A Nation under Our Feet: Black Political Struggles in the Rural South from Slavery to the Great Migration*. Cambridge, Mass.: Belknap Press of Harvard University Press, 2005.

———. *The Political Worlds of Slavery and Freedom*. Cambridge, Mass.: Harvard University Press, 2009.

Hahn, Steven C. *The Invention of the Creek Nation, 1670–1763*. Lincoln: University of Nebraska Press, 2004.

Halbert, H. S., and T. H. Ball. *The Creek War of 1813 and 1814*. 1895. Edited by Frank Owsley Jr. Tuscaloosa: University of Alabama Press, 1969.

Hall, Amanda. "San Antonio de Pocotalaca: An Eighteenth-Century Yamasee Indian Town in St. Augustine, Florida, 1716–1752." MA thesis, University of North Florida, 2016.

Hall, Gwendolyn Midlo. *Africans in Colonial Louisiana: The Development of Afro-Creole Culture in the Eighteenth Century*. Baton Rouge: Louisiana State University Press, 1992.

———. *Slavery and African Ethnicities in the Americas: Restoring the Links*. Chapel Hill: University of North Carolina Press, 2005.

Hall, Neville A. T. *Slave Society in the Danish West Indies: St. Thomas, St. John, and St. Croix*. Edited by B. W. Higman. Baltimore: Johns Hopkins University Press, 1992.

Handler, Jerome. "Freedmen and Slaves in the Barbados Militia." *Journal of Caribbean History* 19, no. 1 (1984): 1–25.

———. "Slave Revolts and Conspiracies in Seventeenth-Century Barbados." *New West Indian Guide* 56, nos. 1/2 (1982): 5–42.

Handler, Jerome, Frederick Lange, and Robert Riordan. *Plantation Slavery in Barbados: An Anthropological and Historical Investigation*. Cambridge, Mass.: Harvard University Press, 1978.

Hanger, Kimberly. *Bounded Lives, Bounded Places: Free Black Society in Colonial New Orleans, 1769–1803*. Durham, N.C.: Duke University Press, 1997.

Hannum, Patrick. "Norfolk, Virginia, Sacked by North Carolina and Virginia Troops." *Journal of the American Revolution*, November 6, 2017. https://allthingsliberty.com/2017/11/norfolk-virginia-sacked-north-carolina-virginia-troops/#:~:text=The%20Americans%2C%20Patriots%20from%20North,the%20British%20in%20the%20future.

Hanserd, Robert. "The Gold Coast, Jamaica and New York: Akan Ideas of Freedom in the Afro-Atlantic during the Eighteenth Century." PhD diss., Northern Illinois University, 2011.

———. "Okomfo Anokye Formed a Tree to Hide from the Akwamu: Priestly Power, Freedom, and Enslavement in the Afro-Atlantic." *Atlantic Studies* 12, no. 4 (2015): 522–544.

Harpham, John Samuel. "'Tumult and Silence' in the Study of the American Slave Revolts." *Slavery and Abolition* 36, no. 2 (2015): 257–274.

Harrell, Isaac Samuel. *Loyalism in Virginia: Chapters in the Economic History of the Revolution*. Durham, N.C.: Duke University Press, 1926.

Harris, William. *The Hanging of Thomas Jeremiah: A Free Black Man's Encounter with Liberty*. New Haven, Conn.: Yale University Press, 2009.

Hart, Richard. *Slaves Who Abolished Slavery*. Kingston: University of the West Indies Press, 2002.

Hartgrove, W. B. "The Negro Soldier in the American Revolution." *Journal of Negro History* 1, no. 2 (April 1916): 110–131.

Hatfield, April. *Atlantic Virginia: Intercolonial Relations in the Seventeenth Century*. Philadelphia: University of Pennsylvania Press, 2004.

Helg, Aline. *Slave No More: Self Liberation before Abolitionism in the Americas.* Chapel Hill: University of North Carolina Press, 2019.

Hendrick, George, and Willene Hendrick. *The Creole Mutiny: A Tale of Revolt Aboard a Slave Ship.* Chicago: Ivan R. Dee, 2003.

Herrera-Paz, Edwin Francisco, Miereya Matamoros, and Angel Carracedo. "The Garifuna (Black Carib) People of the Atlantic Coasts of Honduras: Population Dynamics, Structure, and Phylogenetic Relations Inferred from Genetic Data, Migration Matricies, and Isonymy." *American Journal of Human Biology* 22 (2010): 36–44.

Heuman, Gad. "A Tale of Two Jamaican Rebellions." In *Born Out of Resistance: On Caribbean Cultural Creativity*, edited by Wim Hoogbergen, 196–204. Utrecht: Isor, 1995.

Hewatt, Alexander. *An Historical Account of the Rise and Progress of the Colonies of South Carolina and Georgia.* 2 vols. London: Alexander Donaldson, 1779.

Heywood, Linda, and John Thornton. *Central Africans, Atlantic Creoles, and the Foundation of the Americas, 1585–1660.* New York: Cambridge University Press, 2007.

Higgins, Kathleen. *"Licentious Liberty" in a Brazilian Gold-Mining Region: Slavery, Gender, and Social Control in Eighteenth-Century Sabará, Minas Gerais.* University Park: Pennsylvania State University Press, 1999.

Higginson, Thomas Wentworth. *Black Rebellion: Five Slave Revolts from "Travelers and Outlaws" Episodes in American History.* Boston: Lee & Shepherd, 1889.

Hodges, Graham Russell. "Black Revolt in New York City and the Neutral Zone in New York." In *New York in the Age of the Constitution, 1775–1800*, edited by Paul Gilje and William Pencak, 20–47. Cranbury, N.J.: Associated University Press, 1992.

———. *Slavery and Freedom in the Rural North: African Americans in Monmouth County, New Jersey, 1665–1865.* Madison, Wisc.: Madison House, 1997.

———. *Slavery, Freedom, and Culture among Early American Workers.* Armonk, N.Y.: M. E. Sharpe, 1998.

Hoffman, Paul. *Florida Frontiers.* Bloomington: Indiana University Press, 2002.

Holden, Vanessa. "Generation, Resistance, and Survival: African American Children and the Southampton Rebellion of 1831." *Slavery and Abolition* 38, no. 4 (April 2017): 673–696.

Holmes, Jack D. L. "The Abortive Slave Revolt at Pointe Coupée, Louisiana, 1795." *Louisiana History* 11 (1970): 341–362.

Holsoe, Svend. "The 1848 St. Croix Slave Rebellion: The Day of the Rebellion." In *Negotiating Enslavement: Perspectives on Slavery in the Danish West Indies*, edited by Arnold Highfield and George Tyson, 191–210. Christiansted, St. Croix: Antilles Press, 2009.

Holton, Woody. *Forced Founders: Indians, Debtors, Slaves, and the Making of the American Revolution in Virginia.* Chapel Hill: University of North Carolina Press, 1999.

———. "'Rebel against Rebel': Enslaved Virginians and the Coming of the American Revolution." *Virginia Magazine of History and Biography* 105, no. 2 (Spring 1997): 157–192.

Honychurch, Lennox. *The Dominica Story: A History of the Island*. 2nd ed. London: Macmillan, 1995.

———. *In the Forests of Freedom: The Fighting Maroons of Dominica*. London: Papillote Press, 2017.

Hoogbergen, Wim. *The Boni Maroon Wars in Suriname*. Leiden: Brill, 1990.

Horne, Gerald. *The Dawning of the Apocalypse: The Roots of Slaves, White Supremacy, Settler Colonialism, and Capitalism in the Long Sixteenth Century*. New York: New York University Press, 2020.

———. *Negro Comrades of the Crown: African Americans and the British Empire Fight the U.S. before Emancipation*. New York: New York University Press, 2012.

Howard, Rosalyn. *Black Seminoles in the Bahamas*. Gainesville: University Press of Florida, 2002.

———. "Black Towns of the Seminole Indians: Florida's Maroon Communities." In *Africa in Florida: Five Hundred Years of African Presence in the Sunshine State*, edited by Amanda Carlson and Robin Poynor, 107–121. Gainesville: University of Florida Press, 2014.

Hulme, Peter. "French Accounts of the Vincentian Caribs." In *The Garifuna: A Nation across Borders. Essays in Social Anthropology*, edited by Joseph Palacio, 21–42. Benque Viejo del Carmen, Belize: Cubola Productions, 2005.

Hume, Ivor Noel. *1775: Another Part of the Field*. London: Eyre & Spottiswoode, 1966.

Ivers, Larry. *This Torrent of Indians: War on the Southern Frontier, 1715–1717*. Columbia: University of South Carolina Press, 2016.

Jacobs, Curtis. "Fedon's Rebellion in Grenada (1795–1796)." University of York Centre for Eighteenth Century Studies, Eighth Cultural History Conference, May 2018.

James, Arlington. *Freshwater Swamps and Mangrove Species in Dominica*. Roseau: Forestry Division, Ministry of Agriculture Dominica, 1980.

Jennings, Mathew. *New Worlds of Violence: Cultures and Conquests in the Early American Southeast*. Knoxville: University of Tennessee Press, 2011.

Johnson, Amy. "Captivity among the Maroons of Jamaica in the Seventeenth and Early Eighteenth Centuries: A Comparative Analysis." *International Journal of Humanities and Cultural Studies* 1, no. 3 (December 2014): 1–16.

Johnson, Lyman. *Workshop of Revolution: Plebian Buenos Aires and the Atlantic World, 1776–1810*. Durham, N.C.: Duke University Press, 2011.

Jones, Rhett. "White Settlers, Black Rebels: Jamaica in the Era of the First Maroon War, 1655–1738." PhD diss., Brown University, 1976.

Jones, Terry. "The Free Men of Color Go to War." *New York Times*, October 19, 2012.

Kai, Nubia. "Black Seminoles: The Maroons of Florida." *African and Black Diaspora: An International Journal* 8, no. 2 (April 2015): 146–157.

Kaplan, Sidney. "'The Domestic Insurrections' of the Declaration of Independence." *Journal of Negro History* 61, no. 3 (July 1976): 243–255.

Kaplan, Sidney, and Emma Nogrady Kaplan. *The Black Presence in the Era of the American Revolution*. Rev. ed. Amherst: University of Massachusetts Press, 1989.

Kars, Marjoleine. "'Cleansing the Land': Dutch-Amerindian Cooperation in the Suppression of the 1763 Slave Rebellion in Dutch Guiana." In *Empires and Indigenes: Intercultural Alliance, Imperial Expansion, and Warfare in the Early Modern World*, edited by Wayne Lee, 251–275. New York: New York University Press, 2011.

———. "Dodging Rebellion: Politics and Gender in the Berbice Slave Uprising of 1763." *American Historical Review* 121, no. 1 (February 2016): 39–69.

———. "Policing and Transgressing Borders: Soldiers, Slave Rebels, and the Early Modern Atlantic." *New West Indian Guide* 83, nos. 3/4 (2009): 191–217.

Katz, William Loren. *The Black West*. Garden City, N.Y.: Doubleday, 1971.

Kea, Ray. "Firearms and Warfare on the Gold and Slave Coasts from the Sixteenth to the Nineteenth Centuries." *Journal of African History* 12, no. 2 (1971): 185–213.

———. "'I Am Here to Plunder on the General Road': Bandits and Banditry in the Pre-Nineteenth Century Gold Coast." In *Banditry, Rebellion, and Social Protest in Africa*, edited by Donald Crummy, 109–132. London: James Currey, 1986.

———. *Settlements, Trade, and Polities in the Seventeenth-Century Gold Coast*. Baltimore: Johns Hopkins University Press, 1982.

———. "'When I Die, I Shall Return to My Own Land': An 'Amina' Slave Rebellion in the Danish West Indies, 1733–1734." In *The Cloth of Many Colored Silks: Papers on History and Society, Ghanaian and Islamic in Honor of Ivor Wilks*, edited by John Hunwick and Nancy Lawler, 159–193. Evanston, Ill.: Northwestern University Press, 1996.

Kelley, Sean. "'Mexico in His Head': Slavery and the Texas-Mexico Border, 1810–1860." *Journal of Social History* 37, no. 3 (2004): 709–723.

Kent, R. K. "Palmares: An African State in Brazil." In *Maroon Societies: Rebel Slave Communities in the Americas*, edited by Richard Price, 170–190. Baltimore: Johns Hopkins University Press, 1996.

Kilson, Marion D. "Towards Freedom: An Analysis of Slave Revolts in the United States." *Phylon* 25 (1964): 175–187.

Klein, Martin, and Richard Roberts. "The Banamba Slave Exodus of 1905 and the Decline of Slavery in the Western Sudan." *Journal of African History* 21, no. 3 (1980): 375–394.

Klingberg, Frank. "The Mystery of the Lost Yamasee Prince." *South Carolina Historical Magazine* 63, no. 1 (January 1962): 18–32.

Klooster, Wim. "Slave Revolts, Royal Justice, and a Ubiquitous Rumor in the Age of Revolutions." *William and Mary Quarterly* 71, no. 3 (July 2014): 401–424.

Klooster, Wim, and Gert Oostindie, eds. *Curaçao in the Age of Revolutions, 1795–1800*. Boston: Brill, 2011.

———. *Realm between Empires: The Second Dutch Atlantic, 1680–1815*. Ithaca, N.Y.: Cornell University Press, 2018.

Klos, George. "Blacks and the Seminole Removal Debate, 1812–1835." In *The African American Heritage of Florida*, edited by David Colburn and Jane Landers, 128–156. Gainesville: University Press of Florida, 1995.

Kly, Y. N. "The Gullah War, 1739–1858." In *The Invisible War: The African American Anti-Slavery Resistance from the Stono Rebellion through the Seminole Wars*, edited by Y. N. Kly with assistance from Diana Kly, 50–100. Atlanta: Clarity Press, 2006.

Knetsch, Joe. *Florida's Seminole Wars: 1817–1858*. Charleston, S.C.: Arcadia Publishing, 2003.

Knight, Frederick. *Working the Diaspora: The Impact of African Labor on the Anglo-American World, 1650–1850*. New York: New York University Press, 2010.

Konadu, Kwasi. *The Akan Diaspora in the Americas*. New York: Oxford University Press, 2010.

Kraay, Hendrick. "Arming Slaves in Brazil from the Seventeenth Century to the Nineteenth Century." In Brown and Morgan, *Arming Slaves*, 146–179.

Kruer, Mathew. "Bloody Minds and Peoples Undone: Emotion, Family, and Political Order in the Susquehannock Virginia War." *William and Mary Quarterly* 74, no. 3 (2017): 401–436.

———. "'Our Time of Anarchy': Bacon's Rebellion and the Wars of the Susquehannocks, 1675–1682." PhD diss., University of Pennsylvania, 2015.

Kulikoff, Alan. "Uprooted Peoples: Black Migrants in the Age of the American Revolution, 1790–1820." In *Slavery and Freedom in the Age of the American Revolution*, edited by Ira Berlin and Ronald Hoffman, 143–171. Urbana: University of Illinois Press, 1986.

Kupperman, Karen Ordahl. *Providence Island, 1630–1641: The Other Puritan Colony*. New York: Cambridge University Press, 1993.

Lambert, David. "'A Mere Cloak for Their Proud Contempt and Antipathy towards the African Race': Imagining Britain's West India Regiments in the Caribbean, 1795–1838." *Journal of Imperial and Commonwealth History* 46, no. 4 (April 2018): 627–650.

Lambert, David, and Tim Lockley. "Introduction, Africa's Sons under Arms." *Slavery and Abolition* 39, no. 3 (August 2018): 451–458.

Landers, Jane. "Africans and Native Americans on the Spanish Florida Frontier." In Restall, *Beyond Black and Red*, 53–80.

———. "African-Yamasee Ties in Carolina and Florida." In *The Yamasee Indians*, edited by Denise Bossy, 163–190. Lincoln: University of Nebraska Press, 2018.

———. *Atlantic Creoles in the Age of Revolutions*. Cambridge, Mass.: Harvard University Press, 2010.

———. "The Atlantic Transformation of Francisco Menéndez." In *Biography and the Black Atlantic*, edited by Lisa Lindsay and John Wood Sweet, 209–223. Philadelphia: University of Pennsylvania Press, 2014.

———. "Black-Indian Interaction in Spanish Florida." *Colonial Latin American Historical Review* 2, no. 2 (Spring 1993): 141–162.

———. *Black Society in Spanish Florida*. Urbana: University of Illinois Press, 1999.

———. "Cimarron and Citizen: African Ethnicity, Corporate Identity, and the Evolution of Free Black Towns in the Spanish Circum-Caribbean." In Landers and Robinson, *Slaves, Subjects, and Subversives*, 111–146.

———. "Slavery in the Lower South." *Organization of American Historians Magazine of History* 17, no. 3 (April 2003): 23–27.

———. "Transforming Bondsmen into Vassals: Arming Slaves in Colonial Spanish America." In Brown and Morgan, *Arming Slaves*, 120–145.

Landers, Jane, and Barry Robinson, eds. *Slaves, Subjects, and Subversives: Blacks in Colonial Latin America*. Albuquerque: University of New Mexico Press, 2006.

Lane, Kris. *Quito 1599: City and Colony in Transition*. Albuquerque: University of New Mexico Press, 2002.

Lanning, Michael Lee. *Defenders of Liberty: African Americans in the Revolutionary War*. New York: Citadel Press, 2000.

Larose, Thomas. "African Influences on Seminole Beadwork." In *Africa in Florida: Five Hundred Years of African Presence in the Sunshine State*, edited by Amanda Carlson and Robin Poynor, 86–106. Gainesville: University of Florida Press, 2014.

Law, Robin. "'There's Nothing Grows in the West Indies but Will Grow Here': Dutch and English Projects of Plantation Agriculture on the Gold Coast, 1650s–1780s." In *Commercial Agriculture, the Slave Trade, and Slavery in Atlantic Africa*, edited by Robin Law, Suzanne Schwarz, and Silke Strickrodt, 116–137. Suffolk: Boydell & Brewer, 2013.

Leaming, Hugo. *Hidden Americans: Maroons of Virginia and the Carolinas*. 2nd ed. New York: Garland, 1995.

Le Petit, Mauthurin. *The Natchez Massacre*. Translated by Richard Hart. New Orleans: Poor Richard's Press, 1950.

Lepore, Jill. *New York Burning: Liberty, Slavery, and Conspiracy in Eighteenth-Century Manhattan*. New York: Knopf, 2005.

Linebaugh, Peter, and Marcus Rediker. *The Many-Headed Hydra: Sailors, Slaves, Commoners, and the Hidden History of the Revolutionary Atlantic*. Boston: Beacon, 2000.

Littlefield, Daniel. *Africans and Creeks: From the Colonial Period to the Civil War*. Westport, Conn.: Greenwood, 1979.

Lockley, Tim. "'The King of England's Soldiers': Armed Blacks in Savannah and Its Hinterlands during the Revolutionary War Era, 1778–1787." In *Slavery and Freedom in Savannah*, edited by Leslie Harris and Diana Ramey Berry, 42–54. Athens: University of Georgia Press, 2014.

———. "Mutiny! The Story of the 8th West India Regiment." British Library, 2017. https://www.bl.uk/west-india-regiment/articles/mutiny-the-story-of-the-8th-west-india-regiment.

Lockley, Tim, and David Doddington. "Maroon and Slave Communities in South Carolina before 1865." *South Carolina Historical Magazine* 113 (April 2012): 125–145.

Lokken, Paul. "A Maroon Moment: Rebel Slaves in Early Seventeenth-Century Guatemala." *Slavery and Abolition* 25, no. 3 (December 2004): 44–58.

Lovejoy, Henry. *Prieto: Yorùbá Kingship in Colonial Cuba during the Age of Revolutions*. Chapel Hill: University of North Carolina Press, 2019.

Lovejoy, Paul. "Fugitive Slaves: Resistance to Slavery in the Sokoto Caliphate." In *In Resistance: Studies in African, Caribbean, and Afro-American History*, edited by Gary Okihiro, 71–95. Amherst: University of Massachusetts Press, 1986.

———. "Problems of Slave Control in the Sokoto Caliphate." In *Africans in Bondage: Studies of Slavery and the Slave Trade*, edited by Paul Lovejoy, 235–272. Madison: University of Wisconsin Press, 1976.

———. *Transformations in Slavery: A History of Slavery in Africa*. Cambridge: Cambridge University Press, 1983.

Lovejoy, Paul, and Jan Hogendorn, *Slow Death for Slavery: The Course of Abolition in Northern Nigeria, 1897–1936*. Cambridge: Cambridge University Press, 1993.

Madrilejo, Nicole, Holden Lombard, and Jada Benn Torres. "Origins of Marronage: Mitochondrial Lineages of Jamaica's Accompong Town Maroons." *American Journal of Human Biology* 27, no. 3 (May 6, 2015): 432–437.

Mahon, John. "British Strategy and Southern Indians: War of 1812." *Florida Historical Quarterly* 44, no. 4 (April 1966): 285–302.

———. "The First Seminole War, November 21, 1817–May 24, 1818." *Florida Historical Quarterly* 77, no. 1 (Summer 1998): 62–67.

———. "The Treaty at Moultrie Creek 1823." *Florida Historical Quarterly* 40, no. 4 (April 1962): 350–372.

Malcolm, Joyce Lee. *Peter's War: A New England Slave Boy and the American Revolution*. New Haven, Conn.: Yale University Press, 2009.

Manuel, Keith Anthony. "Slavery, Coffee, and Family in a Frontier Society: Jeremie and Its Hinterland, 1780–1789." MA thesis, University of Florida, 2005.

Marotti, Frank. *Heaven's Soldiers: Free People of Color and the Spanish Legacy in Antebellum Florida*. Tuscaloosa: University of Alabama Press, 2013.

Marques, João Pedro, Seymour Drescher, and P. C. Emmer. *Who Abolished Slavery: Slave Revolts and Abolitionism: A Debate with João Pedro Marques*. New York: Berghahn, 2010.

Marshall, Bernard. "The Black Caribs—Native Resistance to British Penetration into the Windward Side of St. Vincent, 1763–1773." *Caribbean Quarterly* 19, no. 4 (December 1973): 4–19.

Marshall, Woodville. "Provision Ground and Plantation Labour in Four Windward Islands: Competition for Resources during Slavery." In *The Slavery Reader*, edited by Gad Heuman and James Walvin, 470–485. New York: Routledge, 2003.

Martin, Jacqueline. "The Maroons of the Great Dismal Swamp, 1607–1865." MA thesis, Western Washington University, 2004.

Martin, Joel. *Sacred Revolt: The Muskogees' Struggle for a New World*. Boston: Beacon, 1991.

Mathews, Gelien. *Caribbean Slave Revolts and the British Abolitionist Movement*. Baton Rouge: Louisiana State University Press, 2006.

Mattos, Hebe. "'Black Troops' and Hierarchies of Color in the Portuguese Atlantic World: The Case of Henrique Dias and His Black Regiment." *Luso-Brazilian Review* 45, no. 1 (2008): 6–29.

Mattoso, Katia M. de Quiros. *To Be a Slave in Brazil, 1550–1888*. Translated by Arthur Goldhammer. New Brunswick, N.J.: Rutgers University Press, 1986.

Maxwell, Kenneth R. *Conflicts and Conspiracies: Brazil and Portugal, 1750–1808*. Cambridge: Cambridge University Press, 1973.

May, Robert. "Invisible Men: Blacks and the U.S. Army in the Mexican War." *Historian* 49, no. 4 (August 1987): 463–477.

McCusker, John. *Essays in the Economic History of the Atlantic World*. London: Routledge, 1997.

McGowan, Winston. "The Distinctive Features of the 1823 Demerara Slave Rebellion," *Stabroek News* (Georgetown, Guyana), August 1, 2013, http://www.stabroeknews.com.

McKee, Helen Mary. "From Violence to Alliance: Maroons and White Settlers in Jamaica, 1739–1795." *Slavery and Abolition* 39, no. 1 (June 2017): 27–52.

———. "Negotiating Freedom in the Circum-Caribbean: The Jamaican Maroons and Compared." PhD diss., Newcastle University, 2015.

McKnight, Kathryn Joy. "Elder, Slave, and Soldier: Maroon Voices from the Palenque del Limón, 1634." In *Afro-Latino Voices: Narratives from the Early Modern Ibero-Atlantic World, 1550–1812*, edited by Kathryn McKnight and Leo Garofalo, 64–81. Indianapolis: Hackett, 2009.

McPherson, Edward. *The Political History of the United States of America, during the Great Rebellion* . . . Washington, D.C.: Philip & Solomons, 1865.

McPherson, James. *Marching toward Freedom: Blacks in the Civil War, 1861–1865*. New York: Facts on File, 1994.

McRae, Bennie J., Jr., Curtis M. Miller, and Cheryl Trowbridge-Miller. *Nineteenth Century Freedom Fighters: The 1st South Carolina Volunteers*. Chicago: Arcadia Publishing, 2006.

Medina, Charles Beatty. "Alonso de Ellescas (1530s–1590s): African, Ladino, and Maroon Leader in Colonial Ecuador." In *The Human Tradition in the Black Atlantic, 1500–2000*, edited by Beatriz Mamigonian and Karen Racine, 9–22. New York: Rowman & Littlefield, 2010.

Meyer, Howard. *Colonel of the Black Regiment: The Life of Thomas Wentworth Higginson*. New York: Norton, 1967.

Miers, Suzanne, and Igor Kopytoff. "African 'Slavery' as an Institution of Marginality." In *Slavery in Africa: Historical and Anthropological Perspectives*, edited by Suzanne Miers and Igor Kopytoff, 1–81. Madison: University of Wisconsin Press, 1977.

Miles, Tiya, and Celie E. Naylor-Ojurongbe. "African-Americans in Indian Societies." In *Handbook of North American Indians*, edited by Raymond Fogelson, 14:753–759. Washington, D.C.: Smithsonian Institution, 2004.

Millett, Nathaniel. "Britain's 1814 Occupation of Pensacola and America's Response: An Episode of the War of 1812 in the Southeastern Borderlands." *Florida Historical Quarterly* 84, no. 2 (Fall 2005): 229–255.

———. "Defining Freedom in the Atlantic Borderlands of the Revolutionary Southeast." *Early American Studies* 5, no. 2 (Fall 2007): 367–394.

———. *The Maroons of Prospect Bluff and Their Quest for Freedom in the Atlantic World*. Gainesville: University Press of Florida, 2013.

———. "The Radicalism of the First Seminole War and Its Consequences." In *Warring for America: Cultural Contests in the Era of 1812*, edited by Nicole Eustace and Frederika Teute, 164–201. Chapel Hill: University of North Carolina Press, 2017.

Milligan, John. "Slave Rebelliousness and the Florida Maroon." *Prologue* 6, no. 1 (Spring 1974): 4–18.

Milling, Chapman. *Red Carolinians*. Columbia: University of South Carolina Press, 1969.

Mintz, Sidney, and Richard Price. *The Birth of African-American Culture: An Anthropological Perspective*. Boston: Beacon, 1976.

Missall, John, and Mary Lou Missall. *The Seminole Wars: America's Longest Indian Conflict*. Gainesville: University Press of Florida, 2004.

Mock, Shirley Boteler. *Dreaming with the Ancestors: Black Seminole Women in Texas and Mexico*. Norman: University of Oklahoma Press, 2010.

Mohr, Clarence. "Before Sherman: Georgia Blacks and the Union War Effort, 1861–1864." *Journal of Southern History* 45, no. 3 (August 1979): 331–352.

Moitt, Bernard. "Slave Women and Resistance in the French Caribbean." In *More than Chattel: Black Women and Slavery in the Americas*, edited by David Barry Gaspar and Darlene Clark Hine, 239–258. Bloomington: Indiana University Press, 1996.

Monaco, Chris. "Fort Mitchell and the Settlement of the Alachua County." *Florida Historical Quarterly* 79, no. 1 (Summer 2000): 1–25.

Monsalve, M. V., and E. Hagelberg. "Mitochondrial DNA Polymorphisms in Carib People of Belize." *Proceedings, Biological Sciences* 22, no. 264 (August 1997): 1217–1224.

Morgan, Edmund. *American Slavery, American Freedom: The Ordeal of Colonial Virginia*. New York: Norton, 1975.

Morgan, Kenneth. *Slavery and the British Empire: From Africa to America*. Oxford: Oxford University Press, 2007.

Morgan, Philip, and Andrew Jackson O'Shaughnessy. "Arming Slaves in the American Revolution." In Brown and Morgan, *Arming Slaves*, 180–208.

Mullin, Gerald (Michael). *Africa in America: Slave Acculturation and Resistance in the American South and the British Caribbean, 1736–1831*. Urbana: University of Illinois Press, 1992.

———. "British Caribbean and North American Slaves in an Era of War and Revolution, 1775–1807." In *The Southern Experience in the American Revolution*, edited by Jeffrey Crow and Larry Tise, 235–267. Chapel Hill: University of North Carolina Press, 1978.

———. *Flight and Rebellion: Slave Resistance in Eighteenth-Century Virginia*. New York: Oxford University Press, 1972.

Mulroy, Kevin. "Ethnogenesis and Ethnohistory of the Seminole Maroons." *Journal of World History* 4, no. 2 (Fall 1993): 287–305.

———. *Freedom on the Border: The Seminole Maroons in Florida, the Indian Territory, Coachuila, and Texas*. Lubbock: Texas Tech University Press, 1993.

———. *The Seminole Freedmen: A History*. Norman: University of Oklahoma Press, 2007.

Murray, D. J. *The West Indies and the Development of Colonial Government, 1801–1834*. Oxford: Clarendon Press, 1965.

Naisawald, Louis VanLoan. "Robert Howe's Operations in Virginia, 1775–1776." *Virginia Magazine of History and Biography* 60, no. 3 (July 1952): 437–443.

Narayan, Rosalyn. "'Creating Insurrections in the Heart of Our Country': Fear of the British West India Regiments in the Southern U.S. Press, 1838–1860." *Slavery and Abolition* 39, no. 3 (August 2018): 497–517.

Nash, Gary. *The Forgotten Fifth: African Americans in the Age of Revolution*. Cambridge, Mass.: Harvard University Press, 2006.

Nell, William Cooper. *Services of Colored Americans, in the Wars of 1776 and 1812*. Boston: Prentis & Sawyer, 1851.

Northcott, Cecil. *Slavery's Martyr: John Smith of Demerara and the Emancipation Movement, 1817–1834*. London: Epworth Press, 1976.

Northrup, David. *Trade without Rulers: Pre-colonial Economic Development in South-Eastern Nigeria*. Oxford: Clarendon Press, 1978.

Nunez, Theron A., Jr. "Creek Nativism and the Creek War of 1813–1814." *Ethnohistory* 5, no. 2 (Winter 1958): 1–47.

Nwauwa, Apollos. "The Dating of the Aro Chiefdom: A Synthesis of Correlated Genealogies." *History in Africa* 17 (January 1990): 227–245.

Nwokeji, G. Ugo. *The Slave Trade and Culture in the Bight of Biafra: An African Society in the Atlantic World*. Cambridge: Cambridge University Press, 2010.

Oatis, Steven. *A Colonial Complex: South Carolina's Frontiers in the Era of the Yamasee War, 1680–1730*. Lincoln: University of Nebraska Press, 2004.

O'Brien, Sean Michael. *In Bitterness and Tears: Andrew Jackson's Destruction of the Creeks and Seminoles*. Westport, Conn.: Praeger, 2003.

O'Malley, Gregory. *Final Passages: The Intercolonial Slave Trade of British America, 1615–1807*. Chapel Hill: University of North Carolina Press, 2014.

Oostindie, Gert. "Slave Resistance, Colour Lines, and the Impact of the French and Haitian Revolutions in Curaçao." In Klooster and Oostindie, *Curaçao in the Age of Revolutions*, 1–22.

Orser, Charles, Jr. *A Historical Archaeology of the Modern World*. New York: Plenum Press, 1996.

Osei-Tutu, John Kwadwo. *The Asafoi (Socio-military Groups) in the History and Politics of Accra (Ghana) from the 17th to the Mid 20th Century*. Trondheim: Department of History, Norwegian University of Science and Technology, 2000.

Owsley, Frank, Jr. "British and Indian Activities in Spanish West Florida during the War of 1812." *Florida Historical Quarterly* 46, no. 2 (October 1967): 111–123.

———. *Struggle for the Gulf Borderlands: The Creek War and the Battle of New Orleans, 1812–1815*. Gainesville: University Press of Florida, 1981.

Owsley, Frank, Jr., and Gene Allen Smith. *Filibusters and Expansionists: Jeffersonian Manifest Destiny, 1800–1821*. Tuscaloosa: University of Alabama Press, 1997.

Paquette, Robert. "The Drivers Shall Lead Them: Image and Reality in Slave Resistance." In *Slavery, Secession and Southern History*, edited by Robert Paquette and Louis Ferleger, 31–58. Charlottesville: University Press of Virginia, 2000.

Parent, Anthony, Jr. *Foul Means: The Formation of a Slave Society*. Chapel Hill: University of North Carolina Press, 2003.

Parker, Freddie. *Running for Freedom: Slave Runaways in North Carolina, 1775–1840*. New York: Garland, 1993.

Patrick, Rembert. *Florida Fiasco: Rampant Rebels on the Georgia-Florida Border, 1810–1815*. Athens: University of Georgia Press, 1954.

Patterson, Orlando. "Slavery and Slave Revolts: A Socio-historical Analysis of the First Maroon War, Jamaica, 1655–1740." *Social and Economic Studies* 19, no. 3 (September 1970): 289–325.

———. "Slavery and Slave Revolts: A Sociological Analysis of the First Maroon War, 1665–1740." In Price, *Maroon Societies*, 246–292.

———. *Sociology of Slavery: An Analysis of the Origins, Development, and Structure of the Negro Slave Society in Jamaica*. London: McGibbon & Kee, 1967.

Pearson, Edward. "A Countryside Full of Flames: A Reconsideration of the Stono Rebellion." *Slavery and Abolition* 17, no. 2 (1996): 22–50.

Pennington, Edgar Legare. "The South Carolina Indian War of 1715, as Seen by Clergymen." *South Carolina Historical and Genealogical Magazine* 32, no. 4 (October 1931): 251–269.

Pérez de la Riva, Francisco. "Cuban Palenques." In Price, *Maroon Societies*, 49–59.

Peters, Virginia Bergman. *The Florida Wars*. Hamden, Conn.: Archon Books, 1979.

Piecuch, Jim. *Three Peoples, One King: Loyalists, Indians, and Slaves in the Revolutionary South, 1775–1782*. Columbia: University of South Carolina Press, 2013.

Pierce, Edward. "The Freedmen at Port Royal." *Atlantic Monthly* 12 (1863): 291–315.

Poe, Stephen. "Archaeological Excavations at Fort Gadsden, Florida." *Notes in Anthropology* 8 (1963): 1–35.

Pope, Justin. "Inventing an Indian Slave Conspiracy on Nantucket, 1738." *Early American Studies* 15, no. 3 (2017): 505–538.

Popkin, Jeremy. *A Concise History of the Haitian Revolution*. Hoboken, N.J.: Wiley-Blackwell, 2012.

Porter, Kenneth Wiggins. *The Black Seminoles: History of a Freedom-Seeking People*.

Edited by Alcione Amos and Thomas Senter. Gainesville: University Press of Florida, 1996.

———. *The Negro on the American Frontier*. New York: Arno Press, 1971.

———. "Negroes and the East Florida Annexation Plot, 1811–1813." *Journal of Negro History* 30, no. 1 (January 1945): 9–29.

———. "Negroes and the Seminole War, 1817–1818." *Journal of Negro History* 36, no. 3 (July 1951): 249–280.

———. "Negroes on the Southern Frontier, 1670–1763." *Journal of Negro History* 33, no. 1 (January 1948): 53–78.

Posey, John Thornton. *General Thomas Posey: Son of the American Revolution*. East Lansing: Michigan State University Press, 1992.

Price, Richard. *Alabi's World*. Baltimore: Johns Hopkins University Press, 1990.

———, ed. *Maroon Societies: Rebel Slave Communities in the Americas*. 3rd ed. Baltimore: Johns Hopkins University Press, 1996.

———. *Saramaka Social Structure: Analysis of a Maroon Society in Suriname*. Río Piedras, P.R.: Institute of Caribbean Studies, 1975.

———. "Uneasy Neighbors: Maroons and Indians in Suriname." *Tripiti: Journal of the Society for the Anthropology of Lowland South America* 8, no. 2, article 4 (2010): 1–16.

Pybus, Cassandra. *Epic Journeys of Freedom: Runaway Slaves of the American Revolution and Their Global Quest for Liberty*. Boston: Beacon, 2006.

Quarles, Benjamin. "The Colonial Militia and Negro Manpower." *Mississippi Valley Historical Review* 45, no. 4 (1959): 643–652.

———. *The Negro in the American Revolution*. 50th anniversary ed. Chapel Hill: University of North Carolina Press, 2012.

———. *The Negro in the Civil War*. New York: Russell & Russell, 1953.

Rakove, Jack. *Revolutionaries: A History of the Invention of America*. New York: Houghton Mifflin Harcourt, 2010.

Ramos, Donald. "Social Revolution Frustrated: The Conspiracy of the Tailors in Bahia, 1798." *Luso-Brazilian Review* 13, no. 1 (Summer 1976): 74–90.

Ramsey, William. "A Coat for 'Indian Cuffy': Mapping the Boundary between Freedom and Slavery in Colonial South Carolina." *South Carolina Historical Magazine* 103, no. 1 (January 2002): 48–66.

———. *The Yamasee War: A Study of Culture, Economy, and Conflict in the Colonial South*. Lincoln: University of Nebraska Press, 2008.

Rasmussen, Daniel. *American Uprising: The Untold Story of America's Largest Slave Revolt*. New York: Harper Collins, 2011.

———. Interview by Diane Rehm. *The Diane Rehm Show*, WAMU, January 13, 2011.

Rediker, Marcus. *The Amistad Rebellion: An Atlantic Odyssey of Slavery and Freedom*. New York: Viking Penguin Group, 2012.

———. *A Slave Ship: A Human History*. New York: Penguin, 2007.

Reeder, Tyson. "Liberty with the Sword: Jamaican Maroons, Haitian Revolutionaries, and American Liberty." *Journal of the Early Republic* 37, no. 1 (Spring 2017): 81–115.

Reid-Vasquez, Michele. *The Year of the Lash: Free People of Color in Cuba and the Nineteenth-Century Atlantic World*. Athens: University of Georgia Press, 2011.

Reigelsperger, Diana. "Interethnic Relations and Settlement on the Spanish Frontier, 1668–1763." PhD diss., University of Florida, 2013.

Reindorf, Carl. *History of the Gold Coast and Asante*. 3rd ed. Accra: Ghana Universities Press, 2007.

Reis, João José. *Slave Rebellion in Brazil: The Muslim Uprising of 1835 in Bahia*. Translated by Arthur Brakel. Baltimore: Johns Hopkins University Press, 1993.

———. "Slave Resistance in Brazil: Bahia, 1807–1835." *Luso-Brazilian Review* 25, no. 1 (Summer 1988): 111–144.

Restall, Mathew. "Black Conquistadors: Armed Africans in Early Spanish America." *Americas* 57, no. 2 (October 2000): 171–205.

———, ed. Beyond Black and Red: *African-Native Relations in Colonial Latin America*. Albuquerque: University of New Mexico Press, 2005.

Reynolds, David. *John Brown, Abolitionist: The Man Who Killed Slavery, Sparked the Civil War, and Seeded Civil Rights*. New York: Knopf, 2005.

———. *Texas Terror: The Slave Insurrection Panic of 1860 and the Secession of the Lower South*. Baton Rouge: Louisiana State University Press, 2007.

Rice, James. *Tales from a Revolution: Bacon's Rebellion and the Transformation of Early America*. New York: Oxford University Press, 2012.

Richardson, David. "Shipboard Revolts, African Authority, and the Atlantic Slave Trade." *William and Mary Quarterly* 58, no. 1 (January 2001): 69–92. doi: 10.2307/2674419.

Ridley, Milton McFarlane. *Cudjoe of Jamaica: Pioneer for Black Freedom in the New World*. Short Hills, N.J.: Enslow Publishers, 1977.

Riordan, Patrick. "Finding Freedom in Florida: Native Peoples, African Americans, and Colonists, 1670–1816." *Florida Historical Quarterly* 75, no. 1 (Summer 1996): 24–43.

Rivers, Larry. *Rebels and Runaways: Slave Resistance in Nineteenth-Century Florida*. Urbana: University of Illinois Press, 2012.

Rivers, Larry, and Canter Brown Jr. "'The Indispensable Man': John Horse and Florida's Second Seminole War." *Journal of the Georgia Association of Historians* 18 (1997): 1–23.

Robbins, Gerald. "The Recruiting and Arming of Negroes in the South Carolina Sea Islands." *Journal of Negro History* 28, no. 7 (April 1965): 150–167.

Rodriguez, Frederick. "Negro Slavery in New Spain and the Yanga Revolt." MA thesis, DePaul University, 1972.

Rogers, William Warren, ed. "Florida on the Eve of the Civil War as Seen by a Southern Reporter." *Florida Historical Quarterly* 39 (1960–61): 145–158.

Roper, L. H. "The 1701 'Act for the Better Ordering of Slaves': Reconsidering the

History of Slavery in Proprietary South Carolina." *William and Mary Quarterly* 64, no. 2 (April 2007): 395–418.

———. *Advancing Empire: English Interests and Overseas Expansion, 1613–1688*. New York: Cambridge University Press, 2017.

Rose, Willie. *Rehearsal for Reconstruction: The Port Royal Experiment*. Athens: University of Georgia Press, 1964.

Rosen, Deborah. *Border Law: The First Seminole War and American Nationhood*. Cambridge, Mass.: Harvard University Press, 2015.

Rothman, Adam. *Slave Country: American Expansion and the Origins of the Deep South*. Cambridge, Mass.: Harvard University Press, 2005.

Rucker, Walter. *Gold Coast Diasporas: Identity, Culture, and Power*. Bloomington: Indiana University Press, 2015.

———. *The River Flows On: Black Resistance, Culture, and Identity Formation in Early America*. Baton Rouge: Louisiana State University Press, 2006.

Rugemer, Edward. *Slave Law and Politics of Resistance in the Early Atlantic World*. Cambridge, Mass.: Harvard University Press, 2018.

Rushforth, Brett. "The Gauolet Uprising of 1710: Maroons, Rebels, and the Informal Exchange Economy of a Caribbean Sugar Island." *William and Mary Quarterly* 76, no. 1 (January 2019): 75–110.

Russo, Jean, and Elliot Russo. *Planting an Empire: The Early Chesapeake in British North America*. Baltimore: Johns Hopkins University Press, 2012.

Ryan, William. *The World of Thomas Jeremiah: Charles Town on the Eve of the American Revolution*. New York: Oxford University Press, 2010.

Salas, Antonio, et al. "Shipwrecks and Founder Effects: Divergent Demographic Histories Reflected in Caribbean mtDNA." *American Journal of Physical Anthropology* 128 (2005): 855–860.

Sanneh, Lamin. *Abolitionists Abroad: American Blacks and the Making of Modern West Africa*. Cambridge, Mass.: Harvard University Press, 1999.

Saunt, Claudio. "'The English Has Now a Mind to Make Slaves of Them All': Creeks, Seminoles, and the Problem of Slavery." *American Indian Quarterly* 22, nos. 1/2 (Winter-Spring 1998): 157–180.

———. *A New Order of Things: Property, Power, and the Transformation of the Creek Indians, 1733–1816*. Cambridge: Cambridge University Press, 1999.

Sayers, Daniel. *A Desolate Place for a Defiant People: The Archeology of Maroons, Indigenous Americans, and Enslaved Laborers in the Great Dismal Swamp*. Gainesville: University Press of Florida, 2014.

Schama, Simon. *Rough Crossings: Britain, the Slaves and the American Revolution*. London: BBC Books, 2005.

Schuler, Monica. "Akan Slave Rebellions in the British Caribbean." In *Caribbean Slave Society and Economy*, edited by Hilary Beckles and Verene Shepherd, 373–386. New York: New Press, 1991.

Schwaller, Robert. "Contested Conquests: African Maroons and the Incomplete Conquest of Hispaniola, 1519–1620." *Americas* 75, no. 4 (2018): 609–638.

Schwartz, Stuart. "Cantos and Quilombos: A Hausa Rebellion in Bahia, 1814." In Landers and Robinson, *Slaves, Subjects, and Subversives*, 247–270.

———. *Slaves, Peasants, and Rebels: Reconsidering Brazilian Slavery*. Chicago: University of Illinois Press, 1992.

Schwarz, Philip. *Migrants against Slavery: Virginians and the Nation*. Charlottesville: University of Virginia Press, 2001.

———. *Twice Condemned: Slaves and the Criminal Laws of Virginia, 1705–1865*. Baton Rouge: Louisiana State University Press, 1988.

Scott, James C. *Domination and the Arts of Resistance: Hidden Transcripts*. New Haven, Conn.: Yale University Press, 1990.

Scott, Julius Sherrard, III. "The Common Wind: Currents of Afro-American Communication in the Era of the Haitian Revolution." PhD diss., Duke University, 1986.

Scott, Kenneth. "The Slave Insurrection in New York in 1712." *New York Historical Society Quarterly* 45, no. 1 (January 1961): 43–74.

Scott, Rebecca. *Degrees of Freedom: Louisiana and Cuba after Slavery*. Cambridge, Mass.: Harvard University Press, 2005.

Sears, Christine. *American Slaves and African Masters: Algiers and the Western Sahara, 1776–1820*. New York: Palgrave Macmillan, 2012.

Selby, John. *The Revolution in Virginia, 1775–1783*. Williamsburg, Va.: Colonial Williamsburg Foundation, 1988.

Sellick, Gary. "Black Skin, Red Coats: The Carolina Corps and Nationalism in the Revolutionary British Caribbean." *Slavery and Abolition* 39, no. 3 (August 2018): 459–478.

Sensbach, Jon. *Rebecca's Revival: Creating Black Christianity in the Atlantic World*. Cambridge, Mass.: Harvard University Press, 2005.

Sernett, Milton. *Harriet Tubman: Myth, Memory, and History*. Durham, N.C.: Duke University Press, 2007.

Sharples, Jason. "Discovering Slave Conspiracies: New Fears of Rebellion and Old Paradigms of Plotting in Seventeenth-Century Barbados." *American Historical Review* 120, no. 3 (June 2015): 811–843.

———. "The Flames of Insurrection: Fearing Slave Conspiracy in Early America, 1670–1780." PhD diss., Princeton University, 2010.

Shea, William. *The Virginia Militia in the Seventeenth Century*. Baton Rouge: Louisiana State University Press, 1983.

Shepherd, Charles. *An Historical Account of the Island of Saint Vincent*. London: W. Nicol, 1831.

Sheridan, Richard. "The Jamaican Slave Insurrection Scare of 1776 and the American Revolution." In Dubois and Scott, *Origins of the Black Atlantic*, 26–46.

Sidbury, James. *Becoming African in America: Race and Nation in the Early Black Atlantic*. New York: Oxford University Press, 2007.

———. *Ploughshares into Swords: Race, Rebellion, and Identity in Gabriel's Virginia, 1730–1810*. New York: Cambridge University Press, 1997.

Sinha, Manisha. *The Slave's Cause: A History of Abolition*. New Haven, Conn.: Yale University Press, 2016.

Smith, Gene Allen. *The Slaves' Gamble: Choosing Sides in the War of 1812*. New York: Palgrave Macmillan, 2013.

Smith, Mark M. "Remembering Mary, Shaping Revolt: Reconsidering the Stono Rebellion." *Journal of Southern History* 67 (2001): 513–534.

Smith, Robert. *Warfare and Diplomacy in Pre-Colonial West Africa*. London: James Currey, 1989.

———. "Yoruba Armament." *Journal of African History* 8, no. 1 (1967): 87–106.

Snyder, Christina. *Slavery in Indian Country: The Changing Face of Captivity in Early America*. Cambridge, Mass.: Harvard University Press, 2010.

Snyder, Jennifer. "Revolutionary Repercussions." In *The Loyal Atlantic: Remaking the British Atlantic in the Revolutionary Era*, edited by Jerry Bannister and Liam Riordan, 165–184. Toronto: University of Toronto Press, 2012.

"South Carolina Historical Society Recently Processed Manuscripts." *South Carolina Historical Magazine* 105, no. 2 (2004): 157–161.

Sprinkle, John Harold, Jr. "Loyalists and Baconians: The Participants in Bacon's Rebellion in Virginia, 1676–1677." PhD diss., College of William and Mary, 1992.

Stampp, Kenneth. *The Peculiar Institution: Slavery in the Ante-bellum South*. New York: Vintage Books, 1956.

Stein, Robert Louis. *Léger Félicité Sonthonax: The Lost Sentinel of the Republic*. Cranbury, N.J.: Associated Press, 1985.

Sterkx, Henry Eugene, and Brooks Thompson. "Philemon Thomas and the West Florida Revolution." *Florida Historical Quarterly* 39, no. 4 (April 1961): 378–386.

Stilwell, Sean. *Slavery and Slaving in African History*. New York: Cambridge University Press, 2014.

Sturtevant, William. Review of *Africans and Seminoles: From Removal to Emancipation*, by Daniel Littlefield, *American Anthropologist* 81, no. 4 (December 1979): 916–917.

Swanton, John Reed. *Early History of the Creek Indians and Their Neighbors*. Washington, D.C.: Government Printing Office, 1922.

Taylor, Alan. *The Internal Enemy: Slavery in Virginia, 1772–1832*. New York: Norton, 2013.

Taylor, Christopher. *The Black Carib Wars: Freedom, Survival, and the Making of the Garifuna*. Jackson: University Press of Mississippi, 2012.

Taylor, Eric Robert. *If We Must Die: Shipboard Insurrections in the Era of the Atlantic Slave Trade*. Baton Rouge: Louisiana State University Press, 2006.

Tepaske, John. "The Fugitive Slave: Intercolonial Rivalry and Spanish Slave Policy." In *Eighteenth-Century Florida and Its Borderlands*, edited by Samuel Proctor, 2–12. Gainesville: University Press of Florida, 1975.

Theobald, Mary Miley. "Slave Conspiracies in Colonial Virginia." *Colonial Williamsburg Journal* 28 (Winter 2006): 26–31.

Thompson, Alvin. "The Berbice Revolt, 1763–1764." In *Themes in African-Guyanese*

History, edited by Winston McGowan, James Rose, and David Granger, 77–105. London: Hansib Publications, 2009.

———. *Flight to Freedom: African Runaways and Maroons in the Americas*. Kingston: University of West Indies Press, 2006.

Thornton, John. *Africa and Africans in the Making of the Atlantic World, 1400–1800*. Cambridge: Cambridge University Press, 1998.

———. "African Dimensions of the Stono Rebellion." *American Historical Review* 96 (1991): 1101–1113.

———. "The African Experience of the '20 and Odd Negroes' Arriving in Virginia in 1619." *William and Mary Quarterly*, 3rd series, 55 (1998): 421–434.

———. "African Soldiers in the Haitian Revolution." In Dubois and Scott, *Origins of the Black Atlantic*, 195–213.

———. "Armed Slaves and Political Authority in Africa in the Era of the Slave Trade, 1450–1800." In Brown and Morgan, *Arming Slaves*, 79–94.

———. "The Art of War in Angola, 1575–1680." *Comparative Studies in Society and History* 30, no. 2 (April 1988): 360–378.

———. "The Coromantees: An African Cultural Group in Colonial North America and the Caribbean." *Journal of Caribbean History* 32, nos. 1/2 (1998): 161–178.

———. "Les États de l'Angola et la formation de Palmares (Brésil)." *Annals, Histoire, Sciences Sociales* 63, no. 4 (July 2008): 769–797.

———. "I Am the Subject of the King of Congo: African Political Ideology and the Haitian Revolution." *Journal of World History* 4, no. 2 (Fall 1993): 181–214.

———. "War, the State, and Religious Norms in 'Coromantee' Thought: The Ideology of an African American Nation." In *Possible Pasts: Becoming Colonial in Early America*, edited by Robert Blair St. George, 181–200. Ithaca, N.Y.: Cornell University Press, 2000.

———. *Warfare in Atlantic Africa, 1500–1800*. London: UCL Press, 1999.

Toledano, Ehud. *As If Silent and Absent: Bonds of Enslavement in the Islamic Middle East*. New Haven, Conn.: Yale University Press, 2007.

Trudeau, Noah. *Like Men of War: Black Troops in the Civil War, 1862–1865*. New York: Little, Brown, 1998.

Twyman, Bruce Edward. *The Black Seminole Legacy and North American Politics, 1693–1845*. Washington, D.C.: Howard University Press, 1999.

Tyler, Ronnie. "Fugitive Slaves in Mexico." *Journal of Negro History* 57, no. 1 (1972): 1–12.

Ukpabi, S. C. "West Indian Troops and the Defence of British West Africa in the Nineteenth Century." *African Studies Review* 17, no. 1 (1974): 133–150.

United States Adjutant General's Office. *Federal Aid in Domestic Disturbances, 1787–1903*. Washington, D.C.: Government Printing Office, 1903.

Usner, Daniel, Jr. "The Frontier Exchange Economy of the Lower Mississippi Valley in the Eighteenth Century." *William and Mary Quarterly* 44, no. 2 (April 1987): 165–192.

———. *Indians, Settlers, and Slaves in a Frontier Exchange Economy: The Lower Mississippi Valley before 1783*. Chapel Hill: University of North Carolina Press, 1992.

Vaz, Neil. "Dominica's Neg Mawon: Maroonage, Diaspora, and Trans-Atlantic Networks, 1763–1814." PhD diss., Howard University, 2016.

Viotti da Costa, Emilia. *Crowns of Glory, Tears of Blood: The Demerara Slave Rebellion of 1823*. New York: Oxford University Press, 1994.

Voelz, Peter Michael. *Slave and Soldier: The Military Impact of Blacks in the Colonial Americas*. New York: Garland, 1993.

Walker, James W. S. G. *The Black Loyalists: The Search for a Promised Land in Nova Scotia and Sierra Leone, 1783–1870*. Halifax, N.S.: Dalhousie University Press, 1976.

Waller, G. M. "New York's Role in Queen Anne's War, 1702–1713." *New York History* 33, no. 1 (January 1952): 40–53.

Walton, Peter. "54th Massachusetts Infantry Regiment (1863–1865)." December 2007, https://www.blackpast.org/african-american-history/fifty-fourth-massachusetts-infantry-1863-1865/ (accessed April 20, 2020).

Washburn, Wilcomb. *The Governor and the Rebel: A History of Bacon's Rebellion in Virginia*. Chapel Hill: University of North Carolina Press, 1957.

———. "Sir William Berkeley's 'A History of Our Miseries.'" *William and Mary Quarterly* 14, no. 3 (1957): 403–413.

Wax, Darold. "Preferences for Slaves in Colonial America." *Journal of Negro History* 58, no. 4 (1973): 371–401.

Webb, Steven Saunders. *1676: The End of American Independence*. New York: Knopf, 1984.

Weik, Terrance. "The Role of Ethnogenesis and Organization in the Development of African-Native American Settlements: An African Seminole Model." *International Journal of Historical Archaeology* 13, no. 2 (June 2009): 206–238.

Wertenbaker, Thomas Jefferson. *Torchbearer of Revolution: The Story of Bacon's Rebellion and Its Leader*. Princeton, N.J.: Princeton University Press, 1940.

Wesley, Charles, and Patricia Romero. *Negro Americans in the Civil War: From Slavery to Citizenship*. New York: Publishers Company, 1967.

Westergaard, Waldemar. "Account of the Negro Rebellion on St. Croix, Danish West Indies, 1759." *Journal of Negro History* 11, no. 1 (January 1926): 50–61.

———. *The Danish West Indies under Company Rule (1671–1754)*. New York: Macmillan, 1917.

Westwood, Howard. *Black Troops, White Commanders and Freedmen during the Civil War*. Carbondale: Southern Illinois University Press, 2008.

———. "Captive Black Union Soldiers in Charleston—What to Do?" *Civil War History* 29, no. 1 (March 1982): 28–44.

Westwood, Sarah Davis. "'Cedcfo, Sòfa, Tirailleur': Slave Status and Military Identity in Nineteenth-Century Senegambia." *Slavery and Abolition* 39, no. 3 (August 2018): 418–439.

Whitehead, Neil. "Black Read as Red: Ethnic Transgression and Hybridity in

Northeastern South America and the Caribbean." In Restall, *Beyond Black and Red*, 223–244.

Wier, Howard, III. *A Paradise of Blood: The Creek War of 1813–14*. Yardley, Pa.: Westholme, 2016.

Williams, George Washington, and John David Smith. *A History of the Negro Troops in the War of the Rebellion, 1861–1865: Preceded by a Review of the Military Services of Negroes in Ancient and Modern Times*. Reprint. New York: Fordham University Press, 2012.

Willis, William. "Divide and Rule: Red, White, and Black in the Southeast." *Journal of Negro History* 48, no. 3 (July 1963): 157–176.

Willson, Marcius. *History of the United States from the Earliest Discoveries to the Present Time*. New York: Ivison & Phinney, 1854.

Wilson, Ellen Gibson. *The Loyal Blacks*. New York: Capricorn Books, 1976.

Wilson, Joseph. *The Black Phalanx: African American Soldiers in the War of Independence, the War of 1812, and the Civil War*. New York: Arno Press, 1968.

Wilson, Keith. "In the Shadow of John Brown: The Military Service of Colonels Thomas Higginson, James Montgomery, and Robert Shaw in the Department of the South." In *Black Soldiers in Blue: African American Troops in the Civil War Era*, edited by John David Smith, 306–335. Chapel Hill: University of North Carolina Press, 2002.

Wood, Peter. *Black Majority: Negroes in Colonial South Carolina from 1670 through the Stono Rebellion*. New York: Knopf, 1975.

Worden, Nigel. "Revolt in Cape Colony Slave Society." In Alpers et al., *Resisting Bondage*, 10–23.

Worth, John. "Razing Florida: The Indian Slave Trade and the Devastation of Spanish Florida, 1659–1715." In *Mapping the Mississippian Shatter Zone: The Colonial Indian Slave Trade and Regional Stability in the American South*, edited by Robbie Ethridge and Sheri Shuck-Hall, 295–311. Lincoln: University of Nebraska Press, 2009.

———. *The Timucuan Chiefdoms of Spanish Florida*. 2 vols. Gainesville: University Press of Florida, 1998.

Wright, J. Leitch. *Anglo-Spanish Rivalry in North America*. Athens: University of Georgia Press, 1971.

———. "A Note on the First Seminole War as Seen by the Indians, Negroes, and Their British Advisors." *Journal of Southern History* 34, no. 4 (1968): 565–575.

Wright, Philip. "War and Peace with the Maroons, 1730–1739." *Caribbean Quarterly* 16, no. 1 (1970): 5–27.

Wrike, Peter. *The Governor's Island: Gwynn's Island, Virginia, during the Revolution*. Gwynn, Va.: Gwynn's Island Museum, 1995.

INDEX

Aaron (enslaved person), 82
Abikaw Indians, 31
abolitionism, 95, 146, 200–203
Accompong Town Maroon community, 130
Act Concerning Servants who were out in rebellion (Va., 1677), 25
Act for Preventing Negroes Insurrections (Va., 1680), 25
Act for the Better Ordering and Governing of Negroes (Barbados, 1676), 25
Act for the Better Ordering and Governing of Negroes (S.C., 1740), 25
Act for the Better Ordering and Governing of Negroes and Slaves (S.C., 1712), 58–60
Act to prevent the people called Quakers, from bringing Negroes to their Meeting (Barbados, 1676), 25
Adams, John Quincy, 154
Adams-Onís Treaty (1819), 156, 157
Addison, Joseph, 37
Akurio Indians, 130
Alabama Indians, 31, 38
Alberti, Ernestine, 181–183
Allston, Abraham, 195
Alonso (Yamasee cacique), 33
Ambrister, Robert, 151–152, 153–154
Angola Maroon community, 151
Apalachicola Indians, 31, 32
Apalatchee Indians, 31, 32, 38

Arawak Indians, 130
Arbuthnot, George, 151–152, 153–154
Asbury, Francis, 86
Asht, William, 51–52
Atherton, Henry, 45
Atkins, John, 26
Ayala y Escobar, Juan de, 49–50

Bacon, Nathaniel, 18; death of, 16, 20. *See also* Bacon's Rebellion
Bacon's Rebellion: aftermath of, 24; army, composition of, 18–19; defeat of, 20–22; emancipation, promise of, 2, 17–21, 27–28, 207; emancipation, promise of, reneged, 21–22; militarized revolts, comparison to, 22–25; military character of, 22–23; overview of events, 15–17; scholarship on, 16; tactics of, 19; as threat to slave system, 22, 24; Yamasee War, comparison to, 62–63
Bailly (French colonist), 52–53
Barbados uprisings (1673, 1675, and 1685), 7, 23
Barker, Thomas, 34
Barnwell, John, 33, 35, 46
Barr (Dominica captain), 100, 109
Bas-du-Fleuve Maroon community, 238n75
Beard, Oliver, 175–176
Beasley, Daniel, 139
Beaufort National Cemetery, 166
Beck (enslaved person), 1–2, 144

Beckmen, Adrian, 51–52
Benavides Bazán y Molina, Antonio, 49–50
Ben Deford, 176, 180
Bennett, Benjamin, 46
Berbice uprising (1763), 7
Berkeley, William, 25–26. See also Bacon's Rebellion
Bettsey (Ethiopian Regiment), 89
Biassou, Jorge, 127, 137
Bienville, Jean-Baptiste Le Moyne de, 49
Billy (enslaved person), 1–2, 144
Black Carib Maroon community, 147, 159–160
Black Seminoles. See Seminole Maroons
Blair, Hannah, 89
Blount, Willie, 138
Boni Maroon community, 147, 161, 238n75
Boni Maroon Wars (Suriname), 134, 140
Bookman, Dutty, 86
Book of Negroes, 64, 80
Bowlegs (Seminole chief), 129, 145–146, 155
Bowles, William Augustus, 126–127
Bowyer, Henry, 107
Bradford, William, 71
Brasier, Henry, Jr., 51–52
Bray, William, 32, 46
Brent, Robert, 82
Brent, William, 77
Brisbane, William, 177
Britain (Ethiopian Regiment sergeant), 82
Bronson, William, 173
Broughton (Dominica sergeant major), 106
Broughton, Thomas, 34, 35, 36
Brown, John (Black soldier), 174
Brown, John (White abolitionist): legacy of, 201–203; raid at Harpers Ferry, 203
Brown, Uncle York, 175
Bryan, Hugh, 43
Buck, Marcus G., 150
Bureau for Colored Troops, 191
Burrows, Seymour, 33
Bush, Jenny, 89
Bussa's Rebellion (Barbados), 112, 113, 114–115
Butt, Patience, 79
Byrd, Thomas, 77

Calhoun, John, 151, 153, 157
Cameron, Alexander. See Eighth West India Regiment rebellion
Cameron, Allan, 100, 106
Cameron, Allen, 109

Campbell, James, 114
Carolina Corps, 118
Carter, Landon, 72
Cassin (Dominica captain), 100, 106, 109
Catawba Indians, 31, 45, 50
Chanvalon, Jean-Baptiste Thibault de, 127
Chaquetas Indians, 53–54
Charles (enslaved person), 70, 82
Charles II, King of England, 22, 207
Charleston slave conspiracy (1722), 56
Chatoyer (Black Carib), 132
Chépart, Étienne de, 52–53
Cheraw Indians, 45
Cherokee Indians: attacks against, 35; Creek, relationship with, 38; population of, 31; re-enslavement of runaway slaves and, 158; in Yamasee War, 37
Chester (enslaved person), 153
Chickasaw Indians, 158
Chicken, George, 35
Chisholm, Samuel, 195
Choctaw Indians, 48–49, 54
Choptico Indians, 159
Church (Dominica sergeant), 109
Civil War: Black soldiers, 169–173, 176, 200; scholarship on, 167; slavery as central to, 204–205. See also First South Carolina Volunteer Infantry Regiment
Clarke, Archibald, 136
Clifton (First South Carolina Volunteers captain), 181
Clinch, Duncan Lamont, 150
Cochean (Seminole chief), 155
Cochran, James, 43
Cochran, John, 46
Cochrane, Alexander Leslie, 141, 142, 146–147, 169
Cockburn, George, 141
Coffee (enslaved person), 40
Committee of Military Affairs, 154
Congeree Indians, 38
Congo Jack (Eighth West India Regiments rebel), 110
Corbett, John, 51–52
Córcoles y Martínez, Francisco de, 33, 49
Coromantee rebellion (N.Y., 1712), 51–52, 57
Coromantin rebellions (Jamaica, 1760), 84
Corsaboy Indians, 38
Cow Driver (Vacapachasie; Mulatto King), 157–158

Craven, Charles. *See* Yamasee War
Crawford, William, 148, 149
Creek Indians: Cherokee, relationship with, 38; fugitive slaves, aid to, 50–51; fugitive slaves, return to Whites, 46, 158–159; Lower Creeks, 32; on Maroons, 154–155; population of, 31; on Seminole lands in Florida, 156–157; and Yamasee War, 38
Creek War, 122–123, 139–142. *See also* Gulf Coast Borderlands Maroon War
Cresnay, baron de, 55
Cressy (enslaved person), 1–2, 144
Crooke, John, 51
Crouch (Ethiopian Regiment corporal), 82
Cubah (Jamaican queen), 85
Cuffee (enslaved person), 23, 51
Cuffy (Eighth West India Regiments rebel), 110
Cure, John, 51–52
Curry (Eighth West India Regiment sergeant), 79–80, 82, 105
Cynthia (enslaved person), 1–2, 144
Cyrus (enslaved person), 143–144

Dâaga (rebel leader), 118
Darlington (ship), 175
Davey (Dominica corporal), 108
Davis, Jefferson, 200
Davy (enslaved person), 70
Dawes, William, 88
de Bolas, Juan, 9
Delaware Indians, 158
Dexter, Horatio, 128, 157
diseases and illnesses, 58, 75–78, 94, 107
Djuka Maroon community (Suriname), 118–119, 130, 134, 161
Dodds (Dominica sergeant), 100
Doeg Indians, 16
Dokos Maroon community, 148
Douglass, Frederick, 170
Doyle, Edmund, 123, 134, 144, 152–153, 156
Drake, Francis, 147
Duckett, George, 45–46
Dumont de Montigny, Jean-François-Benjamin, 54
Dundas, Henry. *See* West India Regiments
Dunmore, fourth Earl of (John Murray). *See* Dunmore's Proclamation; Ethiopian Regiment
Dunmore, The (ship), 75

Dunmore's Proclamation, 64, 71–73, 78–79, 82, 169. *See also* Ethiopian Regiment
Duvall, William, 157
Du Vallée (Black Carib), 132

Echanachaca, battle of, 122–123, 139
Eden, Charles, 36
Eighth Maine Infantry Regiment, 187
Eighth West India Regiment rebellion, 99–106; aftermath of, 110–112; causes of, 106–110, 208–209; historical marker for, 91; legacy of, 2, 209; loyal soldiers, 100; material deprivation, 107–111, 112; objectives and goals, 119–121; punishments for, 110; rebellions, comparison to others, 112–119; regiment, composition of, 107; ringleader of, alleged (name unknown), 106; scholarship on, 91–93; slave status and, 119–120; as threat to institution of slavery, 101; Whites' fears of spreading rebellions, 111
Elize (enslaved person), 144–145
emancipation (General Order No. 11), 170–171. *See also* Dunmore's Proclamation; Emancipation Proclamation
Emancipation Proclamation, 167, 177; preliminary proclamation, 175; spreading news of, 183, 197, 201
Emoteley (Seminole chief), 157
Ethiopian Regiment: composition of, 78–84; freedom, promise of, 2, 64–65, 208; legacy of, 87–90; material deprivation, 86–87; military incursions, 66–78; noncommissioned officers, 82–83; Nova Scotia, evacuation to, 64–65, 83, 89; Sierra Leone, evacuation to, 83–84, 88, 89; slave rebellions, comparison to others, 84–87
Etowah (ship), 195
Evans, Judith, 89
Evans, Nathan, 199
Excellent (ship), 100

Fédon, Julien, 113
Fédon's Rebellion, Grenada, 112, 113–115
Fellow, James, 61
Fenwick, John, 35, 36
Fifty-Fourth Massachusetts Volunteer Infantry Regiment, 167, 188–190
Finegan, Joseph, 200
First Carib War, Saint Vincent, 133, 134
First Confiscation Act (U.S., 1861), 169

First South Carolina Volunteer Infantry
    Regiment: as eager for action, 181;
    Emancipation Proclamation, celebration
    of, 177–180, 202; families of, 180, 185,
    193–194, 197; former owners, meetings
    with, 185; freedom raids, 175–177, 180–183,
    196–198, 201–202; guerrilla warfare and, 187;
    impressment of enslaved people, 187–188;
    literacy and, 168; members and numbers
    of, 166, 176, 180–181; militarized resistance,
    as culmination of, 166–169, 180, 199–203,
    204–205, 210–212; military engagements
    and, 174–177, 180–187, 188–192; military
    objectives of, 183, 188–192; motivation for
    fighting, 1, 168, 177, 198, 202–203, 204–206,
    210; mustered, initial, 173; mustered,
    second time, 180; mustered out, 192, 203;
    postwar activities of, 203–206; predecessors,
    comparison to, 205; recruitment for,
    192–199; renamed Thirty-Third USCT,
    191; scholarship on, 167; wages for, 173, 193;
    White Union soldiers, fighting with, 187
Fitzgerald, Lucia Braddock, 137
Fleetwood, Christian, 199
Flora (enslaved person), 1–2, 144
Floyd, John, 149
Forbes, John, 2
Forrester, Jake, 187–188
Fort Augusta, Jamaica, 113, 116–119
Fort Clinch, Fla., 187
Fort Mims, 139
Fort Rosalie, 52–54, 55
Fort Scott, 150, 153
Fort Shirley, 91. *See also* Eighth West India
    Regiment rebellion
Fort St. Marks, 155
Fort Sumter, Charleston, 188–190
Fort Wagner, Charleston, 188–189, 191
Forty-Eighth New York Volunteers, 175–176
Fowler (chaplain), 177
France, 93, 107
free Blacks, 136–137
French (chaplain), 177, 179

Gabriel (Yamasee cacique), 33
Gadsden, James, 157
Gage, Francis, 179
Gaines, Edmund, 150, 155
Garçon (enslaved person), 143–144, 151

Gardner, Thomas, 18
Garifuna Maroon community, 130, 131
General Order No. 11, 170–171
General Order No. 143, 191
Genius (Eighth West India Regiments rebel),
    110
George (enslaved person), 78
George, David, 80, 88
George, Phyllis, 80
George I, King of England, 35–36
German Coast rebellion (1811), 6
Giffard (Dominica captain), 100
Gillmore, Quincy, 188
Godin, Benjamin, 34, 40
Gold (Dominica sergeant), 108
Goose Creek conspiracy (S.C.), 56
Gordon, John, 100, 106, 109, 110
Gould, Edward, 175
Gradine, Alfred, 195
Graham, Robert, 46
Grantham, Thomas, 16, 20–21
Grasset, Augustus, 51–52
Great Bridge, Va., battle of, 68–70, 73
Great Britain, 43, 48–49
Green, July, 189
Greenshields (Dominica ensign), 106
Grissoll, John, 70
Grissoll, Ralph, 70
Gulf Coast Borderlands Maroon War: as fight
    against chattel slavery, 2, 142; Maroons,
    numbers of, 140–141; Maroon wars,
    comparison to others, 140. *See also* Prospect
    Bluff, Fla.; Seminole Maroons
Gwynn's Island, Va., battle of, 73–77, 80

Haitian refugees, 127, 137
Haitian Revolution, 85–86, 90, 148
Hambly, William, 156
Hamilton (Dominica major), 101, 102
Hamond, Andrew, 77
Hampton, Va., 66
Hanover Parish conspiracy (Jamaica, 1776),
    84–85, 87
Harris, Buckner, 138–139
Harris, Charles, 139
Harris, Joseph, 66
Harry (enslaved person), 40, 70
Harry (Ethiopian Regiment), 89
Hawke (ship), 66

Hawkins, Benjamin, 128–129, 138, 146, 148, 155
Hazard, Miles, 174
Hearn (Carolina planter), 34
Henry (Ethiopian Regiment), 89
Henry, Patrick, 89
Henry, Robert, 144–145
Heyward, William, 196
Hibberson, Jose, 139
Higginson, Thomas Wentworth: as abolitionist, 201–202; appointment of, 176; Emancipation Proclamation and, 179; on freedom raids, 197; guerrilla warfare and, 187; on soldiers' encounters with former slave owners, 181–183; wounded and left First South, 189, 191. *See also* First South Carolina Volunteer Infantry Regiment
Hinds, Thomas, 140
Hislop, Thomas. *See* West India Regiments
Houston, Jeff, 187
Hugues, Victor, 112
Huiten, Principe (Prince Witten), 127, 136–137
Hunter, David: as abolitionist, 200–201; Department of the South commander, replaced, 188; emancipation proclamation of, 170–171; enslaved soldiers, recruitment of, 171–173; on freedom raids, 196; relationship with soldiers, 199; Tubman, spy for, 202
Hunter, Robert, 52
Huron Indians, 158
hurricane of 1715, 60
hurricane of 1775, 86
Hutchings, Joseph, 2, 68
Hypolite (Dominican private), 118
Hypolite (Dominican slave soldier), 118
Hypolite (Eighth West India Regiment private), 2, 105

indentured servants, restrictions on, 26–27
indigo production, 58
Innerarity, John, 123
Isaac (enslaved person), 153

Jackson (Carolina planter), 35, 36
Jackson, Abraham, 195
Jackson, Andrew, 123, 143, 148, 149, 153–154, 156–157
Jackson, Hannah, 89
Jackson, Judith, 82
Jackson, Peter, 64

Jacobo, Jorge, 137
James (Eighth West India Regiments rebel), 110
James (First South Carolina captain), 187–188
Jane (Ethiopian Regiment), 89
Jaruco Maroon community, 130
Jemmy (enslaved person), 34, 35, 85
Jemy (enslaved person), 56
Jeremiah, Thomas, 84–85, 87
John (enslaved person), 51
John Adams (ship), 180, 181
Johnny (enslaved person), 82
Johnson, John, 71–72
Johnson, Robert, 39–40
Johnston, Gideon, 60
Johnstone, Andrew James Cochrane. *See* West India Regiments
Jones, Charles C., 199–200
Jones, Clara, 195
Jones, David, 195
Jospo (Yamasee chief), 44

Kalingo Indians, 130
Karboegers of Coppename, 160
Kemp's Landing, Va., battle of, 68
Kenhagee (Seminole chief), 155
Kennedy (reverend), 187
Kenty, Judy, 137
Kinache (Seminole chief), 128
Kindelán y O'Regan, Sebastian, 128, 138, 145
King, Boston, 79
King, Edward, 175
King, Mulatto (Vacapachasie; Cow Driver), 157–158
King, Ned, 193–194
Kitt (enslaved person), 70
Kolly, Jean-Daniel, 52

L'Abondance, 64
Lally (enslaved person), 1–2, 144
landownership, 204
Larrimore, Thomas, 20
Lawson, Robert, 68
Lay, John, 200
Leeward Maroon community, 85, 132, 160
Le Maniel Maroon community, 148
Liberty (ship), 66
Lincoln, Abraham, 167, 169, 170–171, 175. *See also* Emancipation Proclamation

Lively (Eighth West India Regiments rebel), 110
Long, Thomas, 1, 187, 198
Loomis, Louis J., 150
Louboëy, Henri de, 54
Low, Johannes, 51–52
Lowndes, Charles, 196
Loyal Dominican Rangers, 94–95
Lyllton, Charles, 9

Mackay (Dominica lieutenant), 100, 109
Mackay, Alexander, 35
Macpherson (slave owner), 56
Madison, James, 71, 151
Magnificent (ship), 100, 101
Major, Sam, 187
Malo, Saint, 238n75
Manby (Eighth West India Regiments rebel), 110
Maroons: in imperial conflicts, 147–148; race and identity of, 125–132, 133; rebellions, participation in, 112, 115, 118–119; as refuge for rebels, 102, 105, 116; running away as form of rebellion, 3; scholarship on, 124–132; slavery, practice of, 132; in Spanish Florida, 122–125; Whites' treaties and dealing with, 158–162. *See also* Seminole Maroons; *individual Maroon communities*
Maroon War, First (Dominica), 140
Maroon War, First (Jamaica), 10, 133–134, 140, 147, 160
Maroon War, Second (Dominica), 118
Maroon War, Second (Jamaica), 133, 134, 147
Marschalck, Joris, 51–52
Mary (enslaved person), 144–145
Mason (enslaved person), 70
Mathew, Thomas, 16
Mathews, George, 135, 136–138
Mattawoman Indians, 159
McDonald (Grenadan lieutenant colonel), 114
McIntosh, William, 138, 150, 155
McIntyre (First South Carolina Volunteer sergeant), 185
Menéndez, Francisco (enslaved soldier), 2, 44
Menéndez Marquez, Francisco, 44
Mercer, Charles Fenton, 152
Mexican-American War, 168
Middleton, Arthur, 36
Militia Act (Jamaica, 1681), 9
Militia Act (U.S., 1862), 193

Mitchell, Bristoll, 80
Mitchell, David, 136–138, 140, 151, 157
Monroe, James, 153–154
Montgomery, David, 183, 188, 196, 201
Moore, Buff, 40
Moore, Maurice, 35, 36, 37
Moreau de Jonnès, Alexandre, 127
Morris, Robert, 20, 22
Morrison, W. William, 195
Mosely, William, 185
Moses (enslaved person), 72
Moultrie Creek, Fla., 156–157
Murchison, Abram, 172–173
Muscogee Indians, 126–127
Mushoe, Henry, 49
Mutiny Acts, 96, 97–98
Mutiny Acts (1807), 98, 117

Nairne, Thomas, 32
Nancy (enslaved person), 138
Nanticoke Indians, 159
Naranjo Maroons, 148
Natchez Indians, 52–56
Natchez rebellion (La., 1729), 52–56, 57
Native Americans: as English allies, 39–40; as enslaved soldiers, 40; enslavement of, 25, 27, 31, 32, 50; fight with Blacks during Patriot War, 122; Maroons, sexual relationships with, 129–132; ransom of enslaved Blacks, 33, 44, 49–50, 53; as refuge for fugitive slaves, 122–125; as slave owners, 128–129. *See also individual nations*
Ndjuka Maroon community, 116
Negro Fort (Prospect Bluff). *See* Eighth West India Regiment rebellion; Prospect Bluff, Fla.
Nelly (enslaved person), 144
Nero (Black Maroon), 129
Nero (enslaved person), 1–2, 144
New London, S.C., 36–37
Newnan, David, 122, 136
Newton, Abigail, 89
Newton, Lydia, 89
Nicholas, Robert, 68
Nicolls, Edward, 123, 141–145, 149, 150, 153, 155
Norfolk, Va., 73, 75

Occaneechee Indians, 18
Ochesee (Creek) Indians. *See* Creek Indians
O'Neal, Charles, 174–175

Oponney (Seminole chief), 157
Oranjebo, Suriname, rebellion (1805), 112–113, 116
Osborne, Nathaniel, 26
Otter (ship), 66, 82

Palmares Maroon community (Palmarian Maroon community), 132, 159
Panton, Leslie and Company, 138
Patriot War, 122, 135–137
Paxley (Dominica major), 101
Payne (Seminole chief), 138
Peck, Rev., 177
Pedee Indians, 38
Pedro (Eighth West India Regiments rebel), 110
Peña, Diego, 39
Périer, Étienne, 55
Perro Bravo (Yamasee Cacique), 33, 44, 49–50
Perry (widow), 40
Perryman, George, 128
Perryman, Joseph, 152–153
Persevall (slave owner), 50–51
Pharcelle (Maroon leader), 115
Philip (Seminole chief), 157
Phoebe (enslaved person), 138
Pierce, Edward, 172
Pight, John, 35
Pinckney's Treaty (1795), 135, 153–154
Pinkett (Dominica sergeant), 108
Piscataway, 159
Planter (ship), 166, 180, 195–196
Pocotaligo (Yamasee village), 32–33
Polinaire, Jean Louis, 115
political participation, 203–204
Polly (enslaved person), 144
Pompey (enslaved person), 35, 45
Pope (enslaved person), 35, 45
Port Royal, S.C., 32–34, 36–37, 38, 42, 45–46
Posey, Thomas, 76
Powell, Thomas, 134, 140
Primus, Thomas, 137
Prince (enslaved person), 143–144
Prince Rupert's, Dominica, 94–95, 99–107, 111
Proctor, Tony, 137–138
Prospect Bluff, Fla. (Negro Fort): battle at, 134–135, 149–151, 155, 209; battle at, aftermath of, 151–152, 156; as refuge for runaway slaves, 123, 128, 138, 140–145, 148. *See also* Eighth West India Regiment rebellion; Seminole Maroons
Prosser, Gabriel, 88
Prosser Rebellion (1800), 8
public welfare fund, 59
Pulteney, William, 45

Quash (enslaved soldier), 108
Queen Anne's War, 41, 48, 57
Quincy, John, 185
Quintyne, Henry, 37

R., James, 190
Ralph (Ethiopian Regiment), 89
Ramsey (Dominica sergeant), 108
Red Caribs, 160
Redwood (English commander), 34
Relyea (captain of CSS *Planter*), 195
Ricard (French colonist), 52
rice, 58
Richebourg (minister), 42
Rivers, Prince, 1, 179, 193, 198, 201–202, 203–204
Robert (Ethiopian Regiment), 89
Robin (enslaved person), 138
Roebuck (ship), 77
Roger (enslaved person), 138
Rogers, Seth, 181, 201
Royal, John, 82
Ruby (ship), 145
running away, 43–48, 70–73, 79, 193–198, 199–202; slave patrols, 38–39, 58–59. *See also* Maroons

Saamaka Maroon community (Suriname), 130, 132, 134, 161
Saint Augustine, Fla. *See* Spanish Florida
Saly (enslaved person), 144–145
Sam (enslaved person), 138, 144
Sambo (enslaved person), 85
Santee Indians, 38
Savanna Indians, 31, 32
Saxton, Rufus, 175; Emancipation Proclamation celebration and, 177–178, 179; on freedom raids, 197. *See also* First South Carolina Volunteer Infantry Regiment
Schenkingh's Fort, 34, 35
Scott (Dominica major), 101, 102
Scott, Charles, 68–70
Sears, Alfred, 187
Seawee Indians, 38

Second Confiscation Act (U.S., 1862), 171
Second South Carolina Volunteers, 183, 187, 188–190, 202. *See also* First South Carolina Volunteer Infantry Regiment
Second West India Regiment rebellion (Jamaica, 1808), 113
Segui, Bernard, 157
Seminole Indians: Black Maroons and, 125–126, 154–155; Black residents, status of, 130–132; land cession and, 158; Maroon warfare and, 126–127; slavery, practice of, 132; on Spanish cession of lands, 156–157. *See also* Seminole Maroons
Seminole Maroons: centrality of, to fighting, 152, 158; chattel slavery, attack on, 132–133, 138–139; as destination for enslaved people, 138–139, 144–145; European alliances, 149, 162–165; free Black militia and, 136–137; guerrilla warfare and terrain knowledge, 134–135, 150; Haitian refugee allies, 137; imperial warfare and, 148–149, 209–210; Maroon warfare, White categorization of, 133–134; Native American alliances, 162–165, 209–210; numbers of, 135–137, 143–146, 152, 157; peace with Whites solidified, 157–162; race, White colonists' understanding of, 127–129; re-enslavements, threat of, 137–138, 151, 158; scholarship on, 124; Whites' fear of insurrection, 137–138, 149, 152. *See also* Gulf Coast Borderlands Maroon War; Seminole Indians
Seminole War, First, 123; White Americans rationale for, 153–154
Seminole War, Second, 162
Seminole War, Third, 162
Seward (Dominica paymaster), 109
Shawnee Indians, 158
Sherman, Thomas, 169
Shova (Dominica corporal), 108
Sierra Leone Company, 88
Simmons, William, 128
Sixth Connecticut Infantry Regiment, 187
Skerrett, John. *See* West India Regiments
slave code (S.C., 1722), 60
slave patrols, 38–39, 58–59
slave trade, intercolonial, 17, 31, 82
slave trade, transatlantic, 17, 31, 57, 82; enslaved soldiers and, 95–97; sex ratios, 129–130
Smalls, Elizabeth Lydia, 195

Smalls, Hannah, 195
Smalls, John, 195
Smalls, Robert, 166, 195–196, 204
Smalls, Robert, Jr., 195
Smalls, Susan, 195
Smith, Thomas Adams, 122, 134, 136–138
Smith, William, 70
Snowball, Nathaniel, 89
Snowball, Violet, 89
Sophy (enslaved person), 144
Sores, Jacques de, 236n48
South Carolina Constitutional Convention (1868), 203–204
Spanish Florida: attacks on United States, 139–140; English, relationship with, 38–39; on Maroons, 155–156; Native Americans, relationship with, 32, 38–39; as refuge for enslaved people, 38–39, 56, 126–127, 135–137; Spanish evacuation of, 156–157. *See also* Gulf Coast Borderlands Maroon War; Seminole Indians; Seminole Maroons
Spaulding, Daniel, 174
Spotswood, Alexander, 45, 49
Squire, Mathew, 66, 82
Stanton, Edwin, 171, 191
Steel (enslaved person), 153
Stephen (enslaved person), 144
St. George's Island, Va., 77–78
St. George's Militia, 100–106
St. John rebellions (1773), 6, 7, 23, 24
St. Kitts uprising (1639), 7
Stone, William, 36
Stono Rebellion (S.C., 1739), 7–8, 56–57, 58
Stopford (Dominica commodore), 100–101
Strong, J. D., 187–188
Stuart (Dominica soldier), 108–109
Success (ship), 37
sugar production, 108, 109
Susquehanna Indians, 18
Sutton, Jeff, 194
Sutton, Robert, 179, 181–183, 194

Tacky's Revolt (Jamaica, 1760), 84, 85, 87
Taíno Indians, 130
Talliboose Indians, 31
Taotal (Natchez Indian), 54
Taylor, Susie King, 180, 191, 193–194
Ted (enslaved person), 78
Texas Revolution, 168

INDEX 299

Third Battalion of Royal Colonial Marines, 142
Thirteenth Amendment, 192
Thirty-Third USCT. *See* First South Carolina Volunteer Infantry Regiment
Thompson, Jane, 2, 64
Thorowgood, Phillis (daughter), 79
Thorowgood, Phillis (mother), 79
Timucua Indians, 32
Titus or Colonel Tye (member of Ethiopian Regiment), 78, 82
tobacco production, 25–26, 57
Treaty at Fort Jackson, 141, 146
Treaty of Amiens (1801), 107
Treaty of Moultrie Creek (1823), 157–162, 209
Treaty of Utrecht (1713), 43, 49
Trial (ship), 46
Trigge, Thomas, 101, 106, 110–112
Trowbridge, Charles, 170, 173; commander for First South Carolina Volunteers, 191–192
Tubman, Harriett, 196, 202–203
Tucker, Robert, 2, 64, 80
Tunfinga Indians, 130
Turner, Nat, rebellion (1831), 6
Turno, Gabriel, 195
Tustunnuggee Hopoy, 155

United States Colored Troops, creation of, 191. *See also* First South Carolina Volunteer Infantry Regiment
Urcullo, José, 144–145

Vacapachasie (Cow Driver; Mulatto King), 157–158
Valour (ship), 36
Vantilborough, Peter, 51
Vaughan, John. *See* West India Regiments
Verdier, William, 166, 189
Virginia Committee of Safety, 68, 72, 78–79

Walker, Chloe, 89
Walker, Henry, 89
Wallace (enslaved person), 34–35, 40
Wanton, John, 187–188
Wareing, Cato "Uncle Cato," 194
Warner, Samuel, 32
War of 1812: enslaved soldiers, British promise of emancipation, 141–146; Native Americans, British recruitment of, 141–143; Patriot War and, 122, 135–137

Washington, George, 89
Wateree Jack, 34
Watts, R. I., 26
Waxaw Indians, 38
Weed, Jacob, 137
Wells, G. M., 171
West, John, 20
Westerneys (Dominica lieutenant), 100, 106
West India Regiments: composition of, 95–97, 107, 116–119; creation of, 10, 93–97; emancipation not promised, 95; enslavement, status of, 97–99, 100, 106, 111, 117–119; Ethiopian Regiment's legacy and, 90; First Regiment, 110, 113, 118; Fourth Regiment, 110, 115–116; language barriers, 98–99; Ninth Regiment, 106; Second Regiment, 113, 116–119; Sixty-Eighth Regiment, 100, 107; Third Regiment, 110; White soldiers, comparison, 97–98 *See also* Eighth West India Regiment rebellion
Westo Indians, 32
White, Annie, 195
Wickliffe, Charles, 171
Wilkinson, Moses "Daddy," 83–84, 89
Willcox, Joseph Morgan, 122
Williams, Harry, 190
Williams, John, 134, 136
Williams, Peter, 187
Willington (captain of *Trial*), 46
Wilson, Lavina, 195
Windward Maroon community, 130, 132, 160
Witten, Glasgow, 137
Witten, Prince, 127, 136–137
Witten, Rafaela "Polly," 137
women and children, 79–81, 85–86, 96, 143, 144–145, 180, 205; running away, 193–198
Woodbine, George, 143–146, 151, 153, 155–156
Woodford, William, 71
Woodward (Carolina planter), 33
Woodward, John, 40
Wright (Loyalist lieutenant), 66
Wright, John, 32
Wyandot Indians, 158
Wyvill, Richard, 96

Yamasee War, 29–30, 31–39, 47; Bacon's Rebellion, comparison to, 62–63; cost of, human, 38; cost of, monetary, 37–38; enslaved Native Americans and, 50;

Yamasee War (*continued*)
    enslaved people, loyalty to British, 39–42;
    enslaved people, recruitment of, 34, 36–37;
    enslaved people fighting with Native Americans, 35; enslaved people fighting with Spanish, 47–48; enslaved soldiers, as insurgents, 42–51; freedom, differing meanings of, 49–50; as imperial conflict, 45–51, 207–208; legacy of, 38–39; material deprivation and, 57–62; motivations and objectives, 62–63, 207–208; Native Americans and English, relationship with, 32, 36–37, 39–40, 207–208; population of colony, 41; population of Yamasee, 31; slave raids, 45–46; slave rebellions, comparison with others, 51–61; Virginia support for English, 36–37, 45

Yanga, Gaspar, 130, 159
Yfallaquisca (Perro Bravo; Yamasee cacique), 33, 44, 49–50
Young, Hugh, 128
Young, William, 133
Ysiopole (Yamasee Cacique), 33
Yucatecan Indians, 130
Yuchi Indians, 31, 32

Zuñiga, Mauricio de, 155–156

EARLY AMERICAN PLACES

On Slavery's Border: Missouri's Small Slaveholding Households, 1815–1865
BY DIANE MUTTI BURKE

Sounds American: National Identity and the Music Cultures of the Lower Mississippi River Valley, 1800–1860
BY ANN OSTENDORF

The Year of the Lash: Free People of Color in Cuba and the Nineteenth-Century Atlantic World
BY MICHELE REID-VAZQUEZ

Ordinary Lives in the Early Caribbean: Religion, Colonial Competition, and the Politics of Profit
BY KIRSTEN BLOCK

Creolization and Contraband: Curaçao in the Early Modern Atlantic World
BY LINDA M. RUPERT

An Empire of Small Places: Mapping the Southeastern Anglo-Indian Trade, 1732–1795
BY ROBERT PAULETT

Everyday Life in the Early English Caribbean: Irish, Africans, and the Construction of Difference
BY JENNY SHAW

Natchez Country: Indians, Colonists, and the Landscapes of Race in French Louisiana
BY GEORGE EDWARD MILNE

Slavery, Childhood, and Abolition in Jamaica, 1788–1838
BY COLLEEN A. VASCONCELLOS

Privateers of the Americas: Spanish American Privateering from the United States in the Early Republic
BY DAVID HEAD

Charleston and the Emergence of Middle-Class Culture in the Revolutionary Era
BY JENNIFER L. GOLOBOY

Anglo-Native Virginia: Trade, Conversion, and Indian Slavery in the Old Dominion, 1646–1722
BY KRISTALYN MARIE SHEFVELAND

Slavery on the Periphery: The Kansas-Missouri Border in the Antebellum and Civil War Eras
BY KRISTEN EPPS

In the Shadow of Dred Scott: St. Louis Freedom Suits and the Legal Culture of Slavery in Antebellum America
BY KELLY M. KENNINGTON

Brothers and Friends: Kinship in Early America
BY NATALIE R. INMAN

George Washington's Washington: Visions for the National Capital in the Early American Republic
BY ADAM COSTANZO

Borderless Empire: Dutch Guiana in the Atlantic World, 1750–1800
BY BRIAN HOONHOUT

Complexions of Empire in Natchez: Race and Slavery in the Mississippi Borderlands
BY CHRISTIAN PINNEN

Toward Cherokee Removal: Land, Violence, and the White Man's Chance
BY ADAM J. PRATT

Generations of Freedom: Gender, Movement, and Violence in Natchez, 1779–1865
BY NIK RIBIANSZKY

A Weary Land: Slavery on the Ground in Arkansas
BY KELLY HOUSTON JONES

Rebels in Arms: Black Resistance and the Fight for Freedom in the Anglo-Atlantic
BY JUSTIN IVERSON

www.ingramcontent.com/pod-product-compliance
Lightning Source LLC
Chambersburg PA
CBHW010719250426
43672CB00033B/2961